VERSE BY VERSE

Acts THROUGH Revelation

VERSE BY VERSE

Acts THROUGH Revelation

Formerly titled *New Testament Apostles Testify of Christ: A Guide for Acts through Revelation*

D. KELLY OGDEN
ANDREW C. SKINNER

DESERET
BOOK

SALT LAKE CITY, UTAH

The descendancy chart of Herod the Great on page 62 is from the Bible Dictionary, LDS edition of the King James Version of the Bible (Salt Lake City: The Church of Jesus Christ of Latter-day Saints, 1979), 701. The chart on pages 395–96 is from the *New Testament Seminary Teacher Outline* (Salt Lake City: Corporation of the President of The Church of Jesus Christ of Latter-day Saints, 1984), 433. The chart on pages 398–99 is from the *New Testament Seminary Student Manual* (Salt Lake City: Corporation of the President of The Church of Jesus Christ of Latter-day Saints, 1984), 279. All are © Intellectual Reserve, Inc. Used by permission.

The illustration on page 105 is adapted and used by permission of Leen Ritmeyer, Ritmeyer Archaeological Design, Harrogate, North Yorkshire, England.

The photo on page 201 is © Val Brinkerhoff; used by permission. All other photos are © D. Kelly Ogden.

Formerly titled *New Testament Apostles Testify of Christ: A Guide for Acts through Revelation.*

Library of Congress Cataloging-in-Publication Data

Ogden, D. Kelly (Daniel Kelly), 1947–
   Verse by verse, acts through revelation / D. Kelly Ogden, Andrew C. Skinner.
      p. cm.
   Includes bibliographical references and index.
   ISBN-10 1-59038-590-X (hardcover : alk. paper)
   ISBN-13 978-1-59038-590-6 (hardcover : alk. paper)
   1. Church of Jesus Christ of Latter-day Saints—Doctrines. 2. Mormon Church—Doctrines. 3. Bible. N.T.—Criticism, interpretation, etc.
I. Skinner, Andrew C., 1951- II. Title.
   BX8675.O43 2006
   230'.9332—dc22
                                                            2006002497

Printed in the United States of America
Publishers Printing, Salt Lake City, UT

10   9   8   7   6   5

CONTENTS

PREFACE vii

MAP: THE WORLD OF THE APOSTLES x

INTRODUCTION 1

TIME CHART 6

1 THE GRAECO-ROMAN WORLD OF THE EARLY APOSTLES . . 7
    ROMAN JUDEA 16
    CHALLENGES FACED BY THE APOSTLES 22

2 THE ACTS OF THE APOSTLES, CHAPTERS 1
    THROUGH 12 26
    PETER, THE CHIEF APOSTLE 38
    PAUL'S LIFE BEFORE HIS CONVERSION 49

3 THE ACTS OF THE APOSTLES, CHAPTERS 13
    THROUGH 28 65
    PAUL'S UNIQUE PREPARATION 71
    THE FOCUS OF PAUL'S MISSIONARY LABORS 72
    PAUL'S TRAVELS 73
    THE TEMPLE IN THE DAYS OF PAUL 100
    THE COURTS OF THE TEMPLE 102

4 FIRST AND SECOND THESSALONIANS 112
    APOSTASY IN THE MERIDIAN DISPENSATION 119
    THE JOSEPH SMITH TRANSLATION 122

5 FIRST AND SECOND CORINTHIANS 128

6 GALATIANS 158

7 ROMANS 169

8 PHILIPPIANS, COLOSSIANS, AND PHILEMON 187

9 EPHESIANS 200
    THE WHOLE ARMOR OF GOD 209

10 FIRST TIMOTHY, TITUS, AND SECOND TIMOTHY 212

Contents

11 The Life of Paul 226

A Tribute to Paul the Apostle 226

The Teachings of Paul, a Witness of Christ . . 229

Paul, the Missionary 233

References to Paul in Latter-day Scripture . . 240

References to Paul by the Prophet
Joseph Smith 242

12 Hebrews 244

Melchizedek and Abraham at Salem 253

13 James and Jude, Brothers of the Lord 264

The Use of Consecrated Olive Oil in
Priesthood Blessings 271

14 First and Second Peter 277

Dealing with Trials, Suffering, and
Afflictions 288

15 First, Second, and Third John 293

Gnosticism 297

John the Apostle 301

16 The Revelation 305

Structure of the Revelation 306

Symbolic Language 306

Understanding Revelation 310

Statements on Revelation 347

17 The Cities of Paul the Apostle and
John the Revelator 350

Appendixes

1 Light, Fire, and Clouds with Celestial Beings . . 383

2 Jews in the Mediterranean World 387

3 The Number Seven in Revelation 395

4 The Seven Churches of Revelation 397

5 Commentary on Armageddon 400

6 Ten Doctrines of Salvation 404

Sources 407

Index 413

PREFACE

All of the New Testament is a precious treasury of scripture, and the books of Acts through Revelation in particular
are invaluable in helping us to understand Deity and doctrine
as they really are, not as the councils of the early Christian
church misunderstood and misinterpreted them to be. For
example, the letters of the apostle Paul unequivocally and
repeatedly affirm that God the Father and Jesus Christ are separate and distinct beings. These sacred texts of the second half
of the New Testament help build our faith in God the Father
and his literal son in the flesh, Jesus of Nazareth, the Messiah.
They corroborate other key doctrines of the Restoration
revealed anew under Joseph Smith's prophetic leadership,
including the sweeping power of the atonement of Jesus
Christ; the nature of the Abrahamic covenant; our premortal
existence, including faithfulness in our first estate, agency, and
accountability; the reality and opposition of Satan; the necessity of priesthood authority; baptism by immersion for the
remission of sins; the laying on of hands for conferring blessings and performing ordinations; the resurrection of the body
to specifically named degrees of glory; and the second coming
of Christ and his millennial reign.

The faith of the Prophet Joseph Smith was rooted in the
Bible, especially the New Testament. In fact, the restoration
of divine truths, begun in 1820 with the appearance of the
Father and the Son to the boy prophet, is directly tied to the
second half of the New Testament—specifically, James 1:5 and
6. Reading that passage motivated Joseph Smith to seek divine

guidance in the Sacred Grove near his home in Palmyra, New York: "If any of you lack wisdom, let him ask of God, that giveth to all men liberally, and upbraideth not; and it shall be given him. But let him ask in faith, nothing wavering . . ."

In a sense, then, we owe the beginning of the Restoration, at least in part, to the second half of the New Testament. New Testament concepts are vital in the Lord's restored Church. How many times do we see a text of the Restoration in the Book of Mormon, the Doctrine and Covenants, or the Pearl of Great Price that has a parallel, or cognate, text in the second half of the New Testament? The theme of James 1:5–6, for instance, is articulated several times in Latter-day Saint scripture (see, for example, D&C 4:7; 42:68; 136:32).

Although many non–Latter-day Saint resources are available for students of the New Testament, no succinct, one-volume study guide aims at touching upon the historical context, geography, and doctrine of the books of Acts through Revelation as a whole. To be sure, Elder Bruce R. McConkie's *Doctrinal New Testament Commentary* is an unparalleled and invaluable tool, but its aim is almost exclusively doctrinal. The present volume seeks to fill a broader need.

Our intent is to combine history, geography, and doctrine to help students of the scriptures see their interconnected-ness—to see that the scriptures were produced and preserved as a result of a number of interrelated factors. To keep such an enterprise to a manageable length, we have omitted the actual scriptural text, assuming that the students of the scriptures who use this book will refer frequently to the standard works of The Church of Jesus Christ of Latter-day Saints. There are several reasons for that assumption. First, the best commentary on any one of the standards works is the other three standard works. Second, no secondary work about the scriptures can replace studying the scriptures themselves regularly and frequently. Finally, this volume is a study *guide;* its use supposes the careful reading of the Latter-day Saint edition of the King James Version of the Bible, including the explanatory footnotes. This volume is not intended to replace the scriptures or to repeat all the annotations of the biblical text. It is intended that this guide be used side by side with the sacred texts of Acts through Revelation.

In the scriptures, as with other texts, whether sacred or secular, some things are more important than others. Thus, we have made choices regarding what to comment upon and what to let pass without comment. We have attempted to discuss fundamental issues as well as to present what we hope will be helpful ideas. Because salvation through Jesus Christ is most important above all other subjects, the nature of the Godhead, grace, faith, works, justification, and the law of Moses have received more discussion than other things.

This study guide follows the chronological structure of the second half of the New Testament itself. One purpose has been to show, where possible, how the different books fit together historically. The two chapters on the book of Acts, for example, contain clear notations about where this or that letter fits at what chronological point in the life of Paul and in the history of the early Church. Also, we have capitalized *Temple* in reference to a proper sanctuary of God but not in reference to pagan shrines.

In summary, then, we have highlighted the people, the places, and the events of the second half of the New Testament that make it come alive and that will help members of the Church of Jesus Christ in the fulness of times see how applicable that ancient record is today. The Bible is a book for all times. Its message is "Jesus Christ, and him crucified" (1 Corinthians 2:2). We truly believe what the Prophet Joseph Smith said about the worth of the biblical text: "He who reads it oftenest will like it best" and will be able to "see God's own handwriting in the sacred volume" (*Teachings of the Prophet Joseph Smith*, 56). Surely, those who study it the most intently will also find the most in it to help them in time of need.

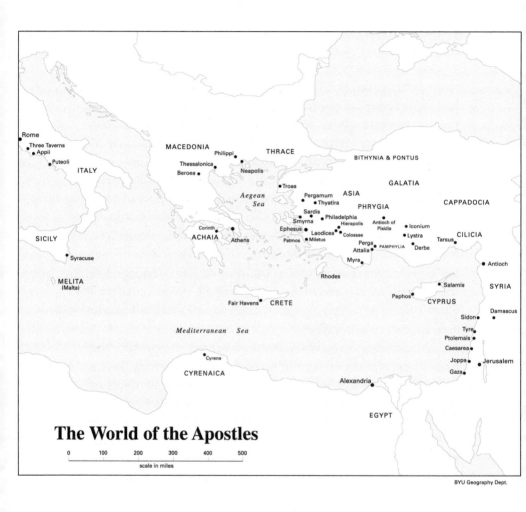

The World of the Apostles

Rome
Three Taverns
Appii
Puteoli
ITALY

MACEDONIA
Philippi
Thessalonica
Beroea
Neapolis

THRACE

BITHYNIA & PONTUS

GALATIA

CAPPADOCIA

Aegean
Sea

Troas

Pergamum
Thyatira

ASIA

PHRYGIA

Sardis
Smyrna
Philadelphia
Hierapolis

Antioch of
Pisidia

Iconium

Corinth
Ephesus
Laodicea
Colossae

Lystra

CILICIA

SICILY

ACHAIA
Athens

Patmos
Miletus

Perga
Attalia

Derbe

Tarsus

Syracuse

Myra

PAMPHYLIA

Antioch

Rhodes

MELITA
(Malta)

Fair Havens
CRETE

Salamis

Paphos

CYPRUS

SYRIA

Damascus

Sidon

Mediterranean   Sea

Tyre
Ptolemais
Caesarea

Cyrene

Joppa
Gaza

Jerusalem

CYRENAICA

Alexandria

EGYPT

| 0 | 100 | 200 | 300 | 400 | 500 |

scale in miles

INTRODUCTION

Joseph Smith loved the New Testament and spent much of his time expounding and explaining it. He felt a special kinship with its principal characters, especially the apostle Paul, whose writings make up a significant part of the New Testament from Acts through Revelation. In telling his own story, the Prophet Joseph stated that he "felt much like Paul" (Joseph Smith–History 1:24). The Book of Mormon, the first book of scripture produced by Joseph Smith in this dispensation through the gift and power of God, reiterates, parallels, and clarifies in a remarkable way the doctrines and principles found in the letters of Paul. Indeed, Church members of the present dispensation who love the Book of Mormon ought to love and delight in the second half of the New Testament, with its own profound discussion of such matters as faith, grace, justification, sanctification, and the Mosaic law as a schoolmaster instituted primarily to bring all unto Christ. In short, the doctrinal gems found in the treasure chest we call the New Testament, bequeathed to us from the Eastern Hemisphere, are polished and set in the Book of Mormon, a second witness from the Western Hemisphere.

Sadly, the second half of the New Testament is sometimes neglected by Latter-day Saints. That is unfortunate because the times in which those books of the New Testament were written were not so different from our own. The information in those books and the lessons we can learn from them could become a towering source of peace and power in coping with life's challenges in our own times. These books speak of the former-day Saints having to endure persecution; sexual temptations and perversions of every kind, including prostitution, adultery, fornication, and homosexuality; recurring and vexing welfare problems; famine and economic uncertainties; sorrow and suffering; trials and tribulations; the allure of reason over revelation; false teachers; and apostasy.

The writers of the individual books of the New Testament teach us about many different facets of the gospel in the meridian dispensation that have unequivocal application to the dispensation of the fulness of times, including training new leaders in expanding areas of the Church, teaching desirable qualities of priesthood holders, building successful marriages, rearing righteous families in wicked and worldly environments, fostering lasting personal relationships, avoiding cliquishness, eschewing prejudice and favoritism and cultivating tolerance, practicing pure religion (visiting the widows and the fatherless), acquiring increased charity, using the scriptures as the most effective gospel teaching method, understanding the importance of balance and perspective in any debate over whether disciples are saved by faith or works, and, above all, adoring Jesus Christ—his mission and his message. Truly, the second half of the New Testament is scripture applicable to our modern world.

The books of Acts through Revelation clearly demonstrate how the first-century Church functioned—what scholars call "primitive" (in the sense of "prime," or "first") Christianity. Through the books of the second half of the New Testament, we are shown the necessity of the Quorum of the Twelve Apostles, the role of that quorum, and how it fits into the structure of the early Church. The apostles were "the foundation," with "Jesus Christ himself being the chief corner stone" (Ephesians 2:20). The apostles were eyewitnesses of the Lord's majesty, power, redeeming grace, and literal resurrection of the body. The testimonies of the apostles found in the second half of the New Testament prepare all honest seekers of truth to recognize the reality of the Great Apostasy, which came in fulfillment of prophetic declaration (see 2 Thessalonians 2:1–3; 1 John 2:18–19). Furthermore, the witness of the apostles recorded in Acts through Revelation prompts careful investigators to look for a *restoration* of all things spoken of by prophets of all previous dispensations of Israelite covenant history (see Acts 3:19–21; Ephesians 1:10).

Latter-day Saints, and all other Christians for that matter, ought to highly prize the second half of the New Testament for the simple reason that within it are the earliest of the writings that make up the New Testament canon. There we find the earliest recorded and circulated testimonies and accounts of the Savior's mission and ministry, written by the apostle Paul. From the hand of Paul alone we have at least ten epistles regarded by many scholars as having been written before A.D. 60 which is earlier than the Gospels were written (see Bruce, *New Testament Documents,* 76).

We more fully appreciate the significance of what that means when we compare the books of the New Testament with other ancient writings. If all of Paul's compositions began circulating in the fledgling Christian community well before the destruction of the Temple in Jerusalem in A.D. 70 (which they did), much of the second half of the New Testament describes contemporaneous and near-contemporaneous events relating to Jesus of Nazareth and first-century Palestinian Judaism. Thus, the books of Acts through Revelation in the New Testament must be deemed among the most reliable of all ancient writings, and they make the case for the reality and historicity of Jesus Christ, including his resurrection, very impressive.

As certain scholars have pointed out, evidence for the historicity and authenticity of the New Testament is ever so much greater than the evidence for many writings of ancient classical authors, whose authenticity no one would dream of questioning. For example, there are extant several manuscripts of Caesar's *Gallic Wars,* which was originally composed between 58 and 50 B.C., but the oldest surviving copy is dated to some nine hundred years after Caesar's day. Of the 142 books written by the Roman historian Livy (59 B.C.–A.D. 17), only 35 have survived, and the manuscript of only one of these is as old as the fourth century after Christ. The work of the Greek historian Thucydides (circa 460–400 B.C.) is known to scholars from eight manuscripts, but here again the earliest full manuscript comes from the tenth century after Christ, with only a few papyrus scraps that can be dated to the beginning of the Christian era. Virtually the same is true of the history of Herodotus (circa 484–425 B.C.). Yet no classical scholar would dare suggest that the authenticity of any of these classical works is to be doubted simply because the earliest manuscripts extant are four hundred to thirteen hundred years later than the originals (see Bruce, *New Testament Documents,* 16–17).

How very different is the situation regarding the New Testament. First, we know of more than five thousand Greek manuscripts of the New Testament, either in whole or in part (see Bruce, *New Testament Documents,* 16). Second, the number of years between the time of composition and the events they describe, as well as the number of years between the time of composition and the dates ascribed to the earliest surviving samples of these New Testament manuscripts, is very small by comparison. The two best and most important, relatively complete New Testament manuscripts date to somewhere around A.D. 350 and include the Codex Vaticanus, the chief treasure of the Vatican Library in Rome, and the Codex Sinaiticus, which is housed in the British Museum. In addition, a considerable number of fragments remain of papyrus copies of books of the New Testament that date from between one hundred to two hundred years *earlier* than these two chief codices. The Chester Beatty Biblical Papyri—a group of papyrus documents and fragments publicized in 1931—consist of portions of several New Testament books, including the four Gospels, the Acts of the Apostles, the Pauline epistles, and the book of Revelation; they date to the early third century, that is, to between A.D. 200 and 250 (see Cross, *Oxford Dictionary of the Christian Church*, 273). A fragment of John's writings has even been dated to around A.D. 120. Truly, the best attested book from antiquity is the New Testament.

All of this should serve as significant evidence of the importance of the books of Acts through Revelation as well as a compelling argument in favor of studying them. In the words of one of the world's leading experts on ancient manuscripts, the late Sir Frederic Kenyon, the interval "between the dates of original composition and the earliest extant evidence becomes so small as to be in fact negligible. . . . Both the *authenticity* and the *general integrity* of the books of the New Testament may be regarded as finally established" (quoted in Bruce, *New Testament Documents*, 20).

TIME CHART

Date A.D. (Approx.)	Details of Events, Travels, Writings	References
30–33	Jesus' ministry and establishment of the Church of Jesus Christ	Gospels
April 33	Atoning sacrifice, death, and resurrection of Jesus Christ; postresurrection ministry and training by the Lord	Acts 1
May 33	Day of Pentecost; disciples receive the gift of the Holy Ghost	Acts 2
33–50	Early missionary efforts to Jerusalem, Judea, Samaria, Antioch, and elsewhere; Stephen is stoned to death; conversion of Saul (Paul); Peter's decisive vision opening the gospel to Gentiles; early ministries of Peter and Paul; Paul's first missionary journey	Acts 3–14 Acts 13:4–14:27
44	Herod Agrippa I: persecution of the Church; James (of the First Presidency) killed; Peter imprisoned and miraculously delivered	Acts 12
45–50	General epistle of James written by Jesus' half-brother	
50	Jerusalem conference convened; circumcision and Gentile conversions	Acts 15
52–53	Paul's second missionary journey; 1 and 2 Thessalonians written by Paul from Corinth	Acts 15:40–18:22
54–58	Paul's third missionary journey	Acts 18:23–21:15
57	1 and 2 Corinthians written by Paul from Ephesus and Macedonia; Galatians written by Paul from Corinth	
57–58	Romans written by Paul from Corinth	
58–60	Paul in Jerusalem and arrested at the Temple; imprisoned for two years at Caesarea	Acts 21:17–23:32 Acts 23:33–26:32
61–62	Paul's journey to and teaching in Rome; Colossians, Ephesians, Philemon, and Philippians written by Paul during his first Roman captivity	Acts 27–28
61–66	Hebrews, 1 Timothy, and Titus written by Paul	
before 68	2 Timothy written by Paul before his martyrdom; 1 and 2 Peter written by the apostle Peter before his martyrdom, possibly from Rome	
70	Jerusalem and the Temple destroyed by the Romans; apparent migration of Christians to Pella (according to Eusebius), and transfer of Church headquarters, likely to Ephesus	
70–100	Jude written; 1, 2, and 3 John and the Revelation written by John the Beloved, possibly from Ephesus	

CHAPTER 1

THE GRAECO-ROMAN WORLD OF THE EARLY APOSTLES

After Israel's return from the Babylonian captivity (538 B.C.), life in the Holy Land was controlled by the Persian empire, which allowed the inhabitants a fair degree of autonomy. By this time, the citizens of Judah were called Jews, though they were a mixture of several tribal elements with Judah predominating. They were obliged to obey a series of prophet-governors, such as Nehemiah, who ruled in concert with the Aaronic high priest. The people and their governors, however, ultimately owed allegiance to the Persian emperor.

In the fifth and fourth centuries before Christ, the course of Judaism changed dramatically in both religious and political realms. According to Jewish belief, sometime after 400 B.C. biblical prophecy ceased. The Talmud declares that with the demise of the last biblical prophets—Haggai, Zechariah, and Malachi—the Holy Spirit, that is, prophetic inspiration, departed from Israel (see Sotah 48b; Sanhedrin 11a). Political authority seems to have devolved solely to the high priest; religious authority was shared between the high priest and learned men called scribes or sages. Thus, Jewish teaching advised, "From now on incline your ear and listen to the instructions of the Sages" (*Seder 'Olam Rabbah* 6, quoted in Talmon, *"Dead Sea Scrolls,"* 16).

In 333 B.C., after two centuries of Persian domination, a new military power arose in the Near East—Alexander the

Great. Alexander's troops, though they were outnumbered, defeated the Persians at the Battle of Issus and began creating a world empire that would stretch from Gibraltar in the west to the Punjab in India in the east. In 332 Alexander conquered Jerusalem, and Hellenistic ("Greek-like") culture was brought firsthand to Judah by the very person who viewed himself as the great emissary of Greek ways. Having been tutored as a boy by Aristotle, Alexander believed his mission was to Hellenize the world.

When Alexander the Great died in 323 B.C., his empire was carved up among four of his commanders and their families, as prophesied in Daniel 7:2–7. The two most important were the Ptolemies, who ruled over Egypt-Judea, and the Seleucids, who ruled over Syria-Mesopotamia. Both dynasties fought incessantly for control of the Holy Land. Both promoted Hellenism. Finally, in 198 B.C., at a place in the northern Galilee region called Panias, a decisive battle was fought. Seleucid forces under Antiochus III (the Great) soundly defeated the Ptolemaic army, and control of the Holy Land passed to the Seleucids. Panias was not only the site of a pivotal battle but was later known in New Testament times as the place where Peter made his notable confession of Jesus as the Christ; Panias is called Caesarea Philippi in Matthew 16.

Antiochus III, the first Syrian (Seleucid) ruler of Judea (from the Greek rendering of *Judah*) granted the Jews many favors, and they took advantage of the situation. A governing council of elders, called in Greek the *Gerousia* ("assembly"), was established to assume the general administrative, political, judicial, and social leadership of the Jewish community under the direction of the Aaronic high priest. This governing body later came to be known as the Sanhedrin, also referred to in the New Testament as "the council" (Acts 4:15) and the "senate of the children of Israel" (Acts 5:21). In New Testament times it was composed of seventy-one members and, under Roman supervision, had far-reaching decision-making powers just short of capital punishment.

Under Antiochus III the pace of Hellenization was accelerated in Judea, and this brought two worldviews into direct conflict. The battleground was Jerusalem. Jews began to coalesce into groups according to their disposition toward Greek cultural influences. As time passed the situation deteriorated and the chasm widened between pro-Hellenistic Jews and anti-Hellenistic Jews. Among the members of the pro-Hellenistic party were aristocratic Jews, the Zadokim or high priestly families (later called the Sadducees). This group was excited by Greek culture and favored the political and economic status quo. The anti-Hellenists formed a group called the Hasidim or Hasideans (Hebrew for "pious ones"; they have no relation to the modern Hasidic Jews). The ancient Hasidim seem to have been the predecessors of the Pharisees; they were orthodox religionists and ardent supporters of God's laws as revealed in the Torah (see 1 Maccabees 2:42–43).

Points of conflict between Judaism and Hellenism were numerous and profound. Hellenism promoted art, appreciation of the human body (including sexuality), athletic competitions (performed without clothing), and philosophy. Essentially, Torah-based Judaism was diametrically opposed to Hellenism. "To the Jews, art, in all its physical forms, was in conflict with the Second Commandment. Nude statuary, swimming, and exercising in the nude or almost nude was offensive to the Jewish people, who, in the courses of several centuries, had built up rigid standards against displaying any part of the body except hands, feet, neck and head in public. . . . The Roman theatre presentations often treated sex in a mode offensive to Jewish sensitivity. Extra-marital relations were discussed or depicted on the stage without any punishment for the sin being presented; this violated the wishes of the Jews, who had insisted that punishment follow such acts. Jewish religion was based on revelation from God, through the prophets and patriarchs. Hellenistic culture substituted human reason, observation, and experience with other humans as the sources from which religion came, apart from any type of communication from divine beings" (Lyon, "Greco-Roman Influences," 20).

In 175 B.C. a new king emerged in Syria, one whose enactments brought Judaism to the brink of disaster. His name was Antiochus IV, and he determined not only to complete the process of Hellenization but also to wipe out the Jewish religion all together. A Greek-style gymnasium was constructed in Jerusalem, and Jews were encouraged to dress after the Greek fashion. An intertestamental text entitled First Maccabees (part of the Apocrypha) describes the situation: "In those days lawless men came forth from Israel, and misled many, saying, 'Let us go and make a covenant with the Gentiles round about us, for since we separated from them many evils have come upon us.' This proposal pleased them, and some of the people eagerly went to the king. He authorized them to observe the ordinances of the Gentiles. So they built a gymnasium in Jerusalem, according to Gentile custom, and removed the marks of circumcision, and abandoned the holy covenant. They joined with the Gentiles and sold themselves to do evil" (1 Maccabees 1:11–15).

The gymnasium changed the whole spiritual and social atmosphere of Jerusalem. It was a place where athletes ran around naked (as the etymology of this Greek word indicates, *gymnos* means "naked"). Eventually, the gymnasium began to rival the Temple as the center of cultural activity and religious-like devotion. Because the gymnasium was under the patronage of the Greek gods Hermes (Mercury) and Hercules, its Jewish patrons seem to have wanted to imitate those gods more than to revere Jehovah.

According to 2 Maccabees 4:12–15, even the priests became caught up in the Hellenistic activities: "There was such an extreme of Hellenization and increase in the adoption of foreign ways because of the surpassing wickedness of Jason, who was ungodly and no high priest, that the priests were no longer intent upon their service at the altar. Despising the sanctuary and neglecting the sacrifices, they hastened to take part in the unlawful proceedings in the wrestling arena after the call to the discus, disdaining the honors prized by their fathers and putting the highest value upon Greek forms of prestige."

Orthodox Jews, especially the Hasidim, or Pious Ones, were outraged at the spread of this virulent and aggressive Hellenism. The split between the two segments of the population widened until fighting broke out in Jerusalem between the pro-Hellenist and pro-Torah parties.

In 168 B.C., Antiochus IV set about to destroy every distinctive feature of the Jewish faith. All Jewish sacrifices were forbidden. The sabbath and feast days were no longer to be observed. The rite of circumcision was forbidden. Books of the Torah were desecrated or destroyed. Jews were forced to eat swine flesh and perform sacrifices at idolatrous altars set up throughout the land. Any disobedience to the various aspects of the Syrian king's decree was punishable by death. To crown his deplorable actions, Antiochus IV desecrated the Temple by erecting an altar to the Greek god Zeus (perhaps molded in the image of Antiochus himself) on the altar of burnt offering within the Temple court (see 1 Maccabees 1:41–61). Antiochus had claimed that Zeus had manifested himself to the Syrian king, and thus he referred to himself as *Epiphanes,* a Greek word meaning "God manifest" (2 Maccabees 4:7). His enemies, however, now applied the epithet and the pun *Epimanes,* which is Greek for "madman."

Naturally, many orthodox Jews chose to die rather than to be defiled by what was to them a Syrian sacrilege, being forced to profane the covenant (see 1 Maccabees 1:62–63). Many fled Jerusalem and crowded into towns where royal agents intent on erasing the Jewish faith pursued them.

Open revolt against Syrian officials began in Modi'in, a village about twenty miles northwest of Jerusalem, where a priest named Mattathias, of the house of Hasmon (the Hasmoneans) lived with his five sons (see 1 Maccabees 2:1–6).

When a Syrian official came to Modi'in to enforce heathen sacrifice, Mattathias slew both the traitorous Jew who offered the sacrifice and the Syrian official. He and his sons fled into the mountains, where they were joined by many zealous Jews, including the Hasidim (see 1 Maccabees 2:23–43). They organized an army, "struck down [the] sinners," and "rescued the law out of the hands of the Gentiles and kings, and they never let the sinner gain the upper hand" (1 Maccabees 2:44, 48).

After the death of Mattathias, the struggle was carried on in turn by three of his sons, Judas (166–160 B.C.) surnamed Maccabeus ("the Hammerer"), Jonathan (160–143 B.C.), and Simon (142–134 B.C.). Success followed success in their campaigns against Syrian forces by using guerrilla warfare tactics. After Judas' fourth victory near Beth-Zur, south of Jerusalem, the freedom fighters were able to occupy the Temple complex. On the 25th of Kislev (December), 164 B.C., the very day on which it had been desecrated three years before (see 1 Maccabees 4:54), the Temple in Jerusalem was cleansed and rededicated under the leadership of Judas, and traditional Mosaic worship restored (see 1 Maccabees 4:36–59; 2 Maccabees 10:1–7). This event has been commemorated ever since as the festival of lights, or Hanukkah.

The Hasmonean dynasty controlled political and religious life in Judea for the next one hundred years (165–63 B.C.). In 141 B.C. a bronze decree was set up in the courtyard of the Temple celebrating Jerusalem's deliverance from the Syrian Greeks and conferring upon Simon the office of high priest as a hereditary possession. Under the Hasmoneans, an independent Jewish state emerged in which the offices of political king and high priest were vested in a single person.

Out of the Hasmonean or Maccabean period also emerged the major Jewish sects, which occupy a prominent place in the New Testament. The Pharisees, as already indicated, seem to have evolved from the Hasidim. Their name, from the Hebrew word *parash,* means "separatists"—either in the sense of resisting Hellenism, or, more likely, in separating themselves from the Jewish masses through strict adherence to a set of ritual purification observances. The Pharisees were determined to have Jewish homes imitate the ritual purity practiced by the priests of the Temple—each home replicating the purity of the Temple (see Neusner, *Glory of God Is Intelligence*, xix–xx). The Pharisees scrupulously avoided "everything which might convey ceremonial impurity to them" (Bruce, *New Testament History*, 72). They were especially concerned with laws governing food. Consumption of forbidden foods was ritually contaminating, but the Pharisees even avoided eating foods that should be tithed unless the tithe had been paid exactly. The prophet Daniel was considered the prototype of the Hasidim (see Daniel 1:8), and hence the prototype of Pharisees as well, in that he refused to defile himself with the impure food and drink of Nebuchadnezzar, king of Babylon (see Bruce, *New Testament History*, 72–73).

With this background, it becomes clear why the Pharisees were often antagonistic toward Jesus and the apostles over such things as Sabbath observance (picking food and healing the sick on that day), cleanliness laws (eating with unwashed hands), and tithing little things but neglecting such things as ethical matters, fasting, and lawful divorce. The Pharisees claimed the right to rule all the Jews by virtue of their possessing the "Oral Torah" of Moses, that is, the body of traditions revealed to Moses alongside what came to be known as the written Torah, or Pentateuch. The oral tradition, or "tradition of the elders," as Jesus called it (Matthew 15:2) was intended to interpret written law to the changing circumstances of life. Though Jesus was sometimes critical of the oral tradition, he also recognized its value (see Matthew 13:52).

The Sadducees seem to have evolved from elements of the pro-Hellenists in Judea and identified themselves or even legitimized themselves by taking their name from that of Zadok, the high priest of the Temple at the time of Solomon. The Zadokite family of high priests had served at the head of the priesthood throughout the First Temple period

(Solomon's Temple) and during Second Temple times (Zerubbabel's Temple) until the Hasmoneans took control of the high priesthood. Ezekiel 44:9–16 had assigned the priestly duties exclusively to this clan. The Sadducees rejected the "Oral Torah," which the Pharisees considered law. That the Sadducees and the Pharisees disagreed intensely with one another over other issues, and yet filled the ranks of the Sanhedrin side by side, is superbly demonstrated in an episode involving the apostle Paul after his third missionary journey: "When Paul perceived that the one part were Sadducees, and the other Pharisees, he cried out in the council, Men and brethren, I am a Pharisee, the son of a Pharisee: of the hope and resurrection of the dead I am called in question. And when he had so said, there arose a dissension between the Pharisees and the Sadducees: and the multitude was divided. For the Sadducees say that there is no resurrection, neither angel, nor spirit: but the Pharisees confess both. And there arose a great cry: and the scribes that were of the Pharisees' part arose, and strove, saying, We find no evil in this man: but if a spirit or an angel hath spoken to him, let us not fight against God" (Acts 23:6–9).

From this passage we also understand that the early apostles encountered another group called scribes. They studied, copied, and interpreted scripture, and they came from the ranks of both the Pharisees and the Sadducees. Scribes could render authoritative judgments according to the Torah and occupied important seats in the Sanhedrin. They were not, strictly speaking, a party or a sect within Judaism but, rather, legal and religious specialists. Their prominence in the New Testament narrative, however, makes them very significant, and they are undoubtedly related in some way to another group encountered in first-century Judaism—the rabbis. The term *rabbi* is an honorific title (Hebrew, "my master" or "my great one") and was bestowed according to one's knowledge of Jewish law, lore, and teaching reputation. Though the term, as most modern scholars contend, may not have been applied as an official title until after the destruction of the Second Temple by the Romans, it seems to have been used in at least unofficial ways by the time of Herod the Great, for we have record that the disciples called Jesus *rabbi* (see Matthew 26:25, 49; Mark 9:5; 11:21; 14:45).

Though not mentioned in the Bible but certainly encountered by Jesus and the apostles was a sect called Essenes. It is probable they originated from different elements of the same Hasidim that produced the Pharisees. Certain numbers of the Essenes reacted to the corrupting influences of Hellenism by withdrawing from Jerusalem in the second century before Christ and establishing a semimonastic community on the shores of the Dead Sea at a place now called Qumran. There the Essene settlement continued to exist on and off from about 150 B.C. until A.D. 68, when the Roman armies swept through the land during the First Jewish War. Realizing that their sacred writings were endangered, they hid their scrolls in at least eleven nearby caves.

The discovery of the Dead Sea Scrolls, beginning in 1947, has provided an extraordinary window into the religious climate that produced both normative, or Pharisaic, Judaism and Christianity—the only two of the more than twenty Jewish-related religious groups to survive the destruction of Jerusalem and the Temple in A.D. 70. Among the hundreds of texts, thousands of parchment fragments, and far fewer rolled-up scrolls, archaeologists have found samples of every book of the Old Testament except Esther. The find also includes apocryphal and pseudepigraphical works, community rulebooks, scriptural commentaries, and prayer texts. The value of the Qumran finds is at least twofold: first, we now have actual scriptures dating from the time period of Jesus and the apostles—the kind they really used in synagogues of the period (before 1947 the oldest biblical texts dated only to the ninth or tenth century after Christ); second, we now know that some of the doctrines Jesus and his apostles taught were almost certainly intended as a direct counter to ideas current in Judaism of that period. For example, some of the sacred texts at Qumran teach that no one had the right to worship the Lord unless a minyan (quorum) of ten men was gathered in the company of a Levitical priest. Also, the Essenes at Qumran taught that they were to love their own kind but hate their enemies. Jesus unmistakably contradicted both notions with true doctrine (Matthew 5:43–44; 18:19–20).

ROMAN JUDEA

Great changes came once again to the Holy Land in 63 B.C. when the Roman general Pompey marched his troops into Jerusalem and proclaimed the Jews subject to the authority of Rome. Though the independent Hasmonean Jewish state came to an end, Hellenism did not. It was simply adopted, adapted, and promoted by the new masters of the Mediterranean world. The Jews were allowed to retain some territories as semiautonomous political districts, including Judea, Perea, the eastern part of Idumea, and Galilee. The Samaritans became independent. Roman overlordship seemed to the Jews very harsh on the once-autonomous Jewish state. For example, in 52 B.C. on the western shore of the Sea of Galilee, thirty-thousand Jews of the district of Tarichae were enslaved.

To give the appearance of independence to this new Roman province, the political administration was eventually entrusted to a man named Antipater. He was the son of a rich man from Idumea, a region that had been forcibly converted to Judaism back in the days of the Hasmonean ruler John Hyrcanus I (134–104 B.C.), who had become king and high priest after his father, Simon, was murdered. Antipater's own political career began under the tutelage of his father who had served as *strategos* ("general") of Idumea. He strengthened his power base when he sided with Julius Caesar in Caesar's struggle for control of the Roman Republic against Caesar's associate in the First Triumvirate, General Pompey. By 47 B.C., Antipater was solidly in control of Judea, and he gave his sons Phasael and Herod (later Herod the Great) the tasks of governing Jerusalem and Galilee respectively.

Though Caesar was assassinated at Rome in 44 B.C., Antipater and his sons held onto the reins of power for a time. But in 43 B.C. Antipater was murdered by one of his opponents, and Herod was left to avenge his father's death and suppress unrest in Galilee and Judea. In 42 B.C. he, together with his brother, was appointed ruler over all the land. A short time later the Parthians invaded, and Herod was forced to flee south, stopping at Masada for protection before continuing to Rome to seek help. When Herod returned to his native land in the winter of 39 B.C., he had Rome's full support. Mark Antony and Octavian, who eventually gained sole control of the Republic and transformed it into the Empire, had Herod appointed king de jure (king by right or by law). Beginning in Galilee, Herod consolidated his strength and in 37 B.C. became king de facto (in fact, as if legally constituted) with the capture of Jerusalem. By 20 B.C. his kingdom included all of Judea and even some of Transjordan (the area east of the Jordan River). He maintained tight control over the entire region until his death just after the birth of Christ.

Throughout his reign Herod encountered fierce opposition. He was doubly odious to the Jewish people. First, most Jews hated having been subjugated by a foreign power, and Herod personified that power. According to Josephus, the Pharisees, who wielded significant influence with common people, refused to swear an oath of loyalty to the Roman emperor. Certain activists, whom the populace apparently supported, vowed to murder Herod for introducing foreign customs. Another example is the story of two rabbis who persuaded several rabbinic students to tear down the image of the Roman golden eagle, which Herod had erected above the Temple gate (for which they were executed). Second, the Pharisees and Essenes refused to recognize an Idumean as king of the Jewish people. Many Jews looked upon Herod's religious sincerity as suspect. Herod had good reason to look over his shoulder constantly, both because of Jewish opponents and because of the changing political winds in Rome. He likely held Galilee and Judea through intimidation and manipulation. He was especially hated in Galilee, as were the Romans.

Immediately after Herod's death, popular outbreaks occurred in virtually every quarter of the land. The people demanded tax reductions, relief from economic and political oppression, and religious reform. The most significant revolt came in Galilee where Judas, son of Hezekiah, raised an army to attack the royal arsenal at Sepphoris and sought to become king. There was almost certainly an element of personal vengeance in these actions, because years earlier (47 B.C.), Herod had first made a name for himself by launching a fierce attack on Hezekiah, who was waging a guerilla war in the north of Galilee—part of Herod's stewardship at the time.

The revolt after Herod's death was crushed when Varus, governor of Syria, entered Judea with two Roman legions and four regiments of cavalry. Galilee was the first region to be subdued. The city of Sepphoris was captured and burned and its people enslaved. The rest of the country was soon brought under control.

After Varus restored apparent stability in the country, Caesar Augustus divided the territory among Herod's sons. They were each to oversee much smaller districts than their father had ruled, and they ruled at the pleasure of an overall governor appointed by Rome in A.D. 6. Archelaus inherited Samaria, Judea, and Idumea in 4 B.C. but was deposed and banished to Gaul in the ninth year of his rule (A.D. 6) because of his tyrannical cruelty. Herod Philip inherited the northern parts of the land and stayed in power from 4 B.C. to A.D. 34. Herod Antipas governed Galilee and Perea from 4 B.C. to A.D. 39.

Jesus of Nazareth grew to manhood in Galilee during the reign of Herod Antipas. A number of his parables (see, for example, Matthew 20:1–15; Mark 12:1–11; Luke 15:11–32; 16:1–12; 16:19–31) give us insight into the social and economic conditions of the Holy Land during the years of his and his apostles' ministries. The main characters are rich men or large landowners. Based on evidence from the Mishnah and from archaeology, scholars have argued that single ownership of large tracts of land increased markedly during the first century after Christ. Increasing numbers of farmers were forced to sell their land as a result of sickness, drought, and above all, exorbitant taxes. Whole villages sometimes came to be owned by one person. Farmers and their sons became day-workers. This situation was nowhere felt more keenly than in Galilee where agriculture was the mainstay of existence. It seems clear from the New Testament that in this period there was tremendous debt, many beggars, and large numbers of slaves. Josephus verifies these dire conditions. He records that during the time of the First Jewish Revolt (A.D. 67–70) Simon bar Gioras, a leader of one of the rebel factions, freed Jewish slaves as part of his plan to claim rule (see Josephus, *Wars*, 4.9.3).

Jewish resistance to Roman domination is extremely complex, but it seems clear that Galilee was a critical focal point of this resistance from 4 B.C. to A.D. 66. In fact, Josephus traces the origins of the Zealot movement (or Fourth Philosophy), which flourished in A.D. 6, to Saddok the Pharisee and Judas the Galilean—a man from the mountain fortress of Gamla, east of the Sea of Galilee. The movement called for armed revolt, saying that such heavy tax assessments amounted to slavery and that only God was master of the Jewish people (Josephus, *Antiquities*, 18.1.1, 6; *Wars*, 2.17.8). Even Jesus may have been suspected of Zealot activity by political officials. He was, after all, from Galilee, had spent most of his time there, and associated with one known Zealot within the ranks of his closest followers (Simon Zelotes). One scholar noted:

"Jesus can hardly have been a Zealot. However, it is quite conceivable that the Roman authorities and the Sadducees, who were sympathetic to them, saw it as such, given his Galilean background, above all because in recent decades Galilee had been regarded as a cradle of rebel movements" (Jagersma, *History of Israel*, 127).

Things went from bad to worse in the first century as banditry and resistance to Roman domination spread through Galilee and Judea. A series of corrupt and incompetent Roman prefects and procurators (governors) exacerbated conditions. In 27 B.C. Caesar Augustus had divided the thirty-two provinces of the Empire into two categories: senatorial and imperial. The eleven senatorial provinces continued to be governed under the supervision of the Senate, while the twenty-one imperial provinces were under the direct control of the emperor. The senatorial provinces were, on the whole, older, richer, and more peaceful territories where there was little danger of an uprising. The imperial provinces were usually frontier areas, recently added to the empire. These territories also contained many revolutionary elements, seething and ready to explode. Such a territory was kept under the direct surveillance of the emperor himself.

Imperial provinces were further broken down into two types. Larger ones were governed by a legate, who served as both military governor and chief magistrate. Smaller imperial provinces were ruled by a governor, who bore the title *praefectus*. From the time of Emperor Claudius (A.D. 41–54) on, however, it became customary to call such a governor by the title of *procurator Augusti*, or, simply, *procurator*. Judea was a smaller imperial province, and its governors resided in an official residence at Caesarea by the sea. They were accustomed to traveling up to Jerusalem at feasts and festival times and sometimes wintered there. When in Jerusalem, the governors occupied either the palace erected by Herod the Great in the Upper City (today's Citadel Museum area) or the Antonia Fortress overlooking the Temple Mount.

Perhaps the best-known governor of Judea was Pontius Pilate (A.D. 26–36), whose administration was depicted by contemporary writers as harsh and corrupt. An inscription found at Caesarea calls him "Praefect of Judaea," though later Jewish and Roman historians, such as Josephus and Tacitus, refer to him as *procurator* because that is the designation that had become current in their day. Throughout the New Testament, the general term *governor* designates Pilate and his successors. Aside from his role in the crucifixion of the Savior, Pilate was widely disliked by his subjects, the Jews, and was finally removed from office and sent to Rome to answer charges of brutality and incompetence.

An example of the venality of the later governors is found in Acts 24:24–27, which recounts the attempt of Felix (who ruled A.D. 52 to 60) to extort a bribe from the apostle Paul, who was under house arrest at Caesarea, waiting to be sent to Rome for an audience with the emperor himself. Josephus tells us that it was also during the administration of Felix that a new group of terrorist-robbers emerged called the Sicarii, a Latin term meaning "men armed with a dagger" (*sica*). They began to disrupt life in Judea by assassinating prominent citizens and those who opposed them (Josephus, *Wars*, 2.13.3). The successors to Felix were no better. Festus (A.D. 60–62) was followed by Albinus (A.D. 62–64), who plundered public and private funds, accepted bribes to release convicts, and emptied prisons of all but the worst criminals.

For a brief time, between A.D. 41 and 44, the rule of the governors was suspended, and the full powers of monarchy were restored to the grandson of Herod the Great, Herod Agrippa I. As a legitimate Jewish king, he ruled over most of the region his grandfather had held. Roman suspicions about Agrippa arose, however, when he began constructing a new wall to enclose and fortify the city of Jerusalem to the north, the weakest point in the city's defenses. Agrippa responded to the suspicions by inaugurating a series of games at Caesarea to celebrate Roman victories in Britain and to honor the emperor. On the second day of the celebrations, while he was presiding over the events in a robe made entirely of silver, Agrippa suddenly fell ill and died. He was fifty-four years of age. Luke depicts this event as divine intervention: the king is smitten by an angel of the Lord as just recompense for his atrocities against the leaders of the early Church (Acts 12). Though Jews mourned his death, Christians and Gentiles were relieved.

Agrippa I had announced that his son Agrippa II would succeed him. The suddenness of his death caused Roman leaders to doubt that a seventeen-year old could handle the challenge of ruling such a kingdom. Emperor Claudius ordered that Judea revert to direct imperial provincial rule but at the same time allowed Agrippa II to hold the title of king. This arrangement lasted for twenty-two years, until the devastation of the First Jewish Revolt.

CHALLENGES FACED BY THE APOSTLES

The early apostles faced at least three major challenges in administering the Church and teaching the gospel of Jesus Christ. First was a significant shift, over time, in the government's attitude toward Christianity. Four of the five Roman emperors who reigned during the period of the New Testament were generally even more corrupt or incompetent than the governors whom they appointed to rule in Judea. The worst of these was the hated Nero (A.D. 54–68), before whom Paul stood trial (Acts 27:24) and under whom both Peter and Paul were executed in Rome. Bad imperial leadership caused instability in the empire and made life difficult. At first, the early Church enjoyed some tolerance under Roman law. As the Church expanded and grew, however, the attitude of tolerance began to change. The worship of other gods was still permitted by Rome, but increasingly the emperor was seen as divine. By the time of Nero it was customary for the emperor to be called by such titles as *theos* ("god") and *soter* ("savior"). By the time of the emperor Domitian (A.D. 81–96) the title *Dominus et Deus* ("lord and god") was added to his imperial majesty. Christians came to see in the emperor a challenge to the singularity and divinity of Christ.

Second was the influence of Hellenism on the preaching of the apostles. Hellenism proved to be a two-edged sword. On the one hand, the early Church missionaries generally found the cultural atmosphere of the empire to be quite congenial and beneficial. It was congenial because it provided a medium through which apostolic teachings could be spread rapidly: the Greek language. Many people throughout the Roman world were bilingual. One language was their native tongue, and the other was often koine, or a common Greek. Koine was the Greek dialect commonly spoken in the Hellenistic and Roman periods, and it became the lingua franca, something resembling a common language among diverse peoples. The Roman cultural atmosphere was beneficial because of the kind of curiosity fostered by the Hellenistic mindset. Rome may have conquered Greece with its armies, but Greece conquered Rome with its ideas and ideology. On the other hand, the very same Hellenistic culture in the empire that made people curious about Christianity also made them lack interest in fully committing to such new and strange ideas. Many early Christians could not resist the temptation to embellish pure revelation with interpretations heavily laced with Greek ideas. The leaders of the early Church struggled to keep the gospel free from false philosophies so prevalent in the empire. The purity of the gospel did not survive, as medieval Christian philosophy and theology testify.

A third challenge faced by the early apostles centered on Jewish resistance to their message. The Jews held God's ancient covenant and thus held themselves superior because of their traditions. Abraham had founded the Hebrew nation. God's covenant was renewed with Moses, who was the great mouthpiece and lawgiver on earth. The Jews were descendants of both, and this spiritual legacy bred a false sense of superiority in the Jewish nation, as is evident in several books of the New Testament. The most striking example is found in John 8. There we are told that the Jews were quick to remind Jesus of their personal exclusiveness: "Abraham is our father," they boasted (v. 39). Any contact with what they perceived to be apostate ideas or persons the Jews regarded as contaminating. Paul summarized the cultural environment, which made missionary work so frustrating: "For the Jews require a sign, and the Greeks seek after wisdom: but we preach Christ crucified, unto the Jews a stumblingblock, and unto the Greeks foolishness" (1 Corinthians 1:22–23).

But even signs were not sufficient for many Jews in the first century after Christ. By that time, tradition had replaced revelation as the guiding principle in Judaism. The Babylonian Talmud contains a fanciful story of an argument between two great and learned rabbis that illustrates this point: After calling forth many impressive and unmistakable signs regarding the correctness of a particular idea, one of the rabbis was finally able to call forth a voice from heaven declaring the truth of his position (in other words, the voice of direct revelation). At this, the other rabbi arose and said: "The Torah declares concerning itself, 'It is not up in heaven'; that is to say, once the Torah was given on Mount Sinai, we pay no heed to heavenly voices but, as the Torah ordains further, we follow the opinion of the majority" (Steinberg, *Basic Judaism,* 68–69).

Jewish resistance to the doctrines of Christ was the most difficult and daunting impediment that Christians faced in the early decades of Church history. A preeminent example is found in Acts 12, which records that Herod Agrippa I killed James, one of the chief apostles: "And because he saw it pleased the Jews, he proceeded further to take Peter also . . . [and] he put him in prison" (Acts 12:3–4). Peter escaped, but things became increasingly difficult as the apostles labored to fulfill their commissions in a world indifferent or hostile to their testimonies. Truly, the ancient apostles faced imposing challenges, and in so doing they taught us much about our own times. We must be wise and learn from them in the pages of the New Testament.

CHAPTER 2

THE ACTS OF THE APOSTLES, CHAPTERS 1 THROUGH 12

The study of the books of Acts through Revelation—the second half of the New Testament—is a course in Church history. Comparable to the history of the rise and growth of the early latter-day Church in the thirty years from 1820 to 1850, the history in Acts through Revelation covers a similar period in the meridian Church, the thirty years from approximately A.D. 34 to 64. In Acts through Revelation we read about the history, the doctrine, and the covenants of the early Church. The second half of the New Testament is a record of the events, or the acts and the revelations of the leaders of the Church that Christ established in the first century.

Because this same Church was restored to the earth in the nineteenth century, one instructive way to study the book of Acts is to make a parallel list of beliefs and practices found in the early Church and in The Church of Jesus Christ of Latter-day Saints. The results show that the book of Acts may be one of the most profound witnesses anywhere that the first-century Church and the latter-day Church match up in an arresting way.

The Lord Jesus Christ established his Church in the meridian of time with an organization whose officers possessed his authority: the leading officers had been given the keys of the kingdom on the Mount of Transfiguration. The chosen leaders were involved in missionary work during his ministry. The Church grew in membership and in organization during the Lord's forty-day ministry after his resurrection, and dramatic changes were promised for the future. Jesus taught that his gospel must expand to "all nations" (Matthew 28:19–20) and that the apostles should "be witnesses unto the uttermost part of the earth" (Acts 1:8). The appearance of the resurrected Lord to the prophet-president, Peter, abruptly altered the course of history. The knowledge and testimony of the resurrection and atoning redemption of the Savior and the blessings of the gift of the Holy Ghost were the moving forces behind the profound new zeal that spread throughout the Mediterranean world.

Notice that the title of the book is The *Acts* of the Apostles, not *Meditations* or *Philosophizing*. A more complete title might be "The Acts of *a Few of* the Apostles." One purpose of the book is to justify the mission to the Gentiles and to explain how the gospel is taken to Rome: Jerusalem to Syria to Asia to Greece to Rome. The book of Acts is an inspired work of historical genius, mentioning no fewer than fifty-four cities and thirty-four countries, tracing the development of the Lord's true Church from the small provincial capital of the Jews, Jerusalem, through the Mediterranean world to the great seat of the Roman Empire, the dazzling city of Rome itself. The Roman Catholic Church in particular would have wanted this record preserved. Perhaps that is one reason the version of the book of The Acts of the Apostles preserved in our King James Version not only survived but triumphed over the other books of the acts of specific apostles such as are found among the compilations of the New Testament Apocrypha and Pseudepigrapha.

Our present book of Acts may be divided into two parts. Part one includes chapters 1 through 12; the center is Jerusalem, and the main figure is Peter. Part two includes chapters 13 through 28; the center is Antioch, and the main figure is Paul.

It is generally agreed that Luke wrote Acts, judging from the parallel introductions of the Gospel of Luke and Acts (compare Luke 1:1–4 and Acts 1:1). It was common practice for historians who wrote around the first century to begin a second volume or sequel to their original work by including a brief summary of the first (Acts 1:1–3) and then laying out the anticipated contents of the second (Acts 1:8). Luke uses the words the Savior spoke to his eleven apostles on the Mount of Ascension to illustrate this pattern. Another outline of Acts is seen in the circles of influence suggested by Luke in Acts 1:8: The apostles are first "witnesses unto me both in Jerusalem," chapters 1 through 7; then "in all Judaea, and in Samaria," chapters 8 through 10; and then "unto the uttermost part of the earth," chapters 11 through 28. The entries "Luke" and "Acts of the Apostles" in the dictionary of the LDS edition of the Bible give us a new appreciation for the ancient author's skill and life's work (see also "New Testament—The Acts of the Apostles," in Ludlow, *Encyclopedia of Mormonism,* 3:1013).

Luke does not name himself as the author of Acts (except perhaps in one variant reading), but internal and external evidence make the issue almost certain. The Muratorian Canon (circa A.D. 170) is the earliest source to state explicitly that Luke was the author of both the third Gospel and The Acts of the Apostles. The early Church theologian Irenaeus (circa A.D. 180) also names Luke as the author of both books. And the fourth-century historian Eusebius, citing several sources, identifies Luke as the author of both the Gospel of Luke and The Acts of the Apostles. The ancient manuscript called the Anti-Marcionite Prologue to the Gospel of Luke regards the author as a real person who also wrote Acts, who came from Antioch of Syria, who served the Lord without distraction, and who died in Boeotia at age eighty-four. In addition, a variant reading of Acts 20:13, which may date to the second century, reads, "But I Luke, and those who were with me, went on board . . ."

Luke became an ardent student of the life of our Lord through his association with the apostles and other eyewitnesses to the Savior's ministry and resurrection (see Luke

1:1–4). Luke also had opportunities to gain first-hand testimonies of the life of Christ as he traveled with and met apostles and prophets of the meridian dispensation. Their testimonies became his testimony and the foundation of his life, just as testimony was the foundation of the entire first-century Church. As one modern non–Latter-day Saint scholar said, "Nothing in history is more certain than that the disciples believed that, after being crucified, dead, and buried, Christ rose again from the tomb on the third day" (Metzger, *New Testament*, 126).

In our time, this same testimony of the resurrection was articulated by the Prophet Joseph Smith: "The fundamental principles of our religion are the testimony of the Apostles and Prophets, concerning Jesus Christ, that He died, was buried, and rose again the third day, and ascended into heaven; and all other things which pertain to our religion are only appendages to it" (*Teachings of the Prophet Joseph Smith*, 121). The implications of this comment are far-reaching, for it means that today we have apostles and prophets, just as in biblical times, who have the same qualifications they possessed anciently—the eyewitness quality of conviction.

The book of Acts serves as a bridge in our New Testament collection between the Gospels, the written testimony of the eyewitnesses regarding "all that Jesus began both to do and teach" (Acts 1:1), and what the eyewitnesses themselves began "to do and teach." In its literary excellence, dramatic description, and presentation of accurate historical detail, The Acts of the Apostles is superb. Archaeological findings support Luke's descriptions of locations and proper terms for the times. He possesses a large vocabulary and employs words that fit the cultural setting he is describing. For example, Luke uses Aramaic idioms when describing events that occurred in the Holy Land (see Acts 1–12). Truly, the Luke-to-Acts sequence is a significant part of our scriptural heritage.

ACTS 1

1:1 *Theophilus,* from the Greek, means "beloved or friend of God"; he was perhaps a non-Christian Roman officer or a Church member. Evidence from Acts 23:26 seems to favor his being an officer, for in the book of Acts, the Roman governor of Judea, Felix, is addressed as "most excellent" one, just as Theophilus is addressed in Luke 1:3.

1:3 The *passion* (from the Latin *patior, passus,* "to suffer") refers to the torturous events of the atoning sacrifice of the Lord Jesus Christ. The "infallible proofs" spoken of in this verse are the Savior's many appearances as a resurrected Being. The Greek word here means, literally, "sure signs or tokens." Jesus bore the sure signs or tokens of his atonement, death, and resurrection in his hands, wrists, feet, and side. We learn about similar things in Latter-day Saint Temples.

The "forty days" refers to Christ's postresurrection ministry among his apostles. Jesus was able to teach the apostles a considerable amount in five to six weeks.

1:4–5 On "the promise of the Father," see Luke 24:49, in which the author uses this same phrase to refer to the Holy Ghost being sent. "Baptized with the Holy Ghost" means immersed in spiritual power and being endowed with the gift of the Holy Ghost. Joseph Smith said:

"When the apostles were raised up, they worked in Jerusalem, and Jesus commanded them to tarry there until they were endowed with power from on high. Had they not work to do in Jerusalem? They did work and prepared a people for the Pentecost. The kingdom of God was with them before the day of Pentecost, as well as afterwards. . . . The endowment was to prepare the disciples for their mission into the world" (Jackson, *Joseph Smith's Commentary on the Bible,* 143).

1:6 Many Jews expected the Messiah to restore Israel's political kingdom (compare Luke 24:21). The Jews in the first century thought that the Messiah would be a great warrior-deliverer in the mold of King David or King Solomon. These two great kings were Israel's archetypal messiahs, or "anointed ones," who took united Israel to its greatest point by establishing the largest, most prosperous, independent political kingdom in its history.

1:8 The question asked in verse 6 is now partially answered. Once the Holy Ghost comes upon the apostles, they will be empowered to build the kingdom. The kingdom will not, however, be an all-powerful military state. The apostles' commission is to be witnesses of the Lord in Jerusalem (see Acts 1–7), and in all Judea and Samaria (see Acts 8–10), and unto the uttermost part of the earth (see Acts 11–28).

1:9 The Ascension. The cloud is a symbol of God's presence and power. For more information about the "cloud" in other scriptures, see Appendix 1, 383.

1:10–11 The messengers refer to "men of Galilee" because all eleven were Galileans; the one Judean, Judas Iscariot, was dead.

The testimony of the two angels that Jesus would come again to the Mount of Olives, as the apostles saw him go, is true. It will happen soon.

1:12 A "Sabbath day's journey" is the distance an orthodox Jew was allowed to walk on the Sabbath. The rabbinical restriction was based on several Old Testament passages, including the Mosaic injunction, "Let no man go out of his place on the seventh day" (Exodus 16:29; see also Numbers 35:5; Joshua 3:4). The maximum distance specified was two thousand cubits (three thousand feet)—about the distance from the city wall of Jerusalem to the Mount of Olives (see Acts 1:12).

1:13 Early meeting places of the Saints in Jerusalem were an upper room (possibly the same as the site of the Last Supper) and at Solomon's Porch, the eastern portico or colonnade of the Temple grounds. Some scholars have proposed that the upper room mentioned here and during the Last Supper was in the home of Mary, the mother of John Mark (see Acts 12:12).

1:14 Mary, Jesus' mother, was active in affairs of the early Church. His stepfather, Joseph, who would likely have been more than fifty years old at this point, is not mentioned during Jesus' ministry or thereafter and was possibly deceased. His "brethren" (brothers), who had previously not believed in him (John 7:5), were now active, too. His brother James seems to have become the leader of the Jerusalem Branch (see Acts 12:17; 15:13) and later still, an apostle (see Galatians 1:19). This verse is the last mention of Mary in the Bible.

1:15–26 Peter is the presiding high priest and apostle and conducts the meeting. The first item on the agenda of the meeting is to fill the vacancy in the Quorum of the Twelve.

1:15 Note the number in attendance. Luke apparently had access to a source preserving exact numbers.

1:16, 20 A prophetic utterance by David (recorded in Psalms; see footnote references to Acts 1:16, 20) is fulfilled in the betrayal and replacement of Judas Iscariot. From this point on, we see Peter teaching and reasoning from the scriptures. Undoubtedly, he learned this method from his Master, who not only encouraged disciples to study the scriptures (see John 5:39) but taught from them himself (see Luke 24:27). Teaching from the scriptures is an important theme for Luke, especially in the book of Acts.

1:18–19 Another burial place has been associated with the southern slopes of the Hinnom Valley since early centuries after Christ: "It was known unto all the dwellers at Jerusalem; insomuch as that field is called in their proper tongue, Aceldama, that is to say, The field of blood" (Acts 1:19). According to Acts 1:18, Judas Iscariot (Hebrew, *ish Kerioth,* "man from Kerioth," a Judean village) had purchased with his betrayal money a field that was to be the scene of his suicide. Matthew 27:5–7, however, preserves the account of Judas casting down the coins in the Temple and going out and hanging himself, whereupon the chief priests bought with the money "the potter's field, to bury strangers in. Wherefore that field was called, The field of blood." *Akeldama* is the Greek rendering of the Aramaic *khakel dema,* "field of blood." According to the New Testament record, then, the renaming of this burial ground in Jerusalem had its origin in the betrayal of Jesus and the death of Judas Iscariot.

1:21–22 Qualifications for apostleship in the early Church: the candidate must have been a member for three years, active from John's baptism to Jesus' resurrection, and an eyewitness of Jesus' return from the grave. John the Baptist had an important role in training those of his own disciples who would later be asked to transfer their allegiance to the Savior and become the Master's apostles.

1:23–26 Candidates to fill the vacancy in the Quorum of the Twelve are narrowed to two, apparently from among several possibilities. The apostles prayed, inspiration came from the Lord, and Matthias was chosen and ordained (this is the only mention of him in the New Testament). The name *Matthias* is in Hebrew *Mattityahu,* or in English, *Matthew,* meaning "gift of God." Casting lots, or voting, was the same as presenting a sustaining vote, in modern terms. It was sometimes done in ancient cultures by each voter putting forward a sherd, or pottery fragment, with the name written on it.

ACTS 2

2:1 Pentecost was fifty days after Passover. In Hebrew the feast is called *Shavuot* (Feast of Weeks, Feast of Harvest, Feast of First Fruits; see Bible Dictionary, "Feasts"). Pentecost is the day of first fruits or the first harvest of the season (see Numbers 28:26). How appropriate to begin the great harvest of souls on this very day on which three thousand persons were added to the Church through baptism (see Acts 2:37–41).

2:2–4 "Cloven tongues like as of fire" (v. 3) is both a literal description and symbolic language. First, the apostles were "on fire" with language ability, able to speak in tongues—that is, in other languages—but not in meaningless gibberish. Second, the Holy Spirit is compared in scripture to fire. Idiomatically, the apostles were "on fire." Compare the two disciples on the road to Emmaus, "did not our heart *burn* within us" (Luke 24:32; emphasis added) and "your bosom shall *burn* within you" (D&C 9:8; emphasis added). Today, we sing "The Spirit of God Like a Fire is Burning." Finally, according to the Prophet Joseph Smith, "God dwells in everlasting burnings" (*Teachings of the Prophet Joseph Smith*, 361). Fire is symbolic of God's glory. Luke is attempting to describe a scene in which God's glory, brought by the third member of the Godhead, settled upon the apostles.

Jesus had conferred the Spirit upon the apostles before (see John 20:22), which allowed them to enjoy the testimony-building power of the Holy Ghost in a temporary sense because Jesus was physically with them. But now they had the right to the enjoyment of the gift of the Holy Ghost, that is, the right to the constant companionship of this member of the Godhead. For some reason the gift of the Holy Ghost did not fully operate during the Savior's ministry, but the Holy Ghost is essential to every conversion experience.

President Brigham Young illustrated the importance of the Holy Ghost in the conversion process: "I had only travelled a short time to testify to the people, before I learned this one fact, that you might prove doctrine from the Bible till doomsday, and it would merely convince a people, but would not convert them. You might read the Bible from Genesis to Revelation, and prove every iota that you advance, and that alone would have no converting influence upon the people. Nothing short of a testimony by the power of the Holy Ghost would bring light and knowledge to them—bring them in their hearts to repentance. Nothing short of that would ever do" (*Journal of Discourses*, 5:327).

In our own dispensation, the dedication of the Kirtland Temple parallels the events at the day of Pentecost: "Probably more Latter-day Saints beheld visions and witnessed other unusual spiritual manifestations than during any other era in the history of the Church. There were reports of Saints' beholding heavenly beings at ten different meetings held during that time. At eight of these meetings, many reported seeing angels. . . . While the Saints were thus communing with heavenly hosts, many prophesied, some spoke in tongues, and others received the gift of interpretation of tongues" (Backman, *Heavens Resound*, 285).

"Prescindia Huntington, who had moved to Kirtland in May 1836 and was baptized the following June, was in her home when an excited young girl rushed to her door and in bewilderment said that a meeting was being held on top of the temple. 'I went to the door,' Prescindia declared, 'and there I saw on the temple angels clothed in white covering the roof from end to end. They seemed to be walking to and fro; they appeared and disappeared. The third time they appeared and disappeared before I realized that they were not mortal men. . . . This was in broad daylight, in the afternoon'" (Backman, *Heavens Resound*, 305).

2:5–11 For the location of lands and peoples named, see Appendix 2, 387.

2:6 The Holy Ghost acts as translator and communicator (see D&C 90:11). The Prophet Joseph Smith taught that "the gift of tongues by the power of the Holy Ghost in the Church, is for the benefit of the servants of God to preach to unbelievers, as on the day of Pentecost" (*Teachings of the Prophet Joseph Smith*, 195).

2:12–15 Jews and other Mediterranean peoples reckoned the time of day from sunrise to sundown. Thus, the first hour began at sunrise, approximately 6 A.M.; the third hour was equivalent to 9 A.M., and so forth. It was customary, especially on feast days, to abstain from food and drink until after the morning synagogue service, which was held about nine in the morning.

2:16–18 The prophecy of Joel was fulfilled in the days of Peter but will be fulfilled again—an example of multiple fulfillment of prophecy. In 1823, Moroni quoted these same words from Joel 2 to Joseph Smith, saying that they were not yet completely fulfilled but were soon to be (see Joseph Smith–History 1:41).

2:19–20 For more on the signs and wonders in the heavens, see Topical Guide, "Jesus Christ, Second Coming" and "Last Days"; see also Joseph Smith–Matthew and Doctrine and Covenants 45. For more on the strange behavior of the heavenly luminaries, see Doctrine and Covenants 133:49.

2:23 The Crucifixion is according to God's plan of redemption (see 2 Nephi 9:5–10), also called "the plan of our God" (2 Nephi 9:13).

2:25–30 Regarding verse 27 on King David, see 1 Samuel 16 and Bible Dictionary, "David." Joseph Smith taught that David would receive forgiveness only through hell but that he would not be left there. David's throne and kingdom were taken from him and given to another "David" in the last days of his lineage (see *Teachings of the Prophet Joseph Smith*, 339). Elder Bruce R. McConkie explained that David was not a son of perdition but that he was fallen (*Doctrinal New Testament Commentary*, 2:39).

2:29, 34 Joseph Smith said: "Even David must wait for those times of refreshing before he can come forth and his sins be blotted out. For Peter speaking of him says, 'David hath not yet ascended into heaven, for his sepulchre is with us to this day.' His remains were then in the tomb. Now we read that many bodies of the Saints arose at Christ's resurrection, probably all the Saints. But it seems that David did not. Why? Because he had been a murderer" (Jackson, *Joseph Smith's Commentary on the Bible,* 144).

2:34–35 "David's Messianic utterance, 'The Lord said unto my Lord' (Psalms 110:1), is here interpreted by Jesus to mean: One God said to another, that is, the Father said to the Son, that, as Paul was later to express it, the 'Son' should sit 'down on the right hand of the Majesty on high'" (*Doctrinal New Testament Commentary,* 1:612).

2:36 The Jews, meaning some Jewish leaders, are guilty of crucifying Jesus, not the Romans.

2:37–39 The simple gospel requires faith, repentance, baptism, and the gift of the Holy Ghost. The promise of salvation is made to all who obey these principles and ordinances.

2:40 *Untoward* means "crooked," "rebellious," "perverse."

2:41 Imagine three thousand baptisms in one day! The brethren must have used a significant number of water cisterns and reservoirs in and around Jerusalem. Certainly such activity must have elicited at least some opposition from Jewish leaders.

2:44–45 The early Saints attempt to live a form of the law of consecration. "All things common" did not mean that everyone pooled all their resources and shared everything in common, all having equal amounts. It meant that every person and family had an equality according to their needs (see Acts 2:45; 4:32, 35; D&C 51:3).

ACTS 3

3:1–11 Two of the three chief apostles (the three chief apostles being equivalent to the First Presidency) are on their way to worship in the Temple, about 3 P.M. A lame man asks for alms at the gate "Beautiful," likely the eastern gate of the

Temple leading into the Court of the Women. The apostles follow Jesus' example in using the priesthood to heal.

3:7 "You cannot lift another soul until you are standing on higher ground than he is" (Lee, *Stand Ye in Holy Places,* 187).

3:11 Solomon's Porch, the eastern portico, or colonnade, of the Temple complex, is one of the meeting places of the early Church members (see Acts 5:12).

3:12–18 Peter, the chief apostle, bears his testimony of the Savior. The power of Jesus healed the lame man, even that same Jesus whom some Jewish leaders had delivered up, denied, and killed. Their rebellion, envy, and jealousy had blinded their eyes to God's own Son.

PETER, THE CHIEF APOSTLE

Peter was a mighty man of God. He and his brother, Andrew, were fishermen. Thus, there were two sets of brothers in the original Quorum of the Twelve: Peter and Andrew, and James and John. Peter and Andrew lived along the northern shore of the Sea of Galilee, first in Bethsaida and then in Capernaum. He was with the Savior constantly and was corrected by the Master on many occasions without displaying any feelings of being offended or angry, which speaks for his humility and teachableness. Peter was on the Mount of Transfiguration with the Savior, where he saw and heard things too sacred to record, was in the presence of heavenly beings (Elohim, Elijah, Moses, John the Baptist, and perhaps others), received the holy endowment, witnessed in vision the transfiguration of the earth (D&C 63:20–21), was taught in plainness of the Savior's death and resurrection (JST Luke 9:31), and perhaps even received a guarantee of exaltation at that time (McConkie, *Doctrinal New Testament Commentary,* 1:399–401). Peter saw the miracles of the Lord, defended

38

Jesus with a sword, bore testimony of the Messiah, and was ultimately a martyr for the cause of Christ.

Though many Christians, Latter-day Saints included, often regard the chief apostle's denial of Christ (Luke 22:34; Mark 14:30) as a fulfillment of the Savior's prophecy to Peter about his lack of conviction, which was spoken just hours before the event, we cannot be so sure. To suppose that such a denial was based on cowardice or weakness is contrary to every other example of Peter's personality and motivations reported in the scriptures. In every other instance, Peter acted courageously, even impetuously, in his protection of Christ. In fact, it is possible to read the Greek text of the Savior's declaration to Peter about the latter's forthcoming denial as a request or instructional command (imperative verb form) rather than as a prediction! In other words, the Greek text indicates that Peter may have been told to deny being associated with the Savior. That seems to be the line of reasoning followed by Elder Spencer W. Kimball in a magnificent address at Brigham Young University entitled *Peter, My Brother:* "Is it possible that there might have been some other reason for Peter's triple denial? Could he have felt that circumstances justified expediency? When he bore a strong testimony in Caesarea Philippi, he had been told that 'they should tell no man that he was Jesus the Christ' (Matthew 16:20)."

3:19 "The times of refreshing" refers to the millennial reign. Joseph Smith said Peter was addressing the murderers who crucified Jesus; that is why he invited them not to repent and be baptized but to repent and hope their sins could be blotted out by the Millennium. "They could not be baptized for the remission of sins, for they had shed innocent blood" (*Teachings of the Prophet Joseph Smith,* 339).

3:20–21 Jesus Christ will come again to the earth at the "times of restitution of all things," which is the restoration of his gospel and Church.

3:22–24 One like unto Moses would come. Moses was

the great deliverer and lawgiver. To fulfill Moses' prophecy, the Mighty One of Israel did come, who was the great Lawgiver and Deliverer (see Joseph Smith–History 1:40).

3:21, 24 All the holy prophets have prophesied of the days of Christ (see Jacob 7:11; Mosiah 13:33; Helaman 8:19–22; Acts 10:43) and even Jewish rabbinical writings record: "All the prophets prophesied only of the days of the Messiah" (Talmud, Sanhedrin 99a).

3:25–26 The Abrahamic covenant, with its blessings and responsibilities, continues in these Jewish descendants of Abraham. They were expected to repent of their iniquities, return to their God, live his laws, and teach them to others so they could be blessed too.

ACTS 4

4:1–7 Peter and John, while preaching of Jesus to thousands of Jerusalemites, were arrested by priests, Sadducees, and the "captain of the temple" (v. 1)—a priest in high authority—with other priests and Levites under his charge.

4:6 Annas was an influential high priest whose five sons all held the position of high priest. His son-in-law, Joseph Caiaphas, was high priest when Jesus was sentenced to die. We know nothing more than this brief reference to John and Alexander.

4:8–10 Peter testifies that Jesus is his source of strength.

4:11–12 The cornerstone (Hebrew, *rosh pinna*, literally, "head of the corner") was a large stone placed in a corner of the building's foundation to secure it, to provide stability and strength to the structure (at least symbolically), and to serve as a guide for laying all other foundation stones in the building. New Testament writers saw in Jesus, as the Messiah, the fulfillment of this prophetic analogy: "This is the stone which was set at nought of you builders, which is become the head of the corner" (Acts 4:11). Thus Jesus is the essential cornerstone upon which we must build. There is no other name under heaven by which we may be saved (see also Mosiah 3:17).

4:13 Being eyewitnesses and now possessing the power of the Holy Ghost to its fullest extent, Peter and the others are changed men. Starting with this verse, look at the following sequence of verses, particularly noting the use of the words *bold, boldness,* and other cognates: Acts 4:18–20, 29, 31; 5:29, 32, 40–42; 9:27, 29; 13:46; 14:3.

President Joseph F. Smith illustrated this transformation: "Not one of the disciples possessed sufficient light, knowledge nor wisdom, at the time of the crucifixion, for either exaltation or condemnation; for it was afterward that their minds were opened to understand the scriptures, and that they were endowed with power from on high; without which they were only children in knowledge, in comparison to what they afterwards become under the influence of the Spirit" (*Gospel Doctrine,* 433).

4:14–16 It is irrefutably true that a man had been healed—there were many eyewitnesses. Though opposed to Jesus and his apostles, these leaders cannot refute such testimony.

4:17–22 The attempt to silence the apostles is futile. Peter essentially declares, "Whether it's better to obey you or to obey God, you decide!" The apostles feel much as Jeremiah did when he wanted to quit. Jeremiah was discouraged and pained at the treatment he was getting in Jerusalem. He almost refused to speak any more in the name of the Lord, but God's "word was in mine heart as a burning fire shut up in my bones, and I was weary with forbearing, and I could not stay" (Jeremiah 20:9). The religious leaders, knowing they were wrong and fearing the people, could only resort to threats.

4:23–31 With new understanding of the scriptures

through the Holy Ghost, the Saints rejoice in Christ and are moved both spiritually and physically.

4:32–35 See commentary on Acts 2:44–45.

4:36–37 An important, new person is introduced: Joses Barnabas, a Levite landowner from the island of Cyprus. He sold his possessions for the gospel cause, served as a missionary companion to Paul (see Acts 13–14), and was regarded as an apostle (see Acts 14:4, 14). Some people even thought he was one of the Graeco-Roman gods come down to earth (Acts 14:11–12).

ACTS 5

5:1–12 "A certain man named Ananias" (Hebrew, *Hananiah*). Luke introduces three different men named Ananias, one here and two later. The other two are the leader of the Church in Damascus (Acts 9:10–17) and the high priest in Jerusalem (Acts 23:2; 24:1).

Ananias and Sapphira, members of the Church, had made sacred covenants with the Lord in addition to their baptismal covenants, and now they were breaking a solemn oath. Ananias and Sapphira had covenanted to live the law of consecration as described in Acts 4:32–35. In fact, the higher covenant they had entered into was the same as that practiced by the people of Enoch and the Book of Mormon society described in 4 Nephi, in which the people were of one heart and one mind, dwelt in righteousness, and had all things in common (compare Moses 7:18–19; Acts 4:32–35; 4 Nephi 15–17, 23–25). Their offense was much greater than simple lying.

In modern times, for violations of higher covenants associated with the new and everlasting covenant, the Lord has prescribed punishments similar to those suffered by Ananias and Sapphira. The punishment for willful violation of this higher law is outlined in Doctrine and Covenants 82:15–21. There the Lord says violators are to "be delivered over to the buffetings of Satan" (D&C 82:21). From Doctrine and Covenants 132:26 we understand that the buffetings involve being "destroyed in the flesh," which is what happened to Ananias and Sapphira.

The placement of the story of Ananias and Sapphira in Acts 5 is no accident—it comes immediately after the enumeration of the principal features of the law of consecration, in Acts 4:32–35. It is meant to show what happens when certain higher laws of God's economy and social order are deliberately transgressed. Can one lie to the prophet? Can one lie to the Lord?

5:15–16 Regarding "the shadow of Peter," see Luke 8:44, healing that resulted from touching Jesus' garment; and Acts 19:12, healing from Paul's handkerchief.

5:17–28 Certain Jewish leaders become more and more frustrated in their efforts to prevent Church leaders from spreading the doctrine of Christ. They object that the Brethren "intend to bring this man's [Jesus'] blood upon us"—but hadn't the Jewish leaders asked for it? (see Matthew 27:25).

5:29–32 From Peter they heard the same response as before: We ought to obey God, not men. Joseph Smith said: "We are reminded of the words of Peter to the Jewish Sanhedrin, when speaking of Christ. He says that God raised him from the dead, 'and we [the apostles] are his witnesses of these things, and so is also the Holy Ghost, whom God had given to them that obey him.' So that after the testimony of the scriptures on this point, the assurance is given by the Holy Ghost, bearing witness to those who obey him, that Christ himself has assuredly risen from the dead" (Jackson, *Joseph Smith's Commentary on the Bible*, 148).

5:33 The frustrated Jewish leaders are "cut to the heart" (see 1 Nephi 16:2), and their first desire is to kill.

5:34–40 Gamaliel was a great Jewish rabbi at the time of

Jesus and grandson of the famous Hillel, who had also been a renowned teacher. Paul studied under Gamaliel in Jerusalem (see Bible Dictionary, "Sanhedrin"). Gamaliel advised the high priest and the council to proceed with caution.

5:37 Gamaliel's point is valid but not accurate. From the movement of "Judas of Galilee" came the anti-Roman party called Zealots, who were not scattered quickly but continued to resist Roman occupation of the land for decades.

5:38–39 What wisdom is there in the great rabbi's counsel to fellow religious leaders?

5:40–42 Again, the command not to speak in the name of Christ. The Brethren disregard the vain authority of men and continue to speak in His name, rejoicing in the opportunity to suffer for His name's sake (see Matthew 5:10–12).

ACTS 6

Adapting to new circumstances and to increasing membership, the apostles saw the need for a new level of Church leadership, just as we in the latter days adapt to progress, too. To resist change and to insist on tradition for the sake of tradition is to be an enemy to continuous revelation. Seven new administrators were called to help with the temporal affairs of the Church. The Greek term describing them is *diakonos,* from which we get our English word *deacon.* This new Church position should not be confused with the modern office in the Aaronic Priesthood. Acts 6 is a fine example of how delegation operated in the early Church and how inspiration can work both from the bottom up and from the top down. For example, the apostles ask for inspired recommendations (compare Acts 1:23–36) which they then confirm through their own inspiration. The apostles simply could not fulfill their divine commission if they became buried under a mountain of requests and details concerning every aspect of administering the Church.

6:1–4 Grecians were Greek-speaking Jewish Christians. See also Bible Dictionary, "Hellenists."

"Widows were neglected in the daily ministration." The people were apparently not living the law of consecration as they should.

6:5–8 Here are the names of the seven Greek-speaking Jewish members of the Church, now authorities in the young Christian Church. Two of them, Stephen and Philip, would particularly distinguish themselves as valiant defenders, preachers, and miracle-workers.

6:7 These priests, or descendants of Aaron, who came to the faith could now become holders of the Melchizedek Priesthood as members of the Church of Jesus Christ.

6:9–14 Whenever a servant of the Lord stands up to defend the cause of truth, there are inevitably antagonists who also rise up to oppose the Lord's work. Stephen is accused of blaspheming against God's law and his holy Temple. They even brought in "false witnesses" (as they did in the case of Jesus; compare Matthew 26:59).

Stephen is teaching that "Jesus of Nazareth shall destroy this place, and shall change the customs which Moses delivered us." Is that blasphemy—or the truth? Stephen is definitely foreshadowing some changes in the Jewish religious establishment and nation and in the Church.

6:15 Stephen (Greek, "crown") is transfigured in front of the Sanhedrin. He is temporarily crowned with the glory of God.

ACTS 7

7:1–50 Stephen reviews the history of Israel to show how great persons, events, doctrines, and practices were all types and shadows of Christ and how all the past culminates in the coming of the Messiah, Jesus.

7:2 Charran is also named Haran in Genesis 11:31 and Abraham 2:4.

7:16 Two different events seem mixed together: Abraham buying the Cave of Machpelah in Hebron (Genesis 23), and Jacob buying the parcel of a field in Sychem (Shechem, in Genesis 33:18–19). Acts 7:16 should apparently refer to the burial place in Hebron, not to that in Shechem/Sychem.

7:22 Just as Moses was immersed in two cultures—that is, educated in Egypt and then educated by Jehovah at Sinai—so Paul was first immersed in the Greek culture and the Judaic culture and then educated by Christ himself.

7:37 It is prophesied that One like unto Moses would arise (Deuteronomy 18:15; Acts 3:22; 7:37), and it is generally recognized that the Messiah would be that Mighty One to come to Israel. Moses was *a* lawgiver and *a* deliverer; the Messiah would be *the* Lawgiver and *the* Deliverer.

7:38 "The church in the wilderness" is the congregation of Israel, the body of the Lord's people.

7:45 The name *Jesus* here refers to the ancient Israelite leader, Joshua son of Nun, and not to Jesus of Nazareth. (*Jesus* and *Joshua* are different forms of the same Hebrew name: *Yehoshua*, or *Yeshua*.)

7:51–54 The guilt felt by members of the Sanhedrin leads them to murderous actions.

7:55–56 Joseph Smith said: "Stephen saw the Son of Man. [He] saw the Son of Man standing on the right hand of God. [There are] three personages in heaven who hold the keys–one to preside over all. . . . Any person that has seen the heavens opened knows that there are three personages in the heavens holding the keys of power" (Jackson, *Joseph Smith's Commentary on the Bible*, 148). Elder Spencer W. Kimball said, "Stephen was a martyr and will inherit eternal life" (Conference Report, April 1969, 29). "Thus he was the first to win the crown called by the same name as he. . . . In Greek

'Stephen' and 'crown' are identical" (Eusebius, *History of the Church*, 35).

7:57–60 For a description of the supposed method of stoning, see Elder Bruce R. McConkie's *Doctrinal New Testament Commentary*, 2:78, which cites the biblical historian Dummelow.

7:58 Luke's inclusion of the intriguing detail of "clothing" being laid at Saul's feet may be a corroboration of the ancient cultural setting of the Book of Mormon. Alma 46 tells us of Captain Moroni's rending his coat and raising it as the "title of liberty," and it also tells of the people making a covenant as "they cast their garments at the feet of Moroni" (Alma 46:22). Among the covenant people of ancient times, clothing appears to have been used to witness or to attest to something, as a token or sign of one's testimony, or as a symbol of one's formal association with an idea or an action.

Paul seems to have represented the Sanhedrin in overseeing the official stoning of Stephen—an action the Jews believed was supported by the Old Covenant, or Mosaic law.

ACTS 8

8:1 "Saul was consenting unto his death." In other words, Saul gave his approval. That does not mean he is a member of the Sanhedrin, but Saul certainly had some kind of authority given to him by the leader of the Sanhedrin, the high priest (see Acts 9:1–2).

8:3 Saul was sincerely dedicated to the wrong cause. He "made havoc of the church." His great energy, now being used to destroy, would soon turn to build the kingdom of God when rechanneled by the Lord himself.

8:5–13 Philip was one of the seven who were called to assist the Twelve (see Acts 6:5; 21:8). He was an early missionary teaching in Samaria and in coastal cities. His home was in Caesarea, with his four prophetess-daughters. He held the Aaronic Priesthood; he taught and baptized but did not confer the Holy Ghost. Joseph Smith said: "In the case of Philip, when he went down to Samaria [he] was under the spirit of Elias. He baptized both men and women. When Peter and John heard of it, they went down and laid hands on them, and they received the Holy Ghost. This shows the distinction between the two powers" (Jackson, *Joseph Smith's Commentary on the Bible*, 149).

Can holders of the Aaronic Priesthood perform miracles? Of course. That priesthood also has the keys to the ministering of angels.

8:9–11 Here is another Simon, this one a sorcerer. As in Pharaoh's court and in Nebuchadnezzar's court, there are always those who counterfeit, who use cheap imitations of the real power of God. Verses 18–20 show that this Simon is one of those who adopt the philosophy that you can buy anything in this world for money. The practice of simony (buying and selling a church office or position) takes its name from this Simon, who was also known as Simon Magus. In early Christian literature Simon is associated with the origins of Gnosticism (see "Gnosticism," 297).

8:16 Joseph Smith taught: "You might as well baptize a bag of sand as a man, if not done in view of the remission of sins and getting of the Holy Ghost. Baptism by water is but half a baptism, and is good for nothing without the other half—that is, the baptism of the Holy Ghost" (*Teachings of the Prophet Joseph Smith*, 314).

8:21–25 Simon Peter, the prophet, rebukes and admonishes Simon, the former sorcerer and new member of the Church.

8:26–40 Philip's ministry was in the southern coastal plain of Judea: first in the sand-desert of Gaza and then in Azotus, the ancient Philistine and Judahite city formerly called Ashdod.

Candace was a name-title for the queen of Ethiopia, as *pharaoh* was for Egyptian kings and *caesar* was for Roman emperors (see also Bible Dictionary, "Eunuch").

The Ethiopian officer is devoted to the worship of Jehovah, as evidenced by his study of the Hebrew prophets. While traveling along the road, Philip stopped him and asked if he would like to know more about the suffering servant he was reading about in Isaiah 53. Note his response and the way Philip taught him about Christ.

8:36–39 This passage is one of the best scriptural references illustrating that baptism is performed by complete immersion in water.

PAUL'S LIFE BEFORE HIS CONVERSION

The persecutor of Christians who became the fearless apostle of the Lord Jesus Christ was born in Tarsus, a distinguished Greek city in Cilicia (see Acts 21:39; 22:3; 23:34; see also "Tarsus," 350). His Hebrew name was Saul; the Graeco-Roman equivalent was Paul (see Acts 13:9). He held Roman citizenship (see Acts 16:37; 22:25–28) and spoke both Greek and Hebrew (see Acts 21:37–40). His Israelite ancestry was through the tribe of Benjamin (see Romans 11:1; Philippians 3:5). He studied at Jerusalem, where he had relatives (see Acts 22:3; 5:34; 23:16). There he was educated as a Pharisee (see Acts 23:6; 26:5; Philippians 3:5) and learned practical skills he could apply in a trade (see Acts 18:3; 20:34; 1 Corinthians 4:12). In summary, then, Paul was the product of three cultures—Judaic, Hellenistic, and Roman (Acts 21:39; 22:27).

Paul said that he had obeyed all Jewish requirements, so he was likely married (see Galatians 1:14; Philippians 3:6). A famous part of the Mishnah, *Pirkei Aboth,* outlines the various stages of a Jewish man's life: "At five years old one is ready for the scripture, at ten years for the Mishnah, at thirteen for the commandments, at fifteen for Talmud, at eighteen for marriage, at twenty for pursuit of righteousness, at thirty for full strength, at forty for discernment, at fifty for counsel, at sixty for old age" (*Aboth* 5:24). The Jewish religion and culture commended marriage and family life to one and all and looked with disfavor on the single state. For example, the Mishnah stipulates that "an unmarried man may not be a teacher of children" (*Kiddushin* 4:13).

Paul may have had a physical disability or infirmity (2 Corinthians 12:7; 10:10). We know he was an early persecutor of the Church (Acts 8:1–4; 22:19–20; 26:9–11; Galatians 1:13; 1 Timothy 1:13), but after his vision on the road to Damascus, he wore out his life in the untiring service of Jesus Christ (see Acts 7:58; 22:3–5; 26:10; Galatians 1:14; Philemon 1:9). For more on Paul, see Ludlow, *Encyclopedia of Mormonism,* "Paul," 3:1068–70.

ACTS 9

9:1 "Breathing out threatenings and slaughter" are strong words. Saul is an ardent persecutor. Is he an evil man? And why such antagonism? There are many reasons. First, oral tradition played an exalted role in Pharisaic Judaism, and Jesus had spoken against it (Matthew 15:1–3; Mark 7:8). Second, belief in revelation from living prophets had ceased. Third, authority was vested in scholar-teachers who promoted the role of tradition. Finally, Jesus, the founder of Christianity, was not highly regarded in some Jewish circles (see John 8:31–59).

Jewish documents dating from after A.D. 70 clearly and explicitly articulate the governing principle that tradition predominated over revelation. This attitude probably existed in the days of Jesus and Paul. For example, the people were astonished when Jesus taught them in an unusual way—from his own authority and not in the scribal or rabbinical method, which was based on prior authority and tradition (Matthew 7:29). Later, the rabbis included in the Babylonian Talmud a fictional account of a debate between Rabbi Eliezer and Rabbi Joshua to emphasize the premier role of tradition. At issue was the possibility that revelation could be given beyond what had been spoken on Sinai. After exhausting every possible argument to no avail, Eliezer, who argued for God's right to continue to reveal his will, called upon the carob tree to prove it. The carob tree, we are told, was immediately torn from the ground and hurled one hundred cubits. This sign was rejected on the grounds that no proof can be brought from a carob tree. Next Eliezer called upon a stream of water to support his point, and the stream started to flow backwards. Joshua objected, "What sort of demonstration does a stream afford?" Eliezer then said, "If the law be according to my opinion, let the walls of the academy prove it," whereupon the walls began to fall. Rabbi Joshua rebuked them, and the walls did not fall but remained at an angle. Seeking an irrefutable witness, Rabbi Eliezer then called on the heavens themselves to state the truth. A heavenly voice sounded forth and said, "What have ye against Rabbi Eliezer after whose opinion the law is always to be framed?" At this, Rabbi Joshua arose and said, "The Torah declares concerning itself, 'It is not up in heaven'; that is to say, once the Torah was given on Mount Sinai, we pay no heed to heavenly voices but, as the Torah ordains further, we follow the opinion of the majority" (Steinberg, *Basic Judaism*, 68–69).

9:2 Damascus lies about 150 miles northeast of Jerusalem. In the first century after Christ it was a member of the association of ten Greek cities known as the Decapolis. Jewish Christians in the Damascus branch of the Church, as elsewhere, were apparently still meeting in synagogues. Paul went to Damascus as a representative of the high priest and the Sanhedrin to stamp out Christianity because the city sat at a prosperous crossroads and was thus an important center of civilization. If Christianity succeeded there, it could spread far and wide.

9:3–4 Paul's first vision. Is Paul's sudden and dramatic conversion fair? Was he deserving of such heavenly grace, to be visited by Jesus himself? Did he grow up in the places he did and in the manner he did for the Lord's own purposes? As we will see in his ensuing apostolic career, the circumstances of his birth, his nationality, and his training were not accidental but all according to a divine plan. Without doubt Paul had been chosen in premortal life and foreordained to be the great apostle and missionary to the Gentiles (Alma 13:1–10). Joseph Smith taught that every man called to minister through the priesthood was foreordained in the Grand Council of God before they came to this earth (*Teachings of the Prophet Joseph Smith*, 365).

9:5 Notice the important question Paul first asked, and notice the important answer.

"It is hard for thee to kick against the pricks": a prick (Greek, *kentra*) was a goad, a sharp stick for pricking the hides of animals to make them move; balking or kicking back made the pain worse. Thus, though Paul is zealous in his quest to keep Judaism and the Mosaic law pure by eradicating the polluting and destructive influence of Christianity, he is kicking against God's foreordained plan. He probably regards Jesus as an apostate and Christianity as a perversion seeking to weaken or destroy the Mosaic system. Nevertheless, Paul is working against the God and creator of this earth. It is possible that Paul may have even experienced pricks or pangs of conscience, perhaps nagging doubts, about the correctness of the course he was pursuing as the Holy Spirit worked on him—a chosen vessel of the Lord.

9:6 A succinct sermon of obedience appears in the response of Saul, "Lord, what wilt thou have me to do?"

9:7 There is a discrepancy between the account in this

verse and the account in Acts 22:9. Joseph Smith Translation Acts 9:7 corrects the discrepancy: "And *they who were journeying* with him *saw indeed the light, and were afraid; but they heard not the voice of him who spake to him*" (italics indicate the Joseph Smith Translation additions).

The three accounts of Paul's vision elicit such questions as, Why is there more than one account? Do differences arise more out of small contradictions or out of silence about details? What do all accounts agree upon? Critics of Joseph Smith's First Vision also ask similar questions. Paul and Joseph Smith told their first visions on more than one occasion because different people in different situations challenged them. "Without memorization or a script, no one will retell any experience in exactly the same way; one will emphasize what he feels important at the time, which is partly determined by whom is listening. For instance, Paul did not emphasize his mission to the Gentiles before the hostile Jewish audience in the temple (Acts 22), but he did to the semi-Gentile, King Agrippa (Acts 26). Paul's experience remained the same, but his reasons for stressing certain facts changed in new circumstances. For both Joseph Smith and Paul, their central experience remained the same in every telling" (Anderson, "Guide to Acts," 24).

9:8–9 Saul is blinded by the brilliance of the light, which is Christ (see also Acts 22:11). Saul's experience of three days without sight or food or drink is similar to Alma's experience in the Book of Mormon (see Mosiah 27; Alma 36).

9:10–19 This Ananias is apparently the leader of the Saints in Damascus. The Lord shows deference to the local authority he has called; the Lord himself could have done what is needed, but he recognizes his local authority. Ananias restores Saul's sight and baptizes him. It is ironic that one of the persons Saul likely intended to arrest and imprison is commissioned to teach, heal, and baptize him.

9:15 Why Saul? Because he had premortal and mortal

qualifications. In him unique and indispensable gifts and skills came together. He is a minister chosen because he possessed these abilities. The Lord knew him; he had been foreordained to the work. Just as Paul was foreordained, so each of us has also been foreordained to this important work and must write our own book of acts. Another lesson comes from Paul's conversion: as miraculous as it was, it didn't sustain him indefinitely. He also had to pray, study scripture, and seek the Spirit constantly. Like each of us, Paul had to struggle daily. He suffered hardship, difficulty, and indignity, as most of us have, although his suffering may have been more intense than any one of us has experienced (see 2 Corinthians 11:24–29).

9:16 This passage teaches us important doctrine. We also gain wisdom and experience, spiritual strength, and leadership ability through our trials. If we want celestial glory, we must withstand trials and struggles of celestial difficulty. There is an elevating purpose in suffering (see Acts 14:22; Hebrews 12:5–7, 10–11; D&C 121:1–10; 122). "Being human, we would expel from our lives physical pain and mental anguish and assure ourselves of continual ease and comfort, but if we were to close the doors upon sorrow and distress, we might be excluding our greatest friends and benefactors. Suffering can make saints of people as they learn patience, long-suffering, and self-mastery" (Kimball, *Faith Precedes the Miracle*, 98).

9:20 Today, although many people question Jesus' divinity, there is no doubt whatsoever about what Jesus and his ancient disciples taught: He "is the Son of God." The first thing that Paul taught after his conversion, and the first thing he taught in all his letters, is the divine Sonship of Jesus Christ. The foundation of all gospel is that Jesus is the Son of God the Father.

9:21–31 These were trying days for Saul in which he encountered varied reactions about his conversion. What would his former friends think as they incredulously heard reports about his abrupt turnabout? What about the suspicions of his new friends, the members of the Church? Could they really trust him? One early leader in the Church, Barnabas, was sure of the reality of Paul's conversion and affirmed the genuineness of it to Church leaders and the Saints at Jerusalem. Paul soon discovered, however, that Jerusalem was a dangerous place for him to be, and the Brethren sent him back to his hometown of Tarsus, more than 350 miles to the north (see "Tarsus," 350).

9:32–42 These verses show the chief apostle, Simon Peter, making a tour of the missions and the branches of the Church on the coastal plain and performing great miracles, just as he had seen Jesus do.

"Saron" in verse 35 refers to the Sharon Plain. The plain covers the area roughly north from modern Tel Aviv and Joppa to Haifa.

The sister in Joppa who is raised from the dead is named Tabitha in Aramaic or Dorcas in Greek (meaning "gazelle").

9:43 About nine people named Simon are mentioned in the New Testament. Peter stays in Joppa with Simon, a tanner, whose house is right along the Mediterranean shore.

ACTS 10

10:1–4 Caesarea is the Roman capital of Judea. It had a temple of Zeus and a temple of Augustus, both built by Herod the Great. It would have been repulsive for Peter to go there; he resided instead in Jewish Joppa, thirty-four miles south (or about eleven hours walking distance).

Cornelius is the first known Gentile to receive the gospel in the meridian of time without converting to Judaism first. His conversion to the Lord's Church took place sometime between A.D. 35 and 44 (see Bible Dictionary, "Cornelius").

At the ninth hour of the day, which was 3 P.M., this Roman centurion of "the Italian band," who had been fasting (v. 30), received an answer to his prayers. God listens to all his children who humbly approach his throne. Cornelius had received a portion of the Holy Ghost; however, "there is a difference between the Holy Ghost and the gift of the Holy Ghost. Cornelius received the Holy Ghost before he was baptized, which was the convincing power of God of the truth of the Gospel, but he could not receive the gift of the Holy Ghost [that is, the right to the constant companionship of that member of the Godhead] until after he was baptized. Had he not taken this sign or ordinance upon him, the Holy Ghost which convinced him of the truth of God, would have left him" (Smith, *Teachings of the Prophet Joseph Smith*, 199; *History of the Church*, 4:555; see also Bible Dictionary, "Holy Ghost").

10:5–8 Cornelius is instructed to send to Joppa for the apostle Peter; again, note the use of local authority. The angel could not baptize him; Peter could. Said Joseph Smith, "No wonder the angel told good old Cornelius that he must send for Peter to learn how to be saved. Peter could baptize, and angels could not, so long as there were legal officers in the flesh holding the keys of the kingdom, or the authority of the priesthood" (Jackson, *Joseph Smith's Commentary on the Bible*, 150).

10:9–33 At the sixth hour (12 noon), Peter "fell into a trance"—that is, he was overcome by the Spirit. It appears that his bodily functions were suspended, similar to the experience of Moses on Mount Sinai, Joseph Smith in the Sacred Grove, and so forth. Peter is the presiding authority of the Lord's kingdom; the message pertains to the whole of the Church, so naturally, the message comes to him.

As is often the case, symbols are used to communicate a profound message. The old laws of clean and unclean were couched in a new setting. For centuries, the Israelites had considered the other nations, or Gentiles, to be unclean. Nevertheless, the Gentiles were children of God and entitled to the same opportunities, if they would accept and live according to God's conditions, as his Israelite children.

The "great sheet knit at the four corners" probably resembled a large prayer shawl of the kind worn by Jewish men during their religious devotions. Nonkosher animals wrapped in a holy prayer shawl would have made a doubly significant impression on Peter.

The dramatic message of Peter's three-time vision is introduced at the end of verse 15. Over time and with considerable thought, Peter came to a clear realization of what God was teaching him, as Luke notes at the end of verse 28.

10:34–35 The message is clear to Peter and to us: God is no respecter of persons. "He inviteth them all to come unto him and partake of his goodness; and he denieth none that come unto him, black and white, bond and free, male and female; and he remembereth the heathen; and *all are alike unto God*" (2 Nephi 26:33; emphasis added).

Elder Bruce R. McConkie illustrated the challenge of taking the gospel to those outside of Israel: "By the time of Jesus, the legal administrators and prophetic associates that he had were so fully indoctrinated with the concept of having the gospel go only to the house of Israel, that they were totally unable to envision the true significance of his proclamation that after the resurrection they should then go to all the world. They did not go to the gentile nations initially. In his own ministration, Jesus preached only to the lost sheep of the house of Israel, and had so commanded the apostles (Matthew 10:6).

"It is true that he made a few minor exceptions because of the faith and devotion of some gentile people. There was one woman who wanted to eat the crumbs that fell from the table of the children, causing him to say, 'O woman, great is thy faith.' (Matthew 15:28; see also Mark 7:27, 28.) With some minor exceptions, the gospel in that day went exclusively to Israel. The Lord had to give Peter the vision and revelation of the sheet coming down from heaven with the unclean meat on it, following which Cornelius sent the messenger to Peter to learn what he, Cornelius, and his gentile associates should do. The Lord commanded that the gospel go to the gentiles; and so it was. There was about a quarter of a century, then, in New Testament times, when there were extreme difficulties among the Saints. They were weighing and evaluating, struggling with the problem of whether the gospel was to go only to the house of Israel or whether it now went to all men. Could all men come to him on an equal basis with the seed of Abraham?

"You know this principle: God 'hath made of one blood all nations of men for to dwell on all the face of the earth and hath determined the times before appointed, and the bounds of their habitation; that they should seek the Lord if haply they might feel after him, and find him' (Acts 17:26, 27)— meaning that there is an appointed time to successive nations and peoples and races and cultures to be offered the saving truths of the gospel.

"We have revelations that tell us that the gospel is to go to every nation, kindred, tongue, and people before the second coming of the Son of Man. And we have revelations which recite that when the Lord comes he will find those who speak every tongue and are members of every nation and kindred, who will be kings and priests, who will live and reign on earth with him a thousand years. That means, as you know, that people from all nations will have the blessings of the house of the Lord before the Second Coming.

"We have read these passages and their associated passages for many years. We have seen what the words say and have said to ourselves, 'Yes, it says that, but we must read out of it the taking of the gospel and the blessings of the temple to the Negro people, because they are denied certain things.' There are statements in our literature by the early brethren, which we have interpreted to mean that the Negroes would not receive the priesthood in mortality. I have said the same things, and people write me letters and say, 'You said such and such, and how is it now that we do such and such?' And all I can say to that is that it is time disbelieving people repented and got in line and believed in a living, modern prophet. Forget everything that I have said, or what President Brigham Young or President George Q. Cannon or whomsoever has said in days past that is contrary to the present revelation. We spoke with a limited understanding and without the light and knowledge that now has come into the world.

"We get our truth and our light line upon line and precept upon precept. We have now had added a new flood of intelligence and light on this particular subject, and it erases all the darkness and all the views and all the thoughts of the past. They don't matter any more.

"It doesn't make a particle of difference what anybody ever said about the Negro matter before the first day of June 1978. It is a new day and a new arrangement, and the Lord has now given the revelation that sheds light out into the world on this subject. As to any sliver of light or any particles of darkness of the past, we forget about them. We now do what meridian Israel did when the Lord said the gospel should go to the gentiles. We forget all the statements that limited the gospel to the house of Israel, and we start going to the gentiles" (McConkie, "The New Revelation on Priesthood," 130–32).

All are indeed alike unto God, yes, but Acts 10:35 makes it clear that God does favor the righteous. One Jaredite king, Kim, "did not reign in righteousness, wherefore he was not favored of the Lord" (Ether 10:13). The Prophet Joseph Smith illustrated this principle: "Who would not love an affectionate and obedient son more than one who was disobedient, and sought to injure Him and overthrow the order of His house? . . . But God seeth not as man seeth, and He is no respecter of persons. (Acts x:34). True, but what saith the next verse, 'He that feareth God and worketh righteousness is accepted of Him;' but it does not say that he that worketh wickedness is accepted, and this is a proof that God has respect to the actions of persons; and if He did not, why should He commend obedience to His law? For if he had no respect to the actions of men, He would be just as well pleased with a wicked man for breaking His law as a righteous man for keeping it; and if Cain had done well, he would have been accepted as well as Abel (Genesis iv:7), and Esau as well as Jacob, which proves that God does not respect persons, only in relation to their acts" (*History of the Church*, 4:262–63).

10:36–43 Peter bears testimony as an eyewitness of Jesus' ministry, death, and resurrection. Peter is also a witness that only through Jesus Christ can all people receive remission of sins and be saved.

10:44–48 With a manifestation of the Holy Ghost among the Gentiles similar to that on the day of Pentecost, Peter testified that they, too, should be baptized and adopted into the household of God and accepted into full fellowship with the Saints.

ACTS 11

11:1–18 Peter reviews with the concerned leaders and members of the Church in Judea how he received the revelation in the coastal cities. He again bears testimony, and the Spirit confirms to those assembled the spiritual propriety of this dramatic revelation.

11:19–26 Truth spreads. Because persecution drove members outward and because of the Church's missionary outreach, the Church expanded farther and farther into the Mediterranean world.

11:26 The passage "disciples were called Christians first in Antioch" refers to that dispensation. In a sense, Adam and Eve were the first "Christians"; they knew of Christ and believed in him, as did many others down through the ages, long before the disciples in Antioch (see "Antioch," 352). The

*Modern Antakya, Turkey, the site of ancient Antioch of Syria,
where Paul's missionary journeys began*

term *Christian* may have been first used as a derisive nick-name, much as *Mormon* was used in the early part of our present dispensation.

11:28 This same prophet Agabus later predicted Paul's imprisonment (see Acts 21:10–11).

Claudius Caesar ruled from A.D. 41–54. Sources other than the Bible corroborate the existence of this famine in the eastern Mediterranean world (see, for example, Josephus, *Antiquities*, 20.2.5). The famine hit Judea in A.D. 46.

11:29–30 One purpose of the journey of Barnabas and Paul to Jerusalem is to deliver the supplies other Saints had contributed for the relief of Church members in Judea.

ACTS 12

12:1–2 The Herod here is Herod Agrippa I, grandson of Herod the Great. This James is a counselor in the First Presidency of the Church, brother of John. He was killed during Passover in Jerusalem in A.D. 44, making him, as far as we

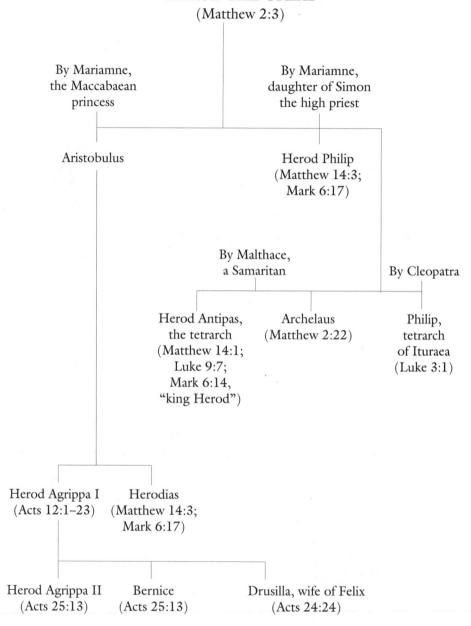

HEROD THE GREAT
(Matthew 2:3)

By Mariamne,
the Maccabaean
princess

By Mariamne,
daughter of Simon
the high priest

Aristobulus

Herod Philip
(Matthew 14:3;
Mark 6:17)

By Malthace,
a Samaritan

By Cleopatra

Herod Antipas,
the tetrarch
(Matthew 14:1;
Luke 9:7;
Mark 6:14,
"king Herod")

Archelaus
(Matthew 2:22)

Philip,
tetrarch
of Ituraea
(Luke 3:1)

Herod Agrippa I
(Acts 12:1–23)

Herodias
(Matthew 14:3;
Mark 6:17)

Herod Agrippa II
(Acts 25:13)

Bernice
(Acts 25:13)

Drusilla, wife of Felix
(Acts 24:24)

know, the first apostle-martyr. The death of James was a pivotal event, for it demonstrated the weakening position and increasing unpopularity of the Christians among the Jews of Jerusalem. This change seems to have resulted from the Church's extending fellowship to the Gentiles. "Luke's account of how, shortly before this, Peter had fraternized with Gentiles in Caesarea and his fellow-apostles had acquiesced in his action, provides a sufficient explanation of their sudden unpopularity with many Jews who had formerly respected them. From this time forth James the brother of Jesus, widely esteemed in Jerusalem as a strictly observant Jew, appears as principal leader of the church of Jerusalem" (Bruce, *New Testament History*, 261). Such an occurrence in ancient times illustrates the opposition that arises in every dispensation to halt the spread of the Gospel and the building up of God's kingdom.

12:3–4 The Feast of Unleavened Bread is a week-long festive occasion, beginning with Passover Day. Use of the word *Easter* here is an anachronism; the Greek is *pascha* from the Hebrew *pesach*, which means "Passover." Christians made Passover into a commemoration of the resurrection.

12:5–19 Prayer works. The Saints' righteous petitions to heaven are answered in the miraculous release of their prophet-leader from prison (see also Daniel 6:22).

12:10 The first and second "ward" means the first and second guard, or detachments of soldiers guarding the prison.

12:12 John Mark is probably the same person who wrote the second Gospel. He accompanied Paul and Barnabas briefly on their first missionary journey (v. 25). His mother, Mary, was a leading member of the Church in Jerusalem. The earliest evidence suggests that he became a scribe and helper to Peter "at Babylon," which is Rome (see 1 Peter 5:13).

12:17 "James" is either the half-brother of Jesus or the son of Alpheus; both men were apparently apostles.

12:21–23 On the second day of the victory games honoring Rome's conquest of Britain, Herod Agrippa, who presided over the events, suddenly fell ill and died at age fifty-four. Luke views Agrippa's death as justice administered by an angel of God.

CHAPTER 3

THE ACTS OF THE APOSTLES, CHAPTERS 13 THROUGH 28

As prophesied by the Savior, there came a time when the apostles and other Church leaders began to take their testimonies beyond the borders of Judea and Samaria "unto the uttermost part of the earth" (Acts 1:8). Acts 13 through 28 report the beginning of the expansion of teaching the gospel outside the Holy Land, starting in Antioch and eventually ending up in Rome.

ACTS 13

13:1–3 Church leaders in Antioch fast and pray and then call and ordain Barnabas and Saul (now called Paul; v. 9) as missionaries. Verse 4 begins the first extended missionary journey, which takes the Brethren at least fourteen hundred miles (see Bible Map 13). Luke writes very little about Paul from the time of his conversion to the time of this first missionary journey, though he does give us a sketchy outline. Paul has been teaching the gospel in Damascus and its environs for quite some time; then, after spending three years in Damascus, he "went up to Jerusalem" (Galatians 1:18). Paul is called by the apostles to serve for several years in his home city of Tarsus before he and Barnabas journey east and south to Antioch. At Antioch they teach "a whole year" (Acts 11:26). Notwithstanding Luke's brief coverage of a ten-year period, we may suppose that Paul has already been involved in considerable missionary work before he begins what we call his first missionary journey.

13:4 The missionaries sail 130 miles from Antioch's port, Seleucia, to Cyprus, probably at the opening of the sailing season, about March.

13:5–13 Journeying overland from Salamis to Paphos on the western end of the island, the missionaries meet and teach Sergius Paulus, who is the Roman proconsul for Cyprus and is also known from other historical records. From Paphos they sail another 180 miles to the port of Attalia, in Pamphylia on the southern coast of modern Turkey.

13:6 "False prophets always arise to oppose the true prophets and they will prophesy so very near the truth that they will deceive almost the very chosen ones" (Smith, *Teachings of the Prophet Joseph Smith*, 365).

13:9 The Latin adjective *paulus* means "little" or "small." Could this word have reference to his physical stature? Joseph Smith gave the following word-portrait of the apostle: "Description of Paul—He is about five feet high; very dark hair; dark complexion; dark skin; large Roman nose; sharp face; small black eyes, penetrating as eternity; round shoulders; a whining voice, except when elevated and then it almost resembled the roaring of a lion. He was a good orator, active and diligent, always employing himself in doing good to his fellow man" (*Teachings of the Prophet Joseph Smith*, 180). This description of Paul suggests that Joseph Smith had personal experience with Paul; perhaps the apostle to the Gentiles appeared to the prophet of the Restoration (see D&C 128:21).

13:10–11 Compare Alma's cursing of Korihor (Alma 30:47–56).

13:13 After arriving in the port of Attalia, Paul, Barnabas, and John Mark walk to the city of Perga, about twelve miles to the northeast. At this point Luke gives a matter-of-fact report of the departure of John Mark. We learn later that his leaving produced some bitter feelings in Paul (Acts 15:36–40).

Lake country of ancient Pisidia

13:14 Luke gives few details of the journey from Perga to Antioch of Pisidia, but it would have taken the missionaries five or six days to climb nearly one hundred miles from the coast up into the mountains of the district of Pisidia. This Antioch and the Antioch in Syria are only two of about sixteen sites named Antioch established during the Hellenistic Seleucid period (see "Antioch of Pisidia," 355).

13:15–41 Paul's discourse at Antioch of Pisidia is one of the most completely recorded in the book of Acts. Paul uses the same approach that Peter and Stephen used previously—reviewing the history of Israel to show how events, people, practices, and prophetic promises were types and foreshadowings of Christ. He further explains how Jesus atoned for sins and resurrected from the dead—all of which makes him, irrefutably, the Messiah.

13:44–48 Paul's talk draws a large crowd on the next Sabbath day, but Jews become envious and oppose him and Barnabas openly. Verse 46 declares that a door is now open for the Gentiles to come directly into the Church without going

The main street (cardo maximus) of Antioch of Pisidia

through the synagogue first. Joseph Smith eloquently illustrates this principle: "After this chosen family had rejected Christ and his proposals, the heralds of salvation said to them, 'Lo, we turn unto the Gentiles.' And the Gentiles received the covenant and were grafted in from whence the chosen family were broken off. But the Gentiles have not continued in the goodness of God but have departed from the faith that was once delivered to the Saints, and have broken the covenant in which their fathers were established, and have become highminded, and have not feared. Therefore, but few of them will be gathered with the chosen family" (Jackson, *Joseph Smith's Commentary on the Bible*, 150).

13:47 See Isaiah 42:6, in which God calls Israel to be a light of the Gentiles. Israel is to provide salvation [Hebrew, *Yeshua*, "Jesus"] that could come unto the ends of the earth.

13:48 Note the important change in the Joseph Smith Translation, as shown in footnote 48*a*: "and as many as *believed* were ordained *unto* eternal life."

13:49–52 The apostles' success often brings jealousy and

68

envy, after which they are persecuted and then cast out or killed. In verse 51 we see the use of one of two priesthood ordinances associated with the feet, each signifying something opposite from that signified by the other. Shaking off the dust from the feet is an action of disapproval and condemnation; the washing of the feet is an ordinance of acceptance and approbation. The shaking off the dust from the feet, like the washing of the feet, is to be performed only by the Lord's authorized servants. The former is initiated as a testimony against those who willfully and maliciously oppose the truth when it is authoritatively presented (see D&C 24:15; 60:15; 75:20; 99:4). It is not invoked against those who simply reject the message of the gospel. As Elder James E. Talmage wrote, "The responsibility of testifying before the Lord by this accusing symbol is so great that the means may be employed *only* under unusual and extreme conditions" (*Jesus the Christ,* 345). Thus, if the ordinance then had the same qualifications and limitations as it does today, we may conclude that in this instance Paul and Barnabas faced grave conditions (see Acts 13:51).

The missionaries move on to Iconium, eighty miles to the southeast, immediately entering the synagogue to teach Jews (see Acts 14:1).

ACTS 14

14:1 See "Iconium," 356.

14:4, 19 Verse 4 contains the first mention of Barnabas and Paul as apostles. Although Paul's relationship to the Twelve has been debated in literature on the New Testament, President Joseph Fielding Smith maintains that "Paul was an ordained apostle, and without question he took the place of one of the other brethren in that Council" (*Doctrines of Salvation,* 3:153).

14:6–12 Lystra lies twenty-five miles south of Iconium in the region called Lycaonia. The Taurus Mountains border this

*Inscription mentioning LVSTRA, found at the
site of Timothy's hometown*

region on the south. Phrygia borders it on the west,
Cappadocia on the east, and Galatia on the north. In Lystra,
the apostles heal a crippled man and are hailed as the gods
Jupiter (Zeus) and Mercury (Hermes). Barnabas, who is pos-
sibly the more imposing of the two in physical stature, is called
Jupiter, and Paul, the spokesman, is called Mercury (see
"Lystra and Derbe," 357).

14:13 The priest of Jupiter brings oxen and garlands.
These two items have been found sculpted into many stone
monuments in the region and were apparently symbols of the
gods Zeus and Hermes.

14:14–20 Paul and Barnabas object to the idolatry of the
populace and teach them to worship the true and living God.
Agitators from Antioch and Iconium follow the Brethren to
Lystra and stir up a mob to stone Paul. Though he has been
thrown out of the city and left for dead, the very next day he
is up again heading toward Derbe to preach the gospel. His
experience is perhaps comparable to Joseph Smith's experience

Paul sailed in and out of this port of Attalia, modern Antalya, Turkey

of having all-night visions and instruction from Moroni and then going out to work in the fields with his father. Similarly, a few years later, after being brutally tarred and feathered, Joseph spent all night cleaning his body and then went to church the next day to give a sermon.

14:21–28 The apostles return to their newly established branches to strengthen the faith of members and set up leadership. They make the return trip to Antioch, where they continue to minister (see "Attalia and Perga," 354).

PAUL'S UNIQUE PREPARATION

Paul was uniquely prepared to take Christianity to the world. He was a Roman citizen of a Benjamite family, perhaps of some prominence, and a native of Tarsus, a distinguished Greek city, whose residents had been given Roman citizenship by Mark Antony. He was also, as he wrote, a Hebrew of the Hebrews. Thus Paul is both the Hellenistic Paul and the Hebraic Saul. Upon his becoming a disciple of Christ, Paul's Pharisaic family would have considered him apostate and

Ruins of ancient Perga, in the southern coastal region anciently called Pamphylia

possibly disowned him. No detail of his preparatory life was accidental; all circumstances were part of God's foreordained plan for Paul. Tarsus, for example, was no arbitrary choice for his birthplace; that city was possibly the single best example of an amalgamation of oriental and occidental ideals—the most successful union of eastern and western character (Ramsay, *Cities of St. Paul*, 79, 88–89).

THE FOCUS OF PAUL'S MISSIONARY LABORS

Paul concentrated his work in the main metropolitan centers of the time. The Roman provincial metropolis served as the regional administrative, civic, cultural, commercial, and religious center for life in Paul's day. Each provincial center served also as Paul's strategic point from which the gospel could spread to surrounding communities. The main centers from which Paul worked included Antioch, for Cilicia and Syria; Perga, for Pamphylia; Antioch, for Pisidia of Galatia; Ephesus, for Asia; Philippi and Thessalonica, for Macedonia; Corinth, for Achaia; and Rome, for Italy.

Paul's letters were written to the Saints in the provincial centers of Galatia, Asia, Macedonia, Achaia, and Italy. The establishment of stable branches of the Church in these centers had far-reaching consequences.

PAUL'S TRAVELS

The apostle Paul journeyed by ship and by foot at least 13,400 airline miles during his years of missionary labors, a figure that would increase enormously could we measure all the circuitous routes that he actually traveled. He was an indomitable laborer for the cause of Christ—despite the usual stress and fatigue that accompany travel. He was even silent about his "thorn in the flesh" (2 Corinthians 12:7), which may have hampered him. Nevertheless, we read nothing of Paul taking a break from his labors; he was on fire, and his desire to save souls energized him.

The following is a description of Paul's journeys, with references and approximate distances noted (adapted from Beitzel, *Moody Atlas of Bible Lands,* 177, 179, 182–83; used by permission):

1. Acts 9:1–30. Jerusalem to Damascus to the Arabian Desert (distance unknown) to Jerusalem to Tarsus—minimum 690 miles (see Bible Map 18).

2. Acts 11:25–26. Tarsus to Antioch—90 miles (see Bible Map 18).

3. Acts 11:30 to 12:25 (compare Galatians 2:1–10). Antioch to Jerusalem to Antioch—560 miles (see Bible Map 18).

4. Acts 13:4 to 14:28. First missionary journey—1,400 miles (see Bible Map 19).

5. Acts 15:12–30. Antioch to Jerusalem to Antioch—560 miles (see Bible Map 18).

6. Acts 15:39 to 18:22. Second missionary journey—2,800 miles (see Bible Map 20).

7. Acts 18:23 to 21:17. Third missionary journey—2,700 miles (see Bible Map 21).

8. Acts 27:1 to 28:16. Journey to Rome—2,250 miles (see Bible Map 22).

9. After the two-year imprisonment in Rome, Paul evidently traveled throughout the Mediterranean world again, visiting Crete (Titus 1:5), Troas (2 Timothy 4:13), Macedonia (1 Timothy 1:3), and Nicopolis (Titus 3:12). He was then imprisoned again in Rome (2 Timothy 1:16–17). If he followed the shortest possible routes, he traveled 2,350 miles.

Total miles traveled: minimum of 13,400 miles traveling direct distances.

ACTS 15

15:1–4 "Certain men which came down from Judaea" (v. 1) arrive at Antioch, teaching that all new converts, such as Greeks, have to be circumcised. Notice the ominous wording: these men "came down . . . [and] taught the brethren." They seem to have been good, honorable men, but they erred regarding circumcision (McConkie, *Doctrinal New Testament Commentary*, 2:139). Their insistence that the old sign of the covenant is still necessary for salvation is false doctrine. The covenant is eternal, but this sign of the covenant is now discontinued: "The law of circumcision is done away in me" (Moroni 8:8; see also Bible Dictionary, "Circumcision").

This matter caused serious division in the early Church and was the subject of a general conference of the Church in Jerusalem. The conference, or council, was held about the year A.D. 50, some fifteen years or so after Paul's conversion.

15:5 Some new members of the Church, converts from the Pharisees, hold to the long-standing requirements for any non-Jew to become a proselyte: circumcision for males and ritual immersion (analogous to baptism) and living the law of Moses. The most pressing question is whether a Gentile convert has to adopt and live the old Mosaic laws—not just circumcision but hundreds of other obligations and scores of traditions the Jews had attached to the old law.

15:6–11 Peter, who is presiding and conducting, stands, bears his testimony, and reminds the Church that the revelation opening the gospel dispensation to the Gentiles did not mean that the old system, the old "yoke" (v. 10) is thrust upon them. Paul and other apostles do not deprecate the law of Moses; they simply acknowledge that the law of Moses is not sufficient to bring a person to salvation. Circumcision is not necessary as a saving ordinance. Salvation is in the Lord Jesus Christ.

15:12–21 Barnabas and Paul give a missionary report, and then James, the Lord's brother (now possibly of the Twelve), confirms the declaration of Peter.

15:18 Latter-day Saints, like the former-day Saints, believe in the omniscience and foreknowledge of God; that is, he knows all things from the beginning.

15:19–20 "My sentence is"—James recommends not to bother the Gentiles with the yoke of the old law and to write to them to abstain from pollutions of idols—avoid eating meat offered to idols and abstain from fornication, things strangled, and blood—all of which were involved in such mystery cults as those of Dionysus and Cybele. In other words, James's advice was to allow Gentiles to abstain from Judaic practices but require all to abstain from pagan practices.

15:23 This verse begins a letter from the Jerusalem leadership (vv. 23–29). Essentially it is what in our day is called an Official Declaration. Nevertheless, the issues of circumcision and adherence to the old law were not definitively resolved. The decision allowed Gentiles into membership without adopting Judaic practices but at the same time seems to have failed to sever Jewish Christians from their Mosaic heritage. Jewish Christians needed to discontinue their dependence on the law of Moses and set their hearts squarely on the gospel of Jesus Christ (see 2 Nephi 25:26–27; 3 Nephi 15:2–5). It seems that the Jerusalem council may have been overly sensitive to Jewish members, not wanting to drive them out of the Church by doctrinal or policy changes that might have seemed too abrupt to some. Upon Paul's return to Jerusalem years later (Acts 21), he found Jewish Christians still holding to the traditions of Judaism.

15:30–35 The Gentiles in the Church rejoice when they hear the word of the Lord from his earthly authorities. Judas Barsabas and Silas were leaders akin to modern-day general or area authorities.

15:36–40 Paul, now back in Antioch, proposes another missionary journey. Barnabas is determined to take his relative John Mark, but Paul resists because of previous experience with him. The exchange of feelings over the matter becomes so acrimonious that they part company. (Paul and Mark were apparently later reconciled, as suggested in Colossians 4:10.) Barnabas takes Mark and sails to his homeland, Cyprus, and Paul selects for his companion Silas, a leader at Jerusalem. Silas is also called by his Latin name Silvanus in Paul's letters.

15:41 A second missionary journey begins (see Bible Map 13; "Cilician Gates," 358).

ACTS 16

16:1–2 At Lystra Paul becomes acquainted with a young man named Timothy, whose friendship he tenderly recalls in epistles written to him. Paul calls him "my own son in the faith" (1 Timothy 1:2).

16:3 Paul vigorously opposed circumcision at the Jerusalem conference, arguing emphatically that his fellow servant Titus, who is a Greek, has no need to be circumcised. Yet Paul circumcises Timothy, who is Jewish, so as not to alienate the Jews. Paul needs Timothy for the missionary work among Jews. His circumcision is a matter of expediency and

sensitivity toward those he would serve rather than a requirement for salvation. Paul often adapted to circumstances of
others to get their attention and teach them (see 1 Corinthians 9:20–22).

16:4–5 The "decrees for to keep" were the decisions of
the Jerusalem council, which the Brethren taught everywhere
they went.

16:6–9 It is a perplexing journey, rushing on from
province to province—Galatia, Phrygia, and Mysia. Paul wants
to go into the provinces of Asia and Bithynia but is forbidden
by the Spirit. Paul and Silas finally arrive at the coastal port of
Troas on the Aegean Sea. Here are some manifestations of
divine guidance: they were cautioned by the Lord not to go
into two particular provinces at that time, and then a vision
came. The reason for all that rushing on and being forbidden
to go elsewhere is that they were needed in Macedonia. They
were called to take the gospel into what we now call continen-
tal Europe (see "Troas," 358).

16:10 At Troas, Luke, a physician by occupation, seems to
have joined the missionaries, for the pronouns *we* and *us* appear
for the first time. The *we* later disappears and then reappears in
20:6; almost certainly this usage indicates the writer's personal
involvement with the traveling company. These verses show
how the Lord directs his apostles where they are needed, just as
modern apostles have also testified of the Lord's divine guidance. For example, Elder Thomas S. Monson recounts how the
president of the Quorum of the Twelve changed his stake visiting assignment to a place where a dying little girl had prayed
for him to come and give her a priesthood blessing. Neither
the president of the Quorum of the Twelve nor Elder Monson
knew about the young girl's prayer before the change was
made (see *Ensign,* November 1975, 20–22).

16:11 The harbor at Troas was the link between Asia and
Macedonia. The journey by sea would have been 150 miles in

Port of Neapolis into which Paul sailed, now called Kavalla, Greece

two days. The missionaries sailed past the island of Samothrace and a day later sailed into the port of Neapolis (Greek, "new city"). The trip may have seemed much like any other city-to-city journey. The apostles probably didn't consider it as traveling from continent to continent—they were just going from one Roman province to another.

16:12 A Roman colony had been established at Philippi, with veteran Roman soldiers settling there (see "Philippi," 359).

16:13 Anyone visiting the ruins of Philippi today will see that there is, indeed, a small river running along the western side of the site.

16:14 As far as we know, the first convert on the continent of Europe is a woman named Lydia, a seller of purple dye from Thyatira in the province of Asia. Her name may reflect her place of origin, the Hellenistic district of Lydia. She is a Gentile who, like Cornelius, believed in God and followed the teachings of scripture though she had not converted to Judaism. She gave Paul hospitality. Because the setting here is

*Paul walked this Roman road, the Via Egnatia,
from Neapolis to Philippi*

Philippi, it is possible that Lydia is Paul's "yokefellow" spoken of in his later letter to the Philippians (Philippians 4:3).

The Israelites, like other societies of the ancient Near East, prized colored dyes—blue, scarlet, and purple in particular. As with other elements and composites in nature that are comparatively rare, such as gold and diamonds, the dyes were treasured because of the limited quantity available. Purple was extracted by the Phoenicians, especially Tyrians, from Murex snails (part of the mollusk phylum) which thrive along the northeastern Mediterranean coast and were used in textile dyeing. Recent experiments by marine biologists and chemists in the Near East have established the certain origin of royal purple and the possible origin of biblical blue from the female and male *rock murex*.

16:16 In Philippi the missionaries encounter a spirit of divination, soothsaying, or sorcery—not unlike the use today of horoscopes, charms, Ouija boards, seances, crystal balls, and so forth.

Ruins of Philippi, where Paul preached and was imprisoned

16:16–18 Joseph Smith said: "They detected the spirit. And although she spake favorably of them, Paul commanded the spirit to come out of her and saved themselves from the opprobrium that might have been heaped upon their heads through an affiance with her in the development of her wicked principles, which they certainly would have been charged with if they had not rebuked the evil spirit" (Jackson, *Joseph Smith's Commentary on the Bible,* 151).

16:19 "Marketplace" is translated from the Greek *agora,* which would have been an effective place to preach because of the many people gathered there. Legal and civil cases could also be heard and official judgments pronounced in the agora.

16:20–34 Although treated badly and illegally committed to prison, and then even placed in stocks, were the Brethren discouraged? No! Late into the night they prayed and sang hymns, perhaps ones similar in feeling to our modern "How Firm a Foundation," "Firm as the Mountains Around Us," and so forth. Then the earthquake came. It is well-known that this part of the world has occasional earthquakes.

Stream at Philippi, possibly where Paul met Lydia and others

The Lord uses this geological phenomenon to miraculously liberate the missionaries and send them on their way.

Consider the following experience from the journal of Elder Wilford Woodruff: "When I arose to speak at Brother Benbow's house [in England], a man entered the door and informed me that he was a constable, and had been sent by the rector of the parish with a warrant to arrest me. I asked him, 'For what crime?' He said, 'For preaching to the people.' I told him that I, as well as the rector, had a license for preaching the gospel to the people, and that if he would take a chair I would wait upon him after meeting. He took my chair and sat beside me. For an hour and a quarter I preached the first principles of the everlasting gospel. The power of God rested upon me, the spirit filled the house, and the people were convinced. At the close of the meeting I opened the door for baptism, and seven offered themselves. Among the number were four preachers and the constable. The latter arose and said, 'Mr. Woodruff, I would like to be baptized.' I told him I would like to baptize him. I went down into the pool and baptized the seven. We then came together. I confirmed thirteen, administered the Sacrament, and we all rejoiced together.

"The constable went to the rector and told him that if he wanted Mr. Woodruff taken for preaching the gospel, he must go himself and serve the writ; for he had heard him preach the only true gospel sermon he had ever listened to in his life. The rector did not know what to make of it, so he sent two clerks of the Church of England as spies, to attend our meeting, and find out what we did preach. They both were pricked in their hearts, received the word of the Lord gladly, and were baptized and confirmed members of the Church of Jesus Christ of Latter-day Saints. The rector became alarmed, and did not venture to send anybody else" (Cowley, *Wilford Woodruff,* 118).

Other prison scenes, in which the Lord's anointed ones are protected and delivered, involve Daniel (Daniel 6), Alma and Amulek (Alma 14), Nephi and Lehi (Helaman 5), and Peter (Acts 12:1–19).

16:27 Roman law stipulated that a jailer would be executed if he allowed capital criminal prisoners to escape.

16:35–40 Upon hearing that their prisoners were Roman citizens, the embarrassed city officials attempt to reverse their injustice privately.

ACTS 17

17:1 The missionaries journeyed on through Amphipolis and Apollonia, an eighty-mile trek along the Egnatian Way to Thessalonica, a city named after the sister of Alexander the Great, who was born near there (see "Thessalonica," 360).

17:2 Paul, "as his manner was," went into the synagogue of the Jews. His approach is to identify scriptures that were fulfilled in Christ and then bear his testimony that Jesus really is the promised Messiah. This pattern seems to have emerged soon after his conversion in Damascus and is consistently

Paul's way of teaching the gospel (Acts 9:20–22; 13:5, 14–43; 14:1–3).

17:3–4 In 1611, when the King James Bible was published, "alleging" meant to bring forth evidence, to present proof. Paul's proof is convincing, and some Jews and many Greeks consorted or joined with the missionaries and believed their words.

17:5 Some envious Jewish antagonists, along with "certain lewd fellows of the baser sort," assault the home of Jason, where they were residing. This Jason is apparently a relative of Paul (see Romans 16:21) and later served in a leadership capacity in the Thessalonian Branch.

17:6–9 Jason and the missionaries are accused of subverting the Roman government by promoting another king named Jesus. Jason posts bond for all of them, and they are released.

"In Acts 17:6–8, Luke refers to the magistrates of Thessalonica as 'politarchs.' While this term appears nowhere else in Greek literature, Luke's accuracy has been confirmed by inscription evidence, which indicates that this was the common title for magistrates not only in Thessalonica but also in Macedonia as a whole. In keeping with Thessalonica's free status, it was these politarchs (five or six in number), rather than any Roman official, who heard the case against Paul and his companions (Acts 17:6–9)" (Harrison, *Major Cities of the Biblical World*, 261).

17:10–11 Paul and Silas escape under cover of night to Berea, fifty miles from Thessalonica. At Berea were Jews whom Luke compliments as "more noble" and gives the reasons why.

17:12–13 Persecution, as usual, followed success.

17:14–15 Paul journeys 250 miles south to Athens, a famous city in modern Greece (Hellas), in the province formerly called Attica. For centuries this region had been a center

The Agora, or marketplace, of Athens, a likely locale for Paul's preaching

of great influence. Although the Greek language and Hellenistic culture had been disseminated very widely throughout the East, it entered directly into scriptural history only in late New Testament times. In Paul's day southern Greece and some Aegean islands made up the province called Achaia. The landscape is extremely mountainous and has twenty-six hundred miles of coastline—more than Italy or Iberia, both of which are much larger areas. It is not possible in this region of Greece to be more than forty miles from the sea (see "Athens," 362).

When Paul arrived in Achaia, he knew he was stepping onto a well-used stage of history. The Mycenaeans were ancient and legendary. Homer's masterpieces were already nine hundred years old. Pericles' age of democracy was long spent. Aeschylus, Sophocles, Socrates, Plato, and Aristotle had long since gone the way of all the earth. The world had seen its finest army out of Macedon, but Alexander's empire had been dissected centuries before. Now with Rome in control of the known world in the first century after Christ, Athens lived mostly off its past glories.

Athens was a quiet university town, still talking philosophy and religion. It was the world center of idol worship; some claim it was easier to find a god in Athens than a man. Paul was appalled at the wholesale idolatry, and he took occasion in the marketplace and at Areopagus to declare not the "unknown god" that the people ignorantly worshipped but the personal God whom he knew well.

17:16–17 Paul is filled with the spirit of Exodus 20:3–4: "Thou shalt have no other gods before me" and "Thou shalt not make unto thee any graven image." He is indignant, but being in Athens he adopted the Socratic method of public discussion and reasoned with his listeners.

17:18 The Epicureans espoused a philosophy of pleasure and avoiding sorrow and pain (though not of embracing licentiousness); the Stoics recognized a supreme governor of the universe and man's constant battle with nature—they ignored the body.

Babbler is the English equivalent of the Greek slang word *spermologos,* "one who picks up scraps of information here and there."

17:19–21 Areopagus (pronounced Ar-ee-AH-pagus) is Greek for Hill of Ares, or Mars, the god of war. This council is the highest court in Athens. Paul is not arraigned or accused; they want to meet and hear him.

17:22–25 On "Too superstitious" see footnote *22a;* Paul's remark is not insulting but praising. In essence, he is saying, I notice you're pretty religious around here. In fact, while I was touring the city, I noticed an altar with the inscription TO THE UNKNOWN GOD. Well, let me tell you about him.

A similar account appears in a biography called the *Life of Apollonius of Tyana,* by Philostratus, who described a visit to the same Athens Paul visited: "Having come to anchor in the Piraeus, he went up from the harbor to the city. Advancing onward, he met several of the philosophers. In his first conversation, finding the Athenians much devoted to Religion, he discoursed on sacred subjects. This was at Athens, where also altars of Unknown gods are set up" (cited in Meinardus, *St. Paul in Greece*, 41).

17:26 Life and life's circumstances do not result from chance. "The race and nation in which men are born in this world is a direct result of their pre-existent life" (McConkie, *Mormon Doctrine*, 616). President Harold B. Lee expounded on this doctrine: "You are all the sons and daughters of God. Your spirits were created and lived as organized intelligences before the world was. You have been blessed to have a physical body because of your obedience to certain commandments in that premortal state. You are now born into a family to which you have come, into the nations through which you have come, as a reward for the kind of lives you lived before you came here and at a time in the world's history, as the Apostle Paul taught the men of Athens and as the Lord revealed to Moses, determined by the faithfulness of each of those who lived before this world was created" (Conference Report, October 1973, 7).

17:27 Note the insight added by the Joseph Smith Translation in footnote 27b: "if *they are willing to* find him *for* he *is* not far from every one of us" (JST alterations in italics). Also compare Abraham 2:12.

17:28 We see Paul's wise teaching method: to quote from a work familiar to his audience, a passage highly regarded by them, and then show its relationship to, and fulfillment in, the gospel of Jesus Christ. Paul may have been referring to the poet Aratus from Tarsus of the third century before Christ; Paul could have studied his *Phaenomena* while he lived in Tarsus. Following is a passage from the poet's work: "From Zeus let us begin; him do we mortals never leave unnamed; full of Zeus are all the streets and all the market-places of men; full is the sea and the havens thereof; always we all have need of Zeus. *For we are also his offspring;* and he in his kindness unto men giveth favourable signs and wakeneth the people to work, reminding them of livelihood" (Aratus, *Phaenomena*, 207; emphasis added).

17:29–31 A warning against idolatry. God may have "overlooked" or tolerated such ignorant worship practices in the past, but now he requires all to repent and return to true worship.

17:32–34 Some Athenians must have thought Paul was out of his mind, preaching that a crucified carpenter from Judea was God and that the human body would be resurrected to live forever. Greek mythology and philosophy of the time considered the body evil. Eternal life was for the spirit, not for the body. Yet other Athenians believed Paul and followed the truth. An early historian recorded: "The Areopagite, Dionysius by name, . . . was, as Luke related in the Acts, the first convert after Paul's address to the Athenians in the Areopagus. He became the first Bishop of Athens, a fact recorded by a very early writer" (Eusebius, *History of the Church*, 67).

ACTS 18

18:1–2 These verses record Paul's journey to Corinth, sixty miles west of Athens. Corinth was the capital of the Roman province of Achaia and its most important commercial center. Corinth is estimated to have had approximately twenty thousand Jews at the time of Paul (see Bible Dictionary, "Corinth"). This large population may have been a result of the expulsion of the Jews from Rome, which several early historians discuss. The Roman historian Suetonius mentioned in his *Life of Claudius,* "The Jews, who by the instigation of one Chrestos were evermore tumultuous, he banished from Rome" (quoted in Meinardus, *St. Paul in Greece,* 66). The fifth-century Spanish historian Paulus Orosius dated the expulsion of Jews from Rome to the ninth

Excavations at ancient Corinth, with the Acrocorinth in the background

year of the reign of Claudius, meaning from January A.D. 49 to January A.D. 50. That fairly accurately dates the arrival of Aquila, Priscilla, and Paul some time thereafter to Corinth (see "Corinth," 364; Bible Dictionary, "Aquila").

18:3 "Jesus was a carpenter, Peter a fisherman, Matthew a tax collector; Brigham Young was a carpenter, painter, and glazier, Heber J. Grant a businessman, David O. McKay a teacher; Paul and Aquila were tentmakers. . . . Work is honorable" (McConkie, *Doctrinal New Testament Commentary*, 2:163).

18:4–11 Paul works for a year and a half in Corinth, teaching on the Sabbath in the synagogue, testifying that Jesus is the long-promised Messiah, and converting and baptizing many, even some leaders of the synagogue. Verse 8 clearly illustrates that baptism follows belief.

18:12 The twelfth year of Claudius' reign was A.D. 52–53. In A.D. 52, Lucius Junius Gallio, the elder brother of the statesman-philosopher Seneca and the deputy or proconsul of Achaia, met Paul at the judgment seat, or *bema*, in Corinth.

An important inscription that helps date Paul's stay in this city was discovered in the late nineteenth century on a limestone slab at Delphi: "Tiberius Claudius Caesar Augustus Germanicus, pontifex maximus, in the 12th year of his tribunal power, acclaimed emperor for the 26th time . . . sends greetings to the city of Delphi . . . but with regard to the present stories and those disputes of the citizens of which a report has been made by Lucius Junius Gallio, my friend a proconsul of Achaia . . ." (quoted in Meinardus, *St. Paul in Greece*, 67).

18:13–16 Gallio seems to have developed a rather expeditious, if not judicious, way of dealing with Jews and their legal polemics!

18:17 Verse 8 mentions Crispus as the *archisynagogos*, or ruler of the synagogue, but now we hear of one Sosthenes. Possibly, the latter is either the successor of Crispus or the head of yet another synagogue.

At this point in the chronology of events recorded in the book of Acts, Paul wrote 1 and 2 Thessalonians from Corinth in about A.D. 52–53. The epistles of Paul are arranged in our New Testament not according to chronological order but according to their length and their theological significance. Thus, Romans, being the longest, comes first; Philemon, the shortest, comes last. The book of Hebrews was placed after the others because the compilers of the New Testament questioned whether or not Paul wrote it (see further on Hebrews). Notwithstanding the present order, we study the books in the sequence they were written, according to the best of our present knowledge (see "The Epistles" in the article entitled "New Testament," in Ludlow, *Encyclopedia of Mormonism*, 3:1013–14). Paul's letters are directed to members of the Church, to those who have already entered the Way. Thus, they emphasize gospel principles and ordinances that keep a person on the straight and narrow path, and pressing forward.

President Joseph Fielding Smith said of Paul's letters:

"Now, the people out in the world have a strange idea about these epistles of Paul and of the men who have written the epistles we have in the Bible. They apply them unto themselves, and they look upon them as being declared as messages to the entire world. But this is not so. Definitely, each of these epistles was written to members of the Church—not to denominations, but to those who heard the words of the apostles of old, had received them, and had been baptized and confirmed members of the Church of Jesus Christ in that dispensation. Therefore, we should have the understanding when we read these epistles that the things said by the apostles are not things that apply to those who have not made covenants through the gospel of Jesus Christ and did not in that day" (Conference Report, April 1967, 119).

18:18 Numbers 6 explains that Israelites could consecrate themselves to the Lord for temporary periods to perform special tasks or seek special blessings. The specific kind of vow was the Nazarite vow (Hebrew, *Nazar*, "dedicate, consecrate"), which a person initiated by shaving his head. During the period for which an individual was under the restrictions of the vow, three areas of life were more intensely regulated: diet, appearance, and associations. A modern analogy might be the special restrictions a full-time missionary places on himself or herself. "As an incentive to greater personal righteousness, it is a wholesome and proper thing for the saints to make frequent vows to the Lord" (McConkie, *Doctrinal New Testament Commentary,* 2:165).

18:23 A third missionary journey commences. This one is the longest in time (four years) and farthest in distance (see Bible Map 13). One of its main purposes is to collect funds for the poor in Jerusalem.

18:24–28 An Alexandrian Jewish member of the Church named Apollos, partially immersed in the gospel of Christ, received a more complete immersion from Aquila and Priscilla

Ruins along a street of Ephesus

in "the way of God" and continued his dedicated service in Ephesus and in Corinth.

ACTS 19

19:1 "Through the upper coasts": Paul's journey carries him overland along the high road through Galatia and Asia. Ephesus became the mission center during his third proselyting journey (see "Ephesus," 367).

19:2–7 John the Baptist's influence is so powerful that it is still being felt many years after and many miles removed from his actual ministry; however, the central truths of John's message have been lost. John the Baptist clearly taught that another baptism (of fire) would follow his baptism of immersion. These, however, were baptisms performed by unauthorized persons and had to be performed again. The reception of the gift of the Holy Ghost followed.

Joseph Smith said: "Baptism was the essential point on which [after receiving it] they could receive the gift of the Holy Ghost. It seems that some sectarian Jew had been baptizing like John but had forgotten to inform them that there was one to follow by the name of Jesus Christ, to baptize with fire and the Holy Ghost, which showed these converts that their first baptism was illegal. And when they heard this, they were gladly baptized, and after hands were laid on them they received the gifts, according to promise, and spake with tongues and prophesied" (Jackson, *Joseph Smith's Commentary on the Bible,* 151).

19:8–10 Paul continued "disputing and persuading"—contending for the cause of Christ in local synagogues. After more than two years of proselyting, "all they which dwelt in Asia heard the word of the Lord Jesus." Here "all" represents a great quantity or large portion. (Other examples of this literary device, called *synecdoche,* are in Matthew 3:5: "Then went out to him Jerusalem, and all Judaea"; and in Mark 1:33: "all the city was gathered together at the door.") Certainly every individual in Asia had not yet listened to the missionaries' discussions, but the purposeful exaggeration demonstrates that the gospel had spread far and wide throughout the Roman province of Asia. By the end of the century, there were seven Church units as a result of labors begun decades before in Ephesus (Revelation 1:11).

19:11–12 Paul performs "special miracles." Compare healing by merely touching the hem of Jesus' garment (Matthew 9:20; 14:36) and healing by the shadow of Peter (Acts 5:15).

On 22 July 1839, numerous healings were seen at Commerce (later Nauvoo), Illinois, when the Prophet Joseph Smith, who himself had been critically ill, rose and began healing people on both sides of the Mississippi River: "After healing the sick in Montrose, all the company followed Joseph to the bank of the river, where he was going to take the boat to return home. While waiting for the boat, a man from the West, who had seen that the sick and dying were healed, asked Joseph if he would not go to his house and heal two of his children who were very sick. They were twins and were three months old. Joseph told the man he could not go, but he would send some one to heal them. He told Elder Woodruff to go with the man and heal his children. At the same time he took from his pocket a silk bandanna handkerchief, and gave to Brother Woodruff, telling him to wipe the faces of the children with it, and they should be healed; and remarked at the same time: 'As long as you keep that handkerchief it shall remain a league between you and me.' Elder Woodruff did as he was commanded, and the children were healed, and he keeps the handkerchief to this day" (Smith, *History of the Church*, 4:4–5).

19:13–20 Joseph Smith taught: "It is very evident that [evil spirits] possess a power that none but those who have the priesthood can control, as in the case of the sons of Sceva" (Jackson, *Joseph Smith's Commentary on the Bible*, 152).

19:19 Book burning, in this case, is good. There is estimated to have been more than ten thousand dollars' worth of books burned.

19:23–41 In Ephesus was a magnificent temple, one of the seven wonders of the ancient world. Dedicated to the Greek goddess Artemis (the Roman Diana), the structure was four times bigger than the Parthenon in Athens. Pliny the Elder, who, like Luke, was writing in the first century after Christ, described the prodigious shrine: "The length of the temple overall is 425 feet, and its breadth 225 feet. There are 127 columns . . . 60 feet in height" (*Natural History*, 36.21.95; see also Bible Dictionary, "Diana"). By comparison, a modern American football field is 300 feet long.

Certain craftsmen who made shrines and figurines of the goddess were now feeling the loss of business brought on by Paul's preaching. It has been well said that the most sensitive part of civilized man is his pocket.

The great theater at Ephesus, scene of near-rioting and mobbing

19:29 The theater at Ephesus had room for twenty-four thousand people.

19:32 The last phrase of this verse is a commentary on typical mob behavior.

19:35–40 Just as Gamaliel had done at Jerusalem and Alexander Doniphan would later do at Far West, Missouri, this town clerk appealed for order and due process of law, if indeed there had been any infraction of law.

19:40 Irresponsible action could jeopardize local autonomy. Roman authorities could cancel freedom for cities whose native officials were unable to maintain peace and order.

First Corinthians fits here chronologically. It was written by Paul from Ephesus in about A.D. 57.

ACTS 20

20:1–6 At least eight men accompanied Paul to Asia—the seven listed in verse 4, plus Luke. In verse 5 and 6 the *us* and

*The theater at Miletus, where Paul bade a tearful
farewell to the elders of Ephesus*

we signal Luke's immediate involvement with the traveling
group once again.

20:7 This verse contains one of the first instances that
indicates the new Sabbath is "the first day of the week,"
Sunday.

20:9 This incident at Troas could be considered a warning to those who would sleep in sacrament meeting. Elder
Bruce R. McConkie wrote of this event, "Sermons can and
sometimes should be long" (*Doctrinal New Testament
Commentary*, 2:175).

Second Corinthians fits here and was written by Paul from
Macedonia about A.D. 57. Galatians was written by Paul, perhaps from Corinth, about late A.D. 57. Romans, too, was written by Paul from Corinth, perhaps in winter A.D. 57–58.

20:13–15 Luke seems very interested in the details of

Paul's overland and maritime itinerary (see "Minor Cities and Other Sites," 381).

20:16–35 In the interest of time, the leaders of the Church at Ephesus are called to meet with Paul in Miletus, and he gives a tearful farewell address, the only one in the book of Acts given to *Christians* (see "Miletus," 371).

20:19 The seventeenth-century word *temptations,* used in the King James Version of the Bible, means "trials, ordeals, or afflictions."

20:28–30 Paul's counsel before he departs. He knows that the gravest dangers to the Church are internal. He warns of savage wolves (by a figure of speech called *hypocatastasis,* wolves represent people) who would attack the Saints with perverse (that is, distorted, corrupted) doctrine. In other words, the Great Apostasy is at hand and was clearly prophesied. We read of betrayal, disobedience, corruptions, deceivers, and perverters; of wresting the scriptures, denying gifts, and quenching the Spirit; turning love into hate, truth into fables, and sheep to wolves; of embracing another gospel, and so forth. Apostasy is already in progress.

Joseph Smith said: "Paul said to the elders of the church at Ephesus, after he had labored three years with them, that he knew that some of their own number would turn away from the faith and seek to lead away disciples after them. . . . After his departure from the church at Ephesus, many, even of the elders, turned away from the truth and, what is almost always the case, sought to lead away disciples after them. Strange as it may appear at first thought, yet it is no less so than true, that with all the professed determination to live godly, after turning from the faith of Christ, apostates have, unless they have speedily repented, sooner or later fallen into the snares of the wicked one and have been left destitute of the Spirit of God, to manifest their wickedness in the eyes of multitudes" (Jackson, *Joseph Smith's Commentary on the Bible,* 152).

20:35 The last sentence of Paul's testimony to the Church as recorded in Acts is a simple but powerful teaching of Jesus not mentioned in the Gospels: "It is more blessed to give than to receive." Paul's life and labors epitomize this great truth.

ACTS 21

21:1–3, 7–8 Paul's voyage to Judea may be traced on Bible Map 13 (see "Minor Cities and Other Sites," 381).

21:4–6 The Saints in Tyre tried to discourage Paul from going up to Jerusalem, unless he felt prepared to face serious trials.

21:8 We have met Philip before (see Acts 6:5; 8:5–13, 26–40). Once he held a priesthood leadership position involved with welfare matters and was a missionary; now he is a patriarch in the Church.

21:9 "Women are not one whit behind [men] in spiritual endowments" (McConkie, *Doctrinal New Testament Commentary*, 2:181).

21:10 We have also met this Judean prophet before, when he prophesied the great famine (see Acts 11:28).

21:11–15 Agabus uses an object lesson to foreshadow Paul's imminent fate in the hands of Jews in Jerusalem. It appears to have been of little concern to Paul what he might suffer for the cause of Christ. The apostle to the Gentiles has a much broader, eternal view of things.

21:18 James, son of Joseph and Mary and the Lord's half-brother, is now apparently one of the apostles.

21:20–26 The remainder of Acts 21 and 22 illustrates what happened to Paul at the Temple in Jerusalem (see "The Temple in the Days of Paul," 100).

"This is an extremely difficult passage to explain in such a way as to do credit to Paul, or to James the Lord's brother, or to the leading brethren in the Church, or to the Jewish segment of the Church established in Jerusalem" (McConkie, *Doctrinal New Testament Commentary*, 2:183).

"Here in the year a.d. 58 we find thousands of Jewish Christians still adhering to the Law of Moses! Twenty-five years after the death of our Lord, the early Church Authorities still have not made it clear to a large portion of the Church membership that the Law of Moses was done away with upon the Advent of the Master. Those of us in the Church today have had little conception of the difficulties that faced the Authorities of the Early Church with respect to this problem. It is obvious from what Paul was told that the Judaizers in Palestine had grievously and even mischievously misrepresented him. Actually the Apostle contended that circumcision mattered nothing. Salvation came only through faith in Christ and not by the rites of the Law of Moses, and Paul would not impose circumcision on Gentile converts; nevertheless he never forbade the Jews to practice it. They could practice it and conform to any Mosaic rites they pleased so long as they knew that salvation came to them through Christ and Christ alone. It is a curious fact that the brethren, knowing Paul's attitude toward the Law, should ask him to give the appearance that he himself obeyed the Law. But the Apostle, realizing the gravity of the problem and knowing that it was important to hold the Jewish and Gentile groups of the Church together, readily agreed to assume the role of peacemaker. Paul . . . probably felt that he would not compromise his principles in any serious respect. The Temple rituals would occupy seven days of purification and sacrifice. Paul would pay for the four lambs and eight pigeons used for sacrifice and would attend the four men in their Temple appearances and rituals, which would end in having their heads shaved and their hair burned on the altar. In so doing the Apostle would be obliged to cross the Court of the Gentiles and Court of the Women, enter the Court of Israel, and finally approach the altar on which burnt offerings were made. He was bound to

98

be in full view of either friend or foe in these Temple areas" (Sperry, *Paul's Life and Letters*, 208–9).

21:27–29 Paul is accused of bringing Gentiles into the sacred precincts of the Inner Temple, beyond the Court of the Gentiles, thus polluting or desecrating the holy place.

21:31–37 The "chief captain" is the tribune in charge of the Roman garrison stationed in the nearby "castle," which word in Hebrew is *Ha Metzad* (same word as *Masada*, the famous site in Israel). *Ha Metzad* is interpreted as "the fortress," that is, the Antonia Fortress. A cohort of approximately six hundred Roman soldiers was regularly stationed there.

21:38 Claudius Lysias mistakenly identifies Paul as an unnamed Egyptian Jew, a revolutionary leader who has won a wide following among Judeans who believe that he possesses prophetic power. He is mentioned only this once in the New Testament and twice by Josephus (*Antiquities*, 20.8.6; *Wars*, 2.13.3–5). The same unnamed Jew "led followers from the desert to the top of the Mount of Olives with the intent of capturing Jerusalem" after the city walls crumbled. They could then drive out the Romans with ease. But he was "driven into hiding by Felix's troops, who crushed his army" (*Anchor Bible Dictionary*, 2:412–13). Perhaps the tribune Lysias mistook Paul for this revolutionary because Lysias believed that the Egyptian had returned to the scene of his former activity and that the angry crowd had seized him with the intent to make him pay for the turmoil his revolutionary actions had caused. The word "murderers" in this verse is used to translate the Greek term for the Latin *Sicarii*, "dagger-men."

21:39 Paul is from the renowned city of Tarsus, the distinguished seat of Greek philosophy and literature that, according to Strabo, ranked with Athens and Alexandria in the number of its schools and learned men.

THE TEMPLE IN THE DAYS OF PAUL

The Temple of Herod was constructed with the help of ten thousand workmen. One thousand priests trained as masons helped to build the holiest parts, and a thousand wagons transported materials. The courtyards and porticoes were under construction for eight years, and the Temple itself took a year and a half. It was said that whoever had not seen the Temple of Herod had never seen a beautiful building. No other temple complex in the Graeco-Roman world compared with it in expansiveness and magnificence. Although the architectural glories of Herod's temple far surpassed those of Solomon's, Herod's did not possess the spiritual atmosphere of Solomon's. The Ark of the Covenant, Mercy Seat, Cherubim, and other holy objects were lacking, as were the Urim and Thummim, which provided revelatory contact with God. And yet it was a place of revelation, as seen in the story of Zacharias (Luke 1). Jesus called it "my Father's house" (John 2:16) and later in his ministry "my house" (Luke 19:46).

Herod nearly doubled the size of the Temple area from what it was during the period of the First Temple, making it nearly forty acres. In expanding it he had to extend the platform of the mount to the north, west, and south. Earth-fill supported the north and west floors, but to the south he supported the floor with vaults—rows of arched colonnades. The area under the floor of the southeast portion of the Temple courtyard, then, was hollow. Now, the large, columned chamber is erroneously labeled Solomon's Stables. The chamber did not exist in Solomon's day, because it was built by Herod. The Crusaders used it later for stabling horses.

The entire Temple Mount was a very large space, measuring more than 132,000 square meters. (The famous Forum in Rome was half that size, and the largest temple complex in the world—Karnak, in Upper Egypt, which was two thousand years in the building—is only a third bigger.) Above ground on all sides were extraordinary colonnaded porticoes or porches (also called cloisters; that is, covered walkways with colonnades opening to the inside). Each portico had a double row of Corinthian columns. Each column was a monolith: cut from one block of stone, the column rose more than thirty-seven feet high.

According to Josephus, Herod was responsible for erecting porticoes inside his newly positioned walls, but Herod built up the eastern portico in the same position as the previous Temple. This eastern portico, called Solomon's Porch (see 1 Kings 6:3), is where Jesus, having come to the Passover at age twelve, conversed with the learned rabbis. Solomon's Porch is also where he walked and taught at the Feast of Dedication (Hanukkah), testifying that he was God's Son, and the Jews tried to stone him (see John 10:22–39). This eastern portico is also where Peter and John, after performing a miracle at the gate of the Temple, drew a large crowd and called for repentance following the denying and killing of the Holy One. And finally, this was where Peter and John were arrested by Temple police and Sanhedrin officials (see Acts 3:1–4:3).

The southern portico—grander than the others—is often called Herod's Basilica. The English word *basilica* (from the Greek *basileus,* "king," and therefore a royal portico) means a public hall that was rectangular in shape and had colonnaded aisles (early Christian churches adopted a similar floor plan). The Royal Basilica or Portico contained 162 Corinthian columns. At its foot were the ramps leading up onto the Temple courtyard from the south.

The eastern gate of the Temple Mount was called the Susa Gate. It faced eastward toward Susa, the Persian capital where the biblical stories of Daniel, Esther, Nehemiah, and others in part unfolded (called "Shushan" in the Bible; see Daniel 8:2; Esther 1:2; Nehemiah 1:1). This gate was said to have been lower than the other gates so that the priests across the bridge on the Mount of Olives watching for the sacrifice of the red heifer might still look directly into the Temple.

THE COURTS OF THE TEMPLE

The outer court of the Temple was called the Court of the Gentiles. It was from this court that Jesus had cast out the moneychangers. Non-Jews were allowed only this far onto the Temple Mount. Surrounding the Temple proper was a balustrade (Hebrew, *soreg*), an elevated stone railing about four and a half feet high with inscriptions posted in both Greek and Latin warning Gentiles not to pass beyond. One of these inscriptions was found in 1935 just outside the Lion's Gate of the Old City and is now on display in the Rockefeller Archaeological Museum. It reads: "No Gentile shall enter inward of the partition and barrier surrounding the Temple, and whosoever is caught shall be responsible to himself for his subsequent death."

Roman authorities conceded control of the sacred inner area to the Jewish religious leaders, even including the right to inflict capital punishment on non-Jews who passed beyond the stone railing. A fortified inner wall with towers and gates surrounded the Court of the Women, where Israelite women were permitted. The main gate into the Court of the Women was called the Beautiful Gate because of its rich decoration. It was at this gate that Peter and John, on their way to worship at the Temple, stopped to hear the petition of a lame man. Peter dramatically healed the man, who joined them in the Temple, "walking, and leaping, and praising God" (Acts 3:1–11). The Women's Court was a large space, nearly 200 feet square. In the four corners were chambers that served various functions. The eastern chambers served the Nazarites as a place where those who had made special vows could prepare their sacrifices. Another chamber was used for storing wood. The western chambers were used for storing olive oil and for the purification of lepers, with their own private ritual bath.

Porticoes surrounded the whole Court of the Women. Against the walls inside the porticoes were chests for charitable contributions. This was likely the place called "the treasury," where the widow cast in her mites (Mark 12:41–44) and where Jesus taught during the Feast of Tabernacles (John 8:20). There Jesus bore witness of his own divinity; proclaimed himself the Light of the World, the Messiah; and bore testimony that he was the God of Abraham. For that the Jews tried to stone him again (John 7–8).

Fifteen curved steps upward, the Gate of Nicanor led into the innermost court. (Nicanor was a wealthy Jew from Alexandria in Egypt who donated the ornate doors of the gate.) Only priests and other authorized Temple officiators entered this court. On one side of its porticoes was the Chamber of Hewn Stone where the Sanhedrin met. This was the place where Stephen was transfigured before them (see Acts 6:12–15), and where Paul testified before them (Acts 22:30–23:10). On the other side of the porticoes was the Chamber of the Hearth, where priests on duty could spend their nights.

On the north side of this court, which is actually a double court (first the Court of the Men of Israel and then the Priests' Court), was the Place of Slaughtering. On the south side was the giant brass wash basin (the Laver) supported on the backs of twelve lions. Millions of gallons of water were brought in to the Temple Mount from Solomon's Pools, south of Bethlehem, and stored in a connected series of rock-cut reservoirs, or cisterns. (Just north of the Temple complex was another water system and set of pools, the Bethesda pools, where Jesus healed a man; John 5:1–9).

Near the Laver stood the great horned Altar of Sacrifice, or Altar of Burnt Offering, measuring 48 feet square and 15 feet high. Some think that the huge rock-mass inside the Dome of the Rock, which now measures approximately 40 feet by 50 feet by 7 feet high, once formed the base of the Altar of Sacrifice. It is clear from scripture (2 Samuel 24:18–25) that King David purchased the Rock to build an altar to the Lord. The Altar of Sacrifice itself was made of whitewashed unhewn stone. A ramp leading up to it from the south was 48 feet long and 24 feet wide. The Altar stood off center in the court so that the priest sacrificing the red heifer on the Mount of Olives could see straight into the giant entryway of the Holy Sanctuary, which stood 66 feet high and 33 feet wide.

The Sanctuary, or Holy Place, was made of marble. Two columns in front were named Jachin and Boaz (meaning "He will establish" and "In him is strength") after those of Solomon's Temple. The Temple proper was more than 150 feet high (today's Dome of the Rock reaches a height of just over 100 feet) and was topped by golden spikes that discouraged birds from landing and tarnishing the stone.

Inside the Holy Place was the veil leading to the most sacred chamber, the Holy of Holies. That same veil was torn from top to bottom at the death of Jesus (see Matthew 27:51). Only the high priest could enter the symbolic Presence of God once a year, but Jesus, through his death, rent that partition, signifying that all people could reach God's presence (see Hebrews 9:11–14; 10:19–22).

Thus the Temple area consisted of a series of rising platforms: from the Court of the Gentiles, one ascended stairs to the Court of the Women; from there one ascended fifteen curved stairs (possibly singing fifteen Psalms of Ascent, or Psalms 120–34) to the Court of the Men of Israel and the Court of the Priests; and finally, another ascent was required to enter the Holy Place itself. One literally went *up* into the Temple.

ACTS 22

22:1–21 Having spoken in Greek with the Roman tribune, Paul tells his conversion story, in Hebrew (or Aramaic), on the steps of the Antonia Fortress to the assembled Jews.

22:17–21 Here we read the account of Jesus' second appearance to Paul while the latter is "in a trance." On this

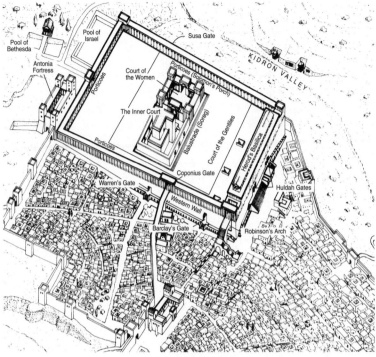

The Temple Mount

occasion Paul received the specific commission to take the gospel to the Gentiles.

22:25–30 The Greek text implies that Paul is "stretched out," as in scourging, not just "bound." Scourging an uncondemned Roman citizen was illegal.

22:28 The "chief captain," that is, the tribune or commander of the Roman garrison, is Claudius Lysias (Acts 23:26). He is impressed with Paul's freeborn status in contrast to his own freedom, which he had had to purchase at a great price.

ACTS 23

23:1–2 Paul had hardly begun his witness before the Sanhedrin when the high priest commanded that he be

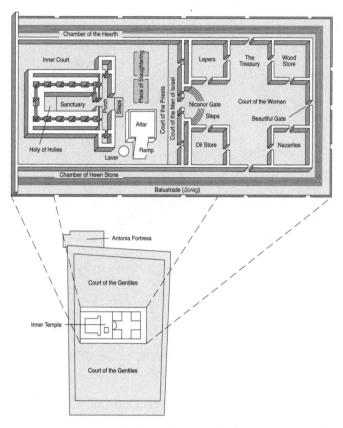

The Floor Plan of the Temple

(unlawfully) slapped. Compare John 18:20–23, where Jesus was also slapped before the high priest (see Bible Dictionary, "Pharisees" and "Sadducees").

23:3 The "whited wall" epithet refers to the custom of whitewashing a wall to hide dirt and stains. Compare Jesus' reference to "whited sepulchres" (Matthew 23:27). Both images depict hypocrisy, and indeed Paul considered any Jewish leader a hypocrite who would order some one to be physically abused contrary to Mosaic law.

23:5 "I wist not"—either Paul really did not know he was the high priest, or Paul's "thorn in the flesh" was an eye disease, allowing him limited vision, or he was being sarcastic, as if to say, I'd never have guessed . . .

23:6–10 Paul cleverly narrows the focus of the accusation to belief in the resurrection. The issue of resurrection was definitely part of the Jewish establishment's antagonism to Paul's work, especially to his preaching that Jesus rose from the dead. But because the various members of the Sanhedrin were themselves divided on the doctrine of resurrection, Paul cleverly raised the issue to take the pressure off himself. Pharisees would naturally side with him in affirming the reality of resurrection.

23:11 Jesus appears a third time to Paul, with comforting assurances that his life would be spared; he had yet to testify of the true God in the empire's capital.

23:12–15 The oaths and curses of certain Jews are reminiscent of secret combinations from the Book of Mormon. The conspiracy extended to members of the Jewish hierarchy, the Sanhedrin.

23:16–23 Paul's sister's son is then living in Jerusalem and overhears the plot to kill Paul. He brings it to the attention of Roman authorities.

23:23 Roman officers escorted Paul to Caesarea with four hundred infantry and seventy cavalry. To avoid possible ambush, the contingent departed Jerusalem at 3 A.M. Paul would be safer in Roman Caesarea than in Jewish Jerusalem (see Bible Dictionary, "Caesarea"). In fact, three times within twenty-four hours Roman troops saved Paul's life.

23:24 Antonius Felix was appointed procurator in A.D. 52 (see Bible Dictionary, "Felix"). Felix's Jewish wife was Drusilla, a sister of Herod Agrippa II. They were living in an adulterous relationship because Drusilla had left her husband and "married" Felix, thus violating Jewish law.

23:25–30 The commander's letter to Governor Felix includes his own assessment of the accusations against Paul:

the whole affair seemed to deal with interpretation of matters of Jewish law, rather than anything illegal by Roman law (v. 29).

23:31 Antipatris is the former (Old Testament) site of Aphek, where, a few decades before Paul, Herod the Great had built a fortress and a city named after his father, Antipater.

ACTS 24

24:1–9 An eloquent orator is brought in to accuse Paul of being "a mover of sedition among all the Jews throughout the world," "a ringleader of the sect of the Nazarenes," and one who goes about profaning the Temple.

24:10–21 Paul energetically defends himself. The accusations, he argues, were without foundation—and these Jews know it.

24:22–26 Felix realizes that these are indeed matters of Jewish law and defers judgment on Paul. The apostle remained under house arrest in Caesarea for two years. Felix, meanwhile, hoped to induce a bribe from Paul.

24:27 Porcius Festus, the new procurator of Judea, arrives and will soon hear the case of Paul (see Bible Dictionary, "Festus").

ACTS 25

25:1–12 Jewish leaders apprise Festus of the case against Paul. Charges and complaints are raised, but with no accompanying evidence. With a potential change of venue to Jerusalem, Paul is obliged to appeal to Caesar, which is his right as a Roman citizen. He had more hope of justice from Nero than from the Sanhedrin.

25:13 Herod Agrippa II, the last of the Herodian dynasty, was living in incest with his sister Bernice (see Bible Dictionary, "Herod").

25:14–27 Festus reviewed the case of Paul with Agrippa.

Paul then had opportunity to bear testimony before yet another ruler and his courtiers.

ACTS 26

26:1–29 Paul's conversion story is related to Herod Agrippa II. Read our modern prophet's parallel situation in Joseph Smith—History 1:24.

26:28–29 Elder Neal A. Maxwell noted that "Agrippa's remark was not a flippant one; he was seriously touched" ("Taking Up the Cross," 255). The Revised Standard Version of the Bible renders this passage as follows: "In a short time you think to make me a Christian!" And Paul said, "Whether short or long, I would to God that not only you but also all who hear me this day might become such as I am—except for these chains."

26:31–32 The verdict is "not guilty." It is the Lord's will that Paul bear testimony in still another court—that of Caesar, in Rome.

ACTS 27

Luke's eyewitness account of Paul's two-thousand-mile voyage to Rome sounds like a chapter from *Kon-Tiki* or *RA II*. In the late 1800s, James Smith sailed the same route as did Paul, using admiralty charts and studying the tides, and so forth, and confirmed the remarkable accuracy of Luke's detailed account (see Cobern, *New Archaeological Discoveries,* 557). But beyond the archeological and physical accuracy of detail, Luke's writing has dramatic effect.

27:1–2 Paul's first ship is from Adramyttium, an Aegean harbor of Mysia, in northwest Asia Minor. Aristarchus from Thessalonica is with *us,* which very likely means Luke is also with Paul (follow the rest of the voyage on Bible Map 22).

27:6 The missionaries transferred to a ship from

Alexandria, Egypt, en route to Italy. The ship's roster included 276 passengers (v. 37).

27:7 Myra to Cnidus is an easy one-day, 130-mile, journey—but they experienced bad winds.

27:9–11 "The fast" is Yom Kippur, the Day of Atonement. After this date, between September and October of each year, the waters were unsafe for travel until weather moderated again early the next spring. Paul warned them against continuing the journey.

27:14 The Euroclydon is today called a "levanter," a small-scale hurricane or cyclone.

27:17 "Helps" were cables or chains under the ship's hull. Some have supposed that "the quicksands" were two areas off North Africa with shallow, marshy whirlpools, infamous graveyards of many ships.

27:20 "Neither sun nor stars in many days appeared"; they couldn't calculate their course.

27:28 "Sounded"—that is, tested the depths with a sounding line. Twenty fathoms is about 120 feet; fifteen fathoms, 90 feet.

ACTS 28

28:1–10 Melita is called Malta today. They remained on the island for three months (v. 11), teaching and healing.

28:11–13 The missionaries boarded a third ship, this one also from Alexandria, on their journey to Rome (follow their course on Bible Map 13). Puteoli became the principal port of southern Italy.

28:14–15 They journeyed on the Via Appia, the most famous of Roman all-weather roads, which stretched from Capua to Rome. Once, after a slave rebellion led by Spartacus, six thousand slaves were crucified on poles along the whole Appian Way.

28:16–31 As far as we know, the first missionary to serve in Rome was Paul. He taught there for two years. The first people he called on were his own people, the Jews. He taught them concerning Jesus, the Messiah, and some of them believed. He taught also the Gentile Romans.

In A.D. 61–62, during his first Roman captivity, Paul wrote Colossians, Ephesians, Philemon, and Philippians. He wrote Hebrews, 1 Timothy, and Titus between A.D. 64–66 and 2 Timothy sometime before his martyrdom (before A.D. 68).

After two years' imprisonment, Paul was released. During that period of freedom, he probably visited again the churches in Asia and Greece and may have visited Spain (see Romans 15:28).

The present book of Acts ends here, but we know that Paul was imprisoned a second time in Rome. Tradition and literary sources indicate that Paul and Peter were both killed during the Neronian persecutions in Rome, sometime before A.D. 68 (see commentary on 2 Timothy 4:6–8).

CHAPTER 4

FIRST AND SECOND THESSALONIANS

1 THESSALONIANS

Though we do not have all of the letters Paul composed, scholars have dated 1 Thessalonians as Paul's first epistle. The letter was likely written near the end of A.D. 52. Paul's usual practice was to dictate to a scribe and then add a few words in his own handwriting. Curiously, the subscriptions at the end of each book were written much later by copyists—probably between the fourth and sixth centuries after Christ. Hence, they are sometimes questionable (see Anderson, *Understanding Paul,* 72). For instance, although the subscription appearing after 1 Thessalonians 5:28 says the epistle was written from Athens, 1 Thessalonians was probably written from Corinth, a city about 250 miles from Thessalonica (see Bible Dictionary, "Epistles to the Thessalonians").

The main theme of 1 Thessalonians is the Second Coming. The Hellenized city of Thessalonica had been named for the sister of Alexander the Great (356–323 B.C.) and was the capital of Macedonia. During Paul's second missionary journey, the apostle and his missionary companions were driven from Thessalonica by Jews who rejected the message of Christ's atonement and resurrection. Nevertheless, the gospel did become established among other Jews and Gentiles living there (see Acts 17:1–10; 1 Thessalonians 1:9; 2:14). Paul knew of the constant persecution directed at the members of the Church and sent Timothy and Silvanus (Silas) back to

112

Thessalonica to check on the condition of the Saints (1 Thessalonians 3:2; Acts 17:15; 18:5). When the two returned from their trip, they brought Paul a favorable report (1 Thessalonians 3:6) but indicated that the members had doctrinal questions about the Second Coming. Those questions included the order of resurrection in relation to the Lord's coming and whether those faithful Saints who had already died before the Second Coming would be damned in their spiritual progress or have part in the great day of the Lord. Paul addressed these doctrinal concerns near the end of his epistle in a section that forms the doctrinal core of his first letter to the Thessalonians, namely 1 Thessalonians 4:13–18.

1 THESSALONIANS 1

1:1 Silvanus is a longer form of the name Silas, who was Paul's second missionary companion. Frequently, Paul introduces his letters by mentioning God the Father and his Son Jesus Christ. There is no doubt that the apostle knew and taught that they were two separate members of the Godhead.

1:2–10 In these verses, the tone of the letter is established. The Thessalonian Saints have proven themselves faithful in the face of "much affliction" (v. 6). It must have been comforting for the early Saints to know that Church leaders were praying for them, just as the Brethren pray for the Saints today. At that time, Greece had been divided by Rome into two provinces, Macedonia and Achaia (see Acts 19:21; Romans 15:26). These Saints had become a model for all believers throughout all of Greece. Their faith was extolled throughout Christendom (see Romans 1:8). They had covenanted to serve the Father and to wait for the Second Coming of his resurrected Son who would deliver them "from the wrath to come" (1 Thessalonians 1:10). In a sense, Christ delivers all people from the "wrath to come," for Christ paved the way for all to escape the effects of physical death. In these verses, Paul discusses deliverance from the wrath of God, "which awaits the wicked, both in this world and in the world to come" (D&C 88:85). Because the Saints were being persecuted by the wicked and hoping for deliverance, Paul's promise undoubtedly lifted the Saints' view to an eternal perspective, helping them to understand the kind of deliverance the gospel provides.

1 THESSALONIANS 2

2:1 "Our entrance" refers to the apostle Paul's visit to the Thessalonian Saints.

2:2–16 In spite of strong opposition, first at Philippi and then at Thessalonica, Paul and his companions boldly proclaimed the gospel without desire for personal or financial gain (see v. 9). In fact, the Greeks disdained manual labor and viewed it as the activity of slaves, but Paul was not embarrassed to do physical work and did not want the Saints to have to support him. In verse 14 Paul acknowledges that at the time of his visit to Thessalonica, the persecution which the Jews had instigated was being promulgated by Gentiles ("your own country men").

2:19 The phrase "in the presence of our Lord Jesus at his coming" is reminiscent of Doctrine and Covenants 88:97, which says "caught up to meet him in the midst of the pillar of heaven" (see also 1 Thessalonians 4:17).

2:17–3:5 Paul speaks of his desire to see the Saints personally but indicates he is hindered by opposition promoted by Satan. He does the next best thing and sends his trusted companions to check on the Saints, hoping that the tempter had not overpowered them (see v. 5). In 1 Thessalonians 3:2, the Greek word translated as "establish" literally means to strengthen a building by adding a buttress to it. The word *comfort* means to encourage.

1 THESSALONIANS 3

3:3–4 Tribulations and afflictions, an inescapable part of mortal experience, can become blessings to the Lord's followers (see Alma 7:5; 17:11; 26:27; 28:8; D&C 58:4).

3:6–13 Because of Timothy's encouraging report of the faith of the Church members, Paul expressed gratitude to God. This is one more hallmark of Paul's greatness, for instead of taking credit for his superior teaching, he thanked God, who is the source of all true and lasting conversion.

1 THESSALONIANS 4

4:1–2 Paul urges the Saints to live "more and more" according to the teachings sanctioned and exemplified by the Lord Jesus Christ. Modern prophets have given similar exhortation. For example, President Howard W. Hunter said, "I would invite all members of the Church to live with ever-more attention to the life and example of the Lord Jesus Christ, especially the love and hope and compassion He displayed" (*Church News,* 11 June 1994, 14).

4:3–4 *Sanctification* means holiness and is discussed in other Pauline epistles, especially Romans. The apostle Paul understood well the nature of personal sanctification. A latter-day counterpart, Elder Bruce R. McConkie said: "To be *sanctified* is to become clean, pure, and spotless; to be free from the blood and sins of the world; to become a new creature of the Holy Ghost, one whose body has been renewed by the rebirth of the Spirit. *Sanctification* is a state of saintliness, a state attained only by conformity to the laws and ordinances of the gospel. The plan of salvation is the system and means provided whereby men may sanctify their souls and thereby become worthy of a celestial inheritance" (*Mormon Doctrine,* 675). The Thessalonian Saints had been taught the same plan of salvation and the same doctrine of sanctification by the apostle Paul that the Saints of the latter days have been taught by modern apostles.

4:5 *Concupiscence* is a Latinate word meaning "to desire ardently." The English word *passion* might be a better translation here of the original Greek.

4:6–12 Paul encourages the Saints to refrain from taking undue interest in other people's affairs and to live lives of brotherly love, quiet dignity, honesty, and hard physical work as they had been taught (see Isaiah 54:13; John 6:45; 1 Corinthians 2:13). In verse 9, the Greek word translated as "brotherly love" is *philadelphia,* which usually denoted the strong mutual love between children and their biological father. Paul uses it here to symbolize the powerful feelings Christians ought to possess for each other.

4:13–18 Here is the core of Paul's teaching on the Second Coming. Those whose friends or family have died ("fallen asleep" is an apt term because Christ's resurrection removes the finality from death) are grieving not only for their loss but also because they wonder if those who have preceded them in death would forfeit progress toward eternal life. Paul teaches that death does not hinder anyone's eternal progression. The phrase "not prevent them which are asleep" (v. 15) means precisely that the living will not have precedence over the dead. This citation is apparently an unrecorded teaching of the Savior's, not found in the Gospels, but, says Paul, is according to the Lord's own word.

Paul further teaches that at the publicly recognized second coming, those covenant disciples who have been dead will be resurrected first as Christ descends out of heaven. Then, those who are alive on the earth at that moment will be caught up together with the resurrected persons to meet the Lord in the clouds. The phrase "caught up" is rendered in the Latin Vulgate *rapiemur,* from the root *rapto.* This word has given rise in English to the word *rapture,* now colloquially used to refer to the second coming of Christ and those who are caught up to meet him. One is immediately reminded of the prophecy of the two angels at Christ's ascension, who informed the apostles that the Savior would come in the same manner as he left (see Acts 1:11). Paul asks the Thessalonian Saints to encourage each other with these comforting and ennobling doctrines.

1 THESSALONIANS 5

5:1–11 Paul continues his discussion on the Second Coming, exhorting the people to be ready for it and emphasizing that salvation is in Christ. "Whether we wake or sleep" (v. 10) is a play on words harking back to the idea of being asleep in Christ, that is, awaiting the resurrection while in the spirit world. Paul reminds the Saints that they already know that "the day of the Lord so cometh as a thief in the night" (v. 2), meaning that it will happen unexpectedly for some people, when they are unprepared spiritually. The phrase "day of the Lord" goes back to Amos 5:18. In Old Testament times the day of the Lord was regarded as a time when God would come and intervene with judgment, instituting blessing or condemnation. The Joseph Smith Translation of Luke 12:44 confirms that Jesus himself was author of the expression "as a thief in the night." This translation also indicates that Jesus told much more about his own second coming than various versions of the New Testament disclose. Paul probably quoted several of the lost teachings of Jesus as part of his own exhortation, just as we saw in 1 Thessalonians 4:15.

5:12–26 Paul lists some of the ways the Saints can prepare their lives for the Second Coming: love Church leaders and live together in peace (vv. 12–13), support the weak (v. 14), pray constantly (v. 17), and avoid even the appearance of evil (v. 22). Much of the same counsel is repeated in latter-day revelation (D&C 20:54; 81:5; 98:11).

2 THESSALONIANS

Paul apparently received word that his first letter to the Thessalonian Saints did not resolve all the questions regarding the Second Coming. He also learned that persecution of the Church had not abated, but the members had followed his counsel and rallied around one another (see 2 Thessalonians 1:3–4). To teach the Saints to stop worrying and theorizing about the Second Coming, especially the precise time of its occurrence, Paul taught that a great rebellion or apostasy from the Lord's true Church must precede it. That is the theme of Second Thessalonians.

2 THESSALONIANS 1

1:1–12 The Saints' patience, faith, endurance, and charity towards one another will be rewarded by the Lord when he comes in glory and power; the wicked will "be punished with everlasting destruction" (v. 9).

2 THESSALONIANS 2

2:2 The day of Christ is "at hand"—according to the Lord's timetable (see JST 2 Peter 3:8).

2:3 "Falling away" sounds rather gradual and passive; the Greek word is *apostasia,* which literally means a "revolt" or "breaking away." Thus apostasy is a defection or desertion, an active movement. The New American Bible renders this term as "mass apostasy." "That man of sin" is, of course, Satan.

2:4 The "temple of God" in this case is the body of believers, that is, the Church.

2:7 The "mystery of iniquity doth already work." It was not the Second Coming that was imminent but the Great Apostasy. In fact, it was already under way by the time of Paul's ministry.

2:8 The evil one and all things evil will be destroyed at the Lord's appearance by the "brightness of [his] coming." The Lord and celestial beings with him will destroy all things telestial by their glory (see D&C 5:19).

2:11 In other words, God shall leave them and allow them to believe a lie.

2:13 Members are foreordained to be exalted.

2 THESSALONIANS 3

3:8 The Brethren chose to set an example of self-support.

3:10–11 A practical problem arose in the Thessalonian branch. Because some members misinterpreted doctrine, some were passively waiting for the Second Coming, some did not want to work, and some refused to work. But work is a commandment.

APOSTASY IN THE MERIDIAN DISPENSATION

The New Testament teaches unequivocally that there was an apostasy from the one and only true Church established by the Lord in the meridian of time. Paul and his associates in the Quorum of the Twelve were primary witnesses of this predicted tragedy. As Paul said good-bye for the last time to some of the Church members at Ephesus that he had grown to love, he gave a chilling prophecy about the coming apostasy: "For I know this, that after my departing shall grievous wolves enter in among you, not sparing the flock. Also of your own selves shall men arise, speaking perverse things, to draw away disciples after them" (Acts 20:29–30).

This may be the most succinct description in all scripture of the nature of apostasy. It is neither passive nor gradual. It is a wrenching conflict, and rebellion is at its heart. Some misunderstanding may derive from the language of 2 Thessalonians 2:3, in which Paul tries to allay the fears of the Saints who believe erroneously that the second coming of Christ is imminent. He says, "That day [the Second Coming] shall not come except there come a falling away first, and that man of sin be revealed, the son of perdition."

The phrase "falling away" may connote to some people a gradual slide from the truth, but a comparison of the wording of the King James Version with other versions of the Bible shows the significance and intent of Paul's comment. The

New International Version renders the Greek as "the rebellion"; the Revised Standard Version, "the rebellion"; the Phillips Bible, "a definite rejection of God"; the Jerusalem Bible, "the Great Revolt"; the Contemporary English Version, "People will rebel against God."

The original Greek text of 2 Thessalonians 2:3 uses the word *apostasia,* meaning literally a "revolt" or "breaking away." Apostasy is a conscious act of rebellion against God in which one deliberately attempts to change divinely appointed doctrine and practice and opposes God's chosen leaders. Apostasy, by definition, is not a gradual drift from divine truth, nor is it waning interest in the gospel. Apostasy, as Paul says, is rebellion, and it always reveals the great motivator of rebellion—Satan, or Perdition (from the Latin *perditus,* "destruction").

As is so clearly demonstrated in Moses 4:1–4 (the detailed account of Satan's rebellion), apostasy occurs from within the covenant community and is the result of pride. Lucifer was, after all, a member of the premortal covenant community, an angel in authority in the presence of God, as Doctrine and Covenants 76:25–26 teaches us. A comparison of Moses 4:1–4 and Joseph Smith's translation of 2 Thessalonians 2:7–9 seems to indicate that Paul knew very well the story of Satan's great rebellion. Paul's associate in the Quorum, John the Beloved, certainly knew that apostasy occurs within the covenant community, for he witnessed the fulfillment of Paul's prophecy. He said: "They [anti-Christs] went out from us, but they were not of us" (1 John 2:19).

Other historical writings besides the scriptures testify of an apostasy. From a post-New Testament document called The Teaching of the Twelve Apostles, we see "that self-seeking and fraudulent claimants to divine guidance were soon preying on the churches" (Walker, *History of the Christian Church,* 40).

The same picture emerges from the writings of a late first-century bishop at Rome named Clement. He was identified by Eusebius of Caesarea, the fourth-century "Father of

Church History," as that same Clement praised by Paul for being among those "whose names are in the book of life" (Philippians 4:3). Clement wrote to correct "the abominable and unholy schism" in the Corinthian branch of the Church, a situation that had resulted from apostates deposing Church officers (bishops and deacons) who had been lawfully and authoritatively appointed by the apostles (1 Clement 1:1–2, in Richardson, *Early Christian Fathers*, 43).

Clement stated emphatically that it was the apostles who had overseen the Church and had appointed converts to be deacons and bishops (see 1 Clement 42:1–4, in Richardson, *Early Christian Fathers*, 62). Therefore, the rebellion against legitimate priesthood leadership was the height of religious sedition. But worse than that, says Clement, is that the "schism has led many astray; it has made many despair; it has made many doubt; and it has distressed us all. Yet it goes on!" (1 Clement 46:9, in Richardson, *Early Christian Fathers*, 65). Here three important truths are corroborated: apostasy involves the rejection of the apostles and their teaching, mass apostasy destroys the faith of many, and it is hard to curtail.

The foundation of the Lord's true Church consists of apostles and prophets, as Paul taught (see Ephesians 2:20). Only the apostles hold the "keys of the kingdom" (Matthew 16:19), the power to direct priesthood authority and to oversee priesthood ordinances. President Brigham Young said: "The keys of the eternal Priesthood, which is after the order of the Son of God, are comprehended by being an Apostle. All the Priesthood, all the keys, all the gifts, all the endowments, and everything preparatory to entering into the presence of the Father and of the Son, are in, composed of, circumscribed by, or I might say incorporated within the circumference of, the Apostleship" (*Journal of Discourses*, 1:134–35).

One by one the apostles chosen by Christ were killed, as he had predicted, and with them went the keys of the kingdom. Institutional revelation for the direction of the Church ceased with the last of the apostles. By the end of the first century after Christ, the apostasy described by Paul was virtually complete.

Then, after centuries of silence and confusion about religion among humankind, God spoke his will again clearly and definitively in 1820. As a result, the true Church of Jesus Christ was reestablished on earth; the apostolic office and authority were restored to the Prophet Joseph Smith and Oliver Cowdery by the ancient apostles Peter, James, and John (see D&C 27:12); and a new Quorum of the Twelve Apostles was established and began to exercise the keys of the priesthood (see D&C 107:35; 124:128). As Joseph Smith said, "The fundamental principles, government, and doctrine of the Church are vested in the keys of the kingdom" (*Teachings of the Prophet Joseph Smith*, 21).

THE JOSEPH SMITH TRANSLATION

First and Second Thessalonians present us with an opportunity to gain important perspectives on the Joseph Smith Translation of the Bible, for it is here that we first encounter some of the Prophet's significant changes in the texts of Acts through Revelation, changes that help clarify the doctrines of the kingdom. Though we do not possess the specific revelation originally commissioning the Joseph Smith Translation, we do have revelations implying that the Lord had commanded it to be undertaken (see D&C 42:56; 76:15). The Prophet referred to his work on the Bible as a "branch of [his] calling" (*History of the Church*, 1:238). In truth, the Joseph Smith Translation is one of the great evidences of Joseph Smith's divine mandate and is a seminal accomplishment of his ministry. It was not just a sideline of his labors nor something of passing interest; it was a central aspect of the restoration of doctrine in this the dispensation of the fulness of times. To neglect or ignore the Joseph Smith Translation is to miss an important dimension of God's work in these latter days and to cut ourselves off from one of God's great gifts to the elect.

In December 1830, as the Prophet was engaged almost daily in making his translation of the Bible, the Lord spoke to his scribe, Sidney Rigdon, and said, "And a commandment I give unto thee—that thou shalt write for him; and the scriptures shall be given, even as they are in mine own bosom, to the salvation of mine own elect" (D&C 35:20). According to the Lord's own voice, the Joseph Smith Translation was given through his special prophet for his elect—for their salvation. There is glorious doctrine in the Joseph Smith Translation, which the elect can possess. The elect of the Lord are those who will use this book and cherish it, for as the Lord also said, "Mine elect hear my voice and harden not their hearts" (D&C 29:7).

The Joseph Smith Translation was not only desirable but necessary, owing to the loss of many plain and precious parts from the scriptures. Prefacing his record of the vision now known as Doctrine and Covenants 76, the Prophet wrote: "Upon my return from Amherst conference, I resumed the translation of the Scriptures. From sundry revelations which had been received, it was apparent that many important points touching the salvation of man had been taken from the Bible, or lost before it was compiled" (D&C 76, headnote). On another occasion Joseph Smith said: "I believe the Bible as it read when it came from the pen of the original writers. Ignorant translators, careless transcribers, or designing and corrupt priests have committed many errors" (*Teachings of the Prophet Joseph Smith*, 327). It seems clear that the Joseph Smith Translation is an anchor to our understanding of revealed truth in its pure and unadulterated form.

On 7 March 1831, Joseph Smith was commanded by the Lord to lay aside his translation of Genesis and begin working on the New Testament (see D&C 45:60). The Lord gave to him the following promise: "Wherefore I give unto you that ye may now translate it, that ye may be prepared for the things to come. For verily I say unto you, that great things await you" (D&C 45:61–62). From the few dates written on the original manuscript pages of the Joseph Smith Translation, it is possible to state only that the Prophet worked on Acts through Revelation sometime between 16 February 1832 and 2 February 1833. On the latter date the Prophet wrote: "I completed the translation and review of the New Testament, on the 2nd of February, 1833 and sealed it up" (*History of the Church*, 1:324). At that point, Joseph Smith resumed work on the Old Testament.

The Prophet's own attitude toward his divinely inspired translation of the New Testament is summarized in a statement he wrote to W. W. Phelps: "We have finished the translation of the New testament [and] great and glorious things are revealed, we are making rapid strides in the old book and in the strength of God we can do all things according to his will" (*Personal Writings of Joseph Smith*, 248). Joseph Smith and his scribes recognized that the translation of the New Testament was far more than busywork. The handwritten entry at the top of page 1 of the manuscript of the Gospel of Matthew reads: "A Translation of the New Testament translated by the power of God" (Matthews, *Plainer Translation*, 276).

The translation of the New Testament was an important way of educating the Prophet at a time when very little "Mormon doctrine" existed. Because of the scriptural and doctrinal education he gained through his work of translation, Joseph Smith became a vessel for much more revelation—revelations now recorded as sections of the Doctrine and Covenants. In other words, the Joseph Smith Translation was the catalyst for the restoration of many of the doctrines of the kingdom we hold dear. The Joseph Smith Translation helps us to understand one way in which revelation comes to all mortals—prophets and ordinary people alike. Revelation may come to us as we pore over existing scripture, allowing new insights to distill upon us, just as they did for Joseph Smith. Many sections of the Doctrine and Covenants came this way. Undoubtedly these revelations are some of the "great things" (D&C 45:62) that awaited the Prophet and the Church.

The greatest proportion of changes in the New Testament are found in the Four Gospels, or "Testimonies," as the Prophet referred to them. It is obvious that Joseph Smith knew the Savior in a profound way and knew what the Savior wanted the New Testament to teach us.

The Prophet also revealed significant changes to the texts of the epistles in the New Testament, as the following table indicates:

Epistle	Number of Verses	Number of Verses Changed	Percentage of Verses Changed
Romans	433	119	27
1 Corinthians	437	70	16
2 Corinthians	257	25	10
Galatians	149	13	9
Ephesians	155	15	10
Philippians	104	14	13
Colossians	95	9	9
1 Thessalonians	89	7	8
2 Thessalonians	47	7	15
1 Timothy	113	15	13
2 Timothy	83	8	10
Titus	46	2	4
Philemon	25	1	4
Hebrews	303	50	17
James	108	20	19
1 Peter	105	24	23
2 Peter	61	20	33
1 John	105	17	16
2 John	13	0	0
3 John	14	0	0
Jude	25	2	8
Total	2,767	438	16

Several chapters in the Joseph Smith Translation have particular significance: Romans 7, on the personality and character of Paul and on the power of Christ to transform human souls; 1 Corinthians 7, 11, and 14, on the true and proper perspective regarding marriage and women; Hebrews 7, on the person and priesthood of Melchizedek; and 1 and 2 Thessalonians, on the Second Coming.

In the book of Revelation, Joseph Smith changed 90 of the 394 verses, or 23 percent of the total but added only three new verses. Those facts bear out the Prophet's statement that the Apocalypse "is one of the plainest books God ever caused to be written" (*Teachings of the Prophet Joseph Smith*, 290). The real value of the Prophet's work on the book of Revelation, however, was that it provided the catalyst for his receiving Doctrine and Covenants 77. The 1 March 1832 entry of the Prophet's history reads: "About the first of March, in connection with the translation of the Scriptures, I received the following explanation of the Revelation of St. John" (*History of the Church*, 1:253). What follows is now recorded in Doctrine and Covenants 77, the master key to understanding the book of Revelation and a tool to which special attention must be paid later on in our study.

Joseph Smith altered chapter 12 in John's revelation more than any other chapter in the book of Revelation. That chapter includes an explanation of "The kingdoms of this world [which] are become the kingdom of our Lord, and of his Christ" (JST Revelation 11:15). The Prophet changed most of the verses in this chapter, rearranged their order, and added one of only three new verses in the entire book. Revelation 12 is of special value to Latter-day Saints, for it tells of an eventual political kingdom led by Christ that will rule all nations. This political kingdom will grow out of the Church of Jesus Christ, which at one point went into apostasy (see Revelation 12:14; D&C 86:3) but which has been restored. And that is the purpose of the Joseph Smith Translation—to help restore God's truths and perspectives in these latter days.

126

Thus, the Joseph Smith Translation is many things. It is a restoration of original text, which was lost early from the first New Testament manuscripts. It is also a restoration of some authentic teachings, dialogues, and episodes that took place but the record of which never made it into the original New Testament collection in the first place. The Joseph Smith Translation is inspired and prophetic commentary given by the Lord's prophet to assist and bless the Lord's elect in the latter days. It is a harmonization of doctrinal concepts in more complete form in latter-day scripture than was originally recorded in the Bible. "The Joseph Smith Translation, or Inspired Version, is a thousand times over the best Bible now existing on earth" (McConkie, "The Bible, a Sealed Book," 5).

CHAPTER 5

FIRST AND SECOND CORINTHIANS

1 CORINTHIANS

Corinth, the capital of the Roman province of Achaia, was one of the richest and most immoral cities in the world. According to the ancient geographer Strabo, the temple of Aphrodite on Acrocorinth (the high hill overlooking the lower city) boasted a thousand ritual prostitutes involved in aberrant rites of worship. Whether that report is accurate or not, it certainly reflects Corinth's reputation at the time.

The Jewish community in Corinth has been estimated to have numbered as many as twenty thousand, perhaps because of Claudius' earlier expulsion of Jews from Rome. Paul says he went to Corinth "in weakness, and in fear, and in much trembling" (1 Corinthians 2:3). He preached at Corinth eighteen months.

First Corinthians is actually Paul's second letter to the Corinthian Saints (see 1 Corinthians 5:9). The first has not survived, and their reply (see 1 Corinthians 7:1) is also lost. The Corinthian members may have sent oral communications to Paul as well (see 1 Corinthians 1:11; 16:17). Thus, 1 and 2 Corinthians represent part of a continuing dialogue between Paul and the Corinthian Saints. These exchanges lasted quite a while. Paul wrote more to the Corinthians than to any other branch of the Church—one-fourth of his surviving writings was directed toward Corinth. In a sense, reading 1 Corinthians without knowing that it was not Paul's first communication with the members at Corinth is like walking in on the middle of a conversation and hearing only the response of one party.

First Corinthians is the most varied of Paul's epistles. It deals with spiritual gifts, resurrection, degrees of glory, baptism for the dead, Jehovah as Christ, charity, unity, moral cleanliness, personal revelation, and the sacrament, to name several important doctrines (see also Bible Dictionary, "Pauline Epistles, Epistles to the Corinthians").

First Corinthians is so good because the Corinthians were not. Paul had to rebuke their lack of unity, spirit of contention, doubts about the resurrection, abuse of spiritual gifts, sophistication of Greek intellectuals, and immorality in a variety of perversions. Aristophanes coined the verb *korinthiazesthai* (note the root *Korinth*), which means, "to fornicate." Another playwright wrote a play entitled *Korinthiastēs,* "The Whoremonger." Plato used the term *korinthia korē,* "a Corinthian girl," to mean "a prostitute" (see *Anchor Bible Dictionary,* 1:1135–36).

By the time Paul wrote his letters to the Corinthian Saints, the Great Apostasy had already begun. In the first stage of apostasy in the early Church, we see Jewish Christians refusing to abandon Judaic traditions (see Acts 15). Now, in the second stage, we see Greek ideas entering Christian theology. For example, the Corinthian Saints held two opposing views of the mortal body. Some believed the physical body was disgusting, evil, and not eternal; believing that sex was evil led, of course, to asceticism—denying the body any pleasures (see 1 Corinthians 7:1). Others subscribed to the opposite view, that a person should have total license to satisfy whatever lusts the body craved. The Saints justified this belief by claiming that God didn't care what people did with their bodies (see 1 Corinthians 5:1; 6:9–10).

Prominent Corinthian Saints appear in both Acts and Corinthians. These include the following:

Apollos was a teacher and leader while Paul was away (see Acts 19:1; 1 Corinthians 1:12; Bible Dictionary, "Apollos").

Sosthenes, a leader of a synagogue (see Acts 18:17), who possibly converted to the Church (1 Corinthians 1:1).

Fortunatus, Achaicus, and Stephanus were apparently Church leaders in Corinth and true to Paul. They visited him in Ephesus (see 1 Corinthians 16:17–18).

Chloe, a sister in the Corinthian branch, notified Paul of divisiveness (see 1 Corinthians 1:11).

Crispus, a former leader of a synagogue (Acts 18:8), was baptized by Paul (see 1 Corinthians 1:14).

Gaius was also baptized by Paul (see 1 Corinthians 1:14).

Justus offered his home for Church meetings (see Acts 18:7).

1 CORINTHIANS 1

1:1–9 Paul leaves no doubt that he is an apostle, that members of the Church are called Saints (just as in our day), and that the members had received a powerful witness of Christ's power and of their fellowship with him.

1:10–15 Paul warns against divisions, factions, and schisms: "Is Christ divided?" A divided Church is the antithesis of the divine intention. "If ye are not one ye are not mine," says the Lord (D&C 38:27). Individuals who promote divisiveness are destined for the telestial kingdom unless they repent of their cliquishness (D&C 76:98–101). Perfection comes as the Saints become *one* in Christ.

1:14 Crispus was in charge of a synagogue at Corinth (see Acts 18:8).

1:23 "Stumblingblock" is the equivalent of the Greek *skandalon,* the movable trigger stick of a trap or snare.

1:26 Not many intellectuals humble themselves to respond to the message of the gospel.

1:28 In the early 1600s, *base* meant lowly or humble.

1 CORINTHIANS 2

2:1–8 Spiritual truths do not always sound scholarly or conventionally logical. Without revelation and the confirming power of the Holy Ghost, the things of God may sound like foolishness.

2:2 "Jesus Christ, and him crucified" is the essence of the gospel (compare 3 Nephi 27:13–14).

2:9 Paul is quoting Isaiah 64:4.

2:10–15 The only way to gain spiritual knowledge, all encompassing knowledge, is by the power of the Spirit. The "natural man" is a person without the enlightening and life-giving Spirit of God and thus is an enemy to God (see Mosiah 3:19).

2:16 Paul is quoting Isaiah 40:13.

1 CORINTHIANS 3

3:1 Insert "men and women" after "spiritual" and after "carnal."

3:2–15 Paul again speaks out against pride and cliquishness in the Church. Such characteristics are carnal (see v. 3). Unity and humility are the great themes of this chapter. The Lord would give the Saints all things if they built their lives on the unifying foundation of eternity, the "Rock of Heaven," Jesus Christ (Moses 7:53; compare D&C 78:17–18). Salvation is not only an individual enterprise but a corporate one as well, each Saint seeking the welfare of his or her neighbor and all coming to Christ (see Moroni 10:32).

3:16–17 We came into mortality to receive a body, because a physical body is necessary to do the work of Gods (Moses 1:39) and to reproduce eternally. Satan knows the importance of reproduction, and he particularly targets that sacred power. Our bodies are sacred; in a sense they are temples of God, and we should protect our chastity as we protect our life.

But Paul's teaching here has another meaning. In a place where several temples were dedicated to Apollo, Aphrodite, and others, Paul taught about the temple of the true God, which is the Church of Jesus Christ. The temple of God spoken of in these verses is the body of believers in Christ, that is, his Church, and "the Spirit of God dwelleth *among* or *within* you [plural]." If any man defiles the temple of God—meaning an apostate who distorts the doctrine and draws away disciples after him—he will be destroyed by God.

One scholar addresses Paul's use of the temple this way: "The real question is how Paul used the word *temple* in his writing. Almost always he used it figuratively—occasionally the body is a temple for God's Spirit, but usually the Church is the temple of God. The members ('ye,' older plural English for the plural Greek) are 'God's building' (1 Corinthians 3:9), with Christ its foundation (1 Corinthians 3:11), or, in summary, 'the temple of God' (1 Corinthians 3:16). Elsewhere Paul teaches about Christ as cornerstone, apostles as foundation, and members fitting into their places as a 'holy temple in the Lord' (Ephesians 2:21). And in one of his last letters, Paul still spoke of 'the house of God, which is the church of the living God' (1 Timothy 3:15). Paul must define Paul, and his own words show that he was here referring to the Church" (Anderson, *Understanding Paul*, 86).

3:19–23 Scholars are fools if they think themselves wiser than apostles and prophets. All the faithful are one in Christ, who is one with the Father in purpose.

1 CORINTHIANS 4

4:1–21 Removing pride by following Christ, his doctrines, and his authorized servants are points of counsel Paul gives. He says, "Be ye followers of me"—in other words, Follow Christ at all costs, as I, Paul, have done.

1 CORINTHIANS 5

5:1 Nine of Paul's fourteen letters contain direct instruction about sexual morality. "Fornication" is derived from the Greek *porneia*, which means any extramarital sexual relations. The early Church clearly taught self-control. "The integrity of the Early Church and the restored Church is shown in their discipline of immorality in wise but firm court decisions on membership" (Anderson, *Understanding Paul*, 103). As with such modern issues as abortion, the true Church is not reluctant, afraid, or passive about declaring the truth.

"That one should have his father's wife" indicates that someone had married his stepmother, which was forbidden by religious law, and must be excommunicated.

5:6–7 The metaphor of leaven is used here in a negative sense. Excommunication is necessary for the good of the Church.

5:9 Evidence of previous correspondence.

5:11–13 Here Paul is saying that we should not do what gross sinners do, nor be influenced by them, nor spend our time going to the places they frequent. We should admonish sinners and love them but stay away from their evil ways (see also 2 Thessalonians 3:14–15). Paul also says it is not his or the Church's business to judge and regulate the whole world but rather to keep the Church pure and leave the world to God. The original Greek of verse 13 is strong: "Drive out the wicked man from among you!"

1 CORINTHIANS 6

6:1–2 When in full operation under a theocratic system, Church disciplinary councils will handle both ecclesiastical and civil matters. For now the Lord has said that those who keep the laws of God will have no need to break the laws of the land. "Wherefore, be subject to the powers that be, until he reigns whose right it is to reign, and subdues all enemies under his feet" (D&C 58:21–22).

6:3 Those who attain exaltation are greater than angels.

6:12–19 This section on sexual morality logically precedes Paul's counsel on marriage recorded in chapter 7.

6:20 We are bought with a price, a painful price—Christ's atoning blood. The Saints ought to reflect their gratitude for that infinite payment in their attitudes and behavior.

1 CORINTHIANS 7

Many have misunderstood Paul's teachings because of mistranslation and misinterpretation. In other words, many have missed the intended points of Paul's instructions. Some have pursued the ascetic life, justified celibacy, and promoted antimarriage traditions because they've taken statements in this chapter out of context. All scriptures, taken together and in context, endorse marriage. Some early Christian apostates, Gnostics and others, believed the highest spirituality and purity could be achieved only by renouncing sexual contact. These groups blamed the fall of Adam and Eve on human sexuality. Paul strongly refutes this notion in 1 Corinthians 7 and affirms the importance of mutual sexual responsibility.

7:1–2 Paul is responding to questions asked in previous correspondence (see 1 Corinthians 7:1; 8:1). Verse 1 could otherwise be translated: "Now to deal with the questions you wrote about: 'Is it good for a man to stay away from women . . . ?'" (see footnotes 1*a*, 2*a*).

7:1–5 These verses contain general counsel on marriage. We all have a sexual nature, and marriage is the solution. Sex is not just for having children; it is also to create emotional bonding between husband and wife. Each has an obligation to meet the other's sexual needs and should not deprive the other (unless both agree to abstain for a time and then resume sexual relations), so that Satan will be less effective in presenting outside distractions and temptations.

This counsel from Paul is a sensitive treatment of sexual responsiveness in marriage, and it may suggest that Paul himself was or had been married—he seems to have understood these things from experience. Other indications that Paul may have been married include the following:

1. His writings portray a positive attitude toward marriage (see 1 Corinthians 11:11; Hebrews 13:4).

2. Of the 613 commandments that the Jews believed to be found in the Old Testament, marriage was the first—and Paul was at one time a strict Pharisee. Marriage was a solemn duty, and he knew it was not good for a man to be alone.

3. If he was a member of the Sanhedrin, or ever hoped to be one, he had to be married.

4. During his missions, he was possibly a widower, or maybe his wife had left him at the time of his conversion. If he had no present wife, he may have chosen not to remarry because his heart was so set on the work (further commentary on Paul's marital status and his views on marriage may be found in Sperry, *Paul's Life and Letters*, 130–32; McConkie, *Doctrinal New Testament Commentary*, 2:345–47; and Anderson, *Understanding Paul*, 104–6).

7:8 "Some translations set up a misleading comparison, as the following examples: 'remain single as I do' (Revised Standard Version); 'remain unattached, as I am' (Phillips); 'stay unmarried, as I am' (New International Version). The Greek text simply does not say this. Twice the comparison is made 'even as I myself' (v. 7) or 'even as I' (v. 8). Any hint of whether or not Paul was married does not come from these verses. The earlier one (v. 7) is strongly used to say that Paul has the gift of self-control (v. 5)—so both verses are asking the Saints to follow Paul in [exemplifying that quality]. Such instruction is appropriate both for the married or unmarried" (Anderson, "Guide to Acts," 59).

7:9 See Joseph Smith Translation alterations and Greek (GR) translations in the footnotes to this verse.

7:10 In a troubled marriage, partners should try to persevere and work it out.

7:12 Paul's view was that in part-member families, a non-member should not be divorced if he or she refuses to convert.

7:14 See Doctrine and Covenants 74.

7:15 If the spouse refuses to live with a Church member, the Church member is forced to choose the Lord.

7:19 Filling in the ellipsis, add "is everything" to the end of the verse.

7:25–40 Missionaries: married or single? This passage discusses marital status in relation to the work of the ministry in the Lord's Church, particularly missionary service. Unquestionably, marriage was approved of and encouraged in the early Church; however, for those unmarried persons engaged in full-time missionary work, marriage was better delayed. For those persons already married but called as full-time servants, it would be as though they were not married because missionary endeavors require so much time, attention, and concentration. We have examples of this principle operating in the present dispensation. Brigham Young, Wilford Woodruff, Heber C. Kimball, and others left home, wives, and children for a time to do the Lord's work.

7:26 "The present distress" would be translated better as "the present necessity," which is the need for missionaries. Today, most missionaries who serve also delay marriage to serve the Lord.

7:29–33 See the Joseph Smith Translation in the Appendix to the Bible. "The time is short" means that the Church needs missionaries—the Great Apostasy is imminent.

7:36 In this verse, a man's "virgin" means his fiancée. The phrase "pass the flower of her age" means she feels she is getting old.

7:38 Note again the Joseph Smith Translation correction; it is better (for the "present necessity") to be a missionary; if not, get married, for that is acceptable.

1 CORINTHIANS 8

Chapters 8 through 11 deal with not offending others whose cultures and customs differ from ours.

8:1 Here is one of Paul's powerful one-liners: "Knowledge puffeth up, but charity edifieth"—that is, knowledge inflates the ego, but charity strengthens.

8:5–6 Note the chapter heading. Today, Christians suppose these verses refer only to the gods of the Greek and Roman pantheons. Joseph Smith, however, interpreted these verses differently: "Paul had no allusion to the heathen gods" (*Teachings of the Prophet Joseph Smith*, 370). These verses were an allusion to the magnificent and ennobling doctrine of the plurality of Gods. The Prophet taught: "If Jesus had a Father, can we not believe that He had a Father also?" (*Teachings of the Prophet Joseph Smith*, 373). Later in this dispensation Elder Bruce R. McConkie wrote: "Those who attain exaltation are Gods" (*Mormon Doctrine*, 57).

8:10–13 Don't eat contaminated meats offered to idols. Avoid even the appearance of evil.

1 CORINTHIANS 9

9:1 We don't know where or when Paul's ordination to the apostleship took place, but according to modern-day revelation, at this point he was probably one of the Twelve (Smith, *Answers to Gospel Questions*, 4:99–100).

9:5 Occasionally, Peter and other apostles apparently traveled with their wives.

9:17 "Dispensation" is used here to translate the Greek word meaning "commission or stewardship."

9:19–23 Paul adapted to the circumstances of each situation he came across and incorporated aspects of each people's culture to teach them. In a spirit of accommodation but not compromise, Paul worked hard to establish common ground with those he taught.

9:24–25 Paul could have attended, or at least heard about, the Isthmian games held every two years at Isthmia, near Corinth. The Isthmian games were second only to the Olympic games in importance to the Greeks. This competition might have been the source for Paul's use of athletic imagery (foot races). The prize for the winner of the Isthmian games was a perishable crown of celery. The gospel race, however, which everyone could win, promises an everlasting crown of glory (see Mosiah 4:27).

1 CORINTHIANS 10

The early apostles often used the experiences of the Israelites in the wilderness to teach important lessons to their disciples.

10:1–4 Christ was Jehovah, the Rock of Salvation for Israel and for us. The Greek word in verse 4 translated "Rock" (*petra*) means "bedrock" and is the same one used by Christ in Matthew 16:18—"thou art Peter [*petros*, 'small rock'], and upon this rock [*petra*, 'bedrock'] I will build my church." The revelation that Jesus is the Christ, the Anointed One, is the bedrock of the Church and of true, saving faith. On verse 4, see also Exodus 17:6.

10:6, 11 Examples, or ensamples, were prefigurative historical events, written as a warning to us who are living in the last days.

10:12 If you think you are firm in the faith, be careful that you don't fall. Compare Proverbs 16:18, "Pride goeth before . . . a fall."

10:13 See footnote *a* to this verse. God protects us against temptations that are thrust upon us, but if we seek out temptations our protection is weakened (see also Alma 13:28).

10:19–21 Paul condemns pagan rituals and sacraments.

10:23 Note important Joseph Smith Translation changes.

10:24 This doesn't sound like good Christian doctrine; "wealth" would be better rendered "well-being" or "welfare" (see footnote 24*b*).

10:27–28 If your host has made an issue of specifying that your food was previously offered to idols, you must take a stand. Do not condone idol worship in any way.

1 CORINTHIANS 11

11:1–15 Paul discusses acceptable behavior, and so forth, in worship.

11:4–6 These verses deal with local customs or traditions.

Verse 3 reminds us that everyone is accountable to somebody else; even Christ is subject to the Father. Verses 3 and 4 combined reflect a play on words, the physiological and the spiritual. Verse 5 discusses women praying and prophesying: it has been said that women are, by nature, generally more spiritually inclined than men (see McConkie, *Doctrinal New Testament Commentary*, 2:361). A woman's head is the husband (see v. 3; see also commentary on Ephesians 5:22–33).

It was the custom then for women to have their hair covered, and it was considered by some to be sexually stimulating to refrain from doing so.

11:11 Men and women cannot be with the Lord eternally without each other; we are exalted only in couples.

11:14 A provocative question!

11:19 There will always be heresies that separate the

"sheep from the goats" (Matthew 25:32). Doctrine is the great divider.

11:20–30 This is a beautiful treatise on the sacrament and an admonition to partake of it worthily. Gluttony and shameful behavior dishonor the sacrament (vv. 20–22). More details and explanations of the purposes of the Last Supper are recorded here than in any other account (vv. 23–25). Paul writes of those details, though he was not present. Thus, the sacred events may have been preserved in writings circulating at the time, or perhaps Paul learned much about the sacred event from his association with others of the Twelve (see, for example, Galatians 1:18). On partaking of the sacrament unworthily (vv. 27–29), compare 3 Nephi 18:28–30.

1 CORINTHIANS 12

12:1–11 Paul's powerful discussion on spiritual gifts parallels those of other prophets of God, namely Joseph Smith (see D&C 46) and Moroni (see Moroni 10:8–18).

12:3 "No man can say that Jesus is the Lord, but by the Holy Ghost." The Prophet Joseph Smith changed "say" to "know" (*Teachings of the Prophet Joseph Smith*, 223).

12:12–31 The body of Christ, the membership of the Church of Christ, is the temple of God. Every member of the body is needed for proper functioning of the whole, just as a car without a battery, distributor, coil, or many other small parts will not run. Every part, or every member, is needed. Some divisiveness existed then, and it exists now. There are those who feel some callings in the Church are more important than others.

> *Father, where shall I work today?*
> *And my love flowed warm and free.*
> *Then He pointed out a tiny spot*
> *And said, "Tend that for me."*
> *I answered quickly, "Oh no; not that!*

Why, no one would ever see,
No matter how well my work was done;
Not that little place for me."
And the word He spoke, it was not stern;
He answered me tenderly:
"Ah, little one, search that heart of thine.
Art thou working for them or for me?
Nazareth was a little place,
And so was Galilee."

(By Meade McGuire; quoted in
Monson, Ensign, *May 1986, 39)*

12:26 Imagine a society with no resentment or jealousy when somebody achieves an honor, a society in which everyone feels bad when someone hurts—such are the aims and realities in a Zion society (see Moses 7:18–19; D&C 82:17–20).

12:31 We should seek after spiritual gifts earnestly, at the same time remembering why they're given (see D&C 46:8–9 concerning proper motives). Spiritual gifts are bestowed so that all members of the Church of Christ may be benefited. The Spirit of God gives every individual a gift (D&C 46:11).

1 CORINTHIANS 13

Paul discusses the greatest attribute or characteristic anyone could be found possessing. His teachings apply to disciples of every dispensation; they are at the heart of Christianity. The Greek *agape* and Latin *caritas,* both of which are translated as "charity," mean love—a selfless concern for others that is not evoked by any love on the part of the other. It is a type of love different from *eros* ("erotic love") and *phileo* ("spontaneous, natural, unreasoned, familial love"). It is the kind of love Christ manifested on the cross (see John 13:34–35; 1 John 3:16). It is the product of a will to be in harmony with God's will (see Moroni 7; 10; Ether 12:28,

33–34). Moroni 7:47 says charity is the pure love of Christ. *Love* is the great teaching of Paul (and Peter, John, Jesus, and Joseph Smith, and all other great teachers). Love is not mere feeling but expressed feeling. We do not love if we do not show our love. Jesus said, "If ye love me, keep my commandments."

One modern scholar discusses the concept of pure love: "The concept of love is not dramatic sacrifice but steady relationship. It is not a giant gift on a special occasion but the continued support of personal caring. . . .

"The tragedy of many unloving people is that they only imagine they love. In truth they want to love but do not pay the price to move from wishful thinking to reality. . . . The impatient jerk on a child, the harsh word to someone trying to assist, or the cold shoulder to a spouse all reveal a smallness of soul. . . . [I]t is subtly disguised in appearing to care but being too busy. . . . Parents in tune with their divine calling know that eternal potential is wrapped up with their helpless and uncoordinated infant. Parents of resistant teenagers are wise if they remember that the potential is still there, and gospel brothers and sisters with this vision will do the same. The future is unlocked by pure love, which 'believes' and 'hopes all things.' . . .

" . . . For Paul, knowledge must be supplemented and revised, but love never fails (1 Cor. 13:8). The gospel experience of unselfish love is closer to eternity than anything else. It may be counterfeited by immorality and cheapened in superficial society. But genuine love is a taste of eternity" (Anderson, *Understanding Paul*, 119, 124).

13:3 Though I give my body to be burned—that is, though I die for the truth.

13:4–8 The ingredients of charity: "suffereth long" means patience; "is kind" means having kindness and generosity; "envieth not" means having no resentment, no discontent over the good fortune of others; "vaunteth not itself" means showing humility and modesty; "is not puffed up" means not contending for superiority; "doth not behave itself unseemly" means having courtesy; "seeketh not her own" means behaving unselfishly; "is not easily provoked" means having gentleness, forbearance; "thinketh no evil" means having purity of thought.

Verse 4 indicates that others' talents, abilities, and successes do not threaten those really converted to Christ.

Verse 8 tells us that charity is celestial, never ending.

13:12 "Glass" is the King James rendering of the Greek word meaning "mirror."

13:13 Hope is not wishing but expectation.

1 CORINTHIANS 14

14:1–6 Paul teaches that all spiritual gifts, especially the gifts of prophecy and tongues ought to be for the benefit of the entire Church (1 Corinthians 12:7; 14:12; D&C 46:9). What good is the gift of tongues if it is not for the building of the kingdom?

Some further instruction on the gift of tongues is found in the *Teachings of the Prophet Joseph Smith:* First, the devil can imitate this gift (see 162). Second, its specific purpose is to teach unbelievers (see 195; 1 Corinthians 14:22). Third, don't be too curious about it (see 247), and don't indulge in it too much (see 229). And finally, as a rule, anything taught by the gift of tongues is not to be received as doctrine (see 229).

14:8 Paul's audience anciently would have been familiar with the use of the trumpet to signal warnings, such as impending battles or other important events (Numbers 10:9; Joshua 6:4, 9). The trumpet (a ram's horn) was also used by the Jews to announce the arrival of the Sabbath.

14:12 Seeking spiritual gifts for the purpose of edifying the Church is an important theme for Paul.

14:21 Here Paul quotes Isaiah 28:11–12 and refers to

such prophetic passages as part of "the law," meaning the whole Old Testament.

14:22 Paul seems to believe that the gift of tongues can be of some benefit to unbelievers, perhaps because it is dramatic, whereas prophecy is for believers because it communicates the mind and will of the Lord.

14:26 If the gift of tongues causes someone to "lose control," it is not of God.

14:34 "Women keep silence in the churches: for it is not permitted unto them to speak"—obviously something is wrong with the text the way we have it; compare 1 Corinthians 11:5, in which women pray and prophesy. The issue is not participation but control. Paul seems to be reminding the sisters to be subject to priesthood leadership, as the priesthood is subject to God. Note Joseph Smith Translation changes in footnotes 34*b* and 35*a*, where "rule" is substituted for "speak." There must be order in the Church on earth, as there is order in heaven (compare v. 40). Women may teach, counsel, testify, and exhort, but God did not intend for them to usurp the authority he designated for priesthood leaders (Smith, *Teachings of the Prophet Joseph Smith*, 212; McConkie, *Doctrinal New Testament Commentary*, 2:387). Yet that is also true for all Church members, male or female, who are asked to follow priesthood leaders.

1 CORINTHIANS 15

15:1–8 These verses introduce Paul's testimony of the resurrection, including an important listing of some appearances of Jesus after his resurrection. Verses 1 through 3 imply that Christ's death and resurrection are the heart of the gospel (compare 3 Nephi 27:13–14). In verse 7 we learn that Jesus appeared to his younger brother James, and then James knew and understood.

15:12–32 How could some say there is no resurrection? Not only did the Sadducees deny the reality of the resurrection, but some of those espousing Greek mythology and philosophy believed that the body was evil, that though there might be eternal life for the spirit, there certainly was none for the body. Paul's response is that the doctrine of the resurrection is pivotal in importance and that all other truths of the gospel of Jesus Christ depend on it. In effect, Paul says the following:

Verse 13—if there's no resurrection, then Christ is dead.

Verse 14—if there's no resurrection, then we're wasting our time, and our faith is a terrible joke.

Verse 15—if there's no resurrection, then we (apostolic preachers) are liars.

Verse 17—if there's no resurrection, there's no spiritual redemption and no redemption from physical death (that is, resurrection is redemption; see 2 Nephi 9:6–9).

Verse 29—if there's no resurrection, why perform baptisms for the dead?

Verse 32—and finally, if there's no resurrection, then why am I working so hard, killing myself off?

15:19–22 What a miserable excuse for religious belief we would have if life ended with this mortal sphere. It has been rightly said, "The object of life is more life." Because of the Fall, physical death comes to all of us, or, "as in Adam all die," but "even so in Christ shall all be made alive" (v. 22; see also Alma 11:42–44). Mosiah 3:16 adds significantly to our understanding of 1 Corinthians 15:22.

15:29 See the epistle written by Joseph Smith in 1842 containing instructions about baptism for the dead: Doctrine and Covenants 128:1–18 (especially vv. 16–18). It is essential to discuss the ordinance of baptism itself when talking about the bold doctrine of baptism for the dead. If baptism by immersion is mandatory for the living for entrance into the kingdom of God, as Jesus and his apostles plainly taught, it should also be a requirement for those who have passed on, who had no opportunity to receive baptism during mortality. There is evidence outside the Bible that the ordinance of baptism for the dead was taught and practiced by early Christians. Even the Roman Catholic *Jerome Biblical Commentary* admits that it seems as though Christians at Corinth "would undergo baptism in the name of their deceased non-Christian relatives and friends, hoping that this vicarious baptism might assure them a share in the redemption of Christ." Nevertheless, the Commentary regards the passage as obscure and the practice strange (Brown, *Jerome Biblical Commentary*, 2:273). Many scholars find no satisfactory explanation for such a practice (see "Baptism for the Dead" in Ludlow, *Encyclopedia of Mormonism*, 1:95–97).

The following is a reconstruction of an interview between Dr. Edgar J. Goodspeed, a renowned Bible translator and scholar, and the late Dr. Paul R. Cheesman, professor of ancient scripture at Brigham Young University. The interview took place on the campus of UCLA in the summer of 1945 (see Anderson, *Understanding Paul*, 413):

Cheesman: Is the scripture found in 1 Corinthians 15:29 translated properly as found in the King James Translation?

Goodspeed: Basically, yes.

Cheesman: Do you believe that baptism for the dead was practiced in Paul's time?

Goodspeed: Definitely, yes.

Cheesman: Does the church to which you belong practice it today?

Goodspeed: No.

Cheesman: Do you think it should be practiced today?

Goodspeed: This is the reason why we do not practice it today. We do not know enough about it. If we did, we would practice it.

Cheesman: May I quote you as a result of this interview?

Goodspeed: Yes.

15:33 According to Jerome, one of the early Church Fathers, this passage may be a quotation from the Greek poet Menander. Menander, however, may have been quoting Euripides. The words have also been ascribed to Plato. In other words, it seems to have been a commonplace saying (see Bullinger, *Figures of Speech Used in the Bible*, 801).

15:36 "That which thou sowest is not quickened, except it die"—compare Jesus' teaching in John 12:24: "except a corn of wheat fall into the ground and die, it abideth alone." The scripture indicates that a kernel of wheat must be planted in the ground and "die"; that is, it must change from its one-time structure to become something bigger and better, to become fruitful. Jesus used this analogy from nature to foreshadow his own death: "The hour is come, that the Son of man should be glorified. . . . If it [the kernal of wheat] die, it bringeth forth much fruit" (John 12:23–24). Sacrifice is what engenders the blessings of eternal life. Burying the carnal man is necessary in order to give birth to the spiritual man.

15:35, 40–42 There are different kinds of bodies in the resurrection (see also D&C 88:20–21, 28–31). Paul's vision of the three degrees of glory is apparently the same as that recorded in 2 Corinthians 12:2–4. "Paul ascended into the third heavens, and he could understand the three principal rounds of Jacob's ladder—the telestial, the terrestrial, and the celestial glories or kingdoms" (Smith, *Teachings of the Prophet Joseph Smith*, 304–5; see Bible Dictionary, "Degrees of Glory," "Paradise," and "Resurrection").

Verse 40 speaks of celestial ("heavenly") and terrestrial ("earthly," where the honorable people of the earth go), but we learn the name of the third heaven from the Prophet Joseph Smith (see JST rendering in footnote 40*a*). *Telestial* may be derived from the Greek *telos,* meaning "end"; telestial bodies come forth at the end, in the last resurrection.

Joseph Smith had a similar vision, as recorded in Doctrine and Covenants 76. "That document," wrote the Prophet, "is a transcript from the records of the eternal world. The sublimity of the ideas; the purity of the language; the scope for action; the continued duration for completion, in order that the heirs of salvation may confess the Lord and bow the knee; the rewards for faithfulness, and the punishments for sins, are so much beyond the narrow-mindedness of men, that every honest man is constrained to exclaim: '*It came from God*'" (*History of the Church*, 1:252–53; emphasis in original).

15:42 Physical perfection is achieved in the resurrection (see also Alma 40:23).

15:45 The "last Adam" is Jesus (Hebrew, *adam*, means "man," or mortal being).

15:50 The life of the mortal body is in the blood (see Leviticus 17:11). Joseph Smith taught that "when our flesh is quickened by the Spirit, there will be no blood in this tabernacle" (*Teachings of the Prophet Joseph Smith*, 367).

1 CORINTHIANS 16

16:1–4 Paul outlines a plan for meeting the Lord's requirement of tithes and offerings, which Church headquarters in Jerusalem would administer.

16:5–18 Paul pleads for diligence in living gospel principles, especially love, unity, charity, kindness towards leaders, and assisting the Lord's work to move forward. As Elder B. H. Roberts later said, "In essentials let there be unity; in nonessentials, liberty; and in all things, charity" (Conference Report, October 1912, 30). Verse 8 indicates this letter was written in the spring.

16:19–20 These verses communicate Paul's warmth and concluding greetings. We see again (compare 1 Thessalonians 5:26) that members of the early Church continued the oriental practice of giving one another a kiss as a salutation and demonstration of respect. Jews practiced the custom in ancient times (see Proverbs 27:6; Matthew 26:49).

2 CORINTHIANS

The best word to describe this epistle may be *defense*. When Paul was accused by some who wanted to see his influence reduced in Corinth, he responded by vigorously defending his status as a teacher, a leader, and an apostle of the Lord Jesus Christ. This letter appears to have been written a few months after 1 Corinthians, this one from Macedonia. Second Corinthians and Philemon are the most personal of Paul's writings, containing more autobiographical material than any of his other letters. Second Corinthians may be divided into three parts, all relating to Paul's imminent third visit to Corinth.

In the first chapters, 1 through 7, Paul explains why he changed his original itinerary, thus answering charges that his word was untrustworthy. In the next two chapters, 8 and 9, Paul encourages the Corinthian Saints to complete their collection of tithes and offerings begun a year earlier. In chapters 10 through 13, Paul defends his apostolic authority and stresses that his arrival in Corinth is imminent.

2 CORINTHIANS 1

1:1–11 Paul's theology obviously shows that Heavenly Father and Jesus Christ are separate and distinct beings, that God the Father and his Son care about the tribulations of the Saints, and that they stand ready to comfort the Saints when they are in need. Knowing the Lord is there, the Saints may then act as God's instruments by comforting one another and supporting the Brethren as they face challenging circumstances.

1:12–2:4 Paul had earlier committed to visit the Corinthian Saints (see 1 Corinthians 4:19; 16:5–7) but could not fulfill his promise. He explains why, indicates his sincerity, and declares his authorized appointment by God (1:21). Paul loves the Saints dearly (2:4).

149

1:22 Here Paul uses an analogy of "earnest money" (in Ephesians 1:14 he calls it "the earnest of our inheritance") to teach the Saints how they can know when the promises of the Atonement are in effect in their behalf. The Saints receive the "earnest of the Spirit," which feeling assures them that they will be inheritors of glory in the future. In other words, the Holy Ghost, or Holy Spirit of Promise, acts as a deposit guaranteeing our inheritance of exaltation. That is what it means to be "sealed with that holy Spirit of promise" (Ephesians 1:13; compare D&C 88:3–4).

2 CORINTHIANS 2

2:1–4 Paul had already made two visits to Corinth, the second of which was painful (made in "heaviness"), though the reason why is not known. Perhaps the visit took place between the writing of 1 and 2 Corinthians. At any rate, Paul intended to make a third visit (see 2 Corinthians 12:14; 13:1). His love for the Saints is obvious (see v. 4).

2:5–11 Paul refers to a particular person on whom Church discipline was imposed. The punishment inflicted by the body of the Church was sufficient (v. 6). It was the duty of the members to forgive the individual. Lack of forgiveness is also one of Satan's devices.

2:12 Paul was anxious to receive news about Corinth from his missionary companion, Titus.

2:14–16 Paul digresses from his narrative about his itinerary to speak out in spontaneous praise and gratitude for Christ's triumph over sin and death.

2 CORINTHIANS 3

3:1–5 Paul doesn't need a letter of thanks from the Corinthian Saints; what is written in their hearts—their being established firmly in the faith—is thanks enough.

3:6 The word here in Greek is *diatheke,* which carries the primary meaning of "covenant." A secondary meaning is "last will, testament," which is why translators improperly associated it with the Latin *testamentum*, which carries only the second meaning. In this verse Paul means that the new covenant (gospel) is based on higher principles and priesthood than the old covenant. To observe Mosaic prescriptions—the lesser law—after the higher law has been given will kill the Saints spiritually.

3:7—4:6 Paul defends his ministry of the "new covenant."

3:14–16 Orthodox and other Jews even in our day know thoroughly the words of the Hebrew Bible, the *Tanakh,* whose name is an acronym: the letters TNK refer to the Torah, the Neviim (prophets), and the Ketuvim (writings, poetic works). They know it backwards and forwards. Yet they do not understand it completely. There is a veil over their minds still. "Nevertheless when [they] shall turn to the Lord, the vail shall be taken away" (v. 16).

2 CORINTHIANS 4

4:7 "We have this treasure in earthen vessels"—a beautiful analogy using clay pots or jugs. Great treasures of the gospel are carried around by such earthly vessels as Peter, a former fisherman; Matthew, a former tax collector; and Paul, a former tentmaker.

4:8–9 This is more than just having a positive mental attitude. Faith in God provides mental stability, knowing that he is ultimately in charge.

4:14 The source of all comfort is Christ's atonement.

4:17 Compare Doctrine and Covenants 121:7–8. Paul had learned great lessons from the Savior. He knew that Jesus' crown of thorns came before his crown of glory.

President Brigham Young said of suffering: "All intelligent beings who are crowned with crowns of glory, immortality, and eternal lives must pass through every ordeal appointed for intelligent beings to pass through, to gain their glory and exaltation. Every calamity that can come upon mortal beings will be suffered to come upon the few, to prepare them to enjoy the presence of the Lord. If we obtain the glory that Abraham obtained, we must do so by the same means that he did. If we are ever prepared to enjoy the society of Enoch, Noah, Melchizedek, Abraham, Isaac, and Jacob, or of their faithful children, and of the faithful Prophets and Apostles, we must pass through the same experience, and gain the knowledge, intelligence, and endowments that will prepare us to enter into the celestial kingdom of our Father and God. How many of the Latter-day Saints will endure all these things, and be prepared to enjoy the presence of the Father and the Son? You can answer that question at your leisure. Every trial and experience you have passed through is necessary for your salvation" (*Discourses of Brigham Young*, 345).

"It is recorded that Jesus was made perfect through suffering. If he was made perfect through suffering, why should we imagine for one moment that we can be prepared to enter into the kingdom of rest with him and the Father, without passing through similar ordeals" (*Discourses of Brigham Young*, 346).

President John Taylor reiterated the words of the Prophet Joseph Smith: "You will have all kinds of trials to pass through. And it is quite as necessary for you to be tried as it was for Abraham and other men of God, and . . . God will feel after you, and He will take hold of you and wrench your very heart strings, and if you cannot stand it you will not be fit for an inheritance in the Celestial Kingdom of God" (*Journal of Discourses*, 24:197).

President George Q. Cannon taught: "Every Latter-day Saint who gains a celestial glory will be tried to the very uttermost. If there is a point in our character that is weak and tender, you may depend upon it that the Lord will reach after that, and we will be tried at that spot for the Lord will test us to the utmost before we can get through and receive that glory and exaltation which He has in store for us as a people" (*Gospel Truth*, 103).

Elder Spencer W. Kimball wrote: "Being human, we would expel from our lives physical pain and mental anguish and assure ourselves of continual ease and comfort, but if we were to close the doors upon sorrow and distress, we might be excluding our greatest friends and benefactors. Suffering can make saints of people as they learn patience, long-suffering, and self-mastery" (Kimball, *Faith Precedes the Miracle*, 98).

Thus, "the greatest trials of life are reserved for the saints" (McConkie, *Doctrinal New Testament Commentary*, 3:318).

2 CORINTHIANS 5

5:1–7 Mortality is a time of testing, trials, and faith, but eternal glory will be our reward. We receive no witness, no sure knowledge, until after the trial of our faith (see Ether 12:6).

5:10–11 This passage sounds as though Paul had read the Book of Mormon on this doctrine (see 3 Nephi 26:4; Alma 11:41).

5:17 After baptism, all followers of Christ become new creatures, our carnal natures are destroyed, and we are spiritually reborn (see Romans 6:4–6).

5:18–20 Note the use in this passage of "reconcile" and "reconciliation." The Greek term from which those words are translated denotes being restored to God's favor. Reconciliation is all part of the Atonement. God himself was willing to come down and make payment for our sins.

5:21 In this verse, Peter, like Paul, testifies that Christ was sinless (see 1 Peter 2:22). All he requires of us as disciples is to repent, which in Hebrew is *lashuv,* meaning "to return to him, to be reconciled to him."

2 CORINTHIANS 6

6:1–10 Paul encourages the Corinthians to remain faithful in the face of affliction by demonstrating the characteristics of true disciples.

6:12 Bowels are the center of pity and kindness. The meaning of the verse could be rendered, You're restricted by your own failure to show love and compassion.

6:14 When two animals plowed together, a yoke made of a wooden beam was laid across the top of the animals' necks and fastened together with leather or rope straps under their necks. The Mosaic law prohibited yoking together two different beasts, such as an ox and an ass; the unequal pull could cause the weaker or smaller of the animals discomfort and pain. Rather than being prejudicial or showing exclusivity, Paul's counsel, "Be ye not unequally yoked together with unbelievers" (2 Corinthians 6:14), was meant to protect the marital partners from experiencing the unequal pull that could cause serious discomfort and pain to one or the other or both.

2 CORINTHIANS 7

Paul did have to chastise some of the Saints, no matter how unpleasant it was (compare Jacob 2).

7:9–10 Alma taught similarly: "Do not endeavor to excuse yourself in the least point because of your sins"; "only let your sins trouble you, with that trouble which shall bring you down unto repentance" (Alma 42:30, 29). In other words, true grief over one's sins produces repentance worthy of eternal life.

2 CORINTHIANS 8

8:14 We should impart of our substance to the less fortunate "by an equality"—that is, according to proper needs and wants (see D&C 51:3; 82:17). The Lord's kind of equality does not refer to sameness of quantity but rather to equal opportunity to satisfy all needs and wants.

2 CORINTHIANS 9

9:2 Usually *provoked* means "aroused to anger," but here it is used in the sense of "aroused, spurred on, encouraged."

9:6–13 Paul encouraged the Saints to be generous with their means and promised them great blessings. The Savior encouraged his disciples to give freely of themselves as well (see Matthew 10:8).

2 CORINTHIANS 10

10:1 "Base" means "lowly, humble."

10:8, 17–18 "Boast" in verse 8 means "to glory," as defined in verses 17 and 18.

10:10 Paul's antagonists in Corinth were ridiculing him. Though they conceded that his letters are "weighty and powerful," these same letters emphasize Paul's physical weaknesses and poor speaking ability. In 2 Corinthians 11:6, Paul is characterized as being "rude in speech"; in 12:7 and the following verses Paul laments and confesses his weaknesses.

All of us are given weaknesses. Moses protested, "I am not eloquent, . . . I am slow of speech, and of a slow tongue" (Exodus 4:10)—that is, I can't talk in front of people.

Enoch exclaimed, "[I] am but a lad, and all the people hate me; for I am slow of speech" (Moses 6:31)—I'm just a youth, and nobody likes me.

Gideon moaned, "My family is poor . . . and I am the least in my father's house" (Judges 6:15)—I'm a nobody.

Saul grieved, "My family [is] the least of all the families of the tribe of Benjamin" (1 Samuel 9:21)—I'm of low birth; I've been brought up in humble circumstances.

Jeremiah, like Moses, lamented, "I cannot speak: for I am

a child" (Jeremiah 1:6)—I'm not mature enough yet to handle this.

Even a modern prophet, Spencer W. Kimball, was worried about his personal weaknesses: "You can't do the work. You are not worthy. You have not the ability" (Conference Report, October 1943, 16).

There are many more excuses: I'm not smart enough; I'm not spiritual enough; I'm not strong enough. Maybe the Lord is trying to teach us something with all these examples. It doesn't necessarily take great speaking ability, high birth, the wisdom of age, popularity, knowledge, or physical strength to fulfill a calling from the Lord. It does take faith and determination to make of ourselves more than we are. The Lord will make us all that we can become, if we let him, as Paul learned.

In 2 Corinthians 10:11, Paul warns his antagonists, "Let such an one think this, that, such as we are in word by letters when we are absent, such will we be also in deed when we are present." When he arrives, he'll deal with them summarily and with authority.

2 CORINTHIANS 11

11:2 "I have espoused you to one husband"—indeed, the Lord's Church is married to her Bridegroom: the disciples of Christ take upon themselves the name of Christ.

11:3 "The simplicity that is in Christ"—compare the "plainness" of the Book of Mormon (2 Nephi 25:4, 7, 20; 26:33; 31:3; Jacob 4:13; Mosiah 2:40; Alma 5:43; 13:23).

11:18 Others boast, or glory, in their immoral conquests and exploits; Paul gloried in his conquests for Christ (on righteous glorifying, see Alma 26).

11:22–28 Some Corinthian Saints have been listening to false teachers ("fools"). Paul matches ridicule with ridicule, speaking as foolishly as some had been doing. Then he lists for us an amazing catalog of perils and sufferings he'd gone through for the cause of Christ (see Acts 9:16).

Beating with rods was a Roman punishment. Paul could have claimed Roman citizenship and escaped the scourging but that would have meant excommunication and being cut off from the synagogues—and that is his missionary approach. He willingly submitted to the shameful punishment in order to continue teaching his own people.

In verse 28 he clearly specifies what caused him the most anxious concern in all his labors.

11:32–33 Aretas IV, the Nabataean king whose capital was at Petra, was then in power over the land of Damascus, and his governor tried to apprehend Paul. Here we learn how. Paul escaped.

2 CORINTHIANS 12

12:1–4 Paul's vision of the three heavens was one of the most sacred events of his life (see commentary on 1 Corinthians 15:35, 40–42).

Verse 4 speaks of "paradise," a word that has various uses in scripture. In this case, Paul refers to the heaven where God dwells.

12:7–10 Much has been written about Paul's "thorn in the flesh." Numerous hypotheses have been advanced by way of identifying the "thorn," including stuttering, epilepsy, a shrewish wife, an eye affliction, malaria, some mortal antagonist, or some spiritual weakness. Whatever it was, he knew why it was there, "lest I should be exalted above measure." He had pleaded with the Lord to take it away, but he learned, as we all do, that the Lord intentionally gives each of us weaknesses to keep us humble. Weaknesses are meant not to humiliate but to humble. If we let them accomplish their appointed purpose, weaknesses will not weaken us but strengthen us.

CHAPTER 6

GALATIANS

Originally a tribe of Celts from Gaul (now France) that migrated to Asia Minor in search of wealth centuries before Christ, the Galatians resided in the political province of Galatia (modern Turkey) during Paul's day. Paul taught them that they were children of God by adoption into the family of Abraham through the grace of Jesus Christ and the power of the Holy Ghost. When Paul left the Galatian Saints they were extremely devoted (Galatians 4:15). Over time, however, they began to adopt false notions, and the Church in Galatia was thrown into turmoil. Paul's apostleship also came under attack. He wrote to the branches of the Church he had established on his first missionary journey—Antioch, Iconium, Lystra, and Derbe—possibly from Corinth in A.D. 57 or 58 (see Bible Dictionary, "Pauline Epistles, Epistle to the Galatians"; "Law of Moses").

The first stage of apostasy that swept through the early Church involved Jewish Christians who seemed unable to abandon their Judaic traditions. The Galatian Saints attempted to revise the gospel by including pagan observances and such Mosaic rituals as circumcision (see Galatians 4:9–10). As adopted members of the Abrahamic covenant, perhaps they believed that the rite of circumcision (so important in Abraham's day; see Genesis 17:10) and other aspects of the Mosaic law were the basis of Christ's gospel. Their zeal led them to keep certain aspects of that law (see Galatians 3:2; 4:21; 5:4, 18) and required all baptized males to be

158

circumcised (see Galatians 5:2, 11; 6:12–13). Paul teaches in this epistle that Christ is not secondary to the law of Moses. The law with its specific requirements cannot bring salvation—only Christ can. Salvation comes through the merits of Christ alone. This epistle has been called a declaration of independence from Judaism. The terms *free* and *freedom* are used eleven times in the brief letter.

Galatians and Romans (the Pauline epistle that most closely resembles Galatians in intent, content, and argument) were the scriptural foundation of the Protestant Reformation. They led Martin Luther to break from the Roman Catholic Church. Thus Paul's words became an impetus to the great religious revolution of the sixteenth century.

A monumental theme in Galatians is that justification comes not by the works of the law but by faith in Jesus Christ (see Galatians 2:16). Thus are we freed from the "curse of the law" (Galatians 3:13). Paul says the same thing in Romans: "For all have sinned, and come short of the glory of God; being justified freely by his grace through the redemption that is in Christ Jesus. . . . Therefore we conclude that a man is justified by faith without the deeds of the law" (Romans 3:23–24, 28). Jesus Christ alone can declare us righteous and put us back into a right relationship with God. This is what it means to be justified, and it is only by the grace of Christ we are justified and saved (2 Nephi 25:23). Galatians supports the truths of grace and justification taught by Nephi in the Book of Mormon.

Galatians shares with Romans several terms and phrases found nowhere else. These include "Love thy neighbour as thyself" as the sum of Christian duty (Galatians 5:14; Romans 13:9), the language of adoption and heirship (Galatians 4:4–7; Romans 8:14–17), and the expressive statement "Abba, Father," uttered by the Savior as his final outcry (Galatians 4:6; Romans 8:15; see Matthew 27:50). This final declaration of the Savior denotes an especially close, uniquely personal, relationship to God; the Aramaic *Abba* may be more accurately translated "Daddy" or "Papa."

GALATIANS 1

1:6–8 There was no other gospel than that which Paul had taught the Saints in Galatia. He cautioned against those who came along with imitations. The Judaizers were preaching a different gospel, attempting to get Christian converts to view the Mosaic law as the foundation and Christianity as an addition.

1:10–13 The true gospel of Jesus was not created by mankind but came by revelation. Just as with Joseph Smith, Jesus Christ revealed himself to Paul and taught him the gospel.

1:14 Paul had been a valedictorian of sorts in his class of rabbinical students in Jerusalem.

1:17–19 These verses give us information about Paul's early years. After the miraculous event on the road to Damascus, he remained for a time in Damascus. Subsequently he spent some preparation time in "Arabia." That didn't necessarily mean that he journeyed hundreds of miles south into the great Syrian-Arabian desert—Damascus itself was in Arabia, which in Paul's day was part of the Nabataean domain of King Aretas IV. After an unstated period of time in the solitude of introspection and spiritual communion (as Moses and Jesus had also done), Paul returned to Damascus. Then "after three years" he went up to become acquainted with the president of the Church, Peter, and to report on the work that he had been called to do by the Lord himself. Peter and Paul spent two weeks together, at which time Paul probably learned about the development of the Church and more about Jesus' life and teachings. Paul also visited with James, Jesus' younger brother, who appears to have become an apostle.

GALATIANS 2

2:1–2 Paul's next trip to Jerusalem was fourteen years later. He went seeking official sanction for the work that he, Barnabas, Titus, and others were engaged in.

2:7–8 Labels commonly used in the early Church were "they of the circumcision," meaning Jews, and "they of the uncircumcision," meaning Gentiles. Peter directed this division of labor and division of responsibility among the apostles.

2:9 The leaders of the Church extended the full hand of fellowship to the missionaries and renewed their commission to continue taking the gospel to the Gentiles while they themselves—the leaders—continued working with the Jews. It is possible that this visit, or the previous one, gave Peter the opportunity to ordain Paul to the apostleship.

2:11–14 A controversy arose between Paul and Peter over basic matters of Church policy. Several serious disagreements appear among early Church leaders in the book of Acts and in Galatians: Paul versus Barnabas (Acts 15:36–40) and Paul versus Peter (Galatians 2:11–14). The men involved in these conflicts were strong, faithful men. Even great leaders can and do disagree; yet they were faithful, and we revere them.

"Apostles and prophets, being mortal and subject to like passions as other men, have prejudices which sometimes are reflected in ministerial assignments and decisions. But the marvel is not the isolated disagreements on details, but the near universal unity on basic principles; not the occasional personality conflicts, but the common acceptance, for the good of the work, of the faults of others. It is not the conflict between Paul and Barnabas which concerns us, but the fact that they (being even as we are) rose thereafter to spiritual heights where they saw visions, received revelations, and made their callings and elections sure—the fact of their disagreement thus bearing witness that we in our weaknesses can also press forward to that unity and perfection which shall assure us of salvation" (McConkie, *Doctrinal New Testament Commentary*, 2:145).

"Even those who stand highest among the Church leaders have their human weaknesses. Paul may have to rebuke Peter (Galatians 2:11–13). But when they forgive each other, God forgives them. 'It is a true sentiment that great men may err; a higher finish with such is, that their greatness is enhanced by acknowledging their errors'" (Smith and Sjodahl, *Doctrine and Covenants Commentary*, 489).

Another modern scholar illustrates the point in this way: "No doubt Peter had his side of the story. Fear may not have been his motive, and Paul may have acted prematurely. Paul admits that the mission of the 'pillars' was to the Jews (Galatians 2:9). If intense Jewish converts reacted negatively to the [Jerusalem] council decision, James and Peter may have sought a transition delay to convince the stubborn. If Peter labored to bring this about, Paul may have pushed conformity to the council's ruling ahead of its time. Paul evidently retold the story because the Judaizers used the episode to give the impression that Peter agreed with them. *The incident is instructive in showing two strong leaders agreeing on a principle that came by revelation but applying the principle with different timing.* Paul does not say that Peter permanently separated himself from the Gentiles. These candid examples show how revelation came after deep searching. Paul reviewed these examples, of course, to show that Church leaders stood with him in teaching salvation through the revealed gospel, not through the Mosaic law" (Anderson, *Understanding Paul*, 158; emphasis added).

2:16–19 Paul, who had, of course, been an ardent disciple of the Mosaic laws and Judaic traditions, now put down the law of Moses, not because it was bad but because it was not enough. The "law" in Paul's day meant the Torah (the books of Genesis through Deuteronomy) plus rabbinical ritualism and oral traditions (the Talmud was compiled later in many,

many volumes containing thousands of rules and regulations). Paul had been liberated from all of that, and he wanted to be sure that no one was required to observe the old law. It was not necessary for salvation. In fact, to adhere to the law of Moses after Jesus Christ had established the gospel was spiritually destructive, especially after approximately twelve hundred years of Israelite history and apostasy, during which many parts of the law were developed. As Paul explains in verse 18, If I try to build (or go back to) what I dismantled because I knew it wasn't right, then I am a sinner.

Justification, or being accounted righteous, comes through faith in Jesus Christ. And though justification comes only through Jesus Christ, salvation also involves works—not the works of the old law but the works of the gospel of Jesus Christ, as Paul wrote. The true way included both faith and faithfulness. The Lord's instructions for salvation are simple and clear: "If ye love me, keep my commandments" (John 14:15).

A modern scholar explained clearly the difference between justification and sanctification in Paul's discussions: "In its theological sense, justification is a forensic, or purely legal, term. It describes what God declares about the believer, not what He does to change the believer. In fact, justification effects no actual change whatsoever in the sinner's nature or character. Justification is a divine judicial edict. It changes our status only, but it carries ramifications that guarantee other changes will follow. . . .

"In biblical terms, justification is a divine verdict of 'not guilty—fully righteous.' It is the reversal of God's attitude toward the sinner. Whereas He formerly condemned, He now vindicates. Although the sinner once lived under God's wrath, as a believer he or she is now under God's blessing. Justification is more than simple pardon; pardon alone would still leave the sinner without merit before God. So when God justifies He imputes divine righteousness to the sinner (Romans 4:22–25). Christ's own infinite merit thus becomes the ground on which the believer stands before God (Romans 5:19; 1 Corinthians 1:30; Phil. 3:9). So justification elevates the believer to a realm of full acceptance and divine privilege in Jesus Christ. . . .

"Justification is distinct from sanctification because in justification God does not make the sinner righteous; he declares that person righteous (Romans 3:28; Galatians 2:16). Justification imputes Christ's righteousness to the sinner's account (Romans 4:11b); sanctification imparts righteousness to the sinner personally and practically (Romans 6:1–7; 8:11–14). Justification takes place outside sinners and changes their standing (Romans 5:1–2); sanctification is internal and changes the believer's state (Romans 6:19). Justification is an event, sanctification a process. The two must be distinguished but can never be separated. God does not justify whom He does not sanctify, and He does not sanctify whom He does not justify. Both are essential elements of salvation" (MacArthur, *Faith Works*, 89–90).

The only true perspective is to emphasize the infinite grace and mercy of Christ and the power of his atonement in the process of salvation. We mortals do not merit salvation on our own. If we could earn salvation, Christ's mercy, by definition, wouldn't be mercy. It wouldn't be needed. Grace, or mercy, is not earned. Still, human behavior cannot be completely ignored. The very act of believing in Christ, having faith in him, is necessary righteous behavior. As Nephi taught (see 2 Nephi 25:23), we are saved only by the grace of Christ apart from any and all good things we might do—but then again, we must do something. We cannot receive salvation in its fullest sense either by doing nothing or by continuing in sin.

2:20 We are all crucified with Christ and yet live when our sinful natures die. We rise from the symbolic watery grave of baptism to newness of life (see Romans 6:3–10). This transformation is made possible through the crucifixion. Christ lives in us when we take upon ourselves his name and we receive his image in our countenances (Alma 5:14).

GALATIANS 3

3:1–6 In some of the strongest language he ever used, Paul rebuked the Galatian Saints for forgetting principles of the gospel that had been taught clearly to them. More specifically, Paul rebuked them for forgetting the doctrine of Christ and its superiority over the Mosaic law and for forgetting the confirming influence of the Holy Spirit, which they clearly had felt. Paul declared how foolish they were to revert to the Mosaic law because they thought it was the agent of their salvation. Were they going to disregard their faith in the gospel and in the grace of Christ and attempt to attain their goal of salvation through frail human effort? he asked.

3:6–14 Paul invites his Judaizing audience to consider Abraham's whole situation, not just his involvement with circumcision. He had faith and was blessed. In the new dispensation, all who live by the gospel are Abraham's children, whether Jew or Gentile. All who observe the law of Moses rather than the gospel of Christ are under a curse. Jesus redeemed us by becoming a curse for us, thus fulfilling the statement in Deuteronomy 21:23 that "cursed is every one that hangeth on a tree" (Galatians 3:13).

3:19 The Prophet Joseph Smith taught: "When the Israelites came out of Egypt they had the Gospel preached to them, according to Paul in his letter to the Hebrews, which says: 'For unto us was the Gospel preached, as well as unto them: but the word preached did not profit them, not being mixed with faith in them that heard it' (see Heb. iv:2). It is said again, in Gal. iii:19, that the law (of Moses, the Levitical law) was 'added' because of transgression. What, we ask, was this law added to, if it was not added to the Gospel? It must be plain that it was added to the Gospel, since we learn that they had the Gospel preached to them" (*Teachings of the Prophet Joseph Smith*, 60). See verse 19 in the Joseph Smith Translation in the Appendix of the Bible.

3:24 See footnote 24*b* and Mosiah 13:29–31. The law of

Moses was a "schoolmaster"; it was meant to prepare Israel for maturity, for the "adult" laws of the gospel of Jesus Christ. The new covenant superseded the old. We may be justified by faith; that is, Christ may save us (see Appendix 6, 404) *Salvation* in the scriptures often means *exaltation* in God's presence, not just resurrection and immortality.

3:26–29 Baptized disciples of Christ are children of God and heirs of the blessings and promises made to Abraham. If we become Christ's seed through discipleship (Mosiah 15:11), then we are Abraham's seed as well, because Christ was the seed of Abraham just as Paul explained earlier in this epistle (see Galatians 3:16).

GALATIANS 4

4:1–7 Though we are sons and daughters of God, only through Christ can we also become joint heirs of God.

4:8–20 Paul expresses his concern about the Galatian Saints and hopes he has not come to be regarded as an enemy because he told the truth in plainness.

4:21–31 These verses detail the "allegory" of Hagar and Sara. Hagar represents the old temporal law and its representative place of origin, Mount Sinai; Sara represents the new spiritual law, which could be symbolized by one of its places of origin, the Mount where Christ gave the Beatitudes.

GALATIANS 5

5:1 This verse contains a call to stand fast in the liberty of the gospel of Christ and not to be burdened by taking back the yoke of the Mosaic law.

5:2 Circumcision was a token of conformity to all of the Mosaic laws, which, in Paul's mind, represented a rejection of the new covenant and a rejection of Christ.

5:4–5 Men and women cannot be justified without Christ.

5:6 Belief alone? No. Jesus said many times, "Keep my commandments." If belief alone were sufficient, then why did Paul write letters encouraging the Saints to live the gospel?

5:13–16 Beautiful counsel. Saints should live according to the promptings of the Holy Ghost, which will serve as a protection.

5:19–21 "Works of the flesh" are sins that will keep us out of the Lord's kingdom: illicit sexual relations, worshipping things other than God, involvement in the occult, lack of love, feuding, factionalism, intrigue, envying, murders, drunkenness, and so forth.

5:22–23 The "fruit of the Spirit" is all the results of righteous behavior. It is the good works that will allow us to reside in the Lord's presence. As in ancient times, a true disciple in modern times will be loving, happy, peaceful, patient, gentle, faithful, and meek and will demonstrate self-control.

GALATIANS 6

6:2 A real Christian will not have passive belief only but will also help bear others' burdens—that's righteous behavior, or works. The covenant of baptism is also explained in Mosiah 18:8–9.

6:3 On inflated ego, see Doctrine and Covenants 136:19.

6:7–9 The law of the harvest: our own life's harvest can consist only of the fruits of what we've sown.

6:11 A better translation of the Greek would be, "You see what large letters I made when I wrote to you in my own hand." Perhaps Paul used a larger script to emphasize a point.

6:14 By a figure of speech called *metalepsis,* the cross represents not the actual cross itself nor even the Crucifixion but the Atonement and the blessings that come from it.

6:17 "Marks" is the English word used here to translate the Greek *stigmata.* These marks are not marks of shame but of faithfulness. Paul indeed had marks on his body, physical marks testifying of his undying efforts in behalf of the Saints: At Antioch of Pisidia he was forcibly expelled, and at Lystra he was stoned and left for dead.

CHAPTER 7

ROMANS

The letter to the Romans appears immediately after the book of Acts in our King James Version because in this translation the epistles are positioned according to length and doctrinal significance (see Bible Dictionary, "Pauline Epistles: The Second Group").

In the first century after Christ, Rome was the center of the civilized world, with anywhere from one to four million inhabitants.

Paul wrote to the Saints in Rome from Corinth, probably during the winter of A.D. 57–58. He wrote to prepare the members there for his visit and to correct false doctrines promulgated by Judaizers. Ten of the sixteen chapters address the relationship of the Mosaic law to the Christian gospel.

The letter is heavily doctrinal, written to Saints who had already received the gift of the Holy Ghost and had been taught basic doctrines of the kingdom. The epistle to the Romans is the most comprehensive treatment of salvation in the New Testament, touching on the doctrines of justification, sanctification, reconciliation, election, making one's calling and election sure, foreordination, adoption, being joint-heirs with Christ, intercession, mediation, sealing by the Holy Spirit of Promise, and the Second Comforter (see Appendix 6, 404). The epistle to the Romans is, arguably, Paul's greatest theological treatise.

Paul's writings, especially in this letter, are not always clear. We encounter obscure words and ideas elaborated in complicated style and syntax. Furthermore, all of this is even more complicated because the literature has been reworked through the process of translation. All of that makes the presentation of some teachings ponderous and difficult. The chief apostle, Peter, admitted that Paul's writings were at times hard to understand: "Our beloved brother Paul also according to the wisdom given unto him hath written unto you; as also in all his epistles, speaking in them of these things; in which are some things hard to be understood, which they that are unlearned and unstable wrest [twist, distort], as they do also the other scriptures, unto their own destruction" (2 Peter 3:15–16).

Unlike Paul's other epistles, Romans was written to a branch of the Church Paul had neither founded nor had previously visited. The origins of the Church in Rome are hazy. The list of visitors to Jerusalem on the day of Pentecost includes "strangers of Rome, Jews and proselytes" (Acts 2:10). Among the three thousand converts to the Church on that day, surely there must have been some who returned to the great capital of the empire. We know only that by the time this epistle was written, the Church had been in existence there "many years" (Romans 15:23).

ROMANS 1

1:1–7 This passage includes an address and a salutation. Paul was an apostle of the Lord Jesus Christ. Speaking to Oliver Cowdery and David Whitmer in June 1829, the Lord said, "I speak unto you, even as unto Paul mine apostle, for you are called even with that same calling with which he was called" (D&C 18:9). Church members were called Saints then, just as they are today.

1:7–9 The theme and language of Romans parallels Galatians, but the tone is vastly different. Here Paul mentions the faithful reputation of the Saints, their beloved standing before God, and his unceasing prayers for them.

1:10–11, 15 Paul had desired to journey to Rome for

quite some time. He longed to see members he had met in Ephesus, in Corinth, and in other places, and to meet with the rest of the Church in the capital of the empire.

1:16 This verse is the window to Paul's heart and soul. It includes Paul's famous declaration of his bold commitment to the revealed gospel—and what that gospel means to both Jew and Gentile.

1:26–27 The early Church clearly condemned homosexual behavior and other perversions. A modern prophet has said of these sins that a heavy penalty is imposed on the unrepentant (see Kimball, *Miracle of Forgiveness,* 81).

1:28 "Convenient" is the King James translation here of the Greek word meaning "fitting" or "proper." The opposite of the elect is the reprobate or depraved. The power of the priesthood seals the elect to eternal life; this same power casts down the reprobate into darkness (D&C 77:8).

1:29–32 The characteristics of the reprobate are enumerated. "Whispers" refers to gossip.

ROMANS 2

2:1–16 This is a section on how God judges.

2:6 "Deeds" is a translation of the Greek word *ergon.* In the New Testament, this word is translated about 20 times as "deeds" but more than 150 times as "works."

2:11–15 A modern prophet said of these verses: "All men—all living souls, whether they have knowledge of gospel law or not—shall be judged by the law of the gospel. Specifically, he says, those who sin, having not the law, shall perish, meaning they will be condemned for disobedience to a law they never had. . . .

"The fact is they are damned through sin whether they had the gospel law or not. . . .

"To show the justice of such a course the Apostle, having previously named the sins of sexual perversion, murder,

171

fornication, and wickedness of every sort, now says that the Gentiles who have not the law given them by revelation, nonetheless have the law written in their hearts so that their minds and consciences bear record that they should not violate the laws of God [verse 15]. This is another and quite an expressive way of saying that 'the Spirit of Christ is given to every man, that he may know good from evil.' (Moroni 7:16; D. & C. 84:46.) Hence every man, in and out of the Church, whether he has the gospel law or not, is accountable for his deeds and will be judged by gospel standards" (McConkie, *Doctrinal New Testament Commentary,* 2:222).

2:13 We are justified by hearing and by doing.

2:29 Inner motives are more important than outer motions. Compare the Old Testament teaching, "To obey is better than sacrifice, and to hearken than the fat of rams" (1 Samuel 15:22), and the modern-day revelation, "I, the Lord, require the hearts of the children of men" (D&C 64:22).

Romans 3 through 5 support the concept of justification through faith and grace (in fact, the two terms are used more often in Romans than in any other New Testament scripture), but chapters 6 through 8 add the necessity of righteous works. Chapters 12 through 14 identify specific works that lead to salvation. The historical and social setting of the Roman branch of the Church helps explain Paul's discussion. The emphasis on justification by grace, apart from the works of the law, had promoted loose or licentious behavior among some Gentile Christians. Observance of Mosaic customs by some Jewish Christians had caused some Gentiles to believe that observance of Jewish dietary customs, for example, was a total refusal of salvation.

We should study any given scripture in context with all other scripture. About twenty percent of this epistle deals with faith and grace and about thirty percent with works. Paul was speaking to both Jews and Gentiles, emphasizing different aspects of the gospel to each group, according to what each needed to hear.

Grace may be defined as "goodwill," "favor," or "spiritual generosity" (see "Grace," in Ludlow, *Encyclopedia of Mormonism*, 2:560–63). Some go so far as to say that we are saved by the grace of God alone, that we can do nothing to promote our own salvation. William Temple summarized that Protestant tradition: "The only thing of my very own which I can contribute to my redemption is the sin from which I need to be redeemed" (cited in Anderson, *Understanding Paul*, 179).

Salvation, or being born again, is not an event—it is a process. It requires not passive expectation but active participation. Renowned evangelist Billy Graham cautioned Protestants about salvation by grace alone: "Too often we have tended toward superficiality—an overemphasis on easy-believism or experience rather than on true discipleship. We have sometimes offered cheap grace and cheap conversions without genuine repentance" (*Christianity Today*, 17 July 1981, 19).

ROMANS 3

3:1–2 Note the clarification provided by the Joseph Smith Translation. Inner motivations and outward motions are critical in bringing disciples closer to God. A spiritual pedigree is more important than a physical lineage.

3:10–18 These verses contain a series of quotations, mostly from Psalms, that emphasize that all people, both Jew and Gentile, are under the power of sin. Often the quotations are not verbatim but give the general sense. Sometimes they are purposefully paraphrased to underscore a principle.

3:24 Note the arresting changes the Joseph Smith Translation makes to this verse. An individual is justified *only* through the grace of Christ. As 2 Nephi 25:23 teaches, ultimately our salvation comes only by the grace of God, by his good pleasure. No matter how many good deeds we accumulate on this earth, we'll never single-handedly earn our place in the eternal world; it is by his goodwill and favor—that is, by his grace—that we are given the greatest of all the gifts, or favors, of God. Thus Paul teaches: "By the deeds of the law there shall no flesh be justified in his sight" (Romans 3:20). Lehi taught exactly the same doctrine: "And by the law no flesh is justified; or, by the law men are cut off" (2 Nephi 2:5). Were it possible for men and women to keep every aspect of the law of Moses with perfect exactness from the time of birth, then individuals could be justified through the law. But such perfect righteousness is not possible: "because of the fall our natures have become evil continually" (Ether 3:2). In other words, because of Satan we live in a fallen world and the deck is stacked against us. Thus, we need Christ! It is *only* "through the merits, and mercy, and grace of the Holy Messiah" that anyone can dwell in the presence of God (2 Nephi 2:8).

3:28 With the help of the Greek text of the New Testament, we understand that, according to Paul, a person is justified by faith in Jesus Christ, apart from observing the law of Moses. Some Judaizers apparently believed that the Mosaic law said one could earn God's pleasure and glory without external intervention.

ROMANS 4

4:1–25 Though the Jews viewed Father Abraham as the supreme example of someone justified by the works of the law, Paul presents him here as an example of righteousness by faith, just as he did in Galatians (see Galatians 3:6–9).

4:15 "Where no law is, there is no transgression" is rendered in 2 Nephi 9:25 as, "Where there is no law given there is no punishment." There is transgression: a law has still been broken. Compare this with 2 Nephi 2:11–15, which teaches that there is transgression and there is punishment because the law *is* given—it is written in their hearts.

4:16 Note the important change in this verse in the Joseph Smith Translation. Faith and works (righteousness) are two sides of the same coin. In fact, faith involves works (see James 2:17–26). Neither faith nor works can operate in behalf of the Lord's disciples without the Lord's grace and mercy. His grace is not negotiable; it cannot be absent from the equation. Compare Jesus' teachings in the Sermon on the Mount as recorded in Matthew 5:16 and 7:21.

ROMANS 5

5:3–5 These verses contain one of the most dynamic and powerful truths of the gospel—a principle that can be a source of peace and comfort to us in our tribulations. Tribulation gives us experience (a primary reason for mortality) and leads to hope and charity (love of God and humankind) as we patiently consider the will of God. To act impatiently suggests we know more than God does. Such things have been taught in modern revelation with the added insight that the endurance of trials and tribulations leads to perfection (see D&C 24:8; 31:9; 54:10; 66:9; 98:23–24; 67:13).

5:11 This is the only use of "atonement" in the New Testament of the King James Version of the Bible.

5:12–19 Paul teaches the greatness and power of the Atonement. Through Adam's fall, sin and death became the inheritance of the human family. Men and women were born into a fallen, sinful environment (see v. 12). Even before the law of Moses was given, sin was in the world; but sin is not charged or ascribed to a person who is ignorant of the law (see v. 13). And though a person does not commit a sin, that person still suffers the consequences of Adam's transgression (see v. 14). But Christ's uncoerced gift, the Atonement, is infinitely greater than Adam's transgression; though one man's actions created infinite problems, Christ's one act rectified all those problems (see vv. 15–19).

5:20 Sin has multiplied over time in the world; grace,

through Christ, has increased all the more to cover the effects of sin.

5:14–21 Compare the dichotomy between Adam and Christ: Adam gave the offense (the Fall); Christ gave the free gift (the Atonement). Adam brought death; Christ brought life. Adam brought condemnation; Christ brought justification. Because of Adam there is an abundance of sin; because of Christ there is an abundance of grace.

ROMANS 6

6:1–2 Romans 5:20 raises the question, Should people continue to sin so that grace may increase? Some, apparently, thought Paul was giving implicit approval to commit sin because Christ's "free" gift would take care of everything anyway. Paul says, no!

6:3–8 Baptism is symbolic of the death and resurrection of Christ—being buried and then being raised up. The very nature of the symbol clearly suggests immersion. Verse 5 says: "We shall be also [raised] in the likeness of his resurrection." Thus the complete ellipsis is supplied. Baptism crucifies, or destroys, the old sinful person and makes every disciple a new person, alive in Christ.

6:11–18 Righteousness, not sin, should be our master after baptism. We can be free from the servitude of sin through the emancipating and life-giving powers of the Atonement.

6:20–23 The rewards of sin and righteousness are described. Sin leads to spiritual death, but the gift of God is eternal life. Being saved in the kingdom of God "is the greatest of all the gifts of God; for there is no gift greater than the gift of salvation" (D&C 6:13).

ROMANS 7

7:1–6 The law of Moses is like a deceased husband; the wife is no longer subject to him when he is dead. "The law hath become dead unto us, and we are made alive in Christ because of our faith" (2 Nephi 25:25).

Chapter 7 elicits two responses:

First, when we read the words of this chapter as they've been transmitted to us over the ages, we read about Paul, who struggles within himself to overcome sin, who is weighed down in captivity to sin, who is warring inside himself, and who exclaims, "O wretched man that I am!" (v. 24). This poignant self-description is similar to that of the great Nephi, who gives us a very personal glimpse of his heart. He exclaims the identical words Paul later uses: "O wretched man that I am!" and details his own sorrow and grief over his sins, over the temptations that so easily beset him, over his anger towards his antagonists (see 2 Nephi 4:17–29). These two valiant disciples of Christ give the rest of us hope. Their lives and words show us that even the greatest have problems. They also struggle to overcome weaknesses. And they both put their trust in the Lord and were able to triumph over their trials and adversities. Every true strength is gained in a struggle. We all need role models, examples of how to overcome.

Second, though there may be a great lesson to learn from chapter 7 as we have received it, it is hard to believe that Paul, nearly twenty years after his conversion, is still struggling with carnality and finding no good in himself (v. 18). The Joseph Smith Translation alters our view of Romans 7 dramatically, as it draws a distinction between Paul's old life under the Mosaic law and his new life under the gospel of Jesus Christ. He was carnal while under the yoke of the law, but now he is spiritual under the yoke of the gospel—now he is able to overcome and find good through the merits of Christ. Romans 7 in the King James Version does not really represent the Paul we read about in the rest of his writings; it does not reflect the great and valiant changes made in his life after his conversion. Romans 7 in the Joseph Smith Translation gives a more proper impression of the apostle's character.

Although both views teach a powerful lesson, the Joseph

Smith Translation more accurately portrays the mind and soul of Paul at the time he wrote to the Roman Saints.

ROMANS 8

8:1–4 Those who are alive in Christ are under no condemnation, in contrast to those who live under the law of Moses, which cannot save anyone. The law is still important, not for salvation, but as a moral, ethical, and cultural guide.

8:5–10 Paul speaks of the natural man versus the man of the Spirit, who is a new creature in Christ. Compare 1 Corinthians 2:10–16.

8:14–18 Paul continues his discussion of the regenerative powers of the Spirit of God. Is there any question about what the scriptures teach us of our eternal nature and glorious destiny? We are the children of God and have the noble potential of being glorified with our Savior and becoming joint-heirs with him, that is, jointly possessing all things that the Father has (see D&C 50:26–28; 84:38; 88:107; 93:22–28; 132:20).

8:19 Compare the translation of verse 19 in the New International Version: "The creation waits in eager expectation for the sons of God to be revealed."

8:19–27 All creation anticipates a future day of redemption and glory.

8:26 Joseph Smith changed "groanings which cannot be uttered" to "striving which cannot be expressed" (*Teachings of the Prophet Joseph Smith*, 278).

8:28 The first phrase is a remarkable promise—to have all things work together for one's ultimate blessing. The Lord has promised similar things in this last dispensation (D&C 90:24).

8:29 "Predestinate" appears four times in the Bible (though the word *predestination* does not occur at all). There is nothing in the Greek implying loss of agency; the word literally means "to determine [our potential destiny] beforehand." The word *foreordain* more aptly describes the concept. Indeed, the Lord has foreordained, or called and elected, each of us to membership in his kingdom. Confirming that ordination, or making that calling and election sure, is now up to us.

The reformer John Calvin misunderstood the doctrine. He wrote: "By predestination we mean the eternal decree of God, by which he determined with himself whatever he wished to happen with regard to every man. All are not created on equal terms, but some are preordained to eternal life, others to eternal damnation. And accordingly, as each has been created for one or other of these ends, we say that he has been predestined to life or to death" (Calvin, *Institutes of the Christian Religion*, 3.21.5).

8:31 Joseph Smith Translation: "If God be for us, who can prevail against us?" Ultimate failure is out of the question for the disciple of Jesus Christ. No person or circumstance will thwart him or her in the end.

8:35–39 These verses contain one of Paul's most sensitive word-pictures of the love of God.

8:36 The Good Shepherd and his disciple-shepherds knew that in ensuing generations some of the sheep would find themselves in peril and would even be sacrificed for the cause of God: "As it is written, For thy sake we are killed all the day long; we are accounted as sheep for the slaughter" (Romans 8:36; see Psalm 44:22). Some of those who were sacrificed must have hoped to follow their Lord's example: "He was led as a sheep to the slaughter; and like a lamb dumb before his shearer, so opened he not his mouth" (Acts 8:32; see Isaiah 53:7). A lamb or sheep is one of the few animals that does not protest at its time of slaughter but actually remains hushed, pacific, and submissive to the end.

ROMANS 9

Chapters 9–11 explain the law of election, referring to conditional opportunity for salvation, not to unconditional predetermination for salvation (see Bible Dictionary, "Election"). Of Romans 9 the Prophet Joseph Smith said: "The whole of the chapter had reference to the Priesthood and the house of Israel; and unconditional election of individuals to eternal life was not taught by the Apostles. God did elect or predestinate, that all those who would be saved, should be saved in Christ Jesus, and through obedience to the Gospel; but He passes over no man's sins, but visits them with correction, and if His children will not repent of their sins He will discard them" (*Teachings of the Prophet Joseph Smith*, 189).

9:1–5 Paul was emphatic in his love for the Jewish people, but their way was not the way of salvation, even though Christ came through them. Because the Jews rejected Jesus as the Messiah, they forfeited great blessings. Still, the word of God had not failed. The Gentiles accepted the gospel and were adopted into the house of Israel.

9:6 "They are not all Israel [spiritually], which are of Israel"—that is, the real covenant people, who ultimately receive the blessings of eternity, do not receive those blessings merely by lineage but by obedience. The New International Version renders this verse as follows: "In other words, it is not the natural children who are God's children, but it is the children of the promise [gospel] who are regarded as Abraham's offspring" (NIV Romans 9:8).

"The house of Israel was a distinct people in pre-existence" (McConkie, *Doctrinal New Testament Commentary*, 2:276). "This election to a chosen lineage is based on pre-existent worthiness and is thus made 'according to the foreknowledge of God'" (McConkie, *Mormon Doctrine*, 216). God does not bestow preferential status or make a certain group his "covenant people" on an arbitrary basis—they received certain blessings and talents through obedience and conformity to God's will before this life. "Chosenness" also implies obligation and accountability.

9:13 "Hated" is used here to translate a Greek verb that also means "displeased with" or "rejected." Jacob and Esau are used here as a hyperbolic contrast, for, of course, the Lord did not hate Esau. Rather, the Lord's preferential regard for one over the other is based on their righteousness in premortal life (see McConkie, *Doctrinal New Testament Commentary*, 2:277).

9:15 Paul quotes Exodus 33:19.

9:16 God's decisions are not controlled by humans.

9:18 See footnote 18*b*.

9:19–21 Paul anticipates an objection to his reasoning: "If God determines who receives mercy and who 'he hardeneth,' how can God blame anyone for having a hardened heart?" Paul answers by asking who are we to be questioning or counseling God? He then uses the analogy of the potter and the clay to emphasize God's omnipotence and sovereignty in dealing with man. Of course, underlying Paul's argument is the understanding that God is perfectly just and merciful and a person's own actions draw him or her toward or away from God. As the wording of verse 18 in Greek implies, Deity merely leaves someone to their own stubbornness or hardness.

9:23–24 Our lineages were chosen in premortality, and we were foreordained to receive certain blessings, including eternal life (compare Acts 17:26; Alma 13:1–8).

9:32–33 The stumbling stone is Jesus (see commentary on 1 Peter 2:7–8).

ROMANS 10

10:3 "Their own righteousness" was Judaism. "The righteousness of God" was the gospel.

10:9 Confess what? "The word of faith" (v. 8), which is Jesus Christ. True faith in Jesus Christ includes works, both hearing and doing, according to Romans 2:13.

10:12 "All are alike unto God, both Jew and Gentile"

(2 Nephi 26:33). The phrase "is rich unto all that call upon him" means "richly blesses all that call upon him."

10:16 Not all hearken, that is, hear *and obey*.

10:17 Joseph Smith said: "Faith comes by hearing the word of God, through the testimony of the servants of God; that testimony is always attended by the Spirit of prophecy and revelation" (*Teachings of the Prophet Joseph Smith*, 148).

10:18–21 Paul uses a series of quotations from the Old Testament: verse 18 corresponds to Psalm 19:4; verse 19, to Deuteronomy 32:21; verse 20, to Isaiah 65:1; verse 21, to Isaiah 65:2.

The basic message Paul attempts to convey follows a logical progression. The heavens testified of the glory of God. But the Gentiles, who were not a single nation forged by God the way the Jews were, understood better than Israel did. Israel itself is responsible for its rejection by God owing to disobedience.

ROMANS 11

11:1–7 Israel rejected God and not the other way around; a righteous remnant remains.

11:8–9 Paul uses quotations from Deuteronomy 29:4 and Psalm 69:22–23 to support his point.

11:13 Note Paul refers to himself as "the apostle of the Gentiles."

11:14 "Emulation" is unrestrained ambition or envy.

11:11–24 This section discusses "ingrafted branches" or adoption into the house of Israel. "Graffed in," or "grafted in," is an agricultural way of saying "adopted in." Paul uses an analogy from agriculture to make the doctrine clearer. The natural olive tree is Israel; the wild branches are the Gentiles. The natural order of things is that the grafted branches control the destiny of the tree. Hence, a good branch from a tame tree could be grafted into a wild tree and make the wild tree tame. But here Paul describes the process in his analogy contrary to nature, not out of ignorance but to make a point. The conversion of the Gentiles was contrary to the expected order of things from Israel's viewpoint. More important, where the house of Israel was concerned, the convert Gentiles did not change the nature and destiny of the house of Israel. Rather, the Gentiles (the branches) became part of Israel (the tree) contrary to the natural order of things regarding olive trees. Paul seems to know that he has changed the natural order in his analogy so that he might teach the Gentiles the power, importance, and meaning of the house of Israel in God's economy. Even though the gospel was then being taken to the Gentiles on a preferential basis, Israel was still the chosen family and the guardian of the Abrahamic covenant.

11:25 "Until the fullness of the Gentiles be come in," means that since Paul's day, the gospel has been and will continue to be taught to the Gentiles on a preferential basis until they have had a full opportunity to accept it. That is "the fullness of the Gentiles." Then, the message will go again to the Jews (see McConkie, *Doctrinal New Testament Commentary,* 2:290).

11:33–35 Compare Isaiah 40:13–14.

ROMANS 12

Romans 12 through 15 are the "Sermon on the Mount of the epistles" (Anderson, *Understanding Paul,* 193). Included in the beautiful counsel of these chapters are at least fifty commandments. Obeying the commandments, especially loving and serving others, helps to make one's calling and election (that is, one's eternal membership, or citizenship, in the kingdom of God) *sure* or guaranteed. Note the significant and numerous parallels in these chapters to principles found in scriptures of the Restoration.

12:2 In other words, be in the world but not of the world.

12:3 "Not to think of himself more highly than he ought to think" (see Galatians 6:3; D&C 136:19).

12:9 Love without "dissimulation" is love without hypocrisy; it is "love unfeigned" (D&C 121:41).

12:12 Patience in tribulation was a principle the Lord often taught through the Prophet Joseph Smith (D&C 31:9; 54:10; 58:2).

12:14 Compare Matthew 5:44.

12:15 Compare Mosiah 18:8–9 and Doctrine and Covenants 42:45.

12:16 Do not be full of pride and haughtiness but associate with all types of people from all walks of life.

12:17 Jesus, being reviled, "reviled not again" (1 Peter 2:23).

12:18 "Live peaceably with all men"—Mosiah clearly explains how to accomplish this feat (see Mosiah 4:9–13).

12:21 "Overcome evil with good" is what Jesus also taught in the Sermon on the Mount (Matthew 5:44). The old law allowed an eye for an eye and a tooth for a tooth (see Exodus 21:24).

ROMANS 13

13:1 Note the Joseph Smith Translation change.

13:9 The Golden Rule (compare Galatians 5:14).

13:11 Here is an appropriate motto for one's bedroom wall: "Now it is high time to awake out of sleep."

ROMANS 14

14:2–3 This section contains counsel that may be applicable to health food enthusiasts.

14:5 For instance, it is not *the* day but *a* day that is important in Sabbath observance.

14:23 "Whatsoever is not of faith is sin"; doubt is spiritual poison.

ROMANS 15

15:4 The purpose of scripture (compare 2 Timothy 3:14–17).

15:19 Illyricum is present-day Albania and Macedonia. Paul is defining the geographical limits of his missionary work.

15:20 Paul specialized in opening new mission fields rather than building on other men's foundations.

15:24, 28 Paul desired to journey to Spain. He may have accomplished his desire, but we have no written record of it.

ROMANS 16

16:1–2 Phebe was a member of the Church from Cenchrea, the port town south of Corinth. She had assisted Paul in the work before this time, and now she carried Paul's letter to Rome.

16:3–15 Paul had apparently become acquainted with many Roman Saints, probably in Corinth and Ephesus. (Roman citizens were hearty travelers). Twenty-eight individuals, a number of them women, are mentioned by name. Some may even have been relatives of Paul (see vv. 7, 11, and 21).

16:23 Erastus was the chamberlain, or city treasurer (Greek, *oikonomos*), of Corinth City. A stone slab has been discovered in the square east of the theater of Corinth with the following inscription: "ERASTVS PRO AEDILITATE S P STRAVIT"—that is, ERASTUS PRO AEDILITATE SUA PECUNIA STRAVIT—translated into the English, the inscription declares: "Erastus, in return for his aedilship [position as city treasurer], laid this pavement at his own expense."

Inscription mentioning Erastus at Corinth

The pavement dates from the middle of the first century after Christ and was therefore in existence when Paul resided in the city of Corinth. If this is the same Erastus spoken of in the New Testament, it appears that this wealthy and influential politician in Corinth became a member of the Church.

CHAPTER 8

PHILIPPIANS, COLOSSIANS, AND PHILEMON

PHILIPPIANS

Philippians, Colossians, Philemon, and Ephesians are Paul's "prison epistles," written during his first Roman imprisonment while he was under house arrest in the imperial capital (see Acts 28:14–31). Three of these letters—Colossians, Philemon, and Ephesians—appear to have been sent at the same time (compare Colossians 4:7–9; Philemon 10; Ephesians 6:21). When Paul wrote Philippians he was in his own rented house, where for two years he was allowed to receive visitors and teach the gospel. The best evidence favors a date of A.D. 61 or 62 for its composition.

The city of Philippi was named after King Philip II of Macedon, father of Alexander the Great. It was a prosperous Roman colony; its inhabitants were Roman citizens who prided themselves on the superiority of Roman customs (see Acts 16:21). Perhaps that was the background for Paul's exhortation to the Saints to look to heaven as the source of their lasting citizenship (see Philippians 3:17–21).

The letter to Philippi may be the happiest, most positive, and most personal of all Paul's writings. His highest compliments were given to this branch of the Church; he called the Philippian Saints "my joy and crown" (Philippians 4:1). They seem to be the most faithful branch in the Church. At the time the letter was written, it had been ten years since Paul's first visit to the city and the conversion of Lydia, the jailer, and others (see Acts 16; Bible Dictionary, "Pauline Epistles, Philippians").

PHILIPPIANS 1

1:1–5 These verses exhibit the standard characteristics of Paul's letters: identification of the sender, the intended audience, a salutation mentioning God the Father *and* Jesus Christ, and mention of prayerful thanksgiving for the members. Members of the Church are called Saints (see v. 1).

1:6 God, not man, is the source of a person's conversion, progress in the kingdom, and exaltation.

1:7–11 Christ shows his love toward the Saints through Paul; Paul hopes the Saints will perpetuate this love.

1:12 The Lord uses negative events that have happened to Paul (imprisonments, floggings, persecutions) to further the work.

1:13 "In all the palace"—that is, in the praetorium, in Rome.

1:15 Some teach Christ by contention; true followers of Christ should teach by love.

1:19 "Supply" means "support, sustenance."

1:21–24 Christ gives Paul's mortal existence meaning. If he were able to go on living, existence would mean fruitful labor; he was torn, however, between tarrying in mortality or dying and being with Christ. Perhaps John the Beloved felt the same way as he struggled within himself whether to go or to stay.

1:27 "Conversation" is the King James translation of the Greek word meaning "conduct."

PHILIPPIANS 2

2:1–9 Paul continues his exhortation to the Saints, asking them to manifest love, unity, humility, and obedience in their lives—these are the great attributes of Christ and a Zion community (see Moses 7:18–19). Verses 6 through 9 recall the doctrine of the condescension of God. The premortal Jehovah divested himself of divine privileges and willingly condescended to mortal conditions. He abased himself in order to be exalted. That doctrine would have been particularly poignant to Paul, who was then abased in prison for the sake of Christ.

The prophet Lorenzo Snow poetically responded to Paul and to John about the elevated concepts described here.

Dear Brother:
Hast thou not been unwisely bold,
Man's destiny to thus unfold?
To raise, promote such high desire,
Such vast ambition thus inspire?

Still, 'tis no phantom that we trace
Man's ultimatum in life's race;
This royal path has long been trod
By righteous men, each now a God:

As Abra'm, Isaac, Jacob, too,
First babes, then men—to gods they grew.
As man now is, our God once was;
As now God is, so man may be,—
Which doth unfold man's destiny.

For John declares: When Christ we see
Like unto him we'll truly be.
And he who has this hope within,
Will purify himself from sin.

Who keep this object grand in view,
To folly, sin, will bid adieu,
Nor wallow in the mire anew;

Nor ever seek to carve his name
High on the shaft of worldly fame;

But here his ultimatum trace:
The head of all his spirit-race.

Ah, well: that taught by you, dear Paul,
'Though much amazed, we see it all;
Our Father God, has ope'd our eyes,
We cannot view it otherwise.

The boy, like to his father grown,
Has but attained unto his own;
To grow to sire from state of son,
Is not 'gainst Nature's course to run.

A son of God, like God to be,
Would not be robbing Deity;
And he who has this hope within,
Will purify himself from sin.

You're right, St. John, supremely right:
Whoe'er essays to climb this height,
Will cleanse himself of sin entire—
Or else 'twere needless to aspire.
(Improvement Era, *June 1919, 660–61*)

2:10 Christ retains all power (see D&C 19:3). A careful reading of this verse and of Isaiah 45:21–23 reveals that Jesus and Jehovah, the God of the Old Testament, are the same person.

2:12 Exaltation comes through obedience, as it did with Jesus (see Hebrews 5:8–9).

2:15 "Ye shine as lights in the world" (see Matthew 5:16).

2:17 "If I be offered . . . "—for Paul, it is a privilege to wear a martyr's crown and receive the joy of eternal life.

2:25–30 Epaphroditus was a noble emissary to Paul. He had served valiantly with Paul and had greatly assisted in the work. But he had been sick, even "nigh unto death" (vv. 27, 30), and had become a little discouraged when his Philippian friends heard about his illness and worried about him. Paul sent him home with high commendation.

PHILIPPIANS 3

3:2 Figuratively, dogs represent unworthy persons. Peter recalled the proverb, "The dog is turned to his own vomit again; and the sow that was washed to her wallowing in the mire" (2 Peter 2:22). Paul said simply, "Beware of dogs, beware of evil workers" (Philippians 3:2).

3:5–6 These verses detail events in Paul's earlier life.

3:8 "The loss of all things"—Paul's family, of Pharisaic persuasion, likely considered him apostate and disowned him.

"Dung" is a rendering of the Greek word meaning "refuse." Both these words are polite translations.

3:12–14 Paul does not promote "push-button salvation." He knows that salvation is a long, hard struggle. Nor does he consider that he has already arrived at ultimate perfection himself. He will continue to press forward to eventually win "the prize of the high calling of God."

3:20–21 Resurrected bodies of the Saints will be fashioned after Christ's.

PHILIPPIANS 4

4:2 Two sisters seem to have had some disagreement in the Philippi branch of the Church.

4:3 Women and men labored with Paul in the gospel and were regarded by Paul as his equals. They are not named here; but their names are known to God and are recorded in the book of life (see Revelation 3:5; D&C 88:2). Scholars have suggested that the "true yokefellow" may have been Lydia, Paul's first European convert at Philippi (see Acts 16:14–15, 40).

Clement is not mentioned elsewhere in the New Testament. Early Church scholars Origen (A.D. 185–254),

Eusebius of Caesarea (260–339), Epiphanius (315–403), and Jerome (331–420) indicate that this Clement was a younger contemporary of Peter and Paul. He eventually became bishop of Rome. "Clement . . . who became the third Bishop of Rome, was, as the Apostle himself testifies, Paul's fellow-worker and fellow-combatant" (Eusebius, *History of the Church*, 67; see also 80).

4:7 The "peace of God, which passeth all understanding" is the harbinger in this life of exaltation in the life to come.

4:8 When Joseph Smith summarized the beliefs of the Church for editor John Wentworth, he concluded his list of thirteen articles of faith with this admonition of Paul.

4:13 Here is a reference to the source of our confidence.

4:15–18 Philippian Saints had been most concerned about attending to Paul's temporal needs, not just in Philippi but also in Thessalonica, Corinth, and Rome.

4:22 "Caesar's household" may be a reference to some of the Saints employed by the emperor in the palace, Saints who had become converted to the gospel through Paul's preaching. Compare Philippians 1:13.

COLOSSIANS

Paul wrote to the Saints in Colossae during his first imprisonment in Rome (A.D. 61–62). Colossae was a small, unimportant town in Phrygia (it's not even shown on our Bible maps). Laodicea and Hierapolis are two other towns mentioned in this letter (Colossians 4:13); all three were located in the Lycus Valley about one hundred miles east of Ephesus. Philemon and Onesimus lived in Colossae.

The problems that Paul wrote about were false doctrines concerning the Godhead and worship of angels (Colossians 2:18). Paul knew that apostates would disseminate perverse doctrines to draw away disciples from the Lord Jesus Christ (see Acts 20:29–30). Some members or apostates were

denying the physicalness of the Savior, just as some of the
Corinthians denied the idea of bodily resurrection. The basic
issue was whether Jesus was God or man (Monophysitism or
Arianism) or both at the same time. Great diversity of belief
prevailed. Some argued that Christ had one mind (Apollonin-
arianism) or one will (Monothelitism), or that he was born a
man and became a God (Nestorianism). Where there were
two Christians, there were three opinions. Some were also
attempting to displace the preeminent Head with mediating
angels (see Bible Dictionary, "Pauline Epistles, Epistle to the
Colossians).

COLOSSIANS 1

1:1–2 Again Paul distinctly refers to two beings in the
Godhead: "God our Father and the Lord Jesus Christ."

1:5 Our hope is the promise of exaltation through Christ.

1:6–7 Apparently, Epaphras was a missionary who spread
the gospel message at Colossae (compare Colossians
4:12–13).

1:15 Paul wrote that God's Son, Jesus Christ, is the image
(Greek, *icon*) of the invisible (meaning unseen) God (meaning the Father). The scriptures do teach *anthropomorphism*—
not "God in the image of man" but "man . . . in the image of
God," just as Genesis 1:27 says. We have bodies; he has a
body. The Bible notes that God has a face (see Exodus 33:20,
23; Deuteronomy 5:4); he has eyes (see Deuteronomy
11:12); ears (see Ezekiel 8:18); a mouth (see Numbers 12:8;
Deuteronomy 8:3); arms (see Exodus 15:16; Isaiah 52:10);
hands (see Job 10:8; 12:9; Isaiah 11:11); fingers (see Exodus
8:19; 31:18); a heart (see Genesis 6:6; 8:21); and feet (see
Isaiah 60:13), and so forth. Paul constantly talks about the
resurrection of Jesus Christ, emphasizing that he has a glorified body. Luke recorded his witness of the risen Lord:
"Handle me, and see; for a spirit hath not flesh and bones, as
ye see me have" (Luke 24:39). The Prophet Joseph Smith

wrote: "That which is without body, parts and passions is nothing. There is no other God in heaven but that God who has flesh and bones" (*Teachings of the Prophet Joseph Smith,* 181).

Today, as in the days of Colossae, false ideas still abound regarding the nature of God. In A.D. 325 a council was held in Nicaea (which lies some fifty miles southeast of today's Istanbul, Turkey). More than three hundred bishops gathered to decide whether or not the body of Christ was corporeal (physical) and whether or not the Son is the same person as the Father. Since that occasion some wrong ideas have circulated and persisted among Christians. For example, a basic Lutheran creed consists of the following statement: "We unanimously hold and teach, in accordance with the decree of the Council of Nicaea, that there is one divine essence, which is called and which is truly God, and that there are three persons in this one divine essence, equal in power and alike eternal: God the Father, God the Son, God the Holy Spirit" (Leith, *Creeds of the Churches,* 67). Roman Catholicism, the Church of England, and the Methodist Church all subscribe to a similar ideological portrayal of God: "There is but one living and true God, everlasting, without body or parts . . . And in the unity of this Godhead there are three persons, of one substance, power, and eternity—the Father, the Son, and the Holy Ghost" (Leith, *Creeds of the Churches,* 354; compare 266–67).

The Old and New Testaments clearly present the doctrine of the Godhead, the same doctrine as revealed through prophets and apostles of the Church of Jesus Christ in our own day: "We believe in God, the Eternal Father, and in His Son, Jesus Christ, and in the Holy Ghost" (Article of Faith 1). "These three constitute three distinct personages and three Gods" (Smith, *Teachings of the Prophet Joseph Smith,* 370). "The Father has a body of flesh and bones as tangible as man's; the Son also; but the Holy Ghost has not a body of flesh and bones, but is a personage of Spirit" (D&C 130:22).

1:16 "Visible and invisible" means seen and unseen.

1:17 This verse is a powerful witness of modern revelation. "By him all things consist" means that all things continue to operate by and through the light of Christ, as Joseph Smith learned (see D&C 88:6–13).

1:18 Christ is the Head of the Church; he is preeminent—a warning against presuming to put angels (see Colossians 2:18) or anyone else ahead of him.

1:19 It pleased the Father to vest in the Son all power in heaven and on earth (see Matthew 28:18) and to share all things with him. The Son is perfect even as the Father is perfect (see 3 Nephi 12:48). Paul teaches the same concept using different words in Colossians 2:9.

1:26 "The mystery" refers to Christ, who is made known only to spiritual persons.

COLOSSIANS 2

2:8 Here is a warning against intellectualism; we must be careful of the philosophies and traditions of men—they are not as credible as scripture.

2:9–10 God is a physical person. Greek *soma* refers to the physical body. The Father and the Son both have all power. Just as Christ shares all things with the Father, so the Saints may share all things through Christ.

2:11 The circumcision of Christ refers to spiritual circumcision, or the cutting away of the carnal nature.

2:12 Compare Romans 6:3–6.

2:16 Don't judge others by the Mosaic law; in other words, avoid legalism. "Sabbath days" are the seventh day.

2:18 Gnostic philosophy held that God's contacts with men and women were through angelic mediators. Paul denounced the idea. Christ is the Head, and somebody was falsely emphasizing the role of angels.

2:21–22 See Joseph Smith Translation.

2:23 "Will worship" was man-made worship. "Neglecting of the body" was a tendency of the Gnostics. They believed that men and women were saved through secret or esoteric knowledge and that the physical body is evil. This led to two extremes: complete denial of marriage and sexual relations; or complete indulgence and satisfaction of the physical urges. Both negated the purpose and value of the human body.

COLOSSIANS 3

3:2 Paul wrote some great one-liners. If only we'd listen to his counsel.

3:3 "Your life is hid with Christ in God": some Colossian Saints had had their calling and election made sure; that is, they were sealed up unto eternal life. Historical records show that on 16 May 1843, Joseph Smith declared that a member of the Church had his calling and election made sure. Later, the Prophet wrote of this occasion, "Putting my hand on the knee of William Clayton, I said: Your life is hid with Christ in God, and so are many others. Nothing but the unpardonable sin can prevent you from inheriting eternal life" (*History of the Church,* 5:391).

3:5–9 "Mortify therefore your members"—in other words, deaden (the literal meaning of *mortify*) and control your carnal desires. On the most basic level, control anger, sexual drives, and dishonesty; beyond basic control, develop real love, or charity.

3:9 "The old man" signifies the natural man.

3:12–14 These verses describe a person filled with charity and spiritual power. Compare Doctrine and Covenants 121:41–45. Both Paul and Joseph Smith were incarcerated when they received strikingly similar counsel for the Saints.

3:18–22 This is beautiful counsel to wives, husbands,

children, fathers, and servants. "Submit" indicates a willingness to give oneself over to the guidance of another.

COLOSSIANS 4

4:1 Regarding masters and servants, see the introduction to Philemon.

4:5–6 Paul counsels the Saints on their conversations with those outside the faith. Salt was a symbol of the covenant in ancient times. Salt is also a preservative and enhances flavor. Christian conversation is to be tasteful and tasty (interesting) and oriented toward the covenant.

4:13 See "Hierapolis," 372.

4:14 This verse refers to the occupation of Luke, the writer of the Gospel of Luke and the book of Acts.

4:16 Some claim that the Bible as presently constituted is the complete word of God and that we should not consider receiving any more revelation. Colossians 4:10 and 16, on the other hand, indicate that some epistles written by Paul are now missing. Therefore, scholars ask, Is the canon of scripture full? Do we now have all the inspired words that prophets and apostles have ever written?

PHILEMON

Philemon was apparently a rich and faithful member of the Church, a resident of Colossae. Paul's personal letter (circa A.D. 61–62) to his convert friend pleads the cause of Onesimus, Philemon's runaway Greek slave, who had joined the Church. Slavery, or servitude, was not viewed as evil by the Judaeo-Christian culture at the time of Christ; it was an institution supported by Roman law. Slaves actually constituted twenty to thirty percent of the population of the empire. Paul wrote about a sensitive problem. He was legally bound to encourage Onesimus to return to Philemon, but Paul's challenge was to help Philemon understand that the man will

The unexcavated mound of Colossae (center right)

be coming back different—not as a slave but as a brother (see v. 16).

Onesimus had done something illegal in running away, and the punishment for runaway slaves was usually death (he possibly had stolen something, too; see v. 18). Paul calls on Philemon to exercise the gospel principle of forgiveness in behalf of his servant (see Bible Dictionary, "Pauline Epistles, Epistle to Philemon"). "He that forgiveth not his brother his trespasses standeth condemned before the Lord; for there remaineth in him the greater sin" (D&C 64:9).

PHILEMON 1

1:2 Apphia is the name of a woman who may have been Philemon's wife. Archippus may have been a local leader of the Church.

1:9 "Paul the aged" (Greek, *presbyteis*, "elder"). That may be a priesthood title, or perhaps Paul was older than Philemon.

1:10–11 The Greek name *Onesimus* means "helpful" or

"profitable" and was a common name for slaves. Note the play on his name in verse 11.

1:18–19 Paul is willing to make up any financial loss to Philemon, but he includes a subtle note about the leverage he has since Philemon owes infinitely more to Paul.

1:22 Paul is interested in making a personal visit soon.

1:23 Epaphras was a resident of Colossae who carried Paul's letter.

1:24 Paul's companions and fellow missionaries: John Mark and Aristarchus were fellow prisoners (see Colossians 4:10). The name *Demas* is probably a contraction of *Demetrius* or *Demarchus*. He had been imprisoned at first with Paul but later apostatized (see 2 Timothy 4:10).

CHAPTER 9

EPHESIANS

Ephesians is addressed to the members of the Church in Ephesus and was written during Paul's first Roman imprisonment (A.D. 61–62). It might have been a circular letter for many branches in Asia. It is a deeply spiritual sermon having no central subject but rather a summary of Church doctrine and an outline of Church organization. Paul wrote of no grave crises in this letter. In fact, many Saints in Ephesus had been living righteously enough to be sealed up to eternal life (see Ephesians 1:13; Bible Dictionary, "Pauline Epistles, Epistle to the Ephesians").

EPHESIANS 1

1:1 Paul emphasizes his apostolic commission from Christ in almost every letter he wrote.

1:2 Paul uses "grace" twelve times and "peace" seven times in Ephesians.

1:3, 17 The separate identity of God the Father and his Son are clearly set forth.

1:4–5 Verse 4 contains a direct allusion to premortal life, and both verses teach the doctrine of foreordination. "Predestinate" is used to translate the Greek *prohoridzo,* which has three variations of meaning: to anticipate, to set before, or to cause in advance. There is no negation of agency in the meaning of the term. The traditional Christian definition of predestination is that God predetermines our destination (according to St. Augustine, Calvin, and others). But Paul

200

Ruins of the Library of Celsus at Ephesus

teaches that foreordination preserves our agency and choice. God can foreordain us to our various callings and assignments in mortality, and he can know in advance our response, because of his omniscience, his perfect foreknowledge. He is not guessing, hoping, or expecting; he knows all things. Still, he does not "fix" our destination beforehand; we are agents and make the choices that will determine our destiny. In essence, we are here not to prove ourselves to God but to prove ourselves to ourselves.

1:10 "The dispensation of the fulness of times" is the last dispensation or bestowal of the Gospel fulness. It is the same as the "last days," the final part of this last millennium of the earth's telestial existence. During this period of time all things that have ever been given to man in previous dispensations will be gathered together and restored to earth (see Bible Dictionary, "Dispensations"). "The dispensation of the fullness of times will bring to light the things that have been revealed in all former dispensations; also other things that have not been before revealed. He shall send Elijah, the Prophet, and so forth, and restore all things in Christ" (Smith, *Teachings of the Prophet Joseph Smith*, 193).

"For it is necessary in the ushering in of the dispensation of the fulness of times, which dispensation is now beginning to usher in, that a whole and complete and perfect union, and welding together of dispensations, and keys, and powers, and glories should take place, and be revealed from the days of Adam even to the present time" (D&C 128:18).

1:13 Being "sealed with that Holy Spirit of promise" is the same as having one's calling and election made sure (Smith, *Teachings of the Prophet Joseph Smith*, 149; see 2 Peter 1:4–19; McConkie, *Doctrinal New Testament Commentary*, 2:493–95).

1:21 Paul emphasizes the exalted status of Christ.

1:22–23 The Church is the body of Christ.

EPHESIANS 2

2:1–5 The Saints are made alive in Christ.

2:8 Ultimately, all are saved by grace. Works cannot save us, but obedience to God's commandments cannot be ignored. Paul taught that we are saved not by faith alone nor by works alone; there must be a balance. The grace versus works controversy is, as C. S. Lewis once commented, like "asking which blade in a pair of scissors is [more] necessary" (*Mere Christianity*, 129). Faith and works are two sides of the same coin. The emphasis is not going to the extreme with either one but maintaining balance.

2:9 Romans 10:9 seemingly teaches the same doctrine as that taught in this verse (but see also Romans 2:13; 2 Nephi 25:23). A spirit body, physical body, resurrection, forgiveness, and the Atonement are unearned gifts of grace bestowed by God's loving kindness. Despite our belief that when we obtain any blessing from God, it is by obedience to the law upon which it is predicated (D&C 130:20–21), it is true that we do not earn or deserve every blessing that comes to us.

2:11–22 "Uncircumcision" and "Circumcision" are symbolic names for Gentiles and Jews (v. 11). Christ reconciles individuals not only to himself and the Father but also to each other. The Saints are united to each other in one body—the Church.

2:12 "Having no hope, and without God in the world" is life without light.

2:14 Surrounding the ancient Temple was a stone balustrade (Hebrew, *soreg*), or partition wall, about four and a half feet high, with inscriptions posted in Greek and Latin warning Gentiles not to pass beyond into exclusively Jewish space. Jesus Christ had now symbolically broken down or taken away that barrier between Gentile and Jew.

2:19 In the gospel the Gentiles are no longer "strangers and foreigners," the latter term being the very word used in the inscription on the balustrade forbidding Gentiles to approach closer to God, as did the Jews. Gentiles could now be fellow citizens and fellow heirs by adoption into the covenant people (see Ephesians 3:6).

2:20–21 The foundation of the Church of Jesus Christ is apostles and prophets—one unmistakable evidence of his true Church. And he, himself, is the chief cornerstone. A cornerstone is the massive stone at the foundation corner that provides stability and strength for the structure and serves as a guide for all other foundation stones. In Christ, Jew and Gentile are bound together to create one unified people.

"The chief cornerstone of the church is Jesus Christ; apostles and prophets constitute the remainder of its authorized foundation. (Ephesians 2:20; 1 Corinthians 12:28.) The superstructure of lesser authorities cannot viably rest upon any other foundation. When God removed that foundation, the edifice collapsed and its debris was used to build the many churches now dotting the Christian landscape" (Turner, "Grace, Mysteries, and Exaltation," 114).

EPHESIANS 3

3:1 Paul's imprisonment came as a result of his unbending commitment to Christ.

3:3–6 A mystery is a sacred truth made known by revelation. The mystery spoken of here is that both Jew and Gentile alike may become heirs of the covenant through Christ, a doctrine not understood by ancient Israel.

3:8 Here is evidence of Paul's sincerity and humility.

3:14–21 This is Paul's prayer for the Ephesian Saints.

3:15 Paul teaches that all those who follow Christ take upon themselves his name and become his seed, just as the Book of Mormon teaches (see Mosiah 15:11; 27:25).

EPHESIANS 4

4:1 See Ephesians 3:1.

4:2–6 Paul constantly preached and prayed for unity among the Church members. The Lord also revealed to Joseph Smith that unity is a key law of the celestial kingdom (D&C 105:3–5). There is only one true Lord, one true faith, one true baptism, and one true Father of all. Unlike the current belief of many Christians, baptism and membership in the true Church of Jesus Christ are necessary for salvation in the fullest sense.

4:9 This passage certainly points us to Christ's condescension, but it could also apply to his visit to the spirits in prison.

4:11 Christ established his Church with apostles and prophets—he considered these offices essential to the salvation of the Church. Because Jesus did not do any unnecessary or unimportant things, one might wonder why there have not been more attempts by others to duplicate the ecclesiastical structure of the Lord's Church as a basis for claiming authority.

"Evangelist" is a flexible title in the New Testament (see Bible Dictionary, "Evangelist"). Its parallel today would be "patriarch." The Prophet Joseph Smith wrote: "An Evangelist is a Patriarch. . . . Wherever the Church of Christ is established in the earth, there should be a Patriarch for the benefit of the posterity of the Saints, as it was with Jacob in giving his patriarchal blessing unto his sons, etc." (*Teachings of the Prophet Joseph Smith*, 151).

The Latin word *pastor* means "shepherd," one who leads a flock, as does a bishop or stake president. The term is translated variously in the English New Testament as "pastor," "shepherd," or "bishop."

4:12–14 The officers and leaders that Paul lists as the heads of the Church of Jesus Christ are still needed today. Paul reasons that we need apostles, prophets, evangelists, pastors, teachers, and others because the Saints are not yet perfected. Moreover, the work of the ministry is not yet accomplished, the body of Christ is not yet wholly edified, we have not yet come to a unity of the faith and knowledge of the Son of God, and we are still children carried about with every wind of doctrine. Until all these objectives are reached, we still need mortal leaders to show us the way.

Verse 12 mentions "saints." "Saints" (or "holy ones") is used to translate *kedoshim* (ten times) and *hassidim* (nineteen times) in the Hebrew Bible (the Old Testament). The English word *saint* comes from the Latin *sanctus* and is used to translate the Greek *hagios* in the New Testament. Today, the name of the Church in Hebrew is *Knesiat Yeshua haMashiah lekdoshei akharit hayamim* [. . . Saints of Latter-days]. All of these terms translated "saints" mean "holy ones." The intent is that the members of the Church are to become a holy people. The term in no way conveys aloofness from sin or any suggestion of superiority over other people. Saints are members of the Lord's Church who are trying to become holy. The members of the Church are given the name because they attempt to live a holy life.

4:18–19 Some individuals have alienated themselves from God through refusing to look to God, by being "past feeling," and giving themselves over to lasciviousness or immoral desires. We must never get to the point of being "past feeling" and consciously ignoring serious consequences of sin.

4:26 "Let not the sun go down upon your wrath"—good counsel to individuals and couples. Before the day ends, try to resolve any friction between you and anyone you may have offended or by whom you may have been offended.

4:30 This is another reference to being sealed by the Holy Spirit of Promise or having a guarantee of exaltation.

EPHESIANS 5

5:4–6 In a list of sins to watch out for, Paul warns against involvement in "filthiness," in a sexual context, "foolish talking," and "jesting" (v. 4). The last term anciently connoted something even more negative than joking: it meant using polished and clever speech to accomplish evil purposes, similar to what the Book of Mormon calls "flattery." Paul also issues a warning against being deceived by flattery (see v. 6).

5:8–14 The righteous are the children of light, the wicked are the children of darkness. The Dead Sea Scrolls from Qumran, discovered and translated during the last half of the twentieth century, also used the light-darkness metaphor.

5:15–17 Paul used contrasts vividly. Here he juxtaposes wisdom and foolishness.

5:22–33 These verses contain counsel on husband-wife relations. Wives are encouraged to "submit" to their husbands, just as the husbands submit to the Lord. The scriptures use the term "submit" in various contexts: we should submit to each other (see Ephesians 5:21); we should submit to government leaders (see Romans 13:1, 5; Titus 3:1); we should submit to Church leaders (see 1 Corinthians 14:32; 16:16; Hebrews 13:17); and we should submit to the Lord (see James 4:7; Mosiah 3:19). In other words, Paul is teaching accountability. Everyone is accountable to someone. The Islamic religion exemplifies the concept of "submission," for the Arabic word *Islam* means, literally, "submission." A Muslim is one who submits to the will of God (Arabic *Allah* is related to Hebrew *Elohim*). Submitting to the will of God is a beautiful and sacred concept. God really does want our hearts, our obedience, our dedication, our loyalty and allegiance; he wants us to turn from doing our own pleasure and submit to his will. "Sanctification cometh because of their yielding their hearts unto God" (Helaman 3:35).

In the same spirit of submission to God, the wife is counseled to submit to her husband—certainly not in the sense of cowering servitude but in the sense of honoring or respecting his leading role in their companionship and in the home. It is clear in the scriptures and in the present-day Church that if the husband himself is not honoring that role, the wife has no obligation to submit to his guidance. The patriarchal order of priesthood and the macho, male chauvinist mentality are not the same. Wives are encouraged to follow the lead of their husbands *in righteousness*. Christ came to serve; husbands should do the same. Doctrine and Covenants 121 gives the most sublime and pointed description of the proper use of priesthood power in the home: "The rights of the priesthood are inseparably connected with the powers of heaven, and . . . the powers of heaven cannot be controlled nor handled only upon the principles of righteousness. That they may be conferred upon us, it is true; but when we undertake to cover our sins, or to gratify our pride, our vain ambition, or to exercise control or dominion or compulsion upon [others], in any degree of unrighteousness, behold, the heavens withdraw themselves; the Spirit of the Lord is grieved; and when it is withdrawn, Amen to the priesthood or the authority of that man. No power or influence can or ought to be maintained by virtue of the priesthood, only by persuasion, by long-suffering, by gentleness and meekness, and by love unfeigned" (vv. 36–37, 41).

With that kind of spirit operating in the home, no one would be abused. In the celestial covenant, both husband and wife must be committed to a celestial lifestyle and celestial attitudes.

In verse 25 husbands are counseled to love their wives, just as Christ loves his bride, the Church. Men ought to love their wives as themselves (see v. 28). Both husbands and wives should love and reverence each other (see v. 33)—the counsel is reciprocal.

EPHESIANS 6

6:1–3 This is good counsel to children.

6:4 Fathers are not to provoke their children. "We seldom get into trouble when we speak softly. . . . The voice of heaven is a still small voice" (Hinckley, *Ensign*, June 1971, 72).

6:5–9 There were millions of slaves in the Roman Empire; perhaps 30 percent of the population was slaves. The Church did not advocate social reform regarding slavery in those days. Counsel is given here to servants and masters.

6:11–17 Here is a series of metaphors about the spiritual guards we set up to protect ourselves from temptation and a comparison of these guards to the armor of a fighting man. In a very real sense, we are waging a war, not against flesh and blood (mortals) but against Satan and his forces, who are the powers of darkness. Our protective shields are truth and righteousness. In these verses, the loins represent the vital organs, typifying virtue, chastity; the breastplate covers the heart, the center of feelings, which translate into conduct; our feet represent goals, or our objectives in life—the path we walk; the helmet covers the head, the center of our thoughts; our weapons are faith and knowledge of the scriptures.

THE WHOLE ARMOR OF GOD

Many years ago Elder Harold B. Lee gave us great insight into how Paul's metaphorical discussion of the Christian soldier can apply to Latter-day Saints. He said that Paul understood that our most deadly contest in life is not with human enemies but with the devil. Paul pictures "each of us as a warrior being clothed with the essential armor to protect the four parts of the human body which apparently Satan and his hosts have found to be the most vulnerable—through which the enemies of righteousness may invade the human soul." Elder Lee then quoted Ephesians 6:14–15, 17 and gave important commentary.

"'Stand therefore, having your loins girt about with truth, and having on the breastplate of righteousness;

"'And your feet shod with the preparation of the gospel of peace;

"'And take the helmet of salvation, . . . '

"Truth is to be the substance of which the girdle about your loins is to be formed if your virtue and vital strength are to be safeguarded. How can truth protect you from one of the deadliest of all evils, unchastity? Remember that the Lord tells us that truth is knowledge—'knowledge of things as they are, and as they were, and as they are to come;' (D&C 93:24.)

"Those who become worthy and enter into the new and everlasting covenant of marriage in the temple will be laying the first cornerstone for an eternal family home in the celestial kingdom. Their reward is to have 'glory added upon their heads forever and forever.' These eternal truths, if you believe them with all your soul, will be as a girdle of armor about your loins to safeguard your virtue as you would protect your life. But if you allow the vain theories of men to cause you to doubt your relationship to God, the divine purpose of marriage, and your future prospects for eternity, you are being victimized by the master of lies because all such is contrary to truth which saves you from these perils.

"Now, what about the breastplate which will safeguard your heart or your conduct in life? It shall be made of a stuff called righteousness. The righteous man strives for self-improvement, knowing that he has daily need of repentance for his misdeeds or his neglect. He endeavors to make each day his masterpiece so that at night's close he can witness in his soul to God that whatever has come to his hand that day, he has done to the best of his ability. His body is not dissipated by the burdens imposed by the demands of riotous living; his judgment is not rendered faulty by the follies of youth; he is clear of vision, keen of intellect, and strong of body. The breastplate of righteousness has given him the 'strength of ten—because his heart is pure.'

"Your feet, which represent your goals or objectives in life, are to be shod with 'The preparation of the gospel of peace.' Preparedness is the way to victory, and 'Eternal vigilance is the price of safety.' Fear is the penalty of unpreparedness and aimless dawdling with opportunity. Whether in speech or in song, in physical or moral combat, the tide of victory rests with him who is prepared.

"And now to the last piece of the prophet teacher's armored dress. We will put a helmet upon the head. Our head or intellect is the controlling member of the body. It must be well protected against the enemy for 'as a man thinketh in his heart, so is he.' Ours is to be the 'helmet of salvation.' Salvation means the attainment of the eternal right to live in the presence of God the Father and the Son as a reward for a good life in mortality. With the goal of salvation ever in our mind's eye as the ultimate to be achieved, our thinking and our decisions which determine action will always challenge all that would jeopardize that glorious future state. The one who confidently looks forward to an eternal reward for his efforts in mortality is constantly sustained through his deepest trials. When he is disappointed in love, he does not commit suicide. When loved ones die, he doesn't despair; when he loses a coveted contest, he doesn't falter; when war and destruction dissipate his future, he doesn't sink into a depression. He lives above his world and never loses sight of the goal of his salvation.

"If we would refrain from murder, we must learn not to become angry; if we would free ourselves from sexual sin, we must control immoral thoughts; if we would avoid the penalty of imprisonment for theft, we must learn not to covet. If we would be strong against all kinds of temptation, we must prepare ourselves ahead of time, to meet the temptation face to face. There must be courage and determination and continual aggressiveness to the right in order to win the 'battle of life' else all the armor in the world suggested for our protection would be of no avail.

"To help us be aggressive in our fight we do what Paul suggested: . . .

"'Above all, taking the shield of faith, wherewith ye shall be able to quench all the fiery darts of the wicked.

"'And take . . . the sword of the Spirit, which is the word of God.' (Eph. 6:16–17).

"Note how the 'shield of faith' and the 'sword of the Spirit, which is the word of God' work together. Guided by faith taught by the Word of God, we view life as a great process of soul training. By faith, as the Word of God teaches, we understand that whatever contributes to our becoming more like him, is good for us, even though painful to us at times" (Lee, "Put on the Whole Armor of God").

CHAPTER 10

FIRST TIMOTHY, TITUS, AND SECOND TIMOTHY

First and Second Timothy and Titus reflect the travels and teachings of Paul after the book of Acts concludes. Written from a "pastor" to "pastors," these three letters are called the Pastoral Epistles and have been so designated for the last 350 years (Latin *pastor* means "shepherd"). Timothy and Titus were indeed shepherds, or leaders, of the flock of God in their respective regions. Timothy was a Church leader and teacher at Ephesus (1 Timothy 1:3), and because one of his duties was to appoint bishops (local unit leaders), he himself was apparently a regional officer, or what we today might call an area authority.

The epistles to Timothy and Titus were probably written not long after the events described in Acts 28, following Paul's first imprisonment (or house arrest) in Rome. That is implied both by his own letters and by the early Church historian Eusebius (*Ecclesiastical History*, 2.22.2–3). Furthermore, Paul wrote Titus to meet him in Nicopolis, apparently after his release from prison (see Titus 3:12). To Timothy he wrote that "no man stood with me, but all men forsook me. . . . Notwithstanding the Lord stood with me, . . . and I was delivered out of the mouth of the lion" (2 Timothy 4:16–17).

Paul had commissioned Titus to act as his representative in Crete and put Timothy in charge of the Church at Ephesus (see 1 Timothy 1:3). Paul then went to Philippi (Macedonia, or northern Greece) where he wrote his first letter to Timothy and one to Titus sometime between A.D. 63

and 66. Later Paul traveled back to Rome, where he was imprisoned a second time, and there he wrote 2 Timothy before being executed around A.D. 67 or 68 (see Bible Dictionary, "Timothy," "Titus," "Pauline Epistles: The Fourth Group").

1 TIMOTHY

The first epistle to Timothy contains counsel on Church and priesthood organization; it also includes encouragement to teach sound doctrine and thus avoid apostasy. Early in the Christian era, theological corruptions were manifested under the generic title of Gnosticism. The Greek word *gnosis* means "knowledge," even secret knowledge. Gnostics were the "deep mystery people." Some of the basic tenets of this theological movement included, first, the idea that corporeality is evil—some Gnostics were against everything with a physical nature. Physical activities, such as sexual relations and even eating, were considered perverse. Some Gnostics were "forbidding to marry" (1 Timothy 4:3). Second, Gnostics believed there were intermediaries between God and mortals; they taught the preeminence of subdeities, or angels (recall the Colossian heresy, worship of angels). Finally, the Gnostics believed salvation comes by secret knowledge—a corruption of a true principle (see "Gnosticism," 297).

1 TIMOTHY 1

1:2–3 Paul mentions Timothy in the beginning verses of seven of his letters; he commends Timothy for his faithfulness and trustworthiness in three of them. Truly, Paul loved and relied on his younger friend and companion. He also gave Timothy important assignments (see 1 Corinthians 4:17; 1 Thessalonians 3:1–2).

1:4 "Endless genealogies" were doubtful, untruthful genealogies, tampered with for improper purposes. A modern apostle has addressed the "endless genealogies" spoken of in this verse: "The scriptures contain condemnation of 'endless genealogies,' rebuking the ancients for seeking their ancestry for the wrong purposes. Those things happen today when a search is made into the past to find some basis for prestige, to make connections with the 'right' family, to run the thread of relationship simply to tie to royalty or to prominence, or to lay claim to properties in an unworthy way. We should be careful of this. The purpose for seeking the names of our kindred and running the chain back as far as we can find it is to give something to our progenitors, not to get something from them" (Packer, *Holy Temple*, 225; see also Smith, *Answers to Gospel Questions*, 1:214–15).

1:5 The ultimate capstone of all the commandments is charity.

1:6 "Vain jangling" is fruitless debate or intellectualizing.

1:8–10 The law of Moses was given by God, but it was a lesser law given for those not ready spiritually for a higher law.

1:13 Before Saul's conversion on the road to Damascus, he was an intense enemy of the Church, and thus of the truth. But he was given mercy—the Atonement operated in his behalf—and he repented.

1:15–16 The way Christ dealt with Paul is a pattern for all of us.

1:20 "Delivered unto Satan" means excommunicated.

1 TIMOTHY 2

2:1–3 We ought to pray for those in authority—we would get better leadership.

2:4 The Savior desires all to be saved but will force no one—in contrast to Satan (Moses 4:1–4).

2:5–6 Modern revelation also testifies that Jesus is the mediator of the new covenant. He justifies men and women and then perfects them (see D&C 76:69; 107:19; 2 Nephi 2:9).

2:9–12 This passage is a sort of honor code as well as dress and grooming standards for women of the first century after Christ.

2:9 In other words, women should avoid vain styles and practices adopted from pagan temples and from Roman society of the time.

2:11–12 The Greek word translated here as "silence" means quietness, tranquillity. For "silence" and "subjection," see commentary on 1 Corinthians 14:34 (144). The intent of this passage is to counsel that women should support their leaders and not try to dominate or usurp authority over those who are called of God as priesthood leaders.

2:14 Rather than being criticized, Eve should be honored for her bold willingness to initiate mortality for all humankind. The Greek of verse 14 suggests that Paul believed Eve's transgression consisted in her overstepping her bounds by usurping authority to make a decision that affected both herself and Adam. The Greek word *parabasis*, translated here as "transgression," means, literally, "to overstep."

1 TIMOTHY 3

3:1 Someone facetiously said that the King James Version left out a critical word: "If a man desire the office of a bishop, he desireth a good work*out!*"

3:2–7 This passage lists the first century qualifications for being a bishop. The title "bishop" derives from the Greek *episcopos: epi*, which means "over" (as in the *epi*center of an earthquake, or the spot over which the quake centers), and *scopos*, meaning "look" or "watch." Therefore, an *episcopos*, or bishop, is one who watches over the flock as an overseer or supervisor. (The Episcopalian denomination is so named because of its emphasis on bishops.)

3:2 "The husband of one wife" means not practicing polygamy but being absolutely faithful to his one spouse.

3:3 "Not greedy of filthy lucre"—Elder Spencer W. Kimball (Conference Report, October 1953, 52) commented: "I feel strongly that men who accept wages or salary and do not give commensurate time, energy, devotion, and service are receiving money that is not clean."

3:4 Any abuse of wife or child would disqualify a man from leadership in the Lord's Church.

3:5 A bishop must be a good father to his own children, for he becomes a father to an entire congregation.

3:8 Other offices, such as deacon, are also described. "We believe in the same organization that existed in the Primitive Church . . ." (Article of Faith 6).

3:12 In Paul's day, the office of deacon carried different responsibilities. In addition, the deacons were often older and married.

3:15 Note the change of emphasis given by the Joseph Smith Translation.

1 TIMOTHY 4

4:1 "In the latter times"—each dispensation has its "latter days"; the prophecy applies to both his day and ours (see also 2 Timothy 3:1–7).

4:2 "Seared with a hot iron"—a loss of sensitivity for doctrine and for others' feelings will burn the apostate's consciences.

4:3 The number one problem listed was "forbidding to marry"—a problem for Gnostics back then and for some in modern times, too. Marriage, to be sure, is part of the heart and soul of the gospel. If there is no marriage, there is no fulfillment of God's "work and glory," the immortality and eternal life of each of us. We are exalted only as couples.

4:12–16 Paul gives personal counsel for each of us.

4:12 "Let no man despise thy youth"—Nephi was a young man, too; Jesus was only twelve when he confounded the learned doctors; Joseph Smith was only fourteen when he walked out of the Sacred Grove with monumental and marvelous truths.

4:14 "We believe that a man must be called of God, by prophecy, and by the laying on of hands by those who are in authority, to preach the Gospel and administer in the ordinances thereof" (Article of Faith 5). A line of authority was just as important to the early Church as it is now. Also, what was the "gift" Paul referred to? Was it the Holy Ghost or Timothy's priesthood stewardship? Modern revelation teaches that "to every man is given a gift by the Spirit of God" (D&C 46:11). But to leaders is given the ability to discern "all those gifts" for the benefit of the Church (D&C 46:27).

1 TIMOTHY 5

This chapter teaches the true principles of welfare.

5:1–4 Respect for one's elders is a godly principle.

5:8 For a man to fail to take care of his family (including alimony payments, if required) is to deny the faith. President Spencer W. Kimball declared: "No true Latter-day Saint, while physically or emotionally able will voluntarily shift the burden of his own or his family's well-being to someone else. So long as he can, under the inspiration of the Lord and with his own labors, he will supply himself and his family with the spiritual and temporal necessities of life" (Conference Report, October 1977, 124).

5:9–11 The Church seems to have kept a list of widows needing welfare assistance. Hence, they were "numbered" (v. 9). Paul clarifies Church policy concerning this issue. The widows must meet certain qualifications, including age and commitment to service in Christ.

5:14 This chapter contains Paul's counsel to young, marriageable women in the Church. President Spencer W. Kimball similarly advised those in the Church today:

"I have told many groups of young people that they should not postpone their marriage until they have acquired all of their education ambitions. I have told tens of thousands of young folks that when they marry they should not wait for children until they have finished their schooling and financial desires. Marriage is basically for the family, and when people have found their proper companions there should be no long delay. They should live together normally and let the children come.

"There seems to be a growing feeling that marriage is for legal sex, for sex's sake. Marriage is basically for the family; that is why we marry—not for the satisfaction of sex, as the world around us would have us believe. When people have found their companions, there should be no long delay. Young wives should be occupied in bearing and rearing their children. I know of no scriptures where an authorization is given to young wives to withhold their families and to go to work to put their husbands through school. There are thousands of husbands who have worked their own way through school and have reared families at the same time. Though it is more difficult, young people can make their way through their educational programs" (Kimball, "Marriage Is Honorable," 263).

5:15 The predicted apostasy had already begun.

5:20 See Doctrine and Covenants 42:88–92.

5:22 "Lay hands suddenly on no man"—in other words, the candidate for priesthood office in the Lord's church should be seasoned, tried, and found worthy before ordination or setting apart.

5:23 "Drink no longer water"—or, don't drink only water. *Water-drinker* was a title used in Paul's day for a rigid ascetic. Was Timothy in delicate health? We do not know what his "often infirmities" were.

5:24 "Open beforehand" is used here to translate the Greek word for "conspicuous."

1 TIMOTHY 6

6:1–5 This section contains Paul's counsel that servants should honor their masters. From Paul's insistence on this point, we might conclude that there were some members who taught differently at the time. If so, they were not in harmony with prophetic counsel of the day.

6:5–19 These verses contain Paul's counsel and warning against focusing on material possessions (as opposed to focusing on eternal life; see v. 12). It is as applicable today as it was in the first century. Riches are a great blessing if used righteously (see Matthew 10:17–27; Jacob 2:17–19; D&C 56:16). Riches can, but do not necessarily, flow from righteousness. In Paul's day, apparently some imitated "godliness" because their real objective was financial gain (see v. 5).

6:6–8 If we have sufficient for our needs, we ought to be content, for we have enough. Contentment combined with godliness brings great blessings to one's soul. Verse 7 is a curt commentary on the vainness, or emptiness, of worldly possessions.

6:10 Here is an apt description of the origin of woes in the lives of the Saints.

6:16 See the important change to this passage in the Joseph Smith Translation.

6:20 See footnote 20*b*—science is really *gnosis* ("knowledge") in Greek. The problem is Gnostic heresies, which are pseudoknowledge.

TITUS

Titus was an early Greek convert to the Church. He was present with Paul at the Jerusalem conference (see Galatians 2:1).

Traditionally, Titus is held to be the first bishop of the Cretans. Paul had left Titus on Crete (see Titus 1:5). Crete is an island approximately 160 miles east to west and averaging twenty-five miles north to south, with many cities and likely quite a few branches of the Church. This epistle was written to strengthen and encourage Titus. This letter, like 1 Timothy, deals also with priesthood organization.

We don't know where Paul was when he wrote this letter, but the date seems to lie between A.D. 64 and 66.

TITUS 1

1:2 "Before the world began"—the Church clearly taught the doctrine of premortal life (see also Ephesians 1:4; 2 Timothy 1:9).

1:6–9 In these verses, Paul again outlines qualifications for the office of bishop; compare 1 Timothy 3:2–7.

1:10 "Unruly" means "insubordinate or rebellious."

1:12 Historically, Cretans had a reputation for avariciousness. "One of themselves, even a prophet of their own"—the early Church Father Jerome thought that Paul was quoting from the poet Epimenides (Bullinger, *Figures of Speech Used in the Bible*, 801–2).

TITUS 2

2:4–5 The former-day Young Women values are given here. The usual translation of the Greek word rendered "obedient" is now usually translated into English as "subject to"— see commentary on Colossians 3:18–22 (196) and on Ephesians 5:22–33 (206).

TITUS 3

3:2 "Speak evil of no man"—Benjamin Franklin adopted this idea as a guideline for his life and work, believing one should exclude "all Libelling and Personal Abuse, which is of late Years become so disgraceful to our country" (*Autobiography*, 165). The authorities of the Church counsel us not to be critical of others, nor to be contentious and quarrelsome but gentle and meek.

3:5 "Not by works . . . but according to his mercy"—again, "We know that it is by grace that we are saved, after all we can do" (2 Nephi 25:23).

"Washing of regeneration" is baptism of water.

"Renewing of the Holy Ghost" is baptism of fire.

3:9 "Foolish questions, and genealogies, and contentions"—for some steeped in Jewish traditions, salvation was made known through genealogical recitations.

3:12 Paul was determined to winter at Nicopolis, on the western coast of Greece.

2 TIMOTHY

The second epistle to Timothy may be the last letter Paul wrote. It speaks of the challenges apostasy has brought and will bring in the last days. It also reveals the faith and hope of a valiant apostle in the face of loneliness and adversity, just before he was executed (for Elder Sterling W. Sill's beautiful tribute to Paul, see 226).

2 TIMOTHY 1

1:3–6 Personal and poignant words to Paul's beloved "son," Timothy. Again it is evident that Paul loved Timothy dearly. Timothy was reared by a mother and grandmother who taught him the scriptures (see 2 Timothy 3:14–15). They were probably converts on Paul's first missionary journey.

1:7 Righteous living dispels fear, replacing it with power, love, and a sound mind.

1:9 This verse refers to foreordination to eternal life during the premortal existence. This foreordination, or election, had its basis in the Grand Council in Heaven. To have this election made sure, or certain, we must take advantage of the Savior's redemption. Alma 13:1–8 contains the record of another premortal calling. Joseph Smith taught that every man called to minister through the priesthood in mortality was foreordained in the Grand Council (see *Teachings of the Prophet Joseph Smith*, 365).

1:15 Paul had warned that "grievous wolves" would enter the flock, promoting perverse doctrines (see Acts 20:29–30). Now, with "all they which are in Asia" turning away, we see evidence of widespread apostasy throughout the Church.

1:16–18 Paul pays tribute to Onesiphorus, one who was not ashamed of the apostle's prison chains, for Onesiphorus ministered to the Church leader while he was in prison and helped him.

2 TIMOTHY 2

2:3–6 Three metaphors: from the military, athletics, and agriculture. Be a good soldier of Jesus Christ; be a good competitor, conforming to rigorous training and the rules of the game; and be a good husbandman, diligently laboring in the vineyard and deserving the fruits of salvation.

2:15 We should study (or in Greek, "be diligent") to merit the approval of God.

2:19 The Lord knows his own.

2:22–25 Avoid debate, argumentation, and criticism that stir up ill feelings; it's better to be gentle and meek.

2 TIMOTHY 3

3:1–7 Paul lists the characteristics of apostate conditions in his day *and* ours. Verse 13 indicates that things will get worse and worse.

3:8 According to Jewish tradition, Jannes and Jambres were two magicians who opposed Moses in the court of Pharaoh.

3:10–12 Actions speak louder than words—Paul's life speaks for itself. His life was his testimony. Paul had suffered persecution and taught that all who live a Christlike life would also (eventually) suffer persecution.

3:14–17 The solution for ungodliness and the misery associated with it (listed in vv. 1–7, 13) is the holy scriptures. Verses 16 and 17 contain one of our best definitions of scripture, along with an indication of its value and usefulness.

2 TIMOTHY 4

As far as we know, this chapter contains the last words of Paul, written not long before his martyrdom. The end of Paul's final letter is a mixture of gloom and glory, of exasperation and exultation.

4:3 Again, Paul knew well in advance that apostates would advocate perverse doctrines, distorting the simple gospel of Jesus Christ (see Acts 20:29–30). Those dissenters would turn to fables—imagined, fabricated stories—whereas the faithful would hold onto the gospel, which is real and true. Early leaders knew that the greatest threat to the Church was not outside opposition but inside corruption.

4:5 "Evangelist" comes from the Greek *euangelion,* meaning "good news." In one sense, an evangelist is a bearer of good news or glad tidings.

4:6–8 Paul's calling and election had become sure; he was sealed up to eternal life. He was aware that his life's work was finished and that his departure was at hand. Our knowledge of his execution in Rome comes from early sources. One records that Rome is the city "where Peter endures a passion like his Lord's" and "where Paul wins his crown in a death like John's [the Baptist]" (Tertullian, *On Prescription Against Heretics,* chap. 36, in *Ante-Nicene Fathers,* 3:260). Another declares that "Paul is beheaded" and "in Rome he springs to life again ennobled by martyrdom" (Tertullian, *Scorpiace,* chap. 15, in *Ante-Nicene Fathers,* 3:648).

Eusebius, quoting an earlier source, states that "to this the Roman Tertullian refers in the following terms: 'Study your records: there you will find that Nero was the first to persecute this teaching when, after subjugating the entire East, in Rome especially he treated everyone with savagery. That such a man was author of our chastisement fills us with pride. For anyone who knows him can understand that anything not supremely good would never have been condemned by Nero.' So it came about that this man, the first to be heralded as a conspicuous fighter against God, was led on to murder the apostles. It is recorded that in his reign Paul was beheaded in Rome itself, and that Peter likewise was crucified" (Eusebius, *History of the Church,* 62).

"Peter seems to have preached in Pontus, Galatia and Bithynia, Cappadocia and Asia, to the Jews of the Dispersion. Finally, he came to Rome where he was crucified, head downwards at his own request. What need be said of Paul, who from Jerusalem as far as Illyricum preached in all its fullness the gospel of Christ, and later was martyred in Rome under Nero? This is exactly what Origen tells us in Volume III of his *Commentary on Genesis*" (Eusebius, *History of the Church,* 65).

4:11 Demas, a former fellow-laborer in the kingdom, had apostatized. Titus was serving a mission in Dalmatia, north of modern-day Greece. Luke was still at Paul's side. Timothy was asked to bring John Mark with him, "for he is profitable to me for the ministry"—which indicates that where there had once been sharp disagreement between them (see Acts 15:37–40), they were now reconciled and rejoiced in each other's company.

4:13 Was "the cloke" needed for the winter in a cold prison? "Parchments" could have been copies of the scriptures (the Old Testament), or possibly copies of his own writings, or memos or membership lists of various branches of the Church.

4:21 "After the martyrdom of Paul and Peter the first man to be appointed Bishop of Rome was Linus. He is mentioned by Paul when writing to Timothy from Rome, in the salutation at the end of epistle" (Eusebius, *History of the Church*, 65; see also 67).

CHAPTER 11

THE LIFE OF PAUL

Eyewitness of the Savior's reality, missionary without peer, tutor of the Prophet Joseph Smith, and model to the Saints of the latter days, Paul was the right man, in the right place, at the right time. Without doubt, Paul loved the Savior more than he loved his own life. After his conversion, his life becomes a study in total consecration. He gave himself wholly to the doctrine of Christ. He explained the mission and message of the Messiah as have few other men in recorded history. He encouraged all he could reach to seek out and live according to the teachings of the Father and the Son. It is hard to find a more dedicated Christian or more persistent missionary.

The following tribute to Paul was penned by Sterling W. Sill, formerly an assistant to the Quorum of the Twelve and an emeritus member of the First Quorum of the Seventy at the time of his death on 25 May 1994. Entitled "Dedication," the article appeared in the *Church News*, 22 April 1967.

A TRIBUTE TO PAUL THE APOSTLE

"One of the most inspiring characteristics of human personality is having the ability to hold persistent, steadfast, constant, and unwavering devotion to a great purpose without complaint or relief.

"Think if you will of Paul the Apostle, as he sits in his prison cell in Rome awaiting his execution. He is an old man. For over thirty-five years he has turned neither to the right nor to the left, but said 'This one thing I do.' He had no sidelines, he made no excuses, and he indulged in no wasteful startings and stoppings; instead he always had that sure and steady quality of always being there, of always going forward, of always keeping in focus the one great aim and purpose of his life.

"How different his career, from what might have been expected thirty-five years before when he was a young and influential member of the Sanhedrin with everything to make his career promising: friends, position, influence, and education.

"Then had come that day on the road to Damascus when 'suddenly there shined around about him a light from heaven: and as he fell to the earth he heard a voice saying unto him, 'Saul, Saul, why persecutest thou me?' and Saul said 'who art thou Lord?' and the Lord said 'I am Jesus whom thou persecutest; it is hard for thee to kick against the pricks.' and Saul trembling and astonished said, 'Lord, what wilt thou have me do?'

"For three days he was without sight, without food, without drink. But the Lord said 'He is a chosen vessel unto me, to bear my name before the Gentiles and Kings and the children of Israel. For I will show him how great things he must suffer for my name's sake.' And from that day onward, Paul ceased not to carry forward with his utmost vigor his assigned task.

"After thirty-five years, he counted his manner of life by saying 'In labors more abundant, in stripes above measure, in prisons more frequent, in deaths oft. Of the Jews five times received I forty stripes save one. Thrice was I beaten with rods, once was I stoned, thrice I suffered shipwreck, a night and a day I have been in the deep. In journeyings often, in perils of water, in perils of robbers, in perils of mine own countrymen, in perils by the heathen, in perils of the city, in perils of the wilderness, in perils by the sea, in perils among false brethren, in weariness and painfulness, in watchings often, in hunger and thirst, in fastings often, in cold and nakedness. Besides those things that are without, that which cometh upon me daily, the care of all the churches.'

"Of all of his experiences, this last must have been the

most wearisome—the care which comes from within the Church. People sometimes get tired and want to quit or they lack the enthusiasm to supply their own initiative and must be encouraged and helped and coaxed. It is easy to fight the battles from without, but the real heartbreak comes when the wavering is from within. But there was no wavering for Paul. He would go on and on and on—alone if need be, and on his own power.

"When we consider the ability which Paul had developed for sustained, continued effort in one direction, it is small wonder that the Lord had said, 'He is a chosen vessel unto me.' This might also be said of many others if we could learn to stick to our convictions as energetically and as enthusiastically and as long. 'His bodily presence was weak, his speech contemptible.' He mentions his 'thorn in the flesh,' but men can get along without money, without name, and without influence; your appearance may be poor and your speech faulty. All these will be as nothing if you know where you're going. We have never heard of Paul taking a vacation or being afraid of wearing out. He was on fire with his determination and never lost sight of his goal.

"It is an interesting thing which he must have thought about, that there is nothing mentioned in all the Revelations about resignations. Occasionally he must have thought of the ease and comfort and affluence that might have been his, and it must have occurred to him long before thirty-five years had passed that he had 'served his term' and would be 'entitled to a release.' But that was not for him. And it is not for us. There can be no such thing as a release in the work in which Paul was engaged. He, and we, must continue to go on and on at an accelerating pace. We can't work out our salvation in two years or ten years or twenty years. 'Only he that endureth to the end shall be saved.' Paul said of himself, 'I fight on lest I myself should be a castaway.'

"Just before the end of his ministry, Paul wrote a letter to Timothy, a young man in whom he had a special interest. He calls him his 'son in the gospel,' and after exhorting Timothy to the utmost of diligence, he expressed the realization that his own mission had been completed. He said, 'For I am now ready to be offered and the time of my departure is at hand. I have fought a good fight; I have finished my course; I have kept the faith.'

"How inspiring are these words when they come at the end of such a life of outstanding devotion and constancy. He was soon to go to Rome to be beheaded. But even in his death, his determination never faltered, and the fervor of his faith shows no sign of any decrease from that first day when blinded and stunned, he said, 'Lord what wilt thou have me do?' And I like to think of Paul on that day, when the ax of the executioner granted him the final release from his earthly labors when he should go to stand a second time before Jesus of Nazareth and I imagine that there will be very few, if any, men who will ever stand before their Maker with greater cause to rejoice than he. And when we come to that point in our lives, and have cause to reflect on the fight we have fought and the course we have run, how insignificant will be the money we have made or the ease we have enjoyed or the affluence we have attained.

"Life was never intended to be only a pleasure trip. It is also a mission, a conquest, a testing, and how bitter must be the final remorse of any wasted life. May God help us to develop the courage, the industry and dedication to live his answers to the great Apostle's question 'Lord what wilt thou have me do?'" (Sill, "Dedication," 13).

THE TEACHINGS OF PAUL, A WITNESS OF CHRIST

Paul the apostle was an eyewitness of the Lord Jesus Christ. At least four different times he saw the Lord or was visited by him. On the road to Damascus, Jesus appeared and spoke to Paul in person; He then presented him a mission call (see Acts 9:3–6, 17, 27; 26:13–18; Galatians 1:12; 1 Corinthians 9:1; 15:8). From the book of Acts we learn that the Savior appeared to Paul once in Corinth (see Acts 18:1, 9) and twice in Jerusalem (see Acts 22:14, 17–21; 23:11). Later, at the end of his ministry, the apostle affirmed that Christ would give him eternal life (see 2 Timothy 4:8, 18). Paul learned that "the truth is in Jesus" (Ephesians 4:21), and that he, and each of us, must teach "wholesome words, even the words of our Lord Jesus Christ" (1 Timothy 6:3).

The first thing that Paul taught after his conversion (see Acts 9:20), and perhaps the most important doctrine he taught throughout his decades of missionary service, was that Jesus is the Son of God the Father (see Romans 1:3–4; 15:6; 2 Corinthians 1:19; 11:31; Galatians 4:4; Ephesians 1:3; 3:14; Colossians 1:3; Hebrews 1:5; 4:14). Jesus was in the image of the Father (see Colossians 1:15; Hebrews 1:3) but was willing to take upon him the likeness of men: He came in the flesh (see Romans 8:3; Philippians 2:7–8; 1 Timothy 3:16; Hebrews 2:9, 14, 17).

Paul began every letter he wrote with the same foundational teaching: the Father and the Son are two separate beings. The apostle's usual reference is to "God our Father, and the Lord Jesus Christ" (Romans 1:7; 5:10–11; 1 Corinthians 1:3; 2 Corinthians 1:2–3; Galatians 1:1, 3; Ephesians 1:2–3; Philippians 1:2; Colossians 1:2–3; 1 Thessalonians 1:1, 3; 3:11, 13; 2 Thessalonians 1:1–2; 2:16; 1 Timothy 1:2; 2 Timothy 1:2; Titus 1:4; Hebrews 1:1–2).

When it came to the identity of God, Paul, like Nephi, delighted in plainness. There would be no mistaking who God is and how he created and saved the world. The apostle used a host of descriptive names and titles to identify Jesus. He is our Savior (see Acts 13:23; Philippians 3:20), our Redeemer (see Hebrews 9:12), and our Mediator, or Intercessor (see Romans 8:34; 1 Timothy 2:5; Hebrews 7:25; 8:6; 9:15, 24; 12:24). He is our peace (see Romans 5:1; 2 Thessalonians 3:16), our hope of glory (see Romans 5:2; 15:7; Colossians 1:27; 2 Thessalonians 2:14; 1 Timothy 1:1; Hebrews 2:10), and our life (see Acts 17:28; Colossians 3:4; 2 Timothy 1:1, 10).

Jesus is the Creator of the worlds and of all things (see Acts 17:24; 1 Corinthians 8:6; Ephesians 3:9; Colossians 1:16; Hebrews 1:2, 10), and he upholds and sustains all things by the word of his power (see Acts 17:25; Hebrews 1:3; 2:10). He is the Judge of all people (see Acts 17:31; Romans 2:16; 14:10; 2 Corinthians 5:10; 2 Timothy 4:1, 8). He is the long-awaited Messiah, or Christ (see Acts 17:3; 18:5, 28), and King (see Acts 17:7). He is the head of the Church (see Ephesians 1:22; 4:15; 5:23; Colossians 1:18), and the head of all principalities and powers (see Colossians 2:10).

Jesus is the author and finisher of our faith (see Hebrews 12:2), the great shepherd of the sheep (see Hebrews 13:20), the foundation and the cornerstone of the temple of God (see 1 Corinthians 3:11; Ephesians 2:19–21). He is the same yesterday, today, and forever (see Hebrews 13:8).

Paul knew and understood significant details of Jesus' mortal life. Not only was Jesus the Firstborn of the Father in the spirit (see Colossians 1:15; Hebrews 1:6) and the Only Begotten of the Father in the flesh, but he was also born of a mortal woman (see Galatians 4:4). Because he was part mortal he experienced temptations and trials (see Hebrews 2:18; 4:15). He suffered on many occasions, including outside the gate of the city (see Hebrews 13:12). He endured the cross for the joy that was set before him (see Hebrews 12:2); he descended below all things in order to ascend above all things (see 2 Corinthians 8:9; Ephesians 4:9–10). And finally, he was made perfect through suffering (see Acts 26:23; Hebrews 2:10; 5:8–9).

Another most important doctrine that Paul taught was the purposes of Jesus' mortal life—his reasons for condescending to earth. The Savior conquered two deaths, overcoming all consequences of the Fall. In the writings of Paul, we find more passages about Jesus' resurrection than about any other

231

subject. The apostle's constant teaching was that the Lord abolished death and was resurrected from the dead so that he might provide the same blessing for us (see Acts 13:30, 33, 34, 37; 17:3, 31; 25:19; 26:23; Romans 4:24; 6:4–11; 8:11, 34; 10:9; 14:9; 1 Corinthians 6:14; 15:4–8, 12–29; 2 Corinthians 4:14; 5:15; Galatians 1:1, 4; Ephesians 1:20; Colossians 2:12; 1 Thessalonians 1:10; 4:14; 2 Timothy 1:10; 2:8; Hebrews 2:9, 14–15; 13:20).

By resurrecting his body, our Redeemer overcame physical death, thereby removing that otherwise permanent result of the Fall; through him all of us are made alive, to live again forever. But even though we all become immortal through the gift of resurrection, we have no assurance or guarantee of life with our Heavenly Father. The other consequence of the Fall was expulsion from the presence of the Father—we are born out of his presence, with no power in ourselves to return. Another prominent theme in Paul's writings is that only our acceptance and application of Christ's atonement will allow us to return to the Father. The apostle frequently taught that salvation, or redemption, is in Christ (see Romans 1:16; 3:24; 1 Thessalonians 5:9; 2 Timothy 2:10; 3:15; Hebrews 5:9; 7:25; 9:28); or, in other words, forgiveness for sins comes only through Christ (see Acts 13:38; Romans 3:25; Ephesians 1:7; Colossians 1:14; 2:13; 3:13; Titus 2:14; Hebrews 9:26, 28; 10:12). Paul used various terms and concepts to explain the process of the Lord's atoning sacrifice. Jesus made reconciliation for our sins (see Romans 5:10–11; 2 Corinthians 5:18–19; Colossians 1:20–22; Hebrews 2:17); he came to save sinners (see 1 Timothy 1:15); he himself purged or cleansed our sins (see Hebrews 1:3). We are sanctified and justified through the offering of Jesus' body, by his blood (see Romans 5:9; 1 Corinthians 6:11; Hebrews 10:10; 13:12). We are justified by faith in Christ and by his grace, not by works of the law (see Romans 3:24, 26, 28; 4:25; 5:1–2, 17–18; Galatians 2:16; Titus 3:7). We are saved through his mercy and grace (see Acts 15:11; Romans 5:15; Ephesians 2:5, 8; Titus 2:11;

3:5). The quintessential message of Paul, and of all the apostles and prophets, is that Jesus loved us and gave himself for us—he died for us (see Romans 5:6, 8; 8:32; 1 Corinthians 5:7; 15:3; 2 Corinthians 5:15; Galatians 2:20; Ephesians 5:2, 25; 1 Thessalonians 5:9–10; 1 Timothy 2:6; Titus 2:14; Hebrews 7:27; 9:14, 26, 28).

In addition to details about Jesus' mortal life and the purposes of his coming into mortality, Paul taught about the Savior's current exalted status and our potential to become like him. The Lord Jesus Christ is now exalted; he sits at the right hand of the Father, the Majesty on high (see Romans 8:34; Philippians 2:9; Hebrews 1:3; 8:1; 10:12; 12:2). His scepter, throne, and kingdom are eternal (see Hebrews 1:8). He is heir of all things (see Hebrews 1:2), and we become heirs of God and obtain an inheritance through Christ (see Romans 8:17, 32; Galatians 4:7; Ephesians 1:11; Hebrews 9:15). Gentiles may also become fellow heirs through Christ (see Ephesians 3:6). We become the children of God by faith in Christ (see Galatians 3:26; Ephesians 1:5). He will change our bodies to a glorified condition like his (see Romans 8:11, 17–18; Philippians 3:21).

The apostle also spoke of the Lord's glorious return to earth at the end of the world. All things will be gathered together in Christ in the dispensation of the fullness of times (see Ephesians 1:10). He will come again in glory (see 2 Thessalonians 1:7–10), whereupon every knee will bow, and every tongue confess, that Jesus is Lord (see Romans 14:11; Philippians 2:10–11).

PAUL, THE MISSIONARY

From that traumatic day on the road to Damascus when the Lord stopped Saul of Tarsus in his tracks, the future apostle to the Gentiles responded positively: "Lord, what wilt thou have me to do?" (Acts 9:6). When he learned what the

Lord wanted him to do, he spent the rest of his life dedicated to that cause. He repented thoroughly and forsook his former ways, "forgetting those things which are behind" (Philippians 3:13). He followed no wasteful sidetracks; his eye was single to his divine calling: "This one thing I do," he wrote (Philippians 3:13).

The Lord explained to his local priesthood leader in Damascus, "he [Saul] is a chosen vessel unto me" and "I will shew him how great things he must suffer for my name's sake" (Acts 9:15–16). Upon his total conversion, after receiving his mission call on the road to Damascus, Paul went out and preached that Christ is the Son of God, the Messiah (see Acts 9:20, 22). He preached boldly, confidently, and fearlessly in the name of the Lord Jesus (see Acts 13:46; 14:3; 19:8; 28:31; Ephesians 6:19–20), teaching that Jesus is the only source of forgiveness of sins (see Acts 13:38). He taught what the Church authorities taught (see Acts 16:4), and he taught from the scriptures (see Acts 17:2).

Paul became one of the greatest missionaries of all time. For more than thirty years he "hazarded his life" for the name of Christ (see Acts 15:26; 2 Corinthians 11:24–27). He was an indomitable traveler, journeying more than thirteen thousand miles over all kinds of terrain, in all kinds of weather, constantly encouraging, exhorting, strengthening, and teaching the doctrines of salvation (see Acts 14:22; 18:23; 20:2; Ephesians 3:16; and all the epistles). His service to the Saints was a "labour of love" (Hebrews 6:10). He worked with his own hands; he preferred not to be burdensome (see Acts 18:1–3; 20:33–34; 1 Thessalonians 2:5–6, 9). He knew how to work; he loved the Lord's work, and he knew how to delegate—he sent out messengers and companions and organized Church units with priesthood leaders (see Acts 14:23). The work began in large cities where there was a greater potential for developing strong leadership, and from those centers of strength it spread into the countryside. He made friends with political leaders (see Acts 19:31), and complimented rulers, making a good first impression (see Acts 26:3). He taught other leaders by word and example. Paul's life illustrated Jesus' teaching: "It is more blessed to give than to receive" (Acts 20:35).

Paul was steadfast and determined. The trials and afflictions that inevitably come to all dedicated missionaries didn't matter to him; all that mattered was his ministry, his life's work (see Acts 20:24; compare also 2 Corinthians 4:8–9, 17 and 6:4–10). The apostle taught, "We must through much tribulation enter into the kingdom of God" (Acts 14:22). He was willing to suffer out of love for the people: "I endure all things for the elect's sakes" (2 Timothy 2:10; see also Colossians 1:24; Philippians 1:12; 2 Corinthians 2:4). He was not discouraged when thrown into prison; he prayed and sang praises to God. A miracle followed which gave him opportunity to convert the jailer and his whole family (see Acts 16:25–34).

Paul took every opportunity to recount his conversion story and bear testimony, even to a hostile audience (see Acts 22:3–21). On one occasion he was almost killed by a mob, but he requested an opportunity to teach and testify to them (see Acts 21:39–40). He defended himself before the Roman governors Felix and Festus, answering accusations and teaching doctrine (see Acts 24:10–21; 25:8–21), and he boldly and powerfully retold his conversion story before King Agrippa (see Acts 26:2–29). He willingly went to Rome, accused and under arrest, in order to teach Jews and even the Caesar (see Acts 28:16–31).

Paul, the missionary, was astute in his control of various situations, as evidenced by his handling of the tendentious debate between Pharisees and Sadducees over the issue of resurrection (see Acts 23:6–10). He became angry at injustice and hypocrisy (see Acts 23:1–5). He was known to be sharp in rebuke, to be direct in conversation, and sometimes to be impetuous in his zeal for the cause of Christ (see Acts 15:39; Galatians 2:11; Galatians 3). Paul was a very real person—he even had companion problems: John Mark abandoned him on their first mission together (see Acts 13:13), but he and Paul were later reconciled (see 2 Timothy 4:11). There was sharp contention between Paul and his former missionary companion, Barnabas (see Acts 15:39). On one occasion Paul even chastised his fellow-apostle Peter, the prophet, in front of others (see Galatians 2:11–14).

But the great missionary was also humble (see 2 Corinthians 12:7–9) and quick to recognize his own weaknesses. He labeled himself the "chief of sinners" (1 Timothy 1:15), and he exclaimed, "I am the least of the apostles, that am not meet to be called an apostle, because I persecuted the church of God" (1 Corinthians 15:9). According to some of his critics, his speech was "contemptible" (2 Corinthians 10:10) and "rude" (2 Corinthians 11:6). But Paul confessed his own nothingness (see 1 Corinthians 3:5–7) and admitted that he had a "thorn in the flesh" (2 Corinthians 12:7), some physical, emotional, social, or spiritual trial, whatever it was, that apparently caused him serious personal anguish—and kept him humble. He lost his life in the service of others. "For though I be free from all men, yet have I made myself servant unto all, that I might gain the more" (1 Corinthians 9:19). He learned by his own experience that it is wise to avoid contentious questions and strife and be gentle and meek (see 2 Timothy 2:23–25).

The great apostle-missionary was anxious to do whatever was necessary to reach everyone. He observed the Christian principle of "accommodation without compromise." Though vehemently denying any necessity for circumcision as a saving ordinance, he had Timothy circumcised so that Timothy would be acceptable to Jews among whom he would teach (see Acts 16:3). He also followed the counsel of leaders in Jerusalem to perform Temple rituals so that he would be acceptable to Jews (see Acts 21:18–26). In Athens he built on common beliefs of the Greeks in order to teach them the whole truth (see Acts 17:16–30). "I am made all things to all men, that I might by all means save some" (1 Corinthians 9:22).

Paul loved to learn and was an avid student (see, for example, 2 Timothy 4:13), but he learned that powerful testimony comes not by man's wisdom, scholarship, or eloquence but by the Holy Ghost (see 1 Corinthians 1:17; 2:1–5, 9, 13).

Paul, the missionary, fasted and prayed much (see Acts 13:3; 14:23). He stayed close to the Spirit and used his priesthood power to bless others. Once, while intent on preaching in the regions of Asia, Bithynia, and Mysia, he listened to the Spirit and pushed on instead to Macedonia for a harvest of souls ready for the gospel (see Acts 16:6–10). He was filled with the Spirit on numerous occasions, causing him to perform miracles in behalf of Saints and believers in God's power (see Acts 13:9–12; 14:8–10; 15:12; 16:25–26). "God wrought special miracles by the hands of Paul" (Acts 19:11)—diseases were healed, evil spirits were cast out, and a young man was raised from the dead (see Acts 20:7–12).

Paul was not building on another man's foundation (see Romans 15:20); he was willing to reach out and work in new areas. He also worked hard to satisfy the temporal needs of others—what we now call humanitarian service (see Romans 15:26–27).

The New Testament record provides us a fairly comprehensive list of Paul's missionary companions: Barnabas, John Mark, Silas, Timothy, Luke, Erastus, Gaius, Aristarchus, Sopater, Secundus, Tychicus, Trophimus, Priscilla and Aquila, Epaphras, Demas, Jesus Justus, Epaphroditus, and Sosthenes.

Some of the most personal glimpses into the great missionary's human relationships come from comments about his companions. Timothy was one of his closest companions, who actually helped write a number of the epistles (see 2 Corinthians 1:1; Philippians 1:1; Colossians 1:1; 1 and 2 Thessalonians 1:1; Philemon 1:1). Paul called Timothy "my own son in the faith" (1 Timothy 1:2) and "my dearly beloved son" (2 Timothy 1:2), and he commended him to the Saints at Philippi with loving, heart-felt words (Philippians 2:19–22). Paul also highly commended another companion,

Epaphroditus, for his faithfulness and devotion even though he was "sick nigh unto death" (Philippians 2:25–30). Paul deeply loved his fellow-laborers in all the many branches he established. One such leader, Onesiphorus, he honored in a letter to Timothy: "he oft refreshed me, and was not ashamed of my chain: But when he was in Rome, he sought me out very diligently, and found me . . . [and in] many things he ministered unto me at Ephesus" (2 Timothy 1:16–18).

Paul was a successful missionary because he learned to love people. He loved them, so they loved him. A scene that beautifully illustrates this truth was his tearful farewell talk to the leaders of Ephesus, their kneeling prayer and subsequent flow of tears as they were told they would not see their beloved leader again in the flesh (see Acts 20:36–38).

There are numerous comments in Paul's letters about his efforts to build relationships of trust and love. He frequently expressed his longing to see certain individuals. "I long to see you," he wrote to the Romans (1:11), and in the final chapter of that letter he extended personal greetings to at least twenty-eight men and women. To others he wrote: "I desire to be present with you now" (Galatians 4:20); "how greatly I long after you all in the [affections] of Jesus Christ" (Philippians 1:8); "so being affectionately desirous of you, we were willing to have imparted unto you, not the gospel . . . only, but also our own souls, because ye were dear unto us" (1 Thessalonians 2:8); "ye have good remembrance of us always, desiring greatly to see us, as we also to see you: . . . Night and day praying exceedingly that we might see your face" (1 Thessalonians 3:6, 10). His deeply compassionate feelings for his beloved companion, Timothy, are revealed in these lines: "Greatly desiring to see thee, being mindful of thy tears, that I may be filled with joy" (2 Timothy 1:4); "do thy diligence to come shortly unto me . . . before winter" (2 Timothy 4:9, 21).

One key to Paul's success as a missionary, which likewise shows his loving concern for the people, was his constant praying for others—and praying for them by name. "Without ceasing I make mention of you always in my prayers," he wrote to the Romans (1:9). And to the Saints in other branches he similarly wrote: "[I] cease not to give thanks for you, making mention of you in my prayers" (Ephesians 1:16); "praying always for you"; "[we] do not cease to pray for you" (Colossians 1:3, 9); "we give thanks to God always for you all, making mention of you in our prayers" (1 Thessalonians 1:2; see also 2 Thessalonians 1:11). He wrote to his convert Philemon, reaffirming his confidence in him: "making mention of thee always in my prayers" (Philemon 1:4). And to his faithful friend and fellow-worker, Timothy, he wrote, "Without ceasing I have remembrance of thee in my prayers night and day" (2 Timothy 1:3).

Paul knew that converts are the glory and joy of missionaries (see 1 Thessalonians 2:19–20). He also knew that the loving relationship between missionary and convert must be reciprocal, so he often requested of the Saints: "Pray for us" (1 Thessalonians 5:25; 2 Thessalonians 3:1; Hebrews 13:18); "I beseech you . . . that ye strive together . . . in your prayers to God for me" (Romans 15:30). He reminded the Ephesian Saints that they should be "praying always . . . [with] supplication in the Spirit . . . for all saints; and for me" (Ephesians 6:18–19), and he counseled the Saints at Colossae: "Continue in prayer . . . praying also for us" (Colossians 4:2–3).

One of the greatest blessings and services of a missionary are his inspired teachings and instructions. Paul wrote some of the most valuable counsel to missionaries ever written. "We are ambassadors for Christ," he told the Corinthians (2 Corinthians 5:20). He spent some time on his knees, talking with Heavenly Father, pleading for the Saints to covet the best of the gifts of God: "That Christ may dwell in your hearts by faith; that ye, being rooted and grounded in love, may be able to . . . *know the love of Christ,* which passeth knowledge, that ye might be filled with all the fulness of God" (Ephesians 3:17–19; emphasis added). "Even so hath the Lord ordained that they which preach the gospel should live of the gospel.

. . . For though I preach the gospel, I have nothing to glory of: for necessity is laid upon me; yea, woe is unto me, if I preach not the gospel! For if I do this thing willingly, I have a reward: but if against my will, a dispensation [Greek, meaning "commission" or "stewardship"] of the gospel is committed unto me. . . . Know ye not that they which run in a race run all, but one receiveth the prize? So run, that ye may obtain. . . . Now they do it to obtain a corruptible crown; but we an incorruptible. . . . I keep under [Greek, "rigorously discipline"] my body, and bring it into subjection: lest that by any means, when I have preached to others, I myself should be a castaway" (1 Corinthians 9:14, 16–17, 24, 25, 27).

Possibly the most powerful and poignant counsel ever written by an ancient apostle, full of meaning for all missionary-ambassadors of the Lord Jesus Christ, is the following, which Paul wrote to Timothy: "Let no man despise thy youth; but be thou an example of the believers, in word, in conversation, in charity, in spirit, in faith, in purity. Till I come, give attendance to reading, to exhortation, to doctrine. Neglect not the gift that is in thee, which was given thee by prophecy, with the laying on of the hands of the presbytery [that is, the priesthood authorities, showing the importance of line of authority then and now]. Meditate upon these things; give thyself wholly to them; that thy profiting may appear to all. Take heed unto thyself, and unto the doctrine; continue in them: for in doing this thou shalt both save thyself, and them that hear thee" (1 Timothy 4:12–16). Paul followed his own counsel.

REFERENCES TO PAUL IN LATTER-DAY SCRIPTURE

Throughout modern-day scripture, the Lord refers to Paul and his writings. The following list details many of these.

Doctrine and Covenants 18:9: "I speak unto you [Oliver

Cowdery and David Whitmer], . . . even as unto Paul mine apostle, for you are called even with that same calling with which he was called."

Doctrine and Covenants 127:2: The Prophet Joseph Smith, reflecting on his life, said: "It all has become a second nature to me; and I feel, like Paul, to glory in tribulation."

Doctrine and Covenants 128:13: "That which is earthly conforming to that which is heavenly, as Paul hath declared, 1 Corinthians 15:46, 47, and 48."

Doctrine and Covenants 128:15: "As Paul says concerning the fathers—that they without us cannot be made perfect."

Doctrine and Covenants 128:16: "And now, in relation to the baptism for the dead, I will give you another quotation of Paul, 1 Corinthians 15:29."

Doctrine and Covenants 74: This section is an explanation of 1 Corinthians 7:14.

Joseph Smith–History 1:24: "However, it was nevertheless a fact that I had beheld a vision. I have thought since, that I felt much like Paul, when he made his defense before King Agrippa, and related the account of the vision he had when he saw a light, and heard a voice; but still there were but few who believed him; some said he was dishonest, others said he was mad; and he was ridiculed and reviled. But all this did not destroy the reality of his vision. He had seen a vision, he knew he had, and all the persecution under heaven could not make it otherwise; and though they should persecute him unto death, yet he knew, and would know to his latest breath, that he had both seen a light and heard a voice speaking unto him, and all the world could not make him think or believe otherwise."

Article of Faith 13: "We believe in being honest, true, chaste, benevolent, virtuous, and in doing good to all men; indeed, we may say that we follow the admonition of Paul— We believe all things, we hope all things, we have endured many things, and hope to be able to endure all things. If there

is anything virtuous, lovely, or of good report or praiseworthy, we seek after these things."

The thirteenth article of faith contains excerpts from two
of Paul's epistles:

"Beareth all things, believeth all things, hopeth all things,
endureth all things" (1 Corinthians 13:7). And, "Finally,
brethren, whatsoever things are true, whatsoever things are
honest, whatsoever things are just, whatsoever things are pure,
whatsoever things are lovely, whatsoever things are of good
report; if there be any virtue, and if there be any praise, think
on these things" (Philippians 4:8).

REFERENCES TO PAUL BY THE PROPHET JOSEPH SMITH

Dr. Robert J. Matthews notes that in *Teachings of the
Prophet Joseph Smith*, which contains only part of the Prophet's
many writings and sermons, the following references are
found under "Paul" (numbers refer to pages in *Teachings*):
"author of Epistle to Hebrews, 59–60; an example of industry and patience, 63; labored unceasingly in the gospel, 63;
summary of life and labors of, 63–64; did not seek honors of
this life, 64; to receive a crown of righteousness at Jesus' second coming, 64; had the Second Comforter, 151; received a
visit from and was taught mysteries of Godliness by Abel,
169–70; was acquainted with and instructed by Enoch, 170;
description of, 180; a good orator, 180; caught up to third
heavens, 247, 301, 304, 311, 323; knew things unlawful to
utter, 247, 305, 323; had to be baptized for remission of sins,
265; was all things to all men to save some, 306; was persecuted, 32; quoted: on hasty ordinations, 42; on sacrifice
offered by Abel, 59; on gospel taught to Abraham, 60; on
necessity of resurrection of Jesus Christ, 62; on second coming of Jesus, 63–65, 286; on receiving crown of righteousness,
63–64; on apostasy in Church at Ephesus, 67; on love of

husbands and wives, 88–89; on doctrine of election, 149, 189; on ministry of angels, 158; on the dispensation of the fulness of times, 159, 168; on baptism of children of Israel, 159; on purposes and order of God, 158; on baptism for the dead, 179, 201, 222; on spiritual gifts, 202, 207, 243–45; on gift of prophecy, 209, 244–46; on order in the Church, 209; on offices in the Church, 244–45; on necessity of having Spirit of God, 247; on three degrees of glory, 311, 359, 374; on rebaptism, 263, 336; on wisdom of the world, 300; on being yoked to unbelievers, 306; on priesthood and ordinances, 308; on seeking after dead, 356; on plurality of gods, 370–71; on earthly likeness to heavenly things, 373" (Matthews, index to *Teachings of the Prophet Joseph Smith*, 422).

Thus we see that the Prophet Joseph Smith made frequent use of the writings of Paul. But, more importantly, the Lord gave Joseph Smith information about Paul beyond what is written in the Bible.

CHAPTER 12

HEBREWS

Scholars and churchmen alike have debated for centuries about the authorship of the work anciently called "To the Hebrews." The thirteen letters previously studied all conspicuously start with Paul's name, but no author's name is given at the beginning of Hebrews. Some scholars claim that differences in style between Paul's other letters and the book of Hebrews preclude attributing this work to Paul. We say that those stylistic differences are negligible and superficial.

The oldest collection of Paul's writings known to us comes from the Chester Beatty Papyri, which dates from around A.D. 200. The text is written in Greek and presents the books of Romans, Hebrews, 1 Corinthians, and others, arranged apparently by size. The book of Hebrews is placed alongside other Pauline writings, with no suggestion that anyone other than Paul wrote it.

One of the early second-century "apostolic fathers," Clement of Alexandria, considered Paul the author of the work: "The Epistle to the Hebrews . . . was written for Hebrews in their own language, and then accurately translated by Luke and published for Greek readers. Hence, in the Greek version of this epistle we find the same stylistic colour as in the Acts. . . . Now, as the blessed presbyter used to say, the Lord, the apostle of the Almighty, was sent to the Hebrews; so through modesty Paul, knowing that he had been sent to the Gentiles, does not describe himself as an apostle of the Hebrews, first because he so reverenced the Lord, and secondly because he was going outside his province in writing to the Hebrews too, when he was an ambassador and apostle of the Gentiles" (Eusebius, *History of the Church*, 192).

Hints within the text also suggest Paul's authorship. Hebrews 13:23 mentions Paul's faithful companion, Timothy, and 13:24 declares, "They of Italy salute you." The reference to Italian Saints, probably of Rome, along with two references to "bonds" (10:34; 13:3) attests possible authorship by Paul. The last line of the letter, "Grace be with you all. Amen," is a typical Pauline closing. Latter-day Saints have additional reason to believe Paul wrote Hebrews: the Prophet Joseph Smith said he did (see *Teachings of the Prophet Joseph Smith*, 59; D&C 128:15).

The date when Hebrews was written is not known, but the book itself clearly presupposes the mid first century after Christ, before the Temple was destroyed in A.D. 70. Scholars have been more definite than that, placing its writing about A.D. 61 or 62. The second half of the epistle focuses on the preeminence of Jesus Christ and his gospel over the Mosaic rituals performed in the Jerusalem Temple and sacrifices offered on the altar of the Temple—certainly, all of these references would be meaningless if the Temple no longer stood and sacrifices were no longer being made.

Paul was probably writing to Jewish Christians in the Holy Land, for his writing is filled with Judaic references: it is packed with Old Testament quotations. For this very reason, the book of Hebrews is an excellent guide to understanding Old Testament teachings and practices. For Paul, Christ was concealed in the Old Testament but revealed in the New Testament. He wrote to Jewish members of the Church to elucidate teachings from the Old Covenant that had been fulfilled in the New Covenant. The Gospel was revealed after the foundation of the preparatory law. In Hebrews, we gain detailed knowledge of priesthood and doctrine on creation, angels, marriage, premortal life, patriarchal blessings, sons of perdition, the unpardonable sin, faith, the Church of the Firstborn, and Zion, the celestial city.

Hebrews may have been written as a missionary tract. This book contains the longest-running argument in the New Testament: the superiority of Jesus and his law over that which was previously taught and lived for centuries. Jesus was superior to angels, to Moses, and to the Levitical high priest. His priesthood was superior to the Levitical Priesthood (all the patriarchs through Melchizedek and Abraham held the higher priesthood before Levi was even born), and his new covenant was superior to the old covenant (see "Hebrews, Epistle to the," in Ludlow, *Encyclopedia of Mormonism*, 2:581–83).

HEBREWS 1 AND 2

1:1–3 These verses detail Paul's understanding of the nature of the Godhead: the Father's word was spoken over the ages by the prophets, but recently the Father spoke more directly by his Son, that same Son by whom he made the worlds (note the plural). The Son is in the express image of the Father. The Son's purpose in coming to earth was to accomplish the Atonement and then to return to the right hand (the place of honor) of his Majesty the Father (see also Colossians 1:2–3, 15).

1:4–2:9 In chapters 1 and 2 Paul cites eight successive quotations from the Old Testament to show that Jesus is greater than angels. To the Jews (Hebrews) angels were highly exalted beings because they were involved in giving the law at Sinai (see Deuteronomy 33:2; Psalm 68:17; Acts 7:53). Apparently, some Jewish leaders even assigned angels a higher station than the Messiah. For example, the Dead Sea Scrolls reflect an expectation that Michael the Archangel would be the premier figure in the great Messianic kingdom at the end of the world. Paul uses the Old Testament, principally the Psalms, to show that Jesus the Messiah was and is Lord, God, and King. He is Son of the Father, with a royal birthright that makes him preeminent among all the children of God. The following verses show Paul's use of the Psalms in this teaching technique:

1:5—See Psalm 2:7; 2 Samuel 7:14; 1 Chronicles 17:13.

1:6—See Deuteronomy 32:43. Note the Joseph Smith Translation change.

1:7—See Psalm 104:4.

1:8–9—See Psalm 45:6–7.

1:10–12—See Psalm 102:25–27.

1:13—See Psalm 110:1.

2:6–8—See Psalm 8:4–6.

Hebrews 1:14 refers both to resurrected angels and to disembodied spirits. The Prophet Joseph Smith clarified that an angel is a resurrected being (such as Moroni) or a translated being (such as Moses or Elijah), who ministers to embodied spirits (that is, to us); a ministering spirit is a disembodied spirit, who ministers to disembodied spirits (as Jesus did between death and resurrection)—that is, spirit to spirit (see *Teachings of the Prophet Joseph Smith*, 191). Angels are under the direction of Michael (see *Teachings of the Prophet Joseph Smith*, 168).

2:10 The Savior was made "perfect through sufferings" (Hebrews 5:8–9). Why a suffering Savior? The important answer is given in Hebrews 2:18 and 4:15 (see also Alma 7:12). He can judge us because he knows the desires of the flesh. He can relate to our infirmities because he, too, has lived through mortality. Truly, he was made like unto us "in all things" (Hebrews 2:17) so that he would know how to nurture us.

2:12 The term *church* in the Old Testament refers to a congregation.

2:17 The purpose of Christ's mortality was to make reconciliation for the sins of the people, that is, to make an atonement for them. The Hebrew term for reconciliation is *kapparah* (from which comes *kippur,* as in "Yom Kippur," meaning "atonement").

HEBREWS 3

3:1–6 Jesus is greater than Moses and all his laws. Jesus is the apostle and high priest of our profession, or confession, the advocate of our testimony and belief. "Christ is the Great High Priest; Adam next" (Smith, *Teachings of the Prophet Joseph Smith,* 158).

3:7–11 This passage is a quotation from Psalm 95:7–11 and summarizes Israel's apostasy in the wilderness. Note its perfect fit with modern revelation, in which we learn that the "rest" of the Lord is "the fulness of his glory" (D&C 84:24; see also 84:6–26).

3:12–17 These verses contain Paul's counsel to help the Hebrews understand and avoid ancient Israel's difficulties. Verse 15 quotes Psalm 95:7–8.

HEBREWS 4

4:1–13 Paul continues teaching about the "rest of the Lord." He includes a sobering warning but also a significant promise. Ancient Israel could have been sanctified and then have entered into the fullness of God's glory (his rest). But they forfeited this blessing through disobedience. Nevertheless, the promise of sanctification still stands and may be obtained by the Saints if they are wiser and more obedient than ancient Israel.

4:3 Compare Psalm 95:11.

4:4 On the seventh period of creation, God entered into the fullness of his glory.

4:7 Compare Psalm 95:7–8.

4:12 On several occasions, when the Lord spoke to Joseph Smith he used the language of Paul (D&C 11:2;

33:1). God is the great discerner of thoughts. Only he can know the thoughts and intents of the heart (see D&C 6:16).

4:15 Righteous living does not protect us from temptation but it does protect us from succumbing to temptation.

4:16 This is one of the greatest promises in all of the New Testament for obtaining help. As our confidence waxes strong in the presence of God through virtuous living (see D&C 121:45), we may approach the throne of grace boldly and receive the help which God knows is best for us.

HEBREWS 5

5:1–4 In ancient Israel, the high priest was selected from among the priestly families to represent the people before God in sacred matters. Aaron and his sons presided over other Levites and were specifically called "high priests." This office was, however, in the Aaronic Priesthood and is comparable to the office of Presiding Bishop of the Church in our day.

Aaron's sons and other Levites performed many tasks, including serving in the tabernacle, bearing the ark of the covenant, conducting the morning and evening sacrifices, keeping watch over the fire on the sacred altar, and teaching the people of Israel the commandments (see Bible Dictionary, "Aaronic Priesthood").

Both the Old and New Testaments show the priesthood functioning through authoritative ordination. Priesthood was a calling and was received by the laying on of hands (see Bible Dictionary, "Laying on of hands"). The Prophet Joseph Smith taught that "Aaron received his call by revelation" (*Teachings of the Prophet Joseph Smith*, 272). In the days of Jesus and Paul, the priesthood had become corrupted and the office of high priest had been bought by a wealthy and influential family. These were times of great corruption in Judaism.

5:5–6 Paul is quoting from Psalm 2:7 and Psalm 110:4.

5:7–8 Though the manuscript of the Joseph Smith

Translation states that when these verses were originally written they were "a parenthesis alluding to Melchizedek and not to Christ," still we remember that Melchizedek was a type of Christ. In a sense, what pertains to the one, excluding the Atonement, also applies to the other.

5:9 This passage refers to Christ again. Perfection comes through trials and suffering. Christ was made perfect through the things which he suffered. There is no perfection without suffering (JST Hebrews 11:40).

5:12 Oracles are scriptures.

HEBREWS 6

6:1 "Leaving the principles of the doctrine of Christ . . ." doesn't sound like good gospel doctrine. The Joseph Smith Translation resolves the problem in a word: "Therefore *not* leaving . . ." (see also Smith, *Teachings of the Prophet Joseph Smith*, 328). A few translations have made a careful reading of the Greek and rendered it similarly to the Joseph Smith Translation (see footnote 1*a:* "having left behind the beginning of the doctrine . . ." or "Therefore, leaving the initial lessons about the Messiah, let us go on to maturity . . ." In other words, after receiving and living the basics let's move on, "not laying again the foundation" (Stern, *Jewish New Testament*, Hebrews 6:1).

6:1–2 The first principles and ordinances of the gospel are the foundation to be built upon.

6:4–6 The sons of perdition are those who would say the sun doesn't shine while they are looking at it (see Smith, *Teachings of the Prophet Joseph Smith*, 358). Paul uses chilling language to describe the kind of unmitigated rebellion that causes one to knowingly reject Christ's atonement: "They crucify to themselves the Son of God afresh" (see also D&C 76:35; 132:27).

6:8 A formidable abundance of thistles and thorns grew

in the Holy Land, and they did not escape the figurative eye of Jesus and his apostles. Thistles and thorns served only the role of affliction and distraction and annoyance. The parable of the four kinds of soil has seeds falling among thorns, which sprang up and choked the seeds (see Matthew 13:7; Mark 4:7; Luke 8:7). Those thorns represented the cares and pleasures of this world and the deceitfulness of riches (see Matthew 13:22; Mark 4:18–19; Luke 8:14). Thorns seem never to symbolize anything good or positive. In short, "that which beareth thorns and briers is rejected, and is nigh unto cursing; whose end is to be burned" (Hebrews 6:8).

6:13–16 Anciently, swearing by an oath was a formal part of Israel's religious life (Numbers 30; 1 Nephi 4:32–33; Genesis 24).

6:19–20 "Veil" is used to translate the Hebrew *parokhet*. Just as the priest entered through the veil into the Holy of Holies on Yom Kippur, the Day of Atonement, to symbolically cleanse Israel, so Jesus, the great High Priest, entered through the veil into heaven to prepare the way for us.

HEBREWS 7

Jesus' priesthood is greater than the Levitical Priesthood.

7:1 In modern times, the Lord has given new, unique information on Melchizedek. For more on this presiding authority in the early days of Abraham and on his role as a prototype for the Savior, see McConkie, *Doctrinal New Testament Commentary*, 3:168–69; Joseph Smith Translation Genesis 14:25–40 (in Bible Appendix); Alma 13:1–19; Doctrine and Covenants 84:6–26; 107:1–4.

7:1–2 Melchizedek (Hebrew, *Malki-Zedek*) was king and (high) priest of the Lord's people in pre-Israelite Canaan. His name means, literally, "King of righteousness," which is what Jesus actually was. Melchizedek was king of Salem (Hebrew, *Shalem*, "peace"), which means "King of peace," which is what Jesus also was (see Bible Dictionary, "Melchizedek" and "Melchizedek Priesthood").

7:3 The first lines of this verse do not refer to the man but to the higher priesthood that Melchizedek held. The Aaronic Priesthood, which was handed down among the Levites in ancient Israel, was received according to lineage. The Melchizedek Priesthood required righteousness for its bestowal (see McConkie, *Mormon Doctrine,* 478).

7:11–12 If perfection and exaltation were attainable through the Levitical Priesthood, why was there a need for a change to the higher priesthood? To be sure, there was a change from the Aaronic/Levitical to the Melchizedek Priesthood.

7:14 Jesus was not from the tribe of Levi; his priesthood was greater.

7:15 Not only was Melchizedek after the likeness of Christ but Christ was in the similitude of Melchizedek. "The priesthood held by Melchizedek is the very priesthood promised [to] the Son of God during his mortal sojourn, which is to say that Christ was to be like unto Melchizedek" (McConkie, *Promised Messiah,* 450).

7:16–17 The Melchizedek Priesthood is the power of endless life and lives because it administers the ordinances that bring endless posterity (D&C 132:19–24).

7:19–21 See the Joseph Smith Translation additions. The "better hope" is the gospel covenant with its attendant Melchizedek Priesthood blessings. The Aaronic Priesthood is not conferred with an oath but given by lineage; the Melchizedek Priesthood is received with an oath and covenant (see D&C 84:39–40).

7:22 In place of "testament" read "covenant." Jesus was made the guarantor of a better covenant—the Melchizedek Priesthood covenant.

7:25 "He ever liveth to make intercession for them" (see D&C 45:3–5). The Savior intercedes on our behalf and pleads our cause before the Father.

MELCHIZEDEK AND ABRAHAM AT SALEM

Abraham's instruction to go to the "land of Moriah" for the offering of his son (Genesis 22:2) is the first biblical reference to a place called Moriah. Numerous and long-standing Jewish and Christian traditions, as well as the historian Josephus, all support the thesis that Moriah is the same place as Jerusalem's Temple Mount. The biblical record itself indicates that "Solomon began to build the house of the Lord at Jerusalem in mount Moriah, where the Lord appeared unto David" (2 Chronicles 3:1).

Partly because of the sanctity of the place, David purchased the rock on Moriah to make an altar to the Lord (see 2 Samuel 24:18–25), and he instructed Solomon to build the holiest edifice in ancient Israel at that spot (see 1 Kings 5:5). But what about Abraham, a millennium earlier? Did he make the long strenuous trek to that same hill to enact one of the most stirring and emotional scenes in all of human history because there was something sacred about that place already?

We do know that Abraham had met with Melchizedek sometime before "at the valley of Shaveh, which is the king's dale" identified in Bible times and today as the confluence of the Kidron, Tyropoeon, and Hinnom Valleys southeast of the City of David—that is, Old Testament Jerusalem (see Genesis 14:17). We know, too, that Melchizedek ruled over his people at Salem, later called Jerusalem. The ancient Israelite psalmist used the names interchangeably in synonymous parallelism: "In Salem also is his tabernacle, and his dwelling place in Zion" (Psalm 76:2). Melchizedek was a type of the Savior: both are called "King of Righteousness" (the literal meaning of *Malki-zedek,* or *Melchizedek*), and both are referred to as "Prince of Peace" (JST Genesis 14:33; Isaiah 9:6). Melchizedek grew up as a prince and then reigned as king in Salem, reigning under or after his father (see Alma 13:18). Jesus, too, was of royal lineage through Mary, and if the country had not been under Roman subjugation at the time, Jesus had the potential to have been king in Jerusalem; as it was, he was accepted by the righteous as their true King. Melchizedek converted his wicked people to righteousness and established such a great degree of peace and righteousness that they "obtained heaven": they were translated to join the City of Enoch (JST Genesis 14:34); Jesus provided the way for all men and women to obtain heaven and be exalted. And it is likely that both Melchizedek and the Savior accomplished their mortal missions at the same place.

Melchizedek was both king and God's high priest (see D&C 107:2). The holy priesthood of God was thus exercised in Jerusalem a thousand years before David established the priestly orders and Solomon built the Temple. Melchizedek was also keeper of the "storehouse of God" at Salem (JST Genesis 14:37), to which, later, Abraham paid tithes. (Anciently, Israel's Temple also served as the storehouse and treasury of the kingdom.)

How could a great high priest function in his priesthood without a tabernacle or Temple? Or how could a people establish such righteousness that they were transferred from this telestial world without having the blessings of the Temple?

The Prophet Joseph Smith taught that the main object of gathering the people of God in any age of the world is "to build unto the Lord a house whereby He could reveal unto His people the ordinances of His house and the glories of His kingdom, and teach people the way of salvation; for there are certain ordinances and principles that, when they are taught and practiced, must be done in a place or house built for that purpose" (*Teachings of the Prophet Joseph Smith,* 308).

It is possible that a Temple or sanctuary existed on Moriah

during Abraham's lifetime. One early historian wrote that "[Melchizedek] the Righteous King, for such he really was; on which account he was [there] the first priest of God, and first built a temple [there], and called the city Jerusalem, which was formerly called Salem" (Josephus, *Wars,* 6.10.1). During the time Melchizedek was the Lord's presiding authority on the earth ("there were many before him, and also there were many afterwards, but none were greater"; Alma 13:19), he and Abraham lived not far from each other in Canaan. Abraham early in his life had wanted to be "a prince of peace" (Abraham 1:2) as was Melchizedek.

Abraham received the priesthood from Melchizedek (see D&C 84:14), though we do not know when or where. Abraham tells us: "I sought for the blessings of the fathers, and the right whereunto I should be ordained to administer the same; having been myself a follower of *righteousness* [possibly a title denoting God and his Son, who is called "Son of Righteousness"; see 2 Nephi 26:9; Ether 9:22; recall that *Malki-Zedek* means "King of *Righteousness*"], desiring also to be one who possessed great knowledge, and to be a greater follower of *righteousness,* and to possess a greater knowledge, and to be a father of many nations, a *prince of peace,* and desiring to receive instructions, and to keep the commandments of God, I became a rightful heir, a *High Priest,* holding the right belonging to the fathers. It was conferred upon me from the fathers" (Abraham 1:2–3; emphasis added), by which we understand (with the help of D&C 84:14) that Melchizedek bestowed on him the priesthood either in the land of the Chaldeans or in the land of Salem. When Abraham "sought for [his] appointment unto the Priesthood" (Abraham 1:4), he either traveled to Canaan or else Melchizedek traveled to Mesopotamia.

We may conclude that for Abraham, Moriah was already a place with holy associations when he took Isaac there to be bound and offered up. Past, present, and future continually come together at this sacred space. To be sure, the mount was for centuries a place of sacrifices in anticipation of the Great Sacrifice that would be accomplished there.

HEBREWS 8

8:1–3 Just as the Levitical high priest was a minister of the Jerusalem Temple or earthly sanctuary and appointed to offer sacrifice, so Christ is the minister (even gatekeeper) of the heavenly sanctuary (celestial kingdom) who offered the ultimate sacrifice—himself.

8:6–7 A mediator is one who resolves differences between two parties. The atonement of Christ reconciles human beings to God the Father, which the law of Moses could not do. Thus, the gospel is a higher covenant.

8:8–13 Paul quotes Jeremiah 31:31–34 and testifies that the gospel of Jesus Christ is the fulfillment of Jeremiah's prophecy concerning that new covenant which God would establish with Israel. Thus, the old covenant is fulfilled.

HEBREWS 9

Note the chapter heading, "Mosaic ordinances prefigured Christ's ministry." The book of Leviticus becomes important to us here, because it helps us to understand sacrificial offerings and how they prefigured, or foreshadowed, the Great Sacrifice. For example in Leviticus 1:3 and 22:20 we learn that the sacrificial lambs were required to be unblemished, thus prefiguring the spotless condition of Jesus, the Lamb of God, whose blood atoned for our spotted, blemished, or sinful condition (Hebrews 9:14). The law of Moses was a preparatory law to make God's people ready for the law of Christ (see Mosiah 13:29–30; 2 Nephi 25:24–27; Alma 25:15–16; 34:13–14).

9:1–10 Paul discusses the order and nature of worship in the ancient Israelite tabernacle, including a description of the arrangement and configuration of the sanctuary, in order to point out the symbolism of Christ and his atonement.

9:7 "Into the second [that is, the second chamber in the Temple proper, the Holy of Holies] went the high priest alone once every year [on Yom Kippur, the Day of Atonement]." All of that was a type, or symbol, of the ultimate Atonement for the "errors," or sins, of all humankind. Christ was not only the High Priest making the offering but he himself was the Offering.

9:11–15 The blood of animals could not atone for our sins. Their sacrifice, or the shedding of their blood, was a shadow of the future shedding of the blood of God. Only that great and last sacrifice could be an atonement.

9:16–17 Changes in the Joseph Smith Translation parallel the intent of the Greek New Testament word *diatheke* here translated as "testament." The word appears in the Greek Old Testament (Septuagint) 280 times and is almost always translated there as "covenant."

Death is the supreme sacrifice for God or man; when a testimony is sealed with one's life, that testimony is binding. Compare Doctrine and Covenants 136:39.

9:22 This verse describes why the blood of Christ had to be shed.

9:23–28 Just as the Levitical high priest entered the holiest place on earth (the Holy of Holies in the Tabernacle or Jerusalem Temple) once a year and sprinkled blood from the sacrificial animal on the mercy seat, so Jesus performed, in parallel fashion, the great sacrificial act of shedding his blood once and for all and entered the most holy place in the universe (heaven itself) to make intercession for all humankind.

In the following verses certain key words define the symbolic nature of the old law and how it served as a type or a similitude of things to come: 9:23 *patterns;* 9:24 *figures;* 10:1 *shadow* and *image;* 10:3 *remembrance.*

HEBREWS 10

10:1–4, 11–12 The animal sacrifices that the high priest performed every year (as well as on a regular, daily basis) could never take away any sins. The one-time great and last sacrifice of the Lamb of God was and is infinitely more important than all the daily sacrifices.

An important part of the Mosaic system of sacrifice included the selection of a goat to become the scapegoat. On the Day of Atonement, the high priest laid his hands on the goat's head and symbolically placed on the goat all the sins of the people. The scapegoat was then chased into the wilderness, figuratively carrying away the nation's sins: "the goat shall bear upon him all their iniquities unto a land not inhabited" (Leviticus 16:22). The blood of goats was shed for centuries to ritually cleanse and sanctify the people (see Hebrews 9). In his elaborate exposition on the purpose of all those sacrifices, however, Paul remonstrated that "it is not possible that the blood of bulls and of goats should take away sins" (Hebrews 10:4).

10:19–22 The ancient high priest entered the earthly sanctuary through rituals of purification; we enter the heavenly sanctuary through Christ's atoning blood.

HEBREWS 11

Chapter 11 constitutes the greatest discourse on faith in the Bible. It includes definitions and examples.

11:1 Here is the classic definition of faith. Note the alternate rendering of the Greek word translated here as "substance": "assurance" (footnote 1*b*). That is the word Joseph Smith substituted in his inspired revision of the text.

11:3 Christ, Adam, Enoch, "Noah, Abraham, Moses, Peter, James and John, Joseph Smith and many other 'noble and great ones' played a part in the great creative enterprise" (Smith, *Doctrines of Salvation*, 1:74–75).

11:4 Abel's sacrifice was acceptable to God; Cain's was not. Joseph Smith explained why: "By faith in this atonement or plan of redemption, Abel offered to God a sacrifice that was accepted, which was the firstlings of the flock. Cain offered of the fruit of the ground, and was not accepted, because he could not do it in faith, he could have no faith, or could not exercise faith contrary to the plan of heaven. It must be shedding the blood of the Only Begotten to atone for man; for this was the plan of redemption; and without the shedding of blood was no remission; and as the sacrifice was instituted for a type, by which man was to discern the great Sacrifice which God had prepared; to offer a sacrifice contrary to that, no faith could be exercised, because redemption was not purchased in that way, nor the power of atonement instituted after that order; consequently Cain could have no faith; and whatsoever is not of faith, is sin. But Abel offered an acceptable sacrifice, by which he obtained witness that he was righteous, God Himself testifying of his gifts. Certainly, the shedding of the blood of a beast could be beneficial to no man, except it was done in imitation, or as a type, or explanation of what was to be offered through the gift of God Himself; and this performance done with an eye looking forward in faith on the power of that great Sacrifice for a remission of sins" (*Teachings of the Prophet Joseph Smith*, 58).

11:6 This verse gives the reason why faith is essential to salvation.

11:8 Abraham left his homeland on faith; he didn't even know exactly where the Lord was taking him.

11:9 Abraham, along with his son and grandson, lived out their lives in a "strange" or foreign land, dwelling in "tabernacles" or tents.

11:10 Abraham wanted to join the celestial city of Zion, Enoch's city, where his predecessor, Melchizedek, had also gone with his people—the city of God, which other prophets also sought for (see v. 16): "Enoch, and his brethren, . . . were separated from the earth, and were received unto myself—a city reserved until a day of righteousness shall come—a day which was sought for by all holy men, and they found it not because of wickedness and abominations; and confessed they were strangers and pilgrims on the earth; but obtained a promise that they should find it and see it in their flesh" (D&C 45:11–14).

11:11 Sara was at least ninety, well past the age of childbearing, but she believed "him faithful who promised."

11:12 "Therefore sprang there even of one, and him as good as dead . . ." is a reference to Isaac.

11:14 "They seek a country" means a place in heaven (see v. 16).

11:17 Notice Paul's carefully chosen words describing Isaac as Abraham's "only begotten son," an obvious association of Abraham and Isaac with the Father and the Son. Jacob 4:5 says, "It was accounted unto Abraham in the wilderness to be obedient unto the commands of God in offering up his son Isaac, which is a similitude of God and his *Only Begotten Son*" (emphasis added). Thus, only two beings in all of scripture have the distinction of being designated "Only Begotten Son." One is the Savior; the other is Isaac.

11:19 Abraham trusted the promise of God: the patriarch would have innumerable posterity from his son Isaac. Abraham must have concluded that if God was serious about taking Isaac's life, then God would raise him up again, even from the dead—because the promise had been made. That's faith.

11:22 Joseph prophesied the "departing" (Greek, *exodus*) of the children of Israel from Egypt and commanded them to take his bones with them. They did as he instructed, burying Joseph's bones eventually in the plot of ground his father,

Jacob, had given him in Shechem (see Genesis 50:25; Joshua 24:32; John 4:5–6).

11:31 Rahab was the harlot (Hebrew, *zona*, "prostitute") who helped the Israelite spies in their reconnaissance for the siege of Jericho (see also James 2:25).

11:33–38 These descriptions may be identified with specific persons throughout scriptural history. For example, "sawn asunder" in verse 37 is traditionally thought to be the way Isaiah was killed by King Manasseh of Judah. One reference we have for that tradition is an apocryphal work called the Ascension of Isaiah, written possibly about the first century after Christ.

11:40 The Joseph Smith Translation brings out a greater lesson: no one will ever approach perfection without suffering. Our Example is the Suffering Servant, our Savior who was made perfect through suffering (see Hebrews 2:10; 12:5–7, 9–11).

HEBREWS 12

12:1 Sin is a great weight.

12:2 "Jesus' cross was a sign of extreme 'shame' (Hebrews 12:2). Paul did not exaggerate when he called the crucified Christ 'a stumbling block to Jews and folly to Gentiles' (1 Cor 1:23; see 2:2; Gal 5:11). A crucified person— so far from being chosen, anointed, and sent by God—was understood to be cursed by God. To the nonbelievers it seemed 'sheer folly' (1 Cor 1:18) to proclaim the crucified Jesus as God's Son, universal Lord, and coming Judge of the world. The extreme dishonor of his death by crucifixion counted against any such claims. A century after Paul, Justin Martyr (ca. 100–65) noted how utterly offensive it was to acknowledge the divine status of a crucified man: 'They say that our madness consists in the fact that we put a crucified man in second place after the unchangeable and eternal God'

(1 *Apol.* 13.4)" (*Anchor Bible Dictionary,* 1:1209–10). Although crucifixion was considered by nonbelievers to be an ignominious way to die, the early Saints saw obedience, humility, love, and power in the Lord's crucifixion. The metaphor of discipleship was "taking up one's cross" and following the Savior (see Matthew 10:38; 16:24; Luke 9:23; 14:27).

12:5–7, 9–11 Divine chastening—correction, instruction—is vital to all of us in an eternal sense. For example, the Israelites were chastened in the wilderness for forty years (see Deuteronomy 8:2, 16). No one really enjoys the trials one must go through, but trials are essential to growth and spiritual progress, and in that sense one can rejoice in them. If we do not become bitter or resentful to God for the painful and often seemingly tragic ordeals of life, but we are properly "exercised" by them, they will yield "the peaceable fruit of righteousness" (see D&C 101:4–5).

12:16–17 This is a strongly-worded characterization of Esau (see Genesis 25:28–34; 27:34–38). "It" in the final line of verse 17 refers to the birthright.

12:22 "Innumerable company of angels"—how many people will be exalted? Millions and millions, according to Daniel 7:10 and Revelation 5:11.

12:23 The Greek word here translated as "firstborn" is plural, referring to Jesus *and* his Saints.

12:24 "The blood of sprinkling, that speaketh better things than that of Abel"—The meaning of this phrase is uncertain.

12:29 "God Almighty Himself dwells in eternal fire" (Smith, *Teachings of the Prophet Joseph Smith,* 367). "The 'fire' of the Second Coming is the actual presence of the Savior, a celestial glory comparable to the glory of the sun (D&C 76:70) or a 'consuming fire' (Heb. 12:29; cf. Mal. 3:2; 4:1). 'So great shall be the glory of his presence that the sun shall hide his face in shame' (D&C 133:49). 'The presence of the Lord shall be as the melting fire that burneth, and as the fire which causeth the waters to boil' (D&C 133:41; cf. Isa. 64:2; JS-H 1:37). 'Element shall melt with fervent heat' (D&C 101:25) and 'the mountains flow down at thy presence' (D&C 133:44)" ("Jesus Christ: Second Coming of Christ," in Ludlow, *Encyclopedia of Mormonism*, 2:738).

HEBREWS 13

13:2 "Angels" are righteous, mortal men sometimes functioning as angels here on earth (see McConkie, *Doctrinal New Testament Commentary*, 3:235).

13:4 "To deliberately refrain from assuming marital or parental obligation is to fail the most important test of this mortal probation" (McConkie, *Doctrinal New Testament Commentary*, 3:236).

13:8 In addition to teaching God's eternal nature, this verse also implies that the Atonement is eternal in its effects and consequences.

13:22 "Suffer the word of exhortation" means to be teachable, to accept correction, chastening.

The short paragraphs in smaller print at the end of Paul's letters were added by later copyists and are often inaccurate.

CHAPTER 13

JAMES AND JUDE,
BROTHERS OF THE LORD

JAMES

The epistle of James is the first of several "general epistles," so called because they were written to all the Saints, not to those in any specific city. Also, they were written by Church authorities other than Paul.

Regarded as one of the earliest New Testament writings, the book of James has been assumed to have been written between A.D. 45 and 50. *James* is the English version of the Hebrew name *Ya'akov* (otherwise rendered *Jacob*). The New Testament records that there were three leaders in the early Church named Ya'akov: the brother of John, son of Zebedee, who was killed by Herod Agrippa around A.D. 44; the son of Alpheus, sometimes called James the Less, another of the Twelve; and finally, the half-brother of Jesus, apparently converted after the Resurrection. This last James might have been the oldest of Jesus' brothers because he is at the head of the list in Matthew 13:55. Scholars and historians traditionally regard this James as the first bishop of Jerusalem (see Eusebius, *History of the Church*, 36, 75). Furthermore, Luke testifies of his significant leadership role in the important general conference or general council of the Church held in Jerusalem (see Acts 15:13). He also apparently became an apostle and finally was stoned by the Sanhedrin in A.D. 62: "He [Ananus] assembled the Sanhedrin of the judges, and brought before them the brother of Jesus, who was called

Christ, whose name was James, and some others . . . he delivered them to be stoned" (Josephus, *Antiquities*, 20.9.1; see also Eusebius, *History of the Church*, 58–61).

The first James, the brother of John and one of the three chief apostles, had been martyred before this epistle was written. We know almost nothing about the second James, and even his fate is unknown. Thus, the author of this epistle was probably the oldest of Jesus' brothers.

Originally James did not believe his brother was the Messiah and even taunted Jesus (see John 7:2–5). At some point, however, he had a powerful conversion experience owing, in part at least, to his brother's postresurrection appearance to him, as recorded by Paul in his list of certain people to whom Jesus appeared (see 1 Corinthians 15:7).

James and Paul seem to have had a special relationship. Paul called James one of the "pillars" of the Church (Galatians 2:9). And when he visited Jerusalem after his conversion, Paul reported he saw only Peter and "James, the Lord's brother" (Galatians 1:19). Luke also made a specific point of mentioning James as the object of Paul's visit to Jerusalem immediately after his third mission (see Acts 21:18).

The teachings in the epistle of James may profitably be compared to practical religion taught in Jesus' Sermon on the Mount (see Matthew 5–7). In fact, another argument in favor of James the brother of Christ being the author of this epistle is that it approximates the language used in Matthew's account of the Sermon on the Mount. In other words, James knew the language of his brother, the Messiah! James presents counsel that centers on themes of enduring tribulation in faith (see 1:2–4, 12), the nature of faith (see 1:6; 2:14–16), applying one's faith in practical Christian living (see 1:26–27; 2:1–10), self-control (1:19; 3:1–18), riches, pride, and lust (see 1:9–11; 4:1–16; 5:1–4), and forgiveness of sin (see 4:17; 5:14–20). See Bible Dictionary, "James"; "James, Epistle of"; and "James, Epistle of," in Ludlow, *Encyclopedia of Mormonism*, 2:716–17).

JAMES 1

1:1 From this verse we learn that the truths of James' letter have great application to the Saints of the latter days, having been given especially for disciples of the latter days. Elder Bruce R. McConkie said: "Paul wrote to the saints of his own day, and if his doctrine and counsel blesses us of later years, so much the better. But James addressed himself to those of the twelve scattered tribes of Israel who belonged to the Church; that is, to a people yet to be gathered, yet to receive the gospel, yet to come into the fold of Christ; and if his words had import to the small cluster of saints of Judah and Benjamin who joined the Church in the meridian of time, so much the better" (*Doctrinal New Testament Commentary*, 3:243).

1:2–4 As Church members bear their tribulations in faith and loyalty to Christ, they not only develop patience but observe one of the important commandments of modern times, and become perfected (see D&C 54:10; 67:13; 101:4–5; JST Hebrews 11:40).

1:5 "This single verse of scripture has had a greater impact and a more far reaching effect upon mankind than any other single sentence ever recorded by any prophet in any age" (McConkie, *Doctrinal New Testament Commentary*, 3:246–47). This great promise applies to us personally as well as to Joseph Smith. God is anxious to answer our earnest pleas, but note the warning in verse 6.

1:6 James' personal experience likely taught him this principle, because he wasn't always a believer. True disciples must not waver in their faith or commitment.

1:9–11 The humblest, most faithful Saint may receive exaltation. Wealth does not guarantee favored status with God. Wealth has been and always will be a fleeting possession.

In the Mediterranean subtropical climate of the land of Israel, the sun can beat down with merciless constancy.

Summer days follow one after another, on and on with unrelenting cloudlessness. The sun's rays fall hard on the earth, scorching any seed or plant that has no root, causing it to wither away (see Matthew 13:6). James saw a parallel in the transitoriness of riches: "For the sun is no sooner risen with a burning heat, but it withereth the grass, and the flower thereof falleth, and the grace of the fashion of it perisheth: so also shall the rich man fade away in his ways."

1:12 He that endures in faith shall overcome the world (D&C 63:47; compare John 16:33).

1:13–16 Even though all men and women are tempted, God is not the source of temptation. He does, however, try or test his sons and daughters, just as the Hebrew text of Genesis 22:1 says concerning Abraham: "God tested Abraham." That truth is confirmed by Doctrine and Covenants 101:4: "Therefore, they must needs be chastened and tried, even as Abraham."

1:22–27 Notice the definition of "pure religion" (v. 27). Pure religion is manifest in one's actions. It is visiting and nurturing those who could easily become forgotten, ignored, or marginalized.

JAMES 2

2:1–9 The Saints cannot be true disciples of Christ and, at the same time, display favoritism. We need to examine our lives if we are partial to persons because of the color of their skin (see 2 Nephi 26:33), their opportunities for learning (see 3 Nephi 6:12), the expensiveness of their clothing (see James 2:2–5), their economic standing (see James 2:6; Alma 32:2), or their national heritage (see 2 Nephi 26:33), or if we belong to groups promoting exclusiveness (see Alma 31:12–18).

If we desire to live "the royal law" we must love our neighbors as ourselves. Elder Marion G. Romney said that caring for the poor is chief among royal laws (see Conference Report, October 1954, 65).

2:10 Joseph Smith said, "Any person who is exalted to the highest mansion has to abide a celestial law, and the whole law too" (*Teachings of the Prophet Joseph Smith*, 331). To be exalted we must be cleansed from all sin (D&C 50:28–29). One sin can damn a person.

2:14–21 Note changes in the Joseph Smith Translation (Bible Appendix).

2:20 Jesus clearly taught that it is not enough to profess belief, "but he that doeth the will of my Father" is the one who is justified; the parable at the end of the Sermon on the Mount pointedly illustrates that truth (Matthew 7:21, 24–27).

2:21–23 James, in seeming contrast to some Pauline passages, uses Abraham as an example of one justified because of his works that issued from his faith. But both apostles are speaking of two sides of the same coin. Abraham became so great that he was called a "Friend of God" (see 2 Chronicles 20:7; Isaiah 41:18). The Savior said his disciples would be his friends if they did whatsoever he commanded them (see John 15:14). Action is critical to faith.

2:25 Both James and Paul cite Rahab, the woman who assisted Israel's "spies" during the initial incursion into the land of Canaan at Jericho, as an example of faith and works (see also Hebrews 11:31).

JAMES 3

Chapter 3 contains a great sermon on controlling the tongue and the temper, interspersed with some remarkable metaphors to illustrate the lessons. A modern general authority has said, "Whenever you get red in the face, whenever you raise your voice, whenever you get 'hot under the collar,' or angry, rebellious, or negative in spirit, then know that the

Spirit of God is leaving you and the spirit of Satan is beginning to take over" (Burton, *Ensign*, November 1974, 56).

3:5 "How great a matter a little fire kindleth!"—or, in other words, How great a forest fire a tiny spark can start!

3:11–12 On avoiding hypocrisy and living with integrity, James metaphorically inquired, "Doth a fountain send forth at the same place sweet water and bitter? Can the fig tree . . . bear olive berries? either a vine, figs? so can no fountain both yield salt water and fresh" (James 3:11–12). The image is fittingly drawn from the background and life experience of these disciples. At various points up and down the Jordan Valley, which is a seismic region, there are mineral springs and fresh water springs, particularly around the Sea of Galilee. Even today salty spring water is channeled south, away from the lake which is modern Israel's central drinking-water reservoir. Sweet water and bitter water are not a felicitous mix, nor is a conscientious life compatible with a devious one.

3:14 Envy is resentment over the good fortune of others. Strife is contention for superiority. And desire for superiority is the quintessential characteristic of Satan (see Moses 4:1).

JAMES 4

4:1 Wars and conflicts arise because of desires for power, fame, and wealth.

There are gems of wisdom in verses 3–4, 7, 8, 10, 14, and 17.

4:14 Both the psalmist, Isaiah, and Peter used "grass" as the symbol of the transitory nature of life—here today, gone tomorrow.

JAMES 5

5:1–3 These words are reminiscent of the Savior's statements uttered during the Sermon on the Mount: "Lay not up for yourselves treasures on earth, where moth and rust doth corrupt" (Matthew 6:19–21).

5:4 "Lord of sabaoth"—"Sabaoth" has nothing to do with "sabbath." The word in Hebrew is *tzava'ot,* which means "hosts." "Lord of hosts" is a familiar title for Jehovah (see Isaiah 51:15; 2 Nephi 8:15; D&C 64:24; 88:2; Bible Dictionary, "Sabaoth").

5:7–11 These verses show the relationship between trials and patience. The prophets are great examples of enduring affliction and exercising patience; Job is the classic example (on the theme of suffering and trials, see 1 Peter).

5:12 Compare the words of Jesus given during the Sermon on the Mount (see Matthew 5:33–37) with the counsel of James given here.

5:13 Are you afflicted? Pray. (Prayer really works; see v. 16.)

5:14 Are you sick? Call the elders, ask for a priesthood blessing, and prepare yourself to receive it.

5:15 The relationship between physical healings and forgiveness of sins is a stunning one. The same kind of faith that produces healing in us through priesthood administration is the same faith by which our sins are remitted, or by which we enter a state of grace and condition of justification. Both are accomplished through the healing power of Christ. As Paul said, "Therefore being justified by faith, we have peace with God through our Lord Jesus Christ" (Romans 5:1; see D&C 42:44–46).

5:17 Elijah gives an example of effective prayer: he prayed for no rain, and no rain fell for three and a half years. That was devastating to the inhabitants of Israel and probably very humbling, which was its purpose (see 1 Kings 17:1–7; Helaman 11:4).

5:19–20 This is another unique biblical insight but not

one surprising to those acquainted with the scripture of the Restoration. Doctrine and Covenants 62:3 tells us we are blessed when we bear testimony—the angels look upon our recorded witness, and our "sins are forgiven"!

THE USE OF CONSECRATED OLIVE OIL IN PRIESTHOOD BLESSINGS

The latter-day Church of Jesus Christ follows the ancient Church in using olive oil for administering to the sick (James 5:14). Why olive oil in particular? Anciently olive oil was considered to be the cleanest, clearest, brightest burning, and longest lasting of all the animal and vegetable oils. It was the purest of oils and would thus be appropriate for holy anointings.

Knowing the pattern of anointing and administration the Lord established among the children of Israel in biblical times and among the Latter-day Saints in modern times, we may with some confidence conclude that this same pattern was instituted from the days of Adam. Our first historical or scriptural mention of anointing with oil dates from the time of Moses. Olive oil was involved in the anointing of the tabernacle of the congregation, the ark of the testimony, other sacred instruments, and Aaron and his sons (see Exodus 30:24–31). Kings and prophets were invested with power, received divine approval, and were consecrated to their holy calling with olive oil. Samuel anointed Saul to be captain over the Lord's people (see 1 Samuel 10:1); he later anointed David to replace Saul as king over Israel (1 Samuel 16:13; compare Psalm 89:20 and Psalm 23:5—"thou anointest my head with oil"). Solomon was anointed by Zadok the priest and Nathan the prophet (see 1 Kings 1:34, 39). Elijah anointed two kings and the man who would succeed him as prophet (see 1 Kings 19:15–16). Priests who ministered in the Temple used olive oil as part of their ritual offerings. The Messiah of whom all the prophets testified was called in Hebrew *Mashiah* and in Greek *Christos,* meaning in both languages, "Anointed One." Pure olive oil is the enduring symbol of the Savior himself and of his atonement. In the Garden of Gethsemane (literally, "oil press" in Hebrew), some of the life blood of Jesus was "pressed out" under the incomprehensible burden, even weight, of sin, suffering and sorrow. In the Garden, Jesus became like unto the olive, whose oil is pressed out.

The use of olive oil for medicinal purposes is illustrated in the parable of the Good Samaritan, who bound up the wounds of the assaulted Jew, "pouring in oil and wine . . ." (Luke 10:34). Oil and wine were believed to have curative and antiseptic properties, as attested also in rabbinical sources of the time.

Jesus healed many times without using oil and sometimes he even healed without physically touching a person, but authorized priesthood holders in his Church were instructed to heal through the anointing of oil and the laying on of hands. Jesus' twelve apostles, while performing their first missionary labors, "anointed with oil many that were sick, and healed them" (Mark 6:13). The Epistle of James records the most detailed description of priesthood administration preserved for us from ancient times:

"Is any sick among you? let him call for the elders of the church; and let them pray over him, anointing him with oil in the name of the Lord: And the prayer of faith shall save the sick, and the Lord shall raise him up" (James 5:14–15).

Throughout the ages the kingdom of God on earth has used symbols—physical objects and substances representing sacred powers and practices. When we baptize, water is the physical property involved in the ordinance. But water does not cleanse a person from sin; it is the faith and repentance that preceded the baptism that allows the God of heaven, through the person's submitting to the ordinance of baptism, to remit sins. When we partake of the sacrament, bread and water become symbols of the body and blood of the Savior.

There is no redeeming value whatsoever in the meager piece of bread and the tiny cup of water, but what they represent is of infinite worth to us. So it is with administrations to the sick: we apply hands and oil, the physical touch and the tangible substance, in the ordinance, but the hands and the oil do not heal. It is faith in Jesus Christ and his incomparable power that heal. James wrote that "the prayer of faith [the priesthood administration uttered with faith] shall save the sick, and the Lord shall raise him up" (James 5:15). Again, pure olive oil is the symbol of the greatest healing agent in the universe—Christ and his atonement.

On one occasion Jesus encountered a man blind from birth. He anointed his eyes with clay and then instructed him to go and wash in the Pool of Siloam (see John 9:6–7). Perhaps he wanted the blind man to be anointed and washed in order to be physically involved in the healing process. So likewise the baptism in water, and the sacramental bread and water, and the laying on of hands and anointing with oil—all involve the faithful participant in the holy ordinance.

Is a priesthood administration valid without the use of olive oil? Again, it is not the oil that heals but the prayer of faith and the use of priesthood power. In time of emergency, with no oil available, it is altogether fitting and proper to administer to a sick or injured member of the Church with no anointing. President Joseph Fielding Smith wrote: "There have been cases, sad to relate, where elders of the Church, through lack of understanding, have refused to administer to the sick under conditions where oil could not be had. It is the privilege and duty of the elders to bless the sick by the laying on of hands. If they have pure olive oil which has been consecrated for this purpose, one of them should use it in anointing the sick, and then they should by the laying on of hands seal the anointing. If no oil is to be had, then they should administer by the laying on of hands in the power of the priesthood and in the prayer of faith, that the blessing sought may come through the power of the Spirit of the Lord. This is in accordance with the divine plan inaugurated in the beginning" (*Doctrines of Salvation,* 3:183).

JUDE

Jude was another half-brother of Jesus (see Eusebius, *History of the Church,* 81; Jude 1:1, where he is identified as the "brother of James"). The Hebrew form of his name is *Yehuda,* or Judah (sometimes "Juda" in the New Testament), and the Greek form of the same name is *Judas,* though the form *Jude* has been preferred in order to avoid any association with the name of the betrayer, Judas Iscariot. Jude is mentioned in Mark 6:3 and Matthew 13:55 and is included with "his brethren" in John 7:5; Acts 1:14; and 1 Corinthians 9:5. We have no indication of his office or calling; he does not claim to be one of the Twelve.

No date or location is suggested in the letter. His audience is those who were "sanctified" (Jude 1:1). The problem on which Jude focuses is apostasy. Important biblical material is exclusive to this general letter and includes the premortal life as "the first estate," the disputation between Michael and Satan over Moses' body, and Enoch's prophecy of the Second Coming. Though short, the book of Jude is a gem, a powerful witness to the truth of Restoration scripture (see Bible Dictionary, "Jude, Epistle of"; "Enoch"; "Apocrypha"; and "Pseudepigrapha").

JUDE 1

1:4 Jude confirms the pattern of apostasy in the ancient Church when he refers to ungodly men who entered the ranks of Church leaders and teachers in a subtle but deliberate fashion ("crept in unawares").

1:6 "Angels which kept not their first estate" is language unique in the Bible. The fate of those who followed Lucifer, rebelling against the Father and the eternal plan of salvation, was expulsion from their "first estate" to await their assignment to outer darkness on the great day of judgment. It is significant corroboration of the doctrine taught in Abraham 3:24–28.

1:7 Here is an interesting note on how Sodom and Gomorrah were destroyed (see commentary on 2 Peter 2:6).

1:9 Concerning Michael, Joseph Smith taught: "The Priesthood was first given to Adam; he obtained the First Presidency, and held the keys of it from generation to generation. . . . He had dominion given him over every living creature. He is Michael the Archangel, spoken of in the Scriptures. . . . The keys have to be brought from heaven whenever the Gospel is sent. When they are revealed from heaven, it is by Adam's authority. . . . He (Adam) is the father of the human family, and presides over the spirits of all men, . . . Christ is the Great High Priest; Adam next" (*Teachings of the Prophet Joseph Smith*, 157–58). The name *mi-ka-el* means "one who is like God."

Jude was apparently quoting an apocryphal work then in circulation, The Assumption of Moses, which teaches that Moses was translated at the end of his mortal life. The text indicates that before his translation, "Michael was commissioned to bury Moses. Satan opposed the burial on the ground (a) that he was the lord of matter and that accordingly the body should be rightfully handed over to him; (b) that Moses was a murderer, having slain the Egyptian. Michael having rebutted Satan's accusations proceeded to charge Satan with having instigated the serpent to tempt Eve. Finally, all opposition having been overcome, the assumption took place in the presence of Joshua and Caleb." Another "Hebrew Apocalypse tells of Moses' transformation into the form of a fiery angel and his ascent through the seven heavens." And yet another deals with "the temporary translation of Moses before his death into heaven. . . . When translated into heaven the heavenly Jerusalem and the Temple were revealed to him, and he was told these would descend to earth after God had gathered

Israel a second time from the ends of the earth" (Charles, *Apocrypha and Pseudepigrapha of the Old Testament*, 2:408–9).

1:14–16 Enoch's prophecy about the second coming of the Lord is another unique contribution from Jude to the New Testament. It may be a quotation from the book of Enoch, which is not in our present canon of scripture, though the book of Moses contains some writings of Enoch (see especially Moses 7:62–66). On one occasion, Joseph Smith said that Enoch appeared to Jude (*Teachings of the Prophet Joseph Smith*, 170).

1:16 Outside persecution is not the most dangerous opposition encountered by the Church in these last days; apostates from within produce the worst forms of antagonism.

1:23 See Doctrine and Covenants 36:6.

CHAPTER 14

FIRST AND SECOND PETER

1 PETER

Simon Peter, or Cephas (Aramaic, "stone"), was the chief apostle and the equivalent of the prophet-president of the Church of Jesus Christ, though he is never called that in the New Testament. Both the book of Acts and the epistles witness that Peter led the Church (see Acts 1:15–22; Galatians 2:7–9). He was active in Jerusalem, Antioch, and Corinth. The Prophet Joseph Smith said of his predecessor, "Peter penned the most sublime language of any of the apostles" (*Teachings of the Prophet Joseph Smith,* 301).

This first letter of Peter was possibly written at Rome, before the Neronian persecutions of the middle 60s after Christ (the Roman Emperor Nero ruled from A.D. 54 to 68). The letter's main theme centers on how the Saints might respond to suffering and persecution in order to receive great blessings, and it gives warnings and preparations for ominous days ahead. Peter knew what he was talking about. He was a man who had grown perfect through his own trials, suffering, and experiences. Tradition has it that Peter and Paul were both executed in Rome at a time of intense persecution and paranoia in Rome owing to Nero (see Bible Dictionary, "Peter"; "Peter, Epistles of"; see also "Peter," in Ludlow, *Encyclopedia of Mormonism,* 3:1077–79).

1 PETER 1

1:1–2 Peter wrote to five major provinces of Asia Minor, to those who became "elect" because of premortal worthiness and obedience to the gospel.

1:5 In the scriptures, the terms *salvation* and *exaltation* are often used to mean the same thing (see McConkie, *Doctrinal New Testament Commentary,* 3:284–85).

1:6 Because of hope in the resurrection and hope for exaltation, the Saints can rejoice, despite the fact that this life brings trials and afflictions. "Temptations" in the sixteenth-century English of the King James Version of the Bible also means "trials, tests, and provings." See commentary on 1 Peter 4:12–16.

1:7 We should feel not bad or sad but *glad* when trials come; they are opportunities to grow in strength and demonstrate our faith, which is more precious than gold. Even the trial itself is to be prized, for if we endure it well it will bring to us a great reward. As Paul said to the Corinthian Saints, "For our light affliction, which is but for a moment, worketh for us a far more exceeding and eternal weight of glory" (2 Corinthians 4:17).

1:9, 11 Salvation of our souls is the goal of our faith. Jesus is our exemplar in all things. His crown of thorns came first and then his crown of glory. There seems to be an eternal principle associated with suffering. The following scriptures illustrate this principle: Alma 7:5: "My joy cometh over them after wading through much affliction and sorrow"; Alma 17:11: "Ye shall be patient in long-suffering and afflictions, that ye may show forth good examples unto them in me, and I will make an instrument of thee in my hands unto the salvation of many souls"; Alma 26:27: "Bear with patience thine afflictions, and I will give unto you success"; Alma 28:8: "This is the account of . . . their sufferings in the land, their sorrows, and their afflictions, and their incomprehensible joy"; Doctrine and Covenants 58:4: "After much tribulation come the blessings"; Doctrine and Covenants 121:7–8: "Thine adversity and thine afflictions shall be but a small moment; and then, if thou endure it well, God shall exalt thee on high."

In other words, after affliction, sorrow, long-suffering,

tribulation, and adversity come joy, success, blessings, and exaltation (see 1 Peter 4:12–16.)

1:13 An interesting idiom: "gird up the loins of your mind," or, as we might say in English idiom: "roll up your sleeves"; that is, prepare yourselves.

1:15 "Holy" is used to translate the Greek *hagios,* meaning "saintly." "Conversation" is the King James rendering of the Greek word meaning "conduct." In other words: "Act like Saints in all your conduct."

1:18–20 Christ was chosen and prepared in premortality, and his future atonement operated retroactively on our behalf before we came to this earth (D&C 93:38). Joseph Smith taught, "At the first organization in heaven we were all present, and saw the Savior chosen and appointed and the plan of salvation made, and we sanctioned it" (*Teachings of the Prophet Joseph Smith,* 181). On verse 19, see Hebrews 9:14. Old Testament sacrifices foreshadowed Christ, who is the true Paschal, or Passover, Lamb (see 1 Corinthians 5:7).

1:24–25 From a psalmist and from the prophet Isaiah we learn the symbolism of grass, the imagery of which persists through both Testaments. For example, "As for man, his days are as grass: as a flower of the field, so he flourisheth. For the wind passeth over it, and it is gone; and the place thereof shall know it no more" (Psalm 103:15–16). "All flesh is grass, and all the goodliness thereof is as the flower of the field: The grass withereth, the flower fadeth: because the spirit of the Lord bloweth upon it: surely the people is grass. The grass withereth, the flower fadeth: but the word of our God shall stand forever" (Isaiah 40:6–8). Grass is a symbol of the transitoriness of man. With the heavy rains of wintertime grass can flourish and even spread over the barren wilderness (*yeshimon*), but it is gone with a wisp of the transitional *khamsin* (an Arabic word for a devastating east wind). The blades are vivacious and vigorous one day—and vanished the next. So is the life of man, but some things, like the word of God, are time-less and permanent. "All flesh is as grass, and all the glory of man as the flower of grass. The grass withereth, and the flower thereof falleth away: But the word of the Lord endureth for ever. And this is the word which by the gospel is preached unto you" (1 Peter 1:24–25). Given the transitory nature of temporal life on earth, it is comforting to know that there is also the permanence of an unchangeable and never-ending Providence: "If God so clothe the grass of the field, which to day is, and to morrow is cast into the oven, shall he not much more clothe you, O ye of little faith?" (Matthew 6:30; compare D&C 124:7).

1 PETER 2

2:1–3 This verse contains Peter's plea for the Saints to be holy people, a people who desire pure gospel teachings, the "sincere milk of the word."

2:4–8 Peter uses significant imagery derived from the rocky terrain of the Holy Land and other areas of the Mediterranean. Christ is the living stone, the bedrock and chief cornerstone of the Saints' faith. Thus, the Saints are themselves living stones (see v. 5). The Messiah is he who gives firmness and sturdiness to the household of God, but something as solid and immovable as a rock can also be a stumblingblock: "The stone which the builders disallowed, the same is made the head of the corner, and a stone of stumbling, and a rock of offence, even to them which stumble at the word, being disobedient" (1 Peter 2:7–8; see also Romans 9:33). "Whosoever shall fall on this stone shall be broken [become humbled, contrite]: but on whomsoever it shall fall, it will grind him to powder" (Matthew 21:44).

2:9 "A peculiar people" in Hebrew is *'am segulla,* meaning "a valued property" or "special treasure." The Greek is similar in meaning. The phrase is used in the Old and New Testaments eleven times, always of the people of Israel. In

Malachi 3:17 *segulla* is translated as "jewels" (compare D&C 60:4).

2:13 We should submit to civil governments where we reside, unless commanded by revelation to do otherwise.

2:20 "Buffeted" means, literally, to be "struck with fists." The same word appears in Matthew 26:67. If we are knocked around or suffer because of our own stupidity and sins, we shouldn't get much credit. But if we suffer for doing good and endure it, that is commendable before God (see D&C 54:10).

2:22 This verse is one of several biblical verses that explicitly state the sinlessness of Jesus.

2:23 "When he suffered, he threatened not"—during Jesus' Roman "trial" and during the scourging, Jesus did not "lash" out verbally but bore his afflictions with dignity (compare Isaiah 53; Matthew 26–27).

2:24–25 Peter here quotes part of Isaiah's tremendous messianic prophecy (see Isaiah 53, especially vv. 3–6).

1 PETER 3

3:1–2 Remember that *conversation* means "conduct." Here is more helpful prophetic counsel for husbands and wives. This time it is encouragement to the wife whose husband is not active in the Church: patiently work with him and be a good example, and he may eventually be won over. There are many examples of that happening.

3:3 Again, to the wife: be modest and conservative in dress (see also 1 Timothy 2:9).

3:4 "We should cultivate a meek, quiet and peaceable spirit" (Smith, *Teachings of the Prophet Joseph Smith*, 316).

3:7 "Weaker vessel"—vessel, in this sense, refers to the physical body. Husbands and wives become partners, joint-heirs.

3:10 Love life.

3:11 Good motto: eschew evil, pursue peace. This counsel came at a time when some might have been tempted to give up a Christian lifestyle out of frustration or to retaliate in the face of persecutions. This verse is an important follow-up to 1 Peter 2:22–23: Jesus did no sin, and "when he was reviled, he reviled not again." Pursuit of peace is a doctrine also given to the Latter-day Saints at a time when they were being sorely persecuted (D&C 98:16). The Lord counsels his disciples to meet persecution with righteousness and peace.

3:15 Bear your testimony, and use boldness but not overbearance (compare Alma 38:10–12).

3:18–20 An inexplicable passage to many people, but the Latter-day Saints have further light and knowledge about Jesus' preaching in the spirit world because of a vision given to a prophet who sat pondering this passage one day in 1918 in Salt Lake City (see D&C 138, especially vv. 1–31).

We do have some extrabiblical corroboration of the idea of preaching to the dead. From early Christian writings we learn of Hermas, whose brother was bishop in Rome, who wrote in the early second century after Christ that Jesus' apostles died and then preached also the name of the Son of God to those who had fallen asleep before them (*Shepherd of Hermas,* Similitudes 9:16, in *Ante-Nicene Fathers,* 2:49).

3:20–21 Souls were "saved by water," which is to say that the Flood was a figure, or type, of baptism. As those souls were saved during the earth's baptism, so we also may be saved by our own baptism.

1 PETER 4

4:1 "Arm yourselves likewise with the same mind" suggests that we should gain the mind of Christ (see 1 Corinthians 2:16).

4:6 Work for the dead is unique to Latter-day Saints. Who is it for? "Salvation for the dead is limited expressly to those who do not have opportunity in this life to accept the gospel but who would have taken the opportunity had it come to them" (McConkie, *Mormon Doctrine,* 686; see also Smith, *Teachings of the Prophet Joseph Smith,* 107).

4:7 "The end of all things is at hand" refers to Peter's foreshadowing of imminent fiery trials for the Saints (see v. 12).

4:8 Joseph Smith said, "Charity, which is love, covereth a multitude of sins, and I have often covered up all the faults among you; but the prettiest thing is to have no faults at all" (*Teachings of the Prophet Joseph Smith,* 316).

4:12–16 Though these verses were given to the Saints nearly two thousand years ago, undoubtedly as a warning to prepare for persecutions that came during the reign of the Emperor Nero, they are still relevant in our day, too. After a devastating fire that burned roughly one-third of the imperial city, Nero instituted a wave of persecutions and terror in the city by blaming the fire on Christians and other groups.

The Latter-day Saints, collectively and individually, will also be tested to see if they will serve the Lord despite all hazards. Can we, as these verses suggest, actually be happy and rejoice when we're called upon to suffer trials? Can we be grateful for pain, suffering, affliction, and conflict in our lives?

Are we not grateful for the ordeals Joseph went through (sold by his brothers into Egypt, falsely accused, unjustly imprisoned, and so forth) to save the Lord's covenant people anciently?

Are we not grateful for the torture and pain Jesus went through to atone for our sins?

Are we not grateful for the confusion in young Joseph Smith's mind that led, despite intervening persecution, to the restoration of the Church and the fulness of the gospel?

Are we not grateful for the physical trials of Brigham Young and thousands of righteous people who persevered in establishing the headquarters of the Church in the Rocky Mountains?

4:17 "And upon my house shall it begin . . ." (D&C 112:25; see also v. 26).

1 PETER 5

5:2 "Feed my sheep" (John 21:17) was instruction Peter himself had received from the Lord. Now he passes on the same instruction to others. See footnotes to this verse.

5:12 Silvanus, or Silas, who served also as a companion to Paul in his labors, was on this occasion Peter's scribe.

5:13 "Babylon" is Rome ("Babylon" is also used figuratively for Rome in John's Revelation, chapters 17–18). Marcus is John Mark, who had left Paul's company during the latter's first missionary journey (see Acts 13:13). He wrote the Gospel of Mark. According to tradition (Papias, circa A.D. 140) Mark received some of his information from his association with Peter (hearing Peter preach). Mark was also the cousin of Barnabas (see Williamson's synopsis at the end of Eusebius, *History of the Church*, 390–91).

2 PETER

Peter's second epistle was likewise apparently written from Rome, just before his martyrdom. It treats three main topics: having one's calling and election made sure (see McConkie, *Doctrinal New Testament Commentary*, 3:325–50), false teachers, and the Lord's glorious return.

2 PETER 1

On at least two occasions the Prophet Joseph Smith preached with this chapter as his text, specifically on making one's calling and election sure (see *Teachings of the Prophet Joseph Smith*, 298–99; 303–6). Having one's calling and election made sure means being sealed up to eternal life, a guarantee of exaltation. We find a specific scriptural definition of this term in Doctrine and Covenants 131:5. Some who have had their calling and election made sure include Abraham, Isaac, and Jacob (D&C 132:37); Enos (Enos 1:27); Alma (Mosiah 26:20); the Nephite Twelve (3 Nephi 28:1–3); Paul (2 Timothy 4:8); Mormon (Mormon 2:19); Moroni (Ether 12:37); Joseph Smith (D&C 132:49). "In this dispensation many have received like assurances," declared Elder Marion G. Romney (Conference Report, October 1965, 22).

Joseph Smith said: "After a person has faith in Christ, repents of his sins, and is baptized for the remission of his sins and receives the Holy Ghost (by the laying on of hands), which is the first Comforter, then let him continue to humble himself before God, hungering and thirsting after righteousness, and living by every word of God, and the Lord will soon say unto him, Son, thou shalt be exalted. When the Lord has thoroughly proved him, and finds that the man is determined to serve Him at all hazards, then the man will find his calling and his election made sure, then it will be his privilege to receive the other Comforter, which the Lord hath promised the Saints" (Smith, *History of the Church,* 3:380).

"Though they might hear the voice of God and know that Jesus was the Son of God, this would be no evidence that their election and calling was made sure, that they had part with Christ, and were joint heirs with Him. They then would want that more sure word of prophecy, that they were sealed in the heavens and had the promise of eternal life in the kingdom of God. Then, having this promise sealed unto them, it was an anchor to the soul, sure and steadfast. Though the thunders might roll and lightnings flash, and earthquakes bellow, and war gather thick around, yet this hope and knowledge would support the soul in every hour of trial, trouble and tribulation" (Smith, *History of the Church,* 5:388–89).

1:4–10 Great and precious promises: how to achieve the divine nature. "Knowledge" is the Greek *gnosis;* "brotherly kindness" is the Greek *philadelphia;* "charity" is the Greek *agape.*

1:14 Peter's death was prefigured already at the end of Jesus' mortal ministry (see John 21:18–19). Now, in this general letter to the Saints, Peter himself foreshadows his imminent death (see commentary on 2 Timothy 4:6–8 about the martyrdom of Peter).

1:16–19 Peter was an eyewitness of the Savior's glorious transfiguration. In these four verses he recounts what happened on the Mount of Transfiguration (see also D&C 63:20–21).

1:19 Joseph Smith commented on this verse, saying, "Peter penned the most sublime language of any of the apostles" (*Teachings of the Prophet Joseph Smith,* 301). Note the Joseph Smith Translation wording.

1:20 "Private" is used here to translate the Greek *idios,* which occurs 113 times in the New Testament and only here is *idios* translated "private." Seventy-seven times it is translated "his own" (see Matthew 25:14, "his own servants"; John 4:44, "his own country"; John 10:3–4, "his own sheep"), which would lead us to understand this passage as meaning that "no prophecy of the scripture is of his (any prophet's) own interpretation."

1:21 "*As they were*"—in most cases the use of italics in the King James Version of the Bible means that words have been supplied to give sense to the passage in English. In this case, however, no italics are necessary, as the three words are represented by the Greek text itself.

2 PETER 2

2:6 Peter's word *overthrow* (the Greek word has come directly into English as *catastrophe*) is used frequently in the Old Testament. In every case that the Hebrew word *mahapekha* is used, it refers to Sodom and Gomorrah and suggests an earthquake. The cities were located at the southern end of the Dead Sea, in the Rift Valley, where one of the longest and deepest cracks in the earth's surface lies. Because the city was located in an earthquake fault-zone, the overthrowing or overturning of Sodom and Gomorrah might have been caused by, or at least accompanied by, an earthquake.

Jude added another dimension to the destructive process: "Even as Sodom and Gomorrha, and the cities about them in like manner, giving themselves over to fornication, and going after strange flesh, are set forth for an example, suffering the vengeance of eternal fire" (Jude 1:7). He labeled the destroying agent as "eternal fire," possibly some radiance or energy from the Divine Power (compare Genesis 19:24; Exodus 3:2; 13:21; and especially Leviticus 10:2; Numbers 16:35—"fire from the Lord" that consumed others). See Hebrews 12:29.

2:10 Rebellion often includes criticism of authorities and leaders. Criticism usually signals the spirit of apostasy.

2:13 "Sporting themselves with their own deceivings while they feast with you"—that is, proudly showing off their "churchiness" while inwardly being out of harmony. Murmuring may be described as half-suppressed complaint or grumbling. We count ourselves "in" because we're not openly critical, but behind the scenes we're disloyal.

2:14 This is a superb example of figurative language: "eyes full of adultery" is the personification of lust.

2:20–21 Once we have committed to accept and live the gospel of Jesus Christ, we are responsible and accountable. It is actually better not to accept the gospel and make the covenants than to do so and then not live up to them.

2 PETER 3

3:8 Regarding the Lord's time, see Abraham 3:4; 5:13; Psalm 90:4; Alma 40:8. Notice the different emphasis of Joseph Smith Translation 2 Peter 3:8: "But concerning the coming of the Lord, beloved, I would not have you ignorant of this one thing, that one day is with the Lord as a thousand years, and a thousand years as one day." When the Lord announced in the nineteenth century after Christ that his coming was imminent, "near at hand," "even at the doors," and so forth, it is true according to the Lord's time schedule.

3:10–14 This is a description of the Second Coming and what will happen on the earth as telestial people and things are removed and a new, terrestrial order is inaugurated. If we're interested in living in such a new world, what kind of people should we be?

3:15–16 This is a commentary of Peter on Paul and also a warning to those who distort Paul's writings and other scripture.

DEALING WITH TRIALS, SUFFERING, AND AFFLICTIONS

There is purpose in suffering (see Hebrews 12:5–7, 10–11; D&C 121:1–10; 122).

The following statements are from great people who themselves knew trials and afflictions:

The Prophet Joseph Smith: "It is a false idea that the Saints will escape all the judgments, whilst the wicked suffer; for all flesh is subject to suffer, and 'the righteous shall hardly escape'" (*History of the Church*, 4:11).

"An actual knowledge to any person, that the course of life which he pursues is according to the will of God, is essentially necessary to enable him to have that confidence in God without which no person can obtain eternal life. It was this that enabled the ancient saints to endure all their afflictions and persecutions, and to take joyfully the spoiling of their goods, knowing (not believing merely) that they had a more enduring substance. (Hebrews x. 34).

"Such was, and always will be the situation of the saints of

God, that unless they have an actual knowledge that the course they are pursuing is according to the will of God they will grow weary in their minds, and faint . . . For a man to lay down his all, his character and reputation, his honor, and applause, his good name among men, his houses, his lands, his brothers and sisters, his wife and children, and even his own life also—counting all things but filth and dross for the excellency of the knowledge of Jesus—requires more than mere belief or supposition that he is doing the will of God; but actual knowledge, realizing that, when these sufferings are ended, he will enter into eternal rest, and be a partaker of the glory of God.

"Let us here observe, that a religion that does not require the sacrifice of all things never has power sufficient to produce the faith necessary unto life and salvation . . .

"Those, then, who make the sacrifice, will have the testimony that their course is pleasing in the sight of God: and those who have this testimony will have faith to lay hold on eternal life, and will be enabled, through faith, to endure unto the end, and receive the crown that is laid up for them . . .

"All the saints of whom we have account, in all the revelations of God which are extant, obtained the knowledge which they had of their acceptance in his sight through the sacrifice which they offered unto him" (*Lectures on Faith*, 57–59).

"Inasmuch as God hath said that He would have a tried people, that He would purge them as gold, now we think that this time He has chosen His own crucible, wherein we have been tried; and we think if we get through with any degree of safety, and shall have kept the faith, that it will be a sign to this generation, altogether sufficient to leave them without excuse; and we think also, it will be a trial of our faith equal to that of Abraham, and that the ancients will not have whereof to boast over us in the day of judgment, as being called to pass through heavier affliction; that we may hold an even weight in the balance with them" (*Teachings of the Prophet Joseph Smith*, 135–36).

"You will have all kinds of trials to pass through. And it is quite as necessary for you to be tried as it was for Abraham and other men of God, and . . . God will feel after you, and He will take hold of you and wrench your very heart strings, and if you cannot stand it you will not be fit for an inheritance in the Celestial Kingdom of God" (John Taylor, *Journal of Discourses*, 24:197).

President Brigham Young taught: "All intelligent beings who are crowned with crowns of glory, immortality, and eternal lives must pass through every ordeal appointed for intelligent beings to pass through, to gain their glory and exaltation. Every calamity that can come upon mortal beings will be suffered to come upon the few, to prepare them to enjoy the presence of the Lord. If we obtain the glory that Abraham obtained, we must do so by the same means that he did. If we are ever prepared to enjoy the society of Enoch, Noah, Melchizedek, Abraham, Isaac, and Jacob, or of their faithful children, and of the faithful Prophets and Apostles, we must pass through the same experience, and gain the knowledge, intelligence, and endowments that will prepare us to enter into the celestial kingdom of our Father and God. How many of the Latter-day Saints will endure all these things, and be prepared to enjoy the presence of the Father and the Son? You can answer that question at your leisure. Every trial and experience you have passed through is necessary for your salvation" (*Discourses of Brigham Young*, 345).

"It is recorded that Jesus was made perfect through suffering. If he was made perfect through suffering, why should we imagine for one moment that we can be prepared to enter into the kingdom of rest with him and the Father, without passing through similar ordeals" (*Discourses of Brigham Young*, 346).

President George Q. Cannon wrote: "Every Latter-day Saint who gains a celestial glory will be tried to the very uttermost. If there is a point in our character that is weak and tender, you may depend upon it that the Lord will reach after that, and we will be tried at that spot, for the Lord will test us to the utmost before we can get through and receive that glory and exaltation which He has in store for us as a people" (*Gospel Truth,* 1:103).

Elder Harold B. Lee said: "I am aware that I have had to submit to some tests, some severe tests, before the Lord, I suppose to prove me to see if I would be willing to submit to all things whatsoever the Lord sees fit to inflict upon me, even as a little child does submit to its father" (Conference Report, October 1967, 98).

Elder Spencer W. Kimball wrote: "Being human, we would expel from our lives physical pain and mental anguish and assure ourselves of continual ease and comfort, but if we were to close the doors upon sorrow and distress, we might be excluding our greatest friends and benefactors. Suffering can make saints of people as they learn patience, long-suffering, and self-mastery" (*Faith Precedes the Miracle,* 98).

Elder Bruce R. McConkie declared: "The greatest trials of life are reserved for the saints" (*Doctrinal New Testament Commentary,* 3:318).

Elder Boyd K. Packer said: "Some are tested by poor health, some by a body that is deformed or homely. Others are tested by handsome and healthy bodies; some by the passion of youth; others by the erosions of old age. Some suffer disappointment in marriage, family problems; others live in poverty and obscurity. Some (perhaps this is the hardest test) find ease and luxury. All are part of the test, *and there is more equality in this testing than sometimes we suspect*" (*Ensign,* November 1980, 21; emphasis added).

Elder Richard L. Evans, quoting Phillips Brooks, said: "You may search all the ages for [a person who has had no problems] . . . you may look through the . . . streets of heaven, asking each [one] how he came there, and you will look in vain everywhere for a man morally and spiritually strong, whose strength did not come to him in a struggle. . . .

Do [not] suppose that [there is any man who] has never wrestled with his own success and happiness. . . . There is no exception anywhere. Every true strength is gained in struggle" (*The Sea of Glass Mingled with Fire*, quoted in *Improvement Era*, April 1964, 306; brackets and ellipses in original).

CHAPTER 15

FIRST, SECOND, AND THIRD JOHN

1 JOHN

John, "the disciple whom Jesus loved," is thought to have written three letters, possibly from Ephesus, sometime between A.D. 70 and 100. These letters were composed, especially the first epistle, in response to Gnosticism, the set of ideas in the early Church that regarded the body as evil and the spirit as the ultimate good. That was an attitude and philosophy that was anti-Christ (see v. 18). John emphasized that Jesus came in the flesh (see 1 John 4:3), countering those who espoused the dogma perpetuated for many centuries thereafter that God is without body, parts, or passions.

As in his Gospel account of Jesus' life, John's letters also emphasized love. "Nothing is so much calculated to lead people to forsake sin," wrote Joseph Smith, "as to take them by the hand, and watch over them with tenderness. When persons manifest the least kindness and love to me, O what power it has over my mind, while the opposite course has a tendency to harrow up all the harsh feelings and depress the human mind" (*Teachings of the Prophet Joseph Smith,* 240). John wrote with tenderness and with the love and light of God (see Bible Dictionary, "John" and "John, Epistles of").

1 JOHN 1

1:1–3 John testifies, for the benefit of those leaning towards the Gnostic view of Jesus, that he personally heard, saw, and touched the Savior. For John and Peter and Paul, God the Father and his biological son, Jesus, are separate and distinct personages.

1:5 An important theme in John's writings is that Christ is the Light of the World (see John 1:4–9; 8:12; 9:1–5; compare D&C 50:23–24; 88:67–68).

1:8 All have sinned, as Paul said to the Romans (see Romans 3:23).

1 JOHN 2

2:1 Note the change in the Joseph Smith Translation and compare Doctrine and Covenants 45:3–5.

2:8–11 As Church members demonstrate Christlike love, they receive and reflect the same light Christ possesses.

2:12–14 These verses contain the effective teaching formula, "I write unto you." The intended audience, "little children," "young men," and "fathers," encompasses the whole Church and is reminiscent of modern prophets who have addressed remarks to all segments and age groups of the Lord's people.

2:15–16 The love of the world is diametrically opposed to the love of God. Note the prominent place of lust and pride in the scheme of the world.

2:18 "It is the last time"—though not yet "last days." John wrote of the Great Apostasy. It had already occurred in John's time. The end of the world was not occurring, but the end of the Church in that day was. We have three classic examples of "antichrists" in the Book of Mormon: Sherem (see Jacob 7), Nehor (see Alma 1), and Korihor (see Alma 30).

2:20 See footnote 20*a* on "unction."

2:23 The italicized ending of the verse does not appear in the Greek manuscripts; it was added from the Latin Vulgate.

2:27 "The anointing" is the gift of the Holy Ghost.

1 JOHN 3

3:2 Here is a one-verse doctrinal sermon about our potential to become like God.

3:4 This verse presents a succinct definition of sin (see also 1 John 5:17).

3:6–9 The Joseph Smith Translation of these verses contains important corrections (as also 1 John 5:18). Spiritual rebirth causes men and women to desire to forsake sin. Satan rebelled against God in the beginning and was thrust out of the presence of Deity to deceive and tempt the rest of Heavenly Father's children (see Moses 4:1–4; Abraham 3:24–28).

3:11 This is always John's message. No wonder he is called John the Beloved. He heard this principle straight from the source of enduring love. It was taught from the beginning, and was reiterated on the last night of the Savior's mortal ministry (see John 15:12).

3:16 The ultimate testimony of love is giving our lives for others, as Jesus did.

3:22 The more righteous a person is, the easier it is to receive communications from heavenly sources. The secret of gaining answers to prayers is prior obedience to the Lord's commandments (see McConkie, *Doctrinal New Testament Commentary,* 3:391, 393).

3:24 "Dwelleth" is used here to translate the Greek word meaning "remains, abides."

1 JOHN 4

4:3 Adherents of *docetism* espoused the idea that Jesus only seemed to live as a mortal and to suffer and die. They claimed that the eternal Messiah did not really come in contact with temporal matter, as that would have desecrated his divinity.

4:7–11 Charity is the essence of God's character and personality. Disciples must come to possess charity. It proceeds from faith, hope, and meekness (see Moroni 7:38–48).

4:12 See the Joseph Smith Translation; see also Doctrine and Covenants 67:11.

1 JOHN 5

5:3 Love of God and obedience, or good works, cannot be separated. "His commandments are not grievous"—"For my yoke is easy, and my burden is light" (Matthew 11:30).

5:5 Salvation is only in and through Christ (see Mosiah 3:17). One cannot merit anything in or of oneself.

5:7 The King James Version has added words in this verse not found in any Greek manuscripts nor in any translation prior to the sixteenth century. Thus, the phrases, "bear record in heaven, the Father, the Word, and the Holy Ghost: and these three are one. And there are three that bear witness in earth . . ." are a late addition. The members of the Godhead are one in purpose, not in physicality or entity.

5:8 Spirit, water, and blood are three elements of mortal and spiritual birth and key elements of the Atonement, which brings renewed life to every creature (see McConkie, *Doctrinal New Testament Commentary,* 3:403–4).

5:9–21 These verses indicate that John wrote to those who were possessors of eternal life through faith in Christ, though they yet lived in mortality. John testified that Church members who have an abiding testimony of Christ (with all that entails and implies) possess eternal life as a present possession, even though the full blessings and conditions of eternity lie in the future.

5:17 This passage leaves little room for rationalization; all unrighteousness is sin.

5:18 Spiritual rebirth causes one to lose the desire for sin (he "continueth not in sin," as the Joseph Smith Translation says). That is the powerful message of Mosiah 5:2: "The Spirit of the Lord Omnipotent . . . has wrought a mighty change in us, or in our hearts, that we have no more disposition to do evil, but to do good continually."

5:18–20 John's testimony in this letter ends with three striking affirmations: "We know that . . ." and summarizes some major points of the epistle.

GNOSTICISM

The word *Gnosticism* (from the Greek *gnosis,* "knowledge") refers to what is generally regarded as a heretical strain of thought in late antiquity, particularly during the period of the early Church. Early Christian writers seem to have used the term as a generic name for various groups that adopted nonorthodox doctrines centering on good, evil, spirit, matter, and the nature of Christ. At the heart of Gnostic teaching was the conviction that spirit was entirely good (the highest good), while matter was entirely evil (the ultimate evil).

The goal of Gnostic teaching was to help the specially chosen people of God (that is, all true Gnostics) understand the correct nature of the universe and escape the fetters of this material world through special knowledge (*gnosis*). Gnostics believed themselves elite; they had been initiated into mysteries revealed through secret *gnosis.* For Gnostics, salvation was not an issue of being delivered from sin and guilt but of freeing the spirit from matter (see *Anchor Bible Dictionary,* 2:1033–34).

The radical dualism that formed the backbone of Gnostic teaching (spirit versus matter, light versus dark) led to significant doctrinal errors. The following outlines many of these

Gnostic beliefs. First, the bodies of men and women, being composed of matter or material substance, were wholly evil. Second, by contrast, God, the highest good, was wholly spirit. Third, because salvation, which is escape from the body, is achieved by special knowledge (*gnosis*), it is not accomplished through faith in Christ. Fourth, out of this perverted view grew a strange justification for licentious behavior. Because escape from the body provided salvation, obedience to the commandments of the literal Son of God was not necessary. Thus, breaking the laws of a code of sexual morality entailed no moral consequence because the physical body was considered evil anyway and the spirit was trapped inside an evil entity. Fifth, because the body was considered evil, it was to be treated harshly. The physical senses were also evil and not to be trusted. That is sometimes referred to as ascetic Gnosticism. Sixth, because Christ was ultimately good and therefore wholly spirit, he only seemed to have a physical body. This belief led to a form of Gnosticism called Docetism (from the Greek, *dokeo*, "to seem"). Finally, some Gnostics, attempting to reconcile their ideas with the person of Christ, said that the divine Christ joined the man Jesus at baptism and then departed from him just before his death (see NIV Study Bible).

The worst thing about Gnosticism is that it was really a sophisticated denial of the most fundamental aspects of the Atonement of the Lord Jesus Christ. By the time the apostles were composing their epistles, Gnosticism had taken hold in some parts of the Church. For example, it forms the background of much of John's message in his three letters now called 1, 2, and 3 John. That can be seen in 1 John 1:1 and 4:2–3, where the beloved apostle counters the false teachings of Gnosticism with his eyewitness testimony of the reality, corporeality, and nature of the Savior. Jesus was the Messiah and he had a physical body that died and was resurrected. John had witnessed these events of the Atonement with all his physical senses.

Ascetic Gnosticism, or harsh treatment of the body and

rejection of the physical senses, also forms the background against which Paul responds to Church members in Colossians 2:21–23. Essentially, he says to members of the Church, "You have died with Christ pertaining to worldly ideas. Why do you act as though you still belong to the world by following notions that certain worldly philosophies promote, such as refusing to acknowledge the senses (handling, tasting, and touching), and treating the body harshly?"

Early Gnosticism is reflected in 1 and 2 Timothy, Titus, 2 Peter, John's letters, and Colossians. Paul's admonishing Timothy to turn away from "disputations of what is falsely called knowledge" (footnote to 1 Timothy 6:20) seems to be an apostolic reference to Gnosticism.

"According to the view of the Church Fathers [Christian writers of the second through the fourth centuries after Christ] the gnostic movement was introduced by the devil. . . . The head of the deceivers was Simon Magus (i.e., 'the Sorcerer') known from Acts 8. His disciple Menander then distributed the gnostic teachings. However, it is very difficult to write the history of Gnosis" (*Anchor Bible Dictionary*, 2:1035–36). Certainly it was closely tied to the dualistic ideas found in Judaism, Zoroastrianism, and Hellenistic traditions, all of which influenced the Church of Jesus Christ in apostolic times.

Though Gnosticism was a pernicious fallacy, Latter-day Saints may recognize in it some elements of truth. God did put into humankind a spirit, soul, or "divine spark." There is a spiritual realm of light to which those spirits yearn to return. And because of Adam's fall, the natural man has become carnal, sensual, and devilish and our natures "evil continually," in the words of Ether 3:2. Our unregenerate physical bodies are incompatible with Deity (see Moses 1). Revelation does communicate special, divine knowledge and wisdom, but all people are not receptive to it. Divine knowledge does give a unique perspective on the universe and teaches certain sacred secrets to those who seek after it.

But all these things point toward the need for a Redeemer, not away from one. At the core of salvation is the mercy, power, and bodily resurrection of Jesus of Nazareth, who is the only true Savior and Lord, omnipotent and omniscient (see Mosiah 3:17), the literal, biological Son of God. One can see that, if for no other reason, scriptures of the Restoration were needed to corroborate the correctness of apostolic teaching in the first century and to lay to rest any notion of the correctness of many Gnostic ideas in the latter days.

2 JOHN

Second and Third John are more personal. Where and when they were written is unknown, though possibly they were written sometime near the turn of the century. It is possible they were written to John's own immediate family.

2 JOHN 1

1:1 John describes himself as "the elder," and the "elect lady" is either figurative for a branch of the Church or literal for a female member, perhaps even his wife. Emma Smith, wife of the Prophet, was called "an elect lady" (D&C 25:3).

1:7 Deceivers and anti-Christs try to promote the idea that Jesus of Nazareth is not the Messiah and teach that "there should be no Christ," just as did Korihor (Alma 30:12). The full pattern of such teaching includes attacks on revelation, prophets, resurrection, and ecclesiastical authority and the promotion of skepticism, empiricism, survival of the fittest, naturalism, and moral relativism (see Alma 30:12–48).

1:10 Don't help those who teach falsely; don't wish them prosperity, and don't support them.

3 JOHN

3 JOHN 1

1:1 Because Gaius is a common first name for a Roman

man, most writers assume the person to be a man, possibly a regional official of the Church.

1:4 There is "no greater joy" than to know that our children walk in truth.

1:9 Diotrephes was an apostate local Church leader.

JOHN THE APOSTLE

Eusebius, an early Christian author, wrote the following of John the apostle:

"In Asia, moreover, there still remained alive the one whom Jesus loved, apostle and evangelist alike, John, who had directed the churches there since his return from exile on the island, following Domitian's death. That he survived so long is proved by the evidence of two witnesses who could hardly be doubted, ambassadors as they were of the orthodoxy of the Church—Irenaeus and Clement of Alexandria. In Book II of his *Against Heresies*, Irenaeus writes:

"'All the clergy who in Asia came in contact with John, the Lord's disciple, testify that John taught the truth to them; for he remained with them till Trajan's time [*Against Heresies*, II. 33.2].'

"In Book III of the same work he says the same thing:

"'The church at Ephesus was founded by Paul, and John remained there till Trajan's time; so she is a true witness of what the apostles taught [*Against Heresies*, III. 3.4].'

"Clement, in addition to indicating the date, adds a story that should be familiar to all who like to hear what is noble and helpful. It will be found in the short work entitled *The Rich Man Who Finds Salvation*. Turn up the passage, and read what he writes:

"'Listen to a tale that is not just a tale but a true account of John the apostle, handed down and carefully remembered. When the tyrant was dead, and John had moved from the island of Patmos to Ephesus, he used to go when asked to the neighboring districts of the Gentile peoples, sometimes to appoint bishops, sometimes to organize whole churches, sometimes to ordain one person of those pointed out by the Spirit. So it happened that he arrived at a city not far off named by some [Smyrna], and after settling the various problems of the brethren, he finally looked at the bishop already appointed, and indicating a youngster he had noticed, of excellent physique, attractive appearance, and ardent spirit, he said: 'I leave this young man in your keeping, with all earnestness, in the presence of the Church and Christ as my witness.' When the bishop accepted him and promised everything, John addressed the same appeal and adjuration to him a second time.

"'He then returned to Ephesus, and the cleric took home the youngster entrusted to his care, brought him up, kept him in his company, looked after him, and finally gave him the grace of baptism. After this he relaxed his constant care and watchfulness, having put upon him the seal of the Lord as the perfect protection. But the youngster snatched at liberty too soon, and was led sadly astray by others of his own age who were idle, dissolute, and evil-livers. First they led him on by expensive entertainments; then they took him with them when they went out at night to commit robbery; then they urged him to take part in even greater crimes. Little by little he fell into their ways; and like a hard-mouthed powerful horse he dashed off the straight road, and taking the bit between his teeth rushed down the precipice the more violently because of his immense vitality. Completely renouncing God's salvation, he was no longer content with petty offenses, but, as his life was already in ruins, he decided to commit a major crime and suffer the same fate as the others. He took these same young renegades and formed them into a gang of bandits of which his was the master mind, surpassing them all in violence, cruelty, and bloodthirstiness.

"'Time went by, and some necessity having arisen, John was asked to pay another visit. When he had dealt with the business for which he had come, he said: 'Come now, bishop, pay me back the deposit which Christ and I left in your keeping, in the presence of the Church over which you preside as my witness.' At first the bishop was taken aback, thinking that he was being dunned for money he had never received. He could neither comply with a demand for what he did not possess, nor refuse to comply with John's request. But when John said 'It is the young man I am asking for, and the soul of our brother', the old man sighed deeply and shed a tear.

""""He is dead."

""""How did he die?"

""""He is dead to God: he turned out wicked and profligate, in short, a bandit; and now, instead of the Church, he has taken to the mountain with an armed gang of men like himself."

"'The apostle rent his garment, groaned aloud, and beat his head. "A fine guardian," he cried, "I left of our brother's soul! However, let me have a horse immediately, and someone to show me the way." He galloped off from the church, then and there, just as he was. When he arrived at the place, and was seized by the bandits' sentry-group, he made no attempt to escape and asked no mercy, but shouted: "this is what I have come for: take me to your leader." For the time being the young man waited, armed as he was; but as John approached he recognized him, and filled with shame, turned to flee. But John ran after him as hard as he could, forgetting his years and calling out: "Why do you run away from me, child—from your own father, unarmed and very old? Be sorry for me, child, not afraid of me. You still have hopes of life. I will account to Christ for you. If need be, I will gladly suffer your death, as the Lord suffered death for us; to save you I will give my own life. Stop! believe! Christ sent me."

"'When he heard this, the young man stopped and stood with his eyes on the ground; then he threw down his weapons; then he trembled and began to weep bitterly. When the old man came up he flung his arms round him, pleading for

303

himself with groans as best he could, and baptized a second time with his tears, but keeping his right hand out of sight. But John solemnly pledged his word that he had found pardon for him from the Savior: he prayed, knelt down, and kissed that very hand as being cleansed by his repentance. Then he brought him back to the church, interceded for him with many prayers, shared with him the ordeal of continuous fasting, brought his mind under control by all enchanting power of words, and did not leave him, we are told, till he had restored him to the Church, giving a perfect example of true repentance and a perfect proof of regeneration, the trophy of a visible resurrection [*The Rich Man Who Finds Salvation,* 42. 1–15].'

"This story from Clement I have included both for its historical interest and for the benefit of future readers" (Eusebius, *History of the Church,* 83–85).

CHAPTER 16

THE REVELATION

The main purpose of the book of Revelation is to testify of Jesus Christ (see Revelation 19:10). That testimony was vital for the Saints when the Revelation was given, and it is vital for the Saints now. John gave us "the big picture," a view of the ultimate triumph of all things good and the ultimate victory of God. The Revelation was written by "St. John the Divine," meaning John the Diviner, or Revelator, who is also known as John the Beloved. John was a member of the original Quorum of the Twelve and of the First Presidency. He was the author of five New Testament books. We also know that John has not yet died but is a translated being (see D&C 7).

Another name for the Revelation is "Apocalypse," a word derived from the Greek *apokalupsis,* which means "uncovering or unveiling," or, indeed, "revelation." Many prophets have seen visions similar to John's: Adam, Enoch, the brother of Jared, Abraham, Joseph, Moses, Isaiah, Nephi, Daniel, Ezekiel, and others. Of all those who saw the grand panorama of history, most received an immediate command to seal it up (see footnotes to 1 Nephi 14:26); John, on the other hand, was assigned to write it down, so it could come to us for our benefit and learning.

Any student preparing to read the Revelation must read at least two passages of scripture: 1 Nephi 14:18–27 and Doctrine and Covenants 77. Ether 4:15–16 also describes the chronological context for the fulfillment of John's revelation.

STRUCTURE OF THE REVELATION

The book of Revelation may be divided into two parts: Chapters 1 through 3 provide a setting for the Revelation and record letters to local churches in John's day; chapters 4 through 22 are an apocalyptic revelation of the grand panorama of the earth's history.

The Revelation is presented in what one author calls "kaleidoscopic structure." It consists of disjointed scenes, conversations, and images—each of these elements is always in motion. Each plays out its brief moment and then shifts to another, jumping from one time period to another, back and forth, constantly refocusing. There seems to be no smooth flow of narrative (see Ryken, *How to Read the Bible as Literature*, 170).

Ryken is correct, to a degree, in depicting the vision as somewhat disjointed or scrambled, which may be part of "the manner of prophesying among the Jews" (2 Nephi 25:1) that relates the present to the past and the future, but still there is a unifying structure to the book of Revelation. The Vision (chapters 4–22) is presented in seven thousand-year periods of this world's temporal existence. In just a few short verses John gives a synopsis of the first five thousand-year periods, and then he describes in considerable detail events in the sixth and seventh periods, with periodic flashbacks or interludes interrupting the smooth flow of history.

SYMBOLIC LANGUAGE

Symbolic or figurative language, a type of "divine code," is often used in the scriptures to reveal truths to the spiritually prepared and to conceal truths from the spiritually unprepared. Some may suppose that careless or evil-disposed scribes or religionists expunged from John's original text many "plain and precious things," resulting in the present text of Revelation, which is often regarded as obscure and unintelligible. Actually John wrote in this manner intentionally so the writing would be deciphered or discerned only by those who pay the price to be spiritually ready. The symbols employed by John may seem weird and grotesque (for example, beasts with many eyes and wings), but they all represent something significant. To gain an understanding of the symbols or figures of speech means to gain an understanding of the message of Revelation.

The symbols used in scripture are understood by the same spirit in which they were given—the spirit of prophecy, which is the testimony of Jesus. Investigating the context of other references to the same or similar symbols will help to increase understanding. It helps to consult known interpretive keys to the apocalyptic writings of Ezekiel, Daniel, and Zechariah. It also helps to consult similar prophetic statements in Matthew 24 (with parallels in Mark 13 and Luke 21), and to consult explanatory passages in Doctrine and Covenants 29, 88, and others. Doctrine and Covenants 77 is particularly important in understanding Revelation; it consists of fifteen questions Joseph Smith asked about the Revelation, and the Lord's fifteen answers. Section 77 is a key that allows us to open the Revelation, to go inside, and to explore it.

Most numbers in the Revelation are symbolic, though it is clear that certain numbers are literal. For example, there actually were seven representative churches, and there are seven thousand-year periods, twelve tribes, and twelve apostles. Individual numbers will be defined as far as we understand them as they appear in the text.

Modern prophets and the scriptures have explained many of the symbolic terms and expressions in the Revelation:

1. Seven spirits, or angels: seven servants (see Revelation 1:4)
2. Seven candlesticks: seven churches (see Revelation 1:12)
3. Nicolaitans: those who want to be Church members *and* worldly (see Revelation 2:6)

4. New Jerusalem from heaven: City of Enoch (see Revelation 3:12)

5. Sea of glass: the celestialized, sanctified earth (see Revelation 4:6)

6. Four beasts: beasts (see Revelation 4:6)

7. Book with seven seals: seven thousand-year periods of world history (see Revelation 5:1)

8. A Lamb: Christ (see Revelation 5:6)

9. Horses: representative of events in the thousand-year periods (see Revelation 6:2, 4–5, 8)

10. Sealing in foreheads: have one's calling and election made sure (see Revelation 7:3)

11. Half hour of silence in heaven: the meaning is unknown (see Revelation 8:1)

12. A star fallen from heaven: Lucifer, or Satan (see Revelation 8:10)

13. Locusts: armies in the battle of Armageddon (see Revelation 9:7)

14. Abaddon or Apollyon: Satan (see Revelation 9:11)

15. The little book: John's mission to gather the tribes of Israel (see Revelation 10:2)

16. Forty and two months: the Great Apostasy (see Revelation 11:2)

17. Two witnesses: two prophets in Jerusalem (see Revelation 11:3)

18. A woman: the Church of God (see Revelation 12:1)

19. Twelve stars: twelve apostles (see Revelation 12:1)

20. Great red dragon: Satan (see Revelation 12:3)

21. Third part of the stars of heaven: the third who followed Satan (see Revelation 12:4)

22. Man child given birth by the woman: millennial kingdom of God (see Revelation 12:5)

23. War in heaven: dispute over eternal plan of salvation (see Revelation 12:7)

24. Michael: Adam (see Revelation 12:7)

25. 666 (the number of the beast): the meaning is unknown (see Revelation 13:18)
26. Mount Zion: New Jerusalem in Missouri (usually) (see Revelation 14:1)
27. 144,000: special missionaries or high priests (see Revelation 14:1)
28. Angel flying in the midst of heaven: Moroni—and others (see Revelation 14:6)
29. Babylon: the wicked world (see Revelation 14:8)
30. The harvest: separation of the righteous and the wicked at Christ's second coming (see Revelation 14:15)
31. Vials: judgments or plagues (see Revelation 15:7)
32. The great whore: church of the devil (see Revelation 17:1)
33. Scarlet apparel: the blood of worldliness (opposite the blood of the Atonement)—(see Revelation 17:4)
34. Marriage of the Lamb: the Second Coming (see Revelation 19:7)
35. Bottomless pit: hell (see Revelation 20:1; 9:1)
36. Gog and Magog: great battle after the Millennium (see Revelation 20:8)
37. Lake of fire and brimstone: torment of disappointment (hell) (see Revelation 20:10)
38. Another book (for judgment): heavenly book of life (see Revelation 20:12)
39. New heaven and new earth (twice): terrestrial and then celestial earth (see Revelation 21:1)
40. The bride, the Lamb's wife: the New Jerusalem (see Revelation 21:9)
41. Twelve names on twelve gates: twelve tribes (see Revelation 21:12)
42. Twelve names on twelve foundations: twelve apostles (see Revelation 21:14)
43. The tree of life and its fruit: love of God, celestial glory (see Revelation 22:2)
44. Root of David: Christ (see Revelation 22:16)

UNDERSTANDING REVELATION

In the middle of the second century after Christ, Irenaeus, bishop of Lyons, quoted John's Revelation many times, attributing it to "John, the Lord's disciple," and even ascribing its writing "towards the end of Domitian's reign [about A.D. 96]" (*Against Heresies*, 4.20.11; 5.30.3, in *Ante-Nicene Fathers*, 1:491, 560). Tertullian, an erudite Christian lawyer writing in the third century, noted that while John was in Rome, he was "plunged, unhurt, into boiling oil, and thence remitted to his island exile" (*On Prescription against Heretics*, 36, in *Ante-Nicene Fathers*, 3:260).

The island of Patmos, about sixty miles southwest of Ephesus, is known from Roman sources to have been a place of exile, an island penitentiary. It is a small island, at most six miles wide and ten miles long. John was probably banished to Patmos during the era of severe persecution of Christians under the emperor Domitian at the end of the first century. When the cult of emperor worship was enforced, Christians found themselves caught in the vise of resentment and antagonism as they worshipped the one and only true God (see references to John's experience on Patmos in *Anchor Bible Dictionary*, 5:179).

"The apostle John, after his exile on the island, resumed residence at Ephesus, as early Christian tradition records" (Eusebius, *History of the Church*, 82).

REVELATION 1–3

In the first three chapters of Revelation, John discusses problems in the seven churches of Asia; he rebukes the Saints' behavior during apostate conditions and encourages them during fiery trials (see Appendix 4). He pleads for the Saints to come unto Christ—to prepare for his coming. Many examples of Temple-centered language and concepts appear in the first three chapters: "And [Jesus Christ] hath made us kings and priests unto God"(1:6); "To him that overcometh will I give to eat of the tree of life"(2:7); "I will give thee a crown of life" (2:17); "To him that overcometh will I give . . . a white stone, and in the stone a new name written, which no man knoweth saving he that receiveth it" (2:10); "And he that overcometh . . . will I give power over many kingdoms" (JST 2:26); "He that overcometh, the same shall be clothed in white raiment; and I will not blot out his name out of the book of life, but I will confess his name before my Father, and before his angels" (3:5); "Him that overcometh will I make a pillar in the temple of my God, and he shall go no more out: and I will write upon him the name of my God . . . and I will write upon him my new name" (3:12); "To him that over-cometh will I grant to sit with me in my throne" (3:21).

REVELATION 1

1:1 Compare the rendering of this passage in the Joseph Smith Translation: "The Revelation of John, a servant of God, which was given unto him of Jesus Christ. . . ."

"Things which must shortly come to pass" is the phrase John uses to begin and end (see 22:6).

1:2 This verse records John's testimony, which centers on Jesus Christ, the Word of God made flesh (see John 1:1, 14).

1:3 Compare this verse with the rendering in the Joseph Smith Translation: "Blessed are they who read" and under-stand—they who hearken and obey. "The time is at hand"—or in other words, "the time of the coming of the Lord draweth nigh" (JST). The coming of the Lord will happen according to the Lord's timetable. The Joseph Smith Translation of 2 Peter 3:8 says, "Concerning the coming of the Lord, beloved, I would not have you ignorant of this one thing, that one day is with the Lord as a thousand years, and a thousand years as one day."

1:4 "Him which is, and which was, and which is to come"

is a reference to the Divine Name (YHWH), which carries the meaning "I WAS, I AM, I WILL BE."

1:4–5 "Now this is the testimony of John to the seven servants who are over the seven churches in Asia . . ." For further changes, see the Joseph Smith Translation in the Appendix to the LDS edition of the Bible.

1:6 This verse was the subject of a great sermon given by the Prophet Joseph Smith on 16 June 1844, just days before his martyrdom. He said of this verse, "It is altogether correct in the translation." The phrase "God and his Father" does not refer to Elohim and his Son, Jesus, who is already spoken of in the previous verse. It refers to Elohim and his Father.

1:7 The Joseph Smith Translation has an important addition (see Bible Appendix).

1:8 "I am Alpha and Omega"—John uses several other descriptive titles for the Savior: the Amen (see Revelation 3:14); the Lion of the tribe of Judah (see Revelation 5:5); the Lamb (see Revelation 5:12); The Word of God (see Revelation 19:13); KING OF KINGS and LORD OF LORDS (see Revelation 19:16); the root and the offspring of David (see Revelation 22:16); the bright and morning star (see Revelation 22:16).

1:9 Some of our greatest revelations have come while the Lord's prophets were imprisoned. John was in exile on the island of Patmos when he recorded Revelation. Paul had also written letters that included great revelation while he was in prison. In this last dispensation Joseph Smith did the same (see D&C 121, 122, 123).

1:10 "I was in the Spirit . . ." Joseph Smith and Sidney Rigdon were also in the Spirit when there was opened up to them "a transcript from the records of the eternal world" (*Teachings of the Prophet Joseph Smith,* 11), that is, Doctrine and Covenants 76 (see 76:113). If we, too, want revelation, we must take the time and make the effort to be "in the

The small island of Patmos, where John received his great revelation

Spirit." Some of us too often dismiss that possibility out of hand; we may feel, as did Laman and Lemuel, that "the Lord maketh no such thing known unto us." But Nephi described the Lord's promise that "if ye will not harden your hearts, and ask me in faith, believing that ye shall receive, with diligence in keeping my commandments, surely these things shall be made known unto you" (1 Nephi 15:9, 11).

"The Lord's day"—Sunday, the new Sabbath (see Bible Dictionary, "Lord's Day").

1:11 The Lord reveals through our mind according to our experience. Though these specific seven churches and twenty-four elders were just a small part of God's work on earth, they were foremost in John's mind. They were representative of all of us. The Lord has revealed, "What I say unto one I say unto all" (D&C 93:49).

The seven churches of Asia were representatives, or types, of the whole Church (*seven* being symbolic of completeness, entirety). *Seven* is used fifty-four times in the Revelation: seven churches, candlesticks, stars, angels, vials, thunders, heads on the beast, kings, mountains, and one-thousand-year periods.

1:12 "I turned to see the voice . . ." How do you "see" a voice? The figure of speech used here is called *catachresis*, or *incongruity*. By another figure called *metonymy*, the voice stands for the person, and we see the person.

"Seven golden candlesticks [menorahs or lampstands]" represented the seven churches (v. 20).

1:13–16 "The Son of man" is, when the name is rendered fully, the Son of "Man of Holiness" (Moses 6:57), meaning the Son of God the Father.

It is not easy to describe God. In fact, Joseph Smith said his "brightness and glory defy all description" (Joseph Smith–History 1:17). Compare other descriptions of what the Lord looks like: Daniel 10:5–9; Ezekiel 1:26–28; Doctrine and Covenants 110:2–3.

1:16 A sharp, two-edged sword: one side would be hurtful to the wicked, cutting them to the very center (see 1 Nephi 16:2), and the other side would be helpful to the righteous, piercing their hearts and causing them to burn with the Spirit (see 3 Nephi 11:3).

1:19 Nephi was told that John would write the vision (see 1 Nephi 14:25).

1:20 "Angels" are servants (JST). In Hebrew and Greek *angels* are messengers, and these servants of the seven churches were leaders or messengers of their respective units of the Church before the Lord.

Candlesticks, or menorahs (representing the seven Church units), were put in place to give light to the world (see Matthew 5:15–16).

REVELATION 2

2:1–7 The letter to Ephesus emphasizes need for the love of Christ.

2:6 The term "Nicolaitans" is unknown outside this verse and verse 15. Their beliefs included the sensual perversions partly described in verse 14. They were apparently individuals who encouraged compromise between Christianity and Graeco-Roman philosophies and lifestyle. They seemed to be saying, "Go ahead and be a member of the pagan clubs and societies; you might have a good influence on them." Nicolaitans appear to have espoused the enthronement of Christ and Augustus side by side. John compared the Nicolaitans to the doctrine of Balaam (see Numbers 22), with subtle and compromising views. Paul, Peter, Jude, and John all denounced this type of doctrine.

2:7 In the messages to the seven churches, the seven promises are made to "him that overcometh"—this verse, plus 2:11, 17, 26; and 3:5, 12, 21. The verb "overcometh" in Greek is *nikao,* a cognate of *nike,* meaning "victory," a word used to describe winning athletic contests.

All of the promises relate to Temple worship: the tree of life (see Revelation 2:7); the crown of life (see Revelation 2:10); the hidden manna and the new name (see Revelation 2:17); the rod (or scepter) and morning star (see Revelation 2:27–28); the white raiment (see Revelation 3:5); the pillar in the Temple (see Revelation 3:12); and the feast, the messianic banquet, and the marriage supper of the Lamb (see Revelation 3:20–21). For an analysis of these promises in their Temple setting, see Madsen, "The Temple and the Restoration," 13–16.

Some have wondered if there is a connection in Ephesians between John's reference to the tree of life in the paradise of God and the temple of Artemis/Diana, which was a tree-shrine. The pagan place of worship was a typical grove of trees, a perversion of a true symbol. In the New Jerusalem, the Temple would be the real glory of God and the tree of life (see Revelation 22:2). The tree, representing the love of God (see 1 Nephi 11:21–22), will provide the fruit of eternal life, in the presence of the Saints' "first love" (Revelation 2:4).

2:8–11 The letter to Smyrna praises the endurance of the

Beautiful port city of Izmir, Turkey, called Smyrna at the time of John

Saints. They receive the greatest commendation for their faithfulness. Smyrna is now called Izmir, Turkey (see "Smyrna," 373).

2:12–17 The letter to Pergamos (usually rendered Pergamum) calls false teachers to repentance (see "Pergamum," 375).

2:13 The Attalid/Pergamene kings had established national cults of the gods Zeus, Athena, Dionysus, and Asclepius and had decreed that they themselves should receive homage as gods. A great sculpted altar was erected for Zeus Soter (Greek, *soter*, meaning "savior"), but most widespread acclaim was given to Asclepius Soter, the god of healing, whose symbol of the serpent was a perversion of a true symbol used by Moses to represent Jehovah/Jesus Christ, the true Savior and Master Healer (see Numbers 21:8–9; John 3:14–15; Alma 33:19–20; Helaman 8:13–15).

The "throne or seat of Satan" may refer to the cult of Asclepius, an imitation of healing and salvation and a corruption of the serpent motif; or it may refer to the altar of Zeus as

316

Site of the altar of Zeus at Pergamum

a type of satanic power; or it may refer to Pergamum itself, a center of pagan religion and especially of the emperor cult. Caesar had become a rival to Christ. In 29 B.C., the first temple to Augustus in all of Asia was established in Pergamum. By the turn of the century all citizens and subjects were obligated by law to make offerings to the imperial god, the divine emperor; otherwise they were condemned to death as traitors and enemies of the state. Christians had to endure state-sponsored persecution and faced the stark choice between Christ and Caesar, with Caesar even appropriating such titles as "Lord" and "Savior."

Antipas is one of the Saints who has been martyred.

2:17 The "white stone" with a "new name" is a "Urim and Thummim" received by those who enter the celestial kingdom (see D&C 130:8–11).

2:18–29 The letter to Thyatira condemns immoral practices. Thyatira does not appear on Bible Map 13, but it is located just east of Smyrna thirty miles north of Sardis (see "Thyatira," 376).

Remains of the Asclepion, the healing center at Pergamum

2:20 "Jezebel" is used in a figurative sense. Apparently, Jezebel was a symbolic name for a woman who was exercising influence in the Church to cause others to compromise true principles and accept perverted, idolatrous practices. Just as the previous Jezebel, wife of Ahab, had introduced pagan idolatry into Israel, so this Jezebel taught followers "to eat things sacrificed unto idols" (Revelation 2:20). Compare her teaching with the apostles' instructions to avoid such things (see Acts 15:20, 29).

2:26 "Will I give power over the nations"—Joseph Smith Translation: " . . . over many kingdoms."

2:27 "Rule them with a rod of iron"—Joseph Smith Translation: " . . . with the word of God."

2:28 The "morning star" is Jesus Christ (see Revelation 22:16).

REVELATION 3

3:1–6 The letter to Sardis calls the Saints to a more spiritual life (see "Sardis," 377).

Remains of the Temple of Artemis at Sardis

3:5 See Bible Dictionary, "Book of Life."

3:7–13 The letter to Philadelphia praises the loyalty of the Saints (see "Philadelphia," 379).

3:7 "The key of David" is the absolute power of Christ (see Isaiah 22:22).

3:12 "The great earthquake of A.D. 17 evidently had so profound an effect upon Philadelphia that the context of the apocalyptic letter must be closely related to it. The disaster made a remarkable impact on the contemporary world as the greatest in human memory. . . . If Sardis suffered catastrophically in the original shock, Philadelphia, probably closer to the epicenter, suffered many lesser tremors, perhaps for years afterwards. After an earthquake people seek protection in the open air. The city was probably slow to recover, and its fears may have been renewed by later shocks in the area, notably that which destroyed life in Philadelphia in the promise to the conqueror: 'he shall no more go outside' (Revelation 3.12)" (Hemer, *Letters to the Seven Churches*, 156–57).

The precariousness of life in Philadelphia is compared to

Partly reconstructed Greek gymnasium at Sardis (background) with adjacent Jewish synagogue (foreground)

the security of life in the city of God, the New Jerusalem. The Saint who overcometh could become a "pillar in the temple of my God" (Revelation 3:12). The pillar symbolizes the firmness and stability of a future abode.

On the "New Jerusalem," see Revelation 21.

3:14–22 The great Jehovah and Creator of the earth was known also by the name "Amen," signifying agreement and commitment. It was for lack of commitment that the Laodiceans were condemned (see "Laodicea," 380).

3:15–16 The Lycus Valley was home to three New Testament cities: Colossae, Hierapolis, and Laodicea. Laodicea, the last of John's seven cities and the one cursed in the strongest terms, was located approximately one hundred miles east of Ephesus and twelve miles from the confluence of the Lycus and Maeander Rivers. The valley has been subject throughout its history to seismic activity. In consequence of its lying in the heart of an earthquake zone, the valley is also characterized by springs of hot mineral waters. Six miles to the north of Laodicea was the city of Hierapolis, famous in antiquity and in modern times for its remarkable terraced travertines. These formations consist mostly of calcium carbonate and look like a series of small, petrified cascading waterfalls similar to those at Yellowstone's Mammoth Hot Springs.

The hot mineral waters of Hierapolis were known for their therapeutic, healing properties. Colossae, ten miles east of Laodicea, featured not only the usual hot, calcareous waters but also some good, cold, fresh waters. In contrast to the cold waters of Colossae and the hot waters of Hierapolis, Laodicea's water was tepid and emetic (inducing vomiting). The water of Laodicea originated at an abundant spring in the upper part of modern Denizli, about five miles to the south, and was transported by stone aqueduct to the city. Remnants of the aqueduct show heavy encrustation in the stone pipes. One of the ancient city's most unusual remains, a sixteen-foot-high water tower that distributed water to all parts of the city, has a number of terra cotta pipes in its center, which are also encrusted by lime deposits.

Laodicea's water was lukewarm, as were its inhabitants' works, according to John. The standard definition of a lukewarm person is somewhere between the "cold" of an unbeliever and the "hot" of a believer, but that definition may be misleading in this case. There is no evidence that the ancients used cold and hot in the metaphorical sense we do now. In the context of the Laodicean letter and in the reality of the Lycus Valley, both cold and hot waters were acceptable and useful, one for refreshing drink and the other for therapy and healing. In this context, either is a commendable option. Lukewarm, emetic waters, on the other hand, would compel the drinker to spew them out of the mouth.

John's use of the local geographical condition in and around Laodicea is effective and profound. The cold, hot, and lukewarm waters of the Lycus Valley were comparable to members of the Lord's Church: cold and hot were commendable and could be a blessing to others ("I would thou wert cold or hot"); lukewarm was distasteful and rejected.

The Laodiceans stood uncommitted between cold and hot, and to the Lord they produced only a reaction comparable to vomiting. Indeed, Laodiceans were "spewed out"—there are no Laodiceans living at that ancient place today.

3:17–18 After a severe earthquake in A.D. 60 the citizens of Laodicea rejected the Roman Senate's relief fund and rebuilt the city themselves. "Thou sayest, I am rich, and increased with goods, and have need of nothing." They were proudly independent of Rome's financial help, and some apparently felt spiritually self-sufficient, sensing no need for the Savior's help. They were now encouraged to seek assistance from the Source of lasting treasure and richness. As Jesus had earlier taught, "Lay not up for yourselves treasures upon earth, where moth and rust doth corrupt, and where thieves break through and steal [and where earthquakes destroy and bury]: But lay up for yourselves treasures in heaven" (Matthew 6:19–20).

"I counsel thee to buy of me . . . white raiment, that thou mayest be clothed, and that the shame of thy nakedness do not appear"—white garments are here contrasted to the celebrated soft, raven-black wool for which Laodicea was famous in John's day. White garments were symbolic of cleanliness and purity, as revealed in the Lord's words to the Church members at Sardis: "He that overcometh, the same shall be clothed in white raiment; . . . and they shall walk with me in white: for they are worthy" (Revelation 3:5, 4).

The Amen also counseled the Laodiceans to "anoint thine eyes with eyesalve, that thou mayest see." The eyesalve seems to refer to a particular powder or ointment used by the famous medical school at Laodicea. Applying the Lord's own kind of eyesalve would cause these Saints to see with spiritual sight, be zealous in his cause, repent, and overcome the world.

3:20 He didn't say he stands at the door waiting for us to knock; he is knocking, calling, inviting; he wants us to come unto him. We may sup with him; he is the Bread of Life.

3:21 Here is the ultimate blessing of faithfulness, of overcoming the world; see also Revelation 21:7.

REVELATION 4–22

The second part of the book of Revelation, chapters 4 through 22, records John's apocalyptic vision of the history of the earth. Chapters 4 and 5 stand as an introduction to the scenes of earth's future and ultimate destiny. Chapters 6 through 20 describe past and future history through important symbols involving the number seven: seven seals, seven trumpets, seven vials, and so forth (see Appendix 3, 395). Chapters 21 and 22 describe the celestialized earth.

John's Revelation "shows not only that the Almighty knew the end from the beginning and contemplated the whole of earth's history, but also that he arranged it. To say it more strongly, before the first soul was ever placed on the earth, God orchestrated the whole of earthly existence. . . .

"God knows how each person will behave at any given time and under any given circumstance. By knowing what each person will do, he knows how the whole of any combination of people will behave. He shapes history by assembling the aggregate while at the same time allowing each individual free reign over his own destiny" (Draper, *Opening the Seven Seals*, 246, 248).

REVELATION 4

4:1 "After this . . ."—now begins the apocalyptic revelation, which continues to the end of the book.

"I will shew thee things which must be hereafter"—the writings are clearly prophetic; anyone who reads with real understanding must believe in prophecy and in the omniscience of God.

4:4 "Four and twenty elders"—These are twenty-four

deceased, faithful elders from the seven churches (see D&C 77:5). White raiment and crowns of gold represent their exalted condition: celestial glory.

4:6 A "sea of glass" is the sanctified earth (see D&C 77:1; 130:6–9).

"Beasts full of eyes before and behind"—see Doctrine and Covenants 77:2–3. In the writings of other prophets, beasts are usually types representing such things as kingdoms (as in Revelation 13), but here in chapter 4, the beasts are beasts, that is, celestialized animals (see Smith, *Teachings of the Prophet Joseph Smith*, 289–92).

REVELATION 5

5:1 The last half of the verse should be punctuated to read: "a book [or a scroll] written within, and on the backside sealed with seven seals." John saw the book sealed with seven seals, representing the history of the earth during seven periods of one thousand years each (see D&C 77:6–7).

5:5–6 Though the Savior was the Root of David and the Lion of the tribe of Judah, salvation (*Yeshua*, or *Jesus*, means "salvation") would be provided not by a "Lion" but by a "Lamb."

The Lamb had twelve horns and twelve eyes (see Joseph Smith Translation), symbolizing the twelve servants of God. Horns represent omnipotence, and eyes represent omniscience.

John the Baptist announced, referring to Jesus, "Behold the Lamb of God" (see John 1:29, 36). Not only were the people of Israel referred to as sheep but Jesus himself was seen as a sheep led to the slaughter (see Acts 8:32). He was also deemed a young and tender sheep, or a lamb. Paul called him "our passover," who was "sacrificed for us," referring to the sacrificial lamb at Passover (see 1 Corinthians 5:7).

Of all the New Testament writers, only John called Jesus the Lamb of God, twice quoting John the Baptist and twenty-eight times mentioning the Lamb in the book of Revelation. There the Lamb is personified. He was slain (see Revelation 5:12), his blood was able to cleanse (see Revelation 7:14), and he was worshipped (see Revelation 5:8). The Lamb felt wrath (see Revelation 6:16) and fought a war (see Revelation 17:14). He had a marriage supper (see Revelation 19:9) and was married to his bride (see Revelation 19:7; 21:9). He possessed a book of life (see Revelation 13:8; 21:27) and a song (see Revelation 15:3), and he served as light for the city of God (see Revelation 21:23).

5:7 Only Christ had the power to put into effect all the terms and conditions of the Father's plan. Only Christ could make an infinite atonement, which is the heart of the great plan and the central operation in the history of earth's salvation.

5:8 Golden vials full of "odours" (Greek, "incense") represent prayers of the Saints. See also Psalm 141:2.

5:9 The lyrics of the new song are given in verses 12–13.

5:10 Kings and priests will rule on a celestialized earth.

5:12–13 After John's weeping and lamentation because no one seemed to be found worthy to open the seals—to initiate the Father's plan for this earth—he saw the Lamb worthy to open the earth life and willing to be slain. There was great rejoicing and praise for him in heaven.

5:13 John saw millions of saved beasts from millions of earths (see Smith, *Teachings of the Prophet Joseph Smith*, 291–92).

REVELATION 6

Seven seals (seven thousand-year periods) are opened by the Lamb (see Revelation 6; 7; 8:1).

6:1–2 The first seal, the first one thousand years, the time of Adam and Enoch, was symbolized by a white horse of conquest, representing the triumph of the righteous over the forces of evil. "A crown" was the wreath of the conqueror. On the wars of Enoch, see Moses 7:13–17.

6:3–4 The second seal, the second thousand years, the time of Noah, was symbolized by a red horse of death. On the corruptness of the earth, see Moses 8:22, 28, 29.

6:5–6 The third seal, the third thousand years, the time of Abraham and others, was symbolized by a black horse of famine.

6:7–8 The fourth seal, the fourth thousand years, the time of the great empires (Assyrian, Babylonian, Persian, Greek, and Roman), was symbolized by a pale horse of death and hell (Greek *chloros* means "pale green").

6:9–10 The fifth seal, the fifth thousand years, was John's own time, in which he saw the souls of those who were martyred for the testimony of Jesus. See also Doctrine and Covenants 135:7.

6:12 The sixth seal, the sixth thousand years, is described in 6:12 to 7:17. A great earthquake (the first one mentioned in the Revelation) and other catastrophic events precede the great day of the Lord.

"The Millennium is dawning upon the world, we are at the end of the sixth thousand years, and the great day of rest, the Millennium of which the Lord has spoken, will soon dawn and the Savior will come in the clouds of heaven to reign over his people on the earth one thousand years" (Woodruff, *Journal of Discourses,* 18:113).

"We are living at the commencement of the Millennium, and near the close of the 6,000th year of the world's history. Tremendous events await this generation" (Woodruff, *Journal of Discourses,* 25:10).

6:14 The lands (continents) come together (see also 16:20). "And he shall utter his voice out of Zion, . . . which shall break down the mountains, and the valleys shall not be found. He shall command the great deep, and it shall be driven back into the north countries, and the islands shall become one land; and the land of Jerusalem and the land of Zion shall be turned back into their own place, and the earth shall be like as it was in the days before it was divided" (D&C 133:21–24).

6:15–16 The wicked want to hide, in their sins, rather than face the Lord.

6:17 The question posed here, "Who shall be able to stand?" is answered in Revelation 7 (especially verse 14).

The following outline of the six thousand years of this earth's telestial existence is from "Great Events" in *Times and Seasons:*

"In the first thousand years, was witnessed the fall of man; the building up of Zion, when Enoch with all his people, walked with God three hundred and sixty five years on earth, and then were taken up into heaven.

"In the second thousand years, the world was deluged with a flood for its wickedness; the tower was built that men might go to heaven; the language was confounded; the earth divided into continents and oceans; the people scattered upon the face of the whole earth; and America was peopled by the Jaredites.

"In the third thousand years, Pharaoh and his host were swallowed up in the Red Sea; Israel, the chosen of the Lord, was overshadowed by his glory in a cloud by day, and a pillar of fire by night; and the building of the temple of the Lord at Jerusalem.

"In the fourth thousand years, the ten tribes of Israel were led away captive out of the land of Canaan, and taken to a place by the hand of the Lord that has not yet been discovered by the Gentiles; the Jaredites were destroyed because of their wickedness; Lehi was guided by the matchless power of God to this continent.

"In the fifth thousand years, the Savior of the world was born, crucified, and rose again from the dead; and most of the apostles were slain for preaching the gospel; and Jerusalem was destroyed.

"In the six[th] thousand years, America, the land of liberty, choice above all others, was settled by the Gentiles; the fulness of the gospel of Jesus Christ came forth in the book of Mormon, the church established, and the gathering of the saints commenced, preparatory to the second coming of their Lord, that in the seventh thousand years the earth may rest" (662).

REVELATION 7

7:1–3 Interpretation is found in Doctrine and Covenants 77:8–10.

7:2 "Another angel" is a "composite" Elias—various beings with various keys and powers to gather Israel and restore all things.

7:3 "Sealed the servants of our God in their foreheads"—that is, their calling and election is made sure (see Smith, *Teachings of the Prophet Joseph Smith*, 321; compare Ezekiel 9:4).

7:4 The number 144,000 is not the number of people saved (see v. 9) but is the number of representatives of the twelve tribes—high priests, missionaries or emissaries (see D&C 77:11).

7:5–8 Twelve tribes are represented, though in this list Dan is missing and Manasseh is substituted. On tribal names being omitted in biblical lists, see Draper, *Opening the Seven Seals*, 267, n. 14.

7:9 An innumerable host of those saved stood before the throne of God, wearing white robes and carrying palms in their hands representing victory over the world.

7:14 Note that all those saved came "out of great tribulation"—that says something about the purpose of this life. President Joseph F. Smith saw in the spirit world the noble and great ones who had "offered sacrifice in the similitude of the great sacrifice of the Son of God, and had suffered tribulation in their Redeemer's name" (D&C 138:13).

REVELATION 8

Much of the rest of the book of Revelation deals with events in the seventh thousand-year period. Most signs of the Second Coming are fulfilled in the seventh period. Chapters 8 and 9 treat events in the seventh period but before the Second Coming (see the two chapter headings and D&C 77:13). A series of woes actually ushers in the Millennium, not the Lord's Coming. His coming in glory is intentionally delayed (see Matthew 24:48 [Joseph Smith–Matthew 1:51]; Matthew 25:5; D&C 45:26). In addition, we might note that the Savior's millennial reign could begin at Adam-ondi-Ahman, even before his glorious appearance to the entire world.

"The Second Coming does not usher in the millennial era. . . . The Millennium . . . begins at the time the Savior commences his reign on the earth. But to begin his rule, he does not have to have appeared to the world. His reign begins as he collects the keys he has given to the prophets through the ages and directs affairs personally. Daniel gives a hint when this will be . . . the great future gathering at Adam-ondi-Ahman. At that time Adam, the Ancient of days, will appear, as will the Savior. An account will be given to the Lord, and he will then begin to personally orchestrate all events from that point (see D&C 116)" (Draper, *Opening the Seven Seals*, 110).

8:1 There will be silence in heaven for "half an hour"—that is, the heavens will be silent. The significance of the silence is unknown, although another description of the same scene is given in Doctrine and Covenants 88:93–96. Some have wondered if the duration could be approximately twenty-one years, based on one thousand earth years being as one day in God's time (see Abraham 3:4; JST 2 Peter 3:8).

Interestingly, after the destructions preceding the Savior's appearance in ancient America there was silence for many hours (see 3 Nephi 10:1).

8:2 The interpretation of this verse is found in Doctrine and Covenants 77:12. Chapters 8 through 11 speak of seven trumpets signaling the pouring out of judgments during the seventh seal. For additional commentary on the seven angels and their plagues, see McConkie, *Millennial Messiah*, 381–88; and Draper, *Opening the Seven Seals*, 95–99.

8:5 "An earthquake"—this is the second mention of an earthquake in the Revelation.

8:7 The rest of chapter 8 and chapter 9 sound like some type of devastating warfare.

8:11 "Wormwood"—in the Bible, the plant usually represents something painful and nearly deadly; in this case, it symbolizes the bitterness of hell.

REVELATION 9

Here we find a description of the final battle, called Armageddon, before the second coming of the Lord. The battle is "woe one"; two others would follow (see v. 12; see also Appendix 5, page 400, for excerpts from Elder Bruce R. McConkie's commentary on Armageddon).

9:1 "I saw a star fall from heaven"—the Greek says, literally, "a star *fallen* from heaven"; that is, Lucifer.

9:3 Armies are compared to a horde of locusts.

9:5 Five months is the actual life span of real locusts.

Humans generally look upon the world of creeping things as ominous and treacherous, particularly such creatures as reptiles and arachnids. In the Revelator's eschatological description of the final battle, scorpions represent danger, harm, and pain: "Their torment was as the torment of a scorpion, when he striketh a man" (Revelation 9:5). "They had tails like unto scorpions, and there were stings in their tails: and their power was to hurt men" (Revelation 9:10).

9:8–10, 17–19 Some have wondered if John could be describing fighter aircraft, tanks, flame throwers, missiles, and so forth.

9:11 The destructive forces are led by their king (Satan), whose name in Hebrew is *Abaddon,* which means "destruction" (same as "perdition"). Satan's name in Greek has the same meaning.

9:15 "The slain will be a third of the inhabitants of the earth itself, however many billions of people that may turn out to be" (McConkie, *Millennial Messiah,* 453).

9:16 "Two hundred million men of war mass their armaments at Armageddon" (McConkie, Conference Report, April 1979, 131). Whether that number is symbolic, as is usual, or real is not known.

9:20–21 One of the greatest tragedies is that the wicked "repented not."

REVELATION 10

This chapter may be described as an interlude, a pause or deliberate interruption in the sequence of events being described by John. He uses this technique in his writing to stop and make supporting points or describe parallel developments that don't fit the flow of earth's unfolding future.

10:1–2 John is given a special mission; an angel appears with a book.

10:3–4 "Seven thunders" are seven angels reciting seven periods of history.

10:9 John's future mission is to gather the tribes of Israel (see D&C 77:14). Ezekiel also ate, or internalized, a book (see Ezekiel 2:6–10; 3:1–3).

10:11 This is John's mission assignment.

REVELATION 11

The two prophets being slain in Jerusalem is "woe two"; a third woe follows (see v. 14).

11:1–2 The Holy City is measured and given over to Gentiles. It is overrun for a period of "forty and two months," which is the same as 1260 days (see commentary on Revelation 12:6).

11:3 Compare Doctrine and Covenants 77:15. The ministry of the two witnesses or prophets in Jerusalem lasts for a period of 1260 days (which is three and one-half years). The number may be literal or it may be symbolic. Three and a half is half of seven, the number of perfection or completion. Thus we understand that their mission is cut short.

11:4 The prophet Zechariah also saw these two witnesses. He referred to them symbolically as two olive trees or two candlesticks (Hebrew, *menorot*). See Zechariah 4:3, 11–14. Olive oil helps to heal, and candlesticks give light.

11:6 The two witnesses will have powers similar to those of two of the great Hebrew prophets of ancient times: shutting the heavens so that it does not rain, as Elijah did (see 1 Kings 17:1), and sending plagues on the earth, as Moses did (see Exodus 7–11).

11:7–13 The two witnesses are killed, and their bodies lie in the streets for three and a half days, with nations viewing their bodies (via satellite-transmitted television?). Then they are resurrected and ascend into heaven while a great earthquake strikes the city (this is the third earthquake mentioned in the Revelation).

11:14 The third woe constitutes much of the rest of the Revelation—seven angels pouring out plagues.

11:15 Here we read the words sung in Handel's famous oratorio *Messiah:* "and he shall reign for ever and ever." The kingdoms of the Egyptians, Assyrians, Babylonians, Persians,

Macedonians, Romans, and even the modern political kingdoms on earth today—all will eventually give way to the kingdom of our Lord, who will reign as King of kings forever and ever.

11:19 Here we read the fourth mention of an earthquake. Plagues continue in 15:1.

REVELATION 12

Study this chapter of the Revelation in the Joseph Smith Translation (Bible Appendix), noting changes in sequence of verses and changes in vocabulary and interpretation. Important revisions are noted also in the following verse-by-verse commentary:

12:1 "A woman" is the Church. "Twelve stars" are twelve apostles.

12:3 "A great red dragon" (the Greek word here means "serpent," or "sea-monster") is Satan.

12:4 "The third part of the stars" is the third part of the hosts of heaven drawn away by Satan.

12:5 (JST v. 3): "A man child" is the millennial kingdom of God. Rule will eventually be through the rod of iron, the word of God.

12:6 (JST v. 5): 1260 years represents the period of the Great Apostasy. The adversary was successful in frustrating the growth of the child in the meridian of time (the child was caught up unto God and his throne [JST v. 3], to be reserved for the time of restoration in the latter days), and the woman (the Church) fled into the wilderness (see D&C 86:3). On the Church coming forth out of the wilderness, see Doctrine and Covenants 5:14; 33:5; 109:73. Eventually she will give birth to the child, and he will overcome the adversary.

12:7 In this flashback to the premortal war, Michael, or

Adam, fought Lucifer, or Satan (see Bible Dictionary, "War in Heaven"). Has the war ended, or just changed battlefields?

12:9 "Devil" means "slanderer." *Satan* is a Hebrew word meaning "adversary."

12:11 Power to overcome Satan and the forces of evil comes in and through the atonement of Jesus Christ, our faithfulness to our testimony of it, and our willingness to sacrifice all things for the cause of God.

12:12 Satan is stepping up his insidious activities because he knows that his time is short. He has known for ages that there is no ultimate victory for him, so his objective is to cause as much damage and misery as possible here and now. What is Satan's misery? Is it that he can never be with Heavenly Father again? That is most unlikely, because he hates the Father. His misery is that he can never be a father himself and he can never be a husband. He will never have a companion in marriage and never have children. He wants to assure that as many as possible of Heavenly Father's other children are eternally denied these ultimate blessings through their disobedience and rebellion and corruption of these sacred powers on earth.

12:14 Daniel (12:7) also mentions this curious numerical sequence: some have suggested that if "time" is 360, then "times" (plural) would be 720 and "half a time" would be 180; the total is 1260 (or 42 months, or 3.5 years). All in all, what these numbers signify is unknown.

12:17 Note with whom Satan wars his fiercest war, with whom he fights his most vicious fights.

REVELATION 13

13:1–8 Study these verses along with *Teachings of the Prophet Joseph Smith*, 287–94.

13:1 Compare Joseph Smith Translation Revelation 13:1. A beast—for John, possibly the Roman Empire (though every age has its equivalent)—rose out of the sea. If the beast represents Rome, then the sea is the Mediterranean. It has seven heads and ten horns (as usual, signifying power).

13:2 "The dragon" is the devil (Smith, *Teachings of the Prophet Joseph Smith*, 293).

13:5 Again, the "forty and two months" signify temporary victory for Satan and his minions.

13:6–8 Satan's campaign of evil achieves considerable success.

13:11–15 Another beast appears "like a lamb" (a "wolf in sheep's clothing"), which proceeds to imitate and counterfeit the true order of things. Satan can imitate the miraculous power of God.

13:16 This verse may refer to the custom in John's culture of marking slaves committed to masters, and persons committed to a certain deity, with a mark on their right palm or on the forehead as a sign of dedication to that master or god (see also Revelation 7:3 and Ezekiel 9:4 for positive use of such a sign).

13:18 The meaning of "666" is yet unknown, although we know that because seven characterizes something complete or perfect, six is always short of perfection.

REVELATION 14

14:1 The Lamb, the Savior, will yet stand on Mount Zion (in what we now call Independence, Missouri), having with him the 144,000 representatives of the tribes of Israel (see D&C 77:11).

14:2–3 The lyrics of the "new song" are written in Doctrine and Covenants 84:98–102.

14:4–5 These verses describe those who are redeemed.

14:6 We have traditionally identified the angel flying through the midst of heaven as Moroni, even though other scriptures clearly suggest a number of angels or messengers; therefore, this is a composite angel involved in the restoration of all things (see also D&C 77:8; 133:36).

14:7 A commandment is given to praise, respect, and worship the God of heaven and earth.

14:8 The fall of "Babylon" is announced (see Bible Dictionary, "Babylon").

"The wine of the wrath of her fornication"—Hebrew and Greek texts indicate that "Babylon" (or the great and abominable church of the devil; 1 Nephi 14:3, 10) has caused all nations to drink of the "poisonous wine of her fornication."

14:9–11 Those who worshipped the beast will suffer and will have no rest; they will not be able to enter into God's glory (see D&C 84:24).

14:12–13 Those who did not worship the beast will be blessed. Doctrine and Covenants 124:86 corrects the last sentence of verse 13 to read, "They shall rest from all their labors here, and *shall continue their works*" (emphasis added).

14:14–20 This event seems to be the same one seen by Daniel (see Daniel 7:13–14). The resurrected Savior comes with a crown of glory and power and with a sickle of judgment. The world is then harvested.

14:17–18 "Another angel" is a destroying angel who is also thrusting in his sickle. The image of the winepress being trodden is reminiscent of Isaiah's similar vision (Isaiah 63:1–4; see also D&C 133:46–51).

REVELATION 15

15:1–8 John saw seven angels preparing vials or bowls of judgment to be poured out on the earth (continued from Revelation 11:19). Chapters 15 and 16 present seven last plagues poured out to cleanse the earth for the Millennium.

15:2–4 The globe where God dwells is like a sea of glass and fire and crystal and is a giant Urim and Thummim (D&C 130:7–9). Righteous Saints will joyfully inherit such a sphere and sing songs of praise to the Lamb of God.

REVELATION 16

16:2 First vial: grievous sore

16:3 Second vial: sea to blood

16:4 Third vial: rivers and fountains to blood

16:6 "They are worthy" that is, deserving (a more accurate translation of the Greek); all other translations indicate they got what they deserved.

16:8–9 Fourth vial: scorching heat

16:10–11 Fifth vial: darkness and pain

16:12–14 Sixth vial: unclean spirits unleashed

16:14, 16 Miracle-working evil spirits gather together to do battle before the great day of God Almighty (the Second Coming). The gathering place, which symbolizes the gatherings of the enemies of God throughout the world, is called "Armageddon," which is in Hebrew *Har Megiddo,* the hill or mound of Megiddo, the great fortress city at the western end of the Jezreel Valley between Galilee and Samaria in the Holy Land. Because many ancient battles were staged in that valley, its name has been attached to the last great battle to end this telestial world. For more scriptural information on the battle of Armageddon, see the cross-references given in footnote 16*a*.

16:17–21 Seventh vial: earthquake and hail

16:18 "A great earthquake, such as was not since men were upon the earth"—the fifth mention of an earthquake in the Revelation. From the succeeding verses we understand that this earthquake signals massive convulsions in the earth's tectonic plates that bring the continents back together into one land mass.

"This is the time when earth's land masses shall unite; when islands and continents shall become one land; when every valley shall be exalted and every mountain shall be made low; . . . It is no wonder that the earthquake shall exceed all others in the entire history of the world" (McConkie, *Millennial Messiah*, 397).

16:20 The time when "every island fled away" also refers to this rejoining of continents into one land. Compare Isaiah 62:4 and Doctrine and Covenants 133:21–24.

REVELATION 17

John was shown the great whore and the judgments upon her (see Revelation 17–19:10). Previously, the woman was the Church of God (see Revelation 12:1), but now the woman, the whore, the mother of harlots and abominations, symbolizes the church of the devil, representing the combined forces of the ungodly.

Nephi also wrote about the church of the devil, "the mother of abominations; . . . the whore of all the earth" (1 Nephi 14:10). "Wherefore, he that fighteth against Zion, both Jew and Gentile, both bond and free, both male and female . . . are they who are the whore of all the earth" (2 Nephi 10:16). Those who belong to the "kingdom of the devil [are] all churches which are built up to get gain, and all those who are built up to get power over the flesh, and those who are built up to become popular in the eyes of the world, and those who seek the lusts of the flesh and the things of the world, and to do all manner of iniquity" (1 Nephi 22:22–23).

17:3–4 In the New Testament, we learn of a "scarlet robe" that was placed on Jesus when Roman soldiers mocked him (Matthew 27:26–28). We also learn that the robe was made of "scarlet wool" (Hebrews 9:19). In the Revelation, a woman, the mother of harlots, is sitting on a "scarlet coloured beast" (Revelation 17:3), wearing "scarlet colour" or simply "scarlet" (Revelation 17:4; 18:12, 16). The red color is derived from the eggs of an insect (*Coccus ilicis*) that lives in oak trees in the Holy Land and is used to dye cloth. The Arabs call it *kirmiz*, which is the source of our English word *crimson*. Scarlet was occasionally symbolic of royalty, but often it is identified with things evil or sinful.

REVELATION 18

The Saints are called out of Babylon, that is, out of the world, which is "spiritual Babylon" (see D&C 133:5, 7, 14).

"In the first and last books of the Bible, Babylon incarnates arrogance, pride, and insatiable corruption in opposition to God and his kingdom. It stands in contrast to the heavenly city, the New Jerusalem, where the law of God thrives. . . . Babylon represents a real historical organization. . . . [I]t is composed of more than one entity. . . . Seeing spiritual Babylon as only one association, either at its inception or today, would therefore be wrong. It symbolizes all leagues that may be properly called Antichrist, that pervert the right way of the Lord, and that promote antichristian principles and life-styles.

"The arrogant Babylonians combined purely sensual and material principles with the lofty striving within the soul of man. Out of this grew the principle of spiritual fornication. Men mistook lust for joy, sought happiness through passion, and pursued security through materialism. The bit of graffiti, 'He who dies with the most toys wins,' could have been written as easily in Babylon as in New York, or Las Vegas. Today many still seek to find heaven through drugs, lust, money, success, or power. People continue to try to escape the deadly round of daily life through material and immoral means. . . .

"God has provided a solution: flee Babylon. The command demands a complete severing of relations. God allows no association whatsoever. There is good reason. Babylon is not to be converted but destroyed: 'We would have healed

Babylon, but she is not healed: forsake her' (Jeremiah 51:9, King James Version). Any that linger in Babylon will be taken with her plagues, 'For after today cometh the burning . . . and I will not spare any that remain in Babylon' (D&C 64:24)" (Draper, *Opening the Seven Seals,* 189–90, 204–5).

18:1 "Earth was lightened with his glory"—literally. See Doctrine and Covenants 88:7–13.

18:2–24 Babylon is the world—where millions of people starve while others spend millions of dollars on luxury living.

REVELATION 19

John sees great events of the earth's final era in vision (chapters 19–22).

19:1–10 Interlude: a song of triumph and celebration of Babylon's fall.

19:7–9 Israel's covenant relationship with their Lord is a marriage covenant, which requires the most fidelity, sacrifice, commitment, and long-suffering of all relationships. God's marriage to his people is featured in the writings of Ezekiel (chapters 16 and 23) and Hosea (chapter 2) and in Matthew 22 (see also Smith, *Teachings of the Prophet Joseph Smith,* 63). The marriage feast of the Son begins at his second coming, and the elders and sisters of the Church of Jesus Christ are even now inviting people throughout the world to attend. The Lamb's (the Son's) wife, his Church, is making herself ready. The fine linen in which she is arrayed is the righteousness of the Saints. Often quoted in ancient and modern scripture is the phrase "put on thy beautiful garments" (Isaiah 52:1), as in Moroni 10:31: "Awake, and arise from the dust, O Jerusalem; yea, and put on thy beautiful garments, O daughter of Zion; and strengthen thy stakes and enlarge thy borders forever."

19:10 "The testimony of Jesus is the spirit of prophecy"—that is, testifying of Jesus is what prophecy is all about. "None of the prophets have written, nor prophesied, save they have spoken concerning this Christ" (Jacob 7:11). "All the prophets who have prophesied ever since the world began—have they not spoken more or less concerning these things?" (Mosiah 13:33). "All the prophets prophesied only of the days of the Messiah" (Talmud, Sanhedrin 99a).

19:11–16 Christ comes as King of kings. The white horse symbolizes war and the conquest of all, in contrast to the donkey, which symbolizes humility as well as peace and royalty. Just days before his atonement, Christ rode into Jerusalem on a donkey. He was the great King as well as the Prince of Peace. At his second coming he will arrive as conqueror over all!

19:13 "Clothed with a vesture dipped in blood"—the red apparel is symbolic of the blood of Christ's atonement (see Isaiah 63:1–4; D&C 133:46–51).

The following comments on Isaiah 63:1–4 may be helpful:

Isaiah 63:1. The Lord comes from *the east* (the priority direction) in his first coming and his second coming.

The Hebrew word for "red" is *Edom*—compare Isaiah 63:2, "red in thine apparel" (compare also D&C 19:15–18). Paintings often portray the Savior coming in glory clad in a brilliant white robe and surrounded by hosts of Saints sounding trumpets. Compare those portrayals to the actual color as described in these verses by Isaiah.

Isaiah 63:2. Redness is from his blood shed in Gethsemane (see Luke 22:44).

"Treadeth in the *winefat,*" or wine*vat,* or wine*press.* The Hebrew word is *gath,* as in the Hebrew word *Gath-shemen,* or "Gethsemane."

Images used here are poignant: the Lord's garments are dyed in the colors of the Atonement—redness is due to the atoning blood pressed from his body as the juice of grapes in a winevat; also the blood of the wicked will be spilled in the day of vengeance (the Second Coming). John envisioned the same event: "He was clothed with a vesture dipped in blood" (Revelation 19:13).

Isaiah 63:3. "I have trodden the winepress alone": that happened in *Gath-shemen* (Gethsemane).

"Trample them in my fury; and their blood shall be sprinkled upon my garments"—the scene portrayed in some of the words of Julia Ward Howe's "Battle Hymn of the Republic":

"Mine eyes have seen the glory of the coming of the Lord;

"He is trampling out the vintage where the grapes of wrath are stored. . . ."

Isaiah 63:4. "The day of vengeance" (see also Isaiah 63:6 and 61:2)—"The day of vengeance is in mine heart"—*justice* (for a "day"); "and the year of my redeemed is come"—*mercy* (for a "year"). Justice and mercy will be meted out by the Savior when he comes again.

This is the "great and dreadful day of the Lord"; destruction of billions of people is the kind of vengeance only God can wreak or allow to occur.

19:15 Note the Joseph Smith Translation change.

19:17–21 The final victory over the beast is announced.

REVELATION 20

20:1–3 "Bottomless pit," "chain," "dragon," and "serpent" are all symbolic terms, but Satan will definitely be bound for a thousand years. How can a spirit be "chained"? Satan will be bound and become powerless because of God's binding or locking him away and because of the righteousness of the Saints (see 1 Nephi 22:26).

20:4–6 Faithful Saints will be resurrected at the beginning of the Millennium (see D&C 88:96–99). John here describes the Millennium in just three verses. His purpose is to dwell not on the era of peace but on the Saints' preparatory era before that time (see Draper, *Opening the Seven Seals,* 220).

20:4 "Them that were beheaded for the witness of Jesus"—for example, John the Baptist.

20:7–10 The "battle of Gog and Magog," the final war for the souls of humankind, or the final conflict in the war that commenced in the premortal life, will occur at the end of the Millennium. Michael will command the forces of good, and Satan will command the forces of evil, who will be released from bonds by God to accomplish His purposes (see D&C 88:111–115.) In the end, the adversary will be cast into "the lake of fire and brimstone."

Of the eight instances of fire and brimstone in the New Testament, seven are in the book of Revelation, where its use portends torment and punishment in the last days for the wicked. Brimstone is sulphur, a yellow-green, highly combustible element commonly found along the shores of the Dead Sea. The same substance is used to make matches and gunpowder and other products today in the chemical and paper industries. When ignited with fire, sulphur liquefies and produces a sharp and suffocating burning odor that can desolate and kill. Apparently in those days, no harsher picture of the hellish fate of the wicked could be portrayed than that of being thrown into a lake of fire, burning with brimstone: "The fearful, and unbelieving, and the abominable, and murderers, and whoremongers, and sorcerers, and idolaters, and all liars, shall have their part in the lake which burneth with fire and brimstone" (Revelation 21:8; see also D&C 63:17).

20:12–13 With final resurrection comes final judgment (see D&C 128:6–7). Books from earth will be opened (scriptures, plus records of baptism, marriage, tithing, missions, callings, and other records of the Church), along with the book of life kept in heaven.

20:13 "*Every* man according to *their* works"—the use of a single collective noun with a plural pronoun is acceptable in ancient languages; see also 2 Nephi 29:11.

REVELATION 21

John sees two phases, terrestrial and celestial, of new heaven and new earth (21:1–22:5).

21:2 John saw the New Jerusalem, or Zion, coming down from heaven. The City of Enoch, including Melchizedek and his people, will descend from heaven to join the earthly New Jerusalem, or Zion, that the Saints will construct in Jackson County, Missouri (see Moses 7:62–64; JST Genesis 14:32–34).

21:3 "He will dwell with them"—"Christ and the resurrected Saints will reign over the earth during the thousand years. They will not probably dwell upon the earth, but will visit it when they please, or when it is necessary to govern it" (Smith, *Teachings of the Prophet Joseph Smith,* 268; *History of the Church,* 5:212). "God himself shall be with them": Hebrew, *Immanuel,* means "God with us."

21:4 "Former things are passed away"—all things telestial will give way to those things terrestrial, translated, or paradisiacal. God's objective, however, is not merely to return the earth to the same Edenic, or paradisiacal, glory it had at the beginning but to give it a glory higher than it has ever had.

21:7 "He that overcometh shall inherit all things"—"all that my Father hath shall be given unto him" (D&C 84:38).

21:10–22:5 These verses contain a description of the holy Jerusalem, the celestial city of God. The vocabulary is elevated in this word-picture of the glorious city in which God the Father and his Son reside. The attempt to describe the city in human language includes dazzling precious stones and jewels, pure gold, and transparent glass. Protection, safety, and peace are symbolically described in terms of high walls and gates. John's angelic guide measured the city and found it to be about 1,400 miles in length, height, and breadth—which is about 2,744,000,000 cubic miles in the City of God (see v.

16). For more on the celestial Jerusalem, see McConkie, *Millennial Messiah*, 700–705.

"A Saint, who is one in deed and in truth, does not look for an immaterial heaven, but he expects a heaven with lands, houses, cities, vegetation, rivers, and animals; with thrones, temples, palaces, kings, princes, priests, and angels; with food, raiment, musical instruments, &c.; all of which are material. Indeed, the Saints' heaven is a redeemed, glorified, celestial, material creation, inhabited by glorified material beings, male and female, organized into families, embracing all the relationships of husbands and wives, parents and children, where sorrow, crying, pain, and death will be no more. Or to speak still more definitely, this earth, when glorified, is the Saints' eternal heaven. On it they expect to live, with body, parts, and holy passions: on it they expect to move and have their being; to eat, drink, converse, worship, sing, play on musical instruments, engage in joyful, innocent, social amusements, visit neighboring towns and neighboring worlds" (Pratt, "Past and Future Existence," 722).

21:22–23; 22:5 The City of God will need no Temple built by human hands nor any man-made lighting. The Lord God Almighty and the Lamb will be the Temple and the light. "The Lamb is the light thereof" (see Isaiah 60:19; D&C 88:7–13).

21:25 The peace and safety of the city of God is epitomized by the fact that its gates need never be closed. Isaiah had the same vision (see Isaiah 60:11).

REVELATION 22

22:1 God the Father and his Son occupy the eternal throne. Out of it proceeds the pure living water, which represents the love of God (see also John 4:14; 1 Nephi 11:25).

22:2, 14 In the celestial world Adam and Eve and all their righteous posterity may finally partake of the fruit of the tree of life and live forever, having repented of all their sins and having been made pure by the blood of the Lamb. The water and the tree both represent the love of God (see 1 Nephi 11:21–22, 25). Love is the quintessential message of John the Beloved. All of his writings focus on and emphasize the love of God (see especially 1 John 4:7–8).

22:6 Here we read John's testimony about all the things he saw, "which must shortly be done"—all according to the Lord's timetable.

22:10 Although the Lord told others to seal up their visions of these things (Ether 3:21–22; 1 Nephi 14:25; Daniel 12:9), John is told not to seal up his writings but to show them to the world.

22:18–19 These verses are sometimes quoted by those antagonistic to the Lord's Church as a warning not to add to what is written in the Bible. These same individuals specifically reject the whole idea of additional scripture—such as the Book of Mormon—and consequentially any new revelation from God. A careful and unbiased examination of this inspired warning reveals its real meaning.

"If any man shall add unto these things . . ."—the first caution is that no *mortal* should tamper with these things, though the Lord may certainly add more if he so desires. A second caution is not to add to "these things"—and the antecedent to "these things" is "the prophecy of this book." John was warning against attempts to alter his revelation as he himself wrote it. He could not have been talking about the whole Bible—the Bible was not yet canonized, in fact, not even in existence, as we know it, at the time John wrote this conclusion to the Revelation. It should also be noted that Moses wrote an identical warning against adding to or diminishing from his revelations, called the Torah (the first five books of the Bible). His warning is recorded in Deuteronomy 4:2, and if the same reasoning were applied to Moses' declaration, then we could accept nothing after the fourth chapter of Deuteronomy (see D&C 20:35).

STATEMENTS ON REVELATION

Elder Bruce R. McConkie wrote: "Are we expected to understand the book of Revelation? Certainly. Why else did the Lord reveal it? The common notion that it deals with beasts and plagues and mysterious symbolisms that cannot be understood is just not true. It is so far overstated that it gives an entirely erroneous feeling about this portion of revealed truth. Most of the book—and it is no problem to count the verses so included—is clear and plain and should be understood by the Lord's people. Certain parts are not clear and are not understood by us—which, however, does not mean that we could not understand them if we would grow in faith as we should.

"The Lord expects us to seek wisdom, to ponder his revealed truths, and to gain a knowledge of them by the power of his Spirit. Otherwise he would not have revealed them to us. He has withheld the sealed portion of the Book of Mormon from us because it is beyond our present ability to comprehend. We have not made that spiritual progression which qualifies us to understand its doctrines. But he has not withheld the book of Revelation, because it is not beyond our capacity to comprehend; if we apply ourselves with full purpose of heart, we can catch the vision of what the ancient Revelator recorded. The apostles in Palestine did not know about the Nephites because they did not seek such knowledge. (See 3 Nephi 15:11–24.) We would have many additional revelations and know many added truths if we used the faith that is in our power to exercise. . . .

" . . . The book of Revelation takes an approach to the plan of salvation that is found nowhere else in all of our inspired writings. The language and imagery is so chosen as to appeal to the maturing gospel scholar, to those who already love the Lord and have some knowledge of his goodness and grace.

"After the baptism of water, after being born of the Spirit, after charting a course of conformity and obedience, the true saint is still faced with the need to overcome the world. Nowhere in any scripture now had among men are there such pointed and persuasive explanations as to why we must overcome the world, and the attendant blessings that flow therefrom, as in this work of the Beloved John" (*Ensign*, September 1975, 87, 89; see also 85–89).

"We are in a much better position to understand those portions of Revelation which we are expected to understand than we generally realize. Thanks be to the interpretive material found in sections 29, 77, 88, and others of the revelations in the Doctrine and Covenants; plus the revisions given in the Inspired Version [Joseph Smith Translation] of the Bible; plus the sermons of the Prophet; plus some clarifying explanations in the Book of Mormon and other latter-day scripture; plus our over-all knowledge of the plan of salvation—thanks be to all of these things (to say nothing of a little conservative sense, wisdom and inspiration in their application), the fact is that we have a marvelously comprehensive and correct understanding of this otherwise hidden book" (McConkie, *Doctrinal New Testament Commentary*, 3:431; see also 3:429–595).

The Prophet Joseph Smith taught: "The subject . . . is one that I have seldom touched upon since I commenced my ministry in the Church.

"It is not very essential for the elders to have knowledge in relation to the meaning of beasts, and heads and horns, and other figures made use of in the revelations; still, it may be necessary, to prevent contention and division and do away with suspense. If we get puffed up by thinking that we have much knowledge, we are apt to get a contentious spirit, and correct knowledge is necessary to cast out that spirit. . . .

" . . . The things which John saw had no allusion to the scenes of the days of Adam, Enoch, Abraham or Jesus, only so far as is plainly represented by John, and clearly set forth by him. John saw that only which was lying in futurity and which was shortly to come to pass. . . .

" . . . The book of Revelation is one of the plainest books God ever caused to be written. . . .

"I make this broad declaration, that whenever God gives a vision of an image, or beast, or figure of any kind, He always holds Himself responsible to give a revelation or interpretation of the meaning thereof, otherwise we are not responsible or accountable for our belief in it. Don't be afraid of being damned for not knowing the meaning of a vision or figure, if God has not given a revelation or interpretation of the subject" (*Teachings of the Prophet Joseph Smith*, 287, 289–91; see also 287–94).

President Wilford Woodruff wrote: "The Lord does communicate some things of importance to the children of men by means of visions and dreams as well as by the records of divine truth. And what is it all for? It is to teach us a principle. We may never see anything take place exactly as we see it in a dream or a vision, yet it is intended to teach us a principle" (*Discourses of Wilford Woodruff*, 286).

Additional valuable information may be found in the Bible Dictionary, "Revelation of John"; Draper, *Opening the Seven Seals;* and "John the Beloved," "John, Revelations of," and "New Testament: Book of Revelation," in Ludlow, *Encyclopedia of Mormonism,* 3:1225–28.

CHAPTER 17

THE CITIES OF
PAUL THE APOSTLE AND
JOHN THE REVELATOR

TARSUS

Tarsus was Paul's hometown. It was an autonomous metropolis in the province of Cilicia and a respected university city. In Paul's day Strabo wrote, "The people of Tarsus have devoted themselves so eagerly, not only to philosophy, but also to the whole round of education in general, that they have surpassed Athens, Alexandria, or any other place that can be named where there have been schools and lectures of philosophers" (*Geography* 14.5.13). Tarsus was one of several Cilician cities that had been granted free status during Rome's civil war, apparently by Mark Antony, who lived there for a time and had a spectacular meeting with Cleopatra there. She adorned herself as Aphrodite/Venus and sailed her luxurious galley up the Cydnus River right into the city. Paul gave notice of his high estimation of his hometown "when he replied to the Roman Tribune, 'I am a Jew, Tarsian of Cilicia, citizen of no mean city.' One would have expected him to claim the Roman rights, as indeed he did a few moments later; but the first words that rose to his lips came direct from his heart and expressed the patriotism and pride in his fatherland, his *patria*, that lay deep in his nature" (Ramsay, *Cities of St. Paul*, 115).

BRIEF HISTORY

The date of the original settlement of Tarsus is unknown.

The first historical reference to Tarsus is on the Black Obelisk of Shalmaneser III (about 850 B.C.), who claims to have captured the city. In the next century a rebellion arose during the reign of Sennacherib and the city was destroyed. When rebuilt, Tarsus came under Persian control and was later freed from the Persians by Alexander the Great. Attempts to Hellenize the inhabitants led to a revolt against Antiochus IV Epiphanes. While Cicero, who was a Roman orator and statesman, was governor of Tarsus, Mark Antony declared it a free city and exempt from taxes in 41 B.C. Tarsus was made the capital of the region of Cilicia and enjoyed some golden years during the reign of Augustus (27 B.C.-A.D. 14).

GEOGRAPHICAL SETTING

Tarsus was located on the Cydnus River eighty feet above sea level on a fertile plain about ten miles from the Mediterranean Sea at the foothills of the Taurus Mountains on the southeastern coast of Asia Minor. In New Testament times, the Cydnus River flowed through Tarsus, allowing navigation of light vessels into the middle of the city. The strategic importance of Tarsus was its crossroads position on the plain leading to the Cilician Gates, one of the key routes in the Mediterranean World.

SCRIPTURAL ASSOCIATIONS

Acts 9:11, 30

Acts 11:25

Acts 21:39 Paul was born into a Jewish family in Tarsus, an important city in Cilicia whose residents had been granted Roman citizenship.

Acts 22:3

Acts 15:41; 18:23 Paul probably visited Tarsus on his second and third missionary journeys.

Consider the implications of these facts: Paul was born Jewish and a Roman citizen in a Greek city in Asia. After being trained as a strict Pharisee in Jerusalem and being converted by the Lord en route to Damascus, he first organized Christian missionary work out of Syrian Antioch.

ANTIOCH

Antioch (modern Antakya, Turkey) was considered the third greatest city in the Roman Empire, after Rome and Alexandria. It is often called "Antioch of Syria" or "Antioch on the Orontes" or "Antioch the Great" to distinguish it from fifteen other Antiochs, all named after the father or the son of Seleucus, the founder of the Seleucid Empire. Antioch of Syria became the second greatest center of early Christianity. All three of Paul's missionary journeys started in this city.

BRIEF HISTORY

Antioch was founded by Seleucus I about 300 B.C. It was conquered by Rome in 64 B.C. and served as the capital of the Roman province of Syria throughout most of its history as a Roman city. At its peak Antioch had a population of more than half a million people. A fire in A.D. 525 and earthquakes in 526 and 528 killed more than 360,000 people. Soon afterwards the Persians sacked Antioch, and those who survived the sacking suffered a plague in 542. By the time Antioch was captured by the Arabs in 637, it had become merely a frontier fortress.

GEOGRAPHICAL SETTING

The city was three hundred miles north of Jerusalem at the foot of Mount Silpius, which extends 1500 feet above the plain. It lay on the Orontes River, which is approximately 125 feet wide, and was less than twenty miles from the Mediterranean Sea. Antioch prospered anciently on account of such geographical advantages as healthy climate, adequate water supply, good drainage, fertile land, and commercial opportunity. It was situated far enough from the sea for protection but close enough for communication. The Orontes River was navigable right up to Antioch.

ARCHAEOLOGICAL REMAINS

The city was laid out in an oblong plan of about 555 acres. Its layout maximized the use of the sun in both winter and summer and caught the wind blowing up the Orontes Valley from the sea to penetrate all sections of the city. Herod the Great built a grand colonnaded street honoring Octavian's visit to Antioch after he established his supremacy over Antony. The street ran northeast to southwest. Paved with marble, it was two miles long and thirty-one feet wide and had more than thirty-two hundred columns. It was one of only three streets in antiquity that enjoyed street lighting. The main street of modern Antakya, *Kurtulus Caddesi,* follows the course of this monumental Herodian street (see Harrison, *Major Cities of the Biblical World,* 8–21).

SCRIPTURAL ASSOCIATIONS

Acts 6:5 Nicolas was a convert from Antioch.

Acts 11:19–30 The beginnings of Christianity at Antioch: Paul and Barnabas; prophets from Jerusalem; relief sent to Jerusalem.

Acts 15:22, 23 Endorsement for missionary work among Gentiles was sent to Antioch.

Galatians 2:11 Paul confronted Peter about circumcision.

Acts 13:1

Acts 14:26 Antioch was the center for Paul's missionary labors.

Acts 15:35

Acts 18:22

Acts 13:4 Paul and Barnabas sailed out of Seleucia, the port for Antioch.

On his first missionary journey Paul, in company with

Barnabas, a Levite from Cyprus, sailed 130 miles to Salamis on the eastern coast of Cyprus and then journeyed overland to Paphos, the capital of Roman Cyprus. At Paphos, the missionaries taught and converted the Roman governor, Sergius Paulus, who was from Antioch of Pisidia and who likely encouraged them to visit that city and meet his acquaintances. From there they sailed another 180 miles to the port of Attalia in Pamphylia and continued on into the interior of Asia Minor.

ATTALIA AND PERGA

Attalia and Perga were cities on the plain of Pamphylia, a hot, humid coastal plain eighty miles long and twenty miles wide off the main route of historical and political action. Attalia (modern Antalya, Turkey) was a port city named after King Attalos II of Pergamum (159–138 B.C.). Paul used the port of Attalia because it was one of the few points along the Mediterranean coast of Asia Minor that was approachable; the Taurus Mountains descend steeply to the sea in most other places. Perga was located twelve miles northeast of Attalia, and there are considerable ruins at the site today. The theater and the stadium (one of the best preserved in Asia Minor) could seat, respectively, fourteen thousand and twelve thousand. The main colonnaded thoroughfare was divided in the middle by a water channel, and wagon-wheel ruts can still be seen. Some believe that Paul left Perga for Pisidian Antioch because of illness. One scholar, Ramsay, wondered if Paul experienced attacks of malaria fever, and others have suggested epilepsy and severe headaches, all due to the enervating climate of Pamphylia with its prevalent fevers and abundant insect pests.

SCRIPTURAL ASSOCIATIONS
ATTALIA
Acts 14:25–26 Paul and Barnabas sailed in and out of the port of Attalia on their first missionary journey.

PERGA

Acts 13:13, 14 Paul and Barnabas were at Perga on their first missionary journey.

Acts 14:25 Paul and Barnabas taught in Perga on their return trip.

ANTIOCH OF PISIDIA

GEOGRAPHICAL SETTING

Antioch of Pisidia was located one kilometer north of present-day Yalvac, Turkey, near the lake region anciently called Pisidia. It was not until the end of the third century after Christ that Antioch was in Pisidia proper; it is now supposed that in Paul's day this Antioch was geographically in Phrygia but politically in Galatia. Pisidian Antioch lay on one of the great commercial highways nearly one hundred miles north of Perga and about three thousand feet higher in elevation. Water was brought by way of an aqueduct from a spring six to seven miles from the city. Most of the aqueduct was underground, but the last mile was above ground on arches, twenty of which are still visible. Antioch boasted a temple to Augustus.

SCRIPTURAL ASSOCIATIONS

Acts 13:14–52 Paul and Barnabas taught in synagogue on the Sabbath; their lives were threatened.

Acts 14:19–24 Antiochian Jews stirred up trouble in Lystra; Paul returned to Pamphylia through Antioch of Pisidia.

Acts 16:6; 18:23 Paul may have revisited the city on his second and third missionary journeys.

2 Timothy 3:11 Paul's persecution at Antioch is mentioned.

ICONIUM

GEOGRAPHICAL SETTING

The New Testament Iconium is now the large, modern Turkish city of Konya, eighty miles southeast of Pisidian Antioch. The site has always been certain, the place-name having been preserved without interruption throughout history at the same location. The city lies at the western end of a vast, level plain 3,370 feet above sea level. Only three to four miles to the west are the Phrygian-Pisidian Mountains with peaks over 5,000 feet (which makes it similar in situation to Damascus in Syria). To the east is a long, broad plain, very fertile and intensely cultivated. Iconian territory actually extended east to Kara Dagh, fourteen hours' journey east of Iconium. Konya was for a time the capital of the Seljuk Turkish Empire, a splendid city that merited the enduring Turkish proverb "See all the world; but see Konia" (Ramsay, *Cities of St. Paul,* 319).

SCRIPTURAL ASSOCIATIONS

Acts 13:51 The Brethren left persecution at Antioch of Pisidia and traveled to Iconium.

Acts 14:1–6 The Brethren taught in the synagogue, and many believed.

Acts 14:19, 21 Some from Iconium were involved in stoning Paul at Lystra; Paul returned to Antioch through Iconium.

Acts 18:23 Paul probably visited Iconium again on his third journey.

2 Timothy 3:11 Paul's persecution at Iconium is mentioned.

LYSTRA AND DERBE

BRIEF HISTORY

Augustus made the city of Lystra a Roman stronghold against the mountain tribes in about 6 B.C. The region around Lystra had a distinct language and boasted a temple to Zeus. The location of Lystra was unknown until 1885, when a Roman altar was found at Zoldera, a mile north of the present-day village of Hatunsaray, Turkey. The altar inscription, discovered by Professor J. R. S. Sterrett, confirms the location of Lystra there. The Latin inscription reads as follows (Lystra is *Lustra* on coins and inscriptions): *Divum Aug(ustum) Col(onia) Iul(ia) Felix Gemina Lustra consecravit d(ecreto) d(ecurionum)* and may be translated as follows: "For divine Augustus, fortunate Julian twin colony, Lustra, consecrated by decree of the town councilors (decurions)" (Ramsay, *Historical Geography of Asia Minor*, 332).

GEOGRAPHICAL SETTING

Lystra is in the region of Lycaonia, about twenty-five miles south of Iconium. The mound of Lystra has not been excavated.

SCRIPTURAL ASSOCIATIONS

Acts 14:6–23 In the cities of Lycaonia, Paul and Barnabas healed a lame man and were hailed as gods; persecutors stoned Paul, and much teaching was accomplished.

Acts 16:1–3 Paul's second journey: Timothy was circumcised and accompanied Paul.

2 Timothy 3:11 Paul's persecutions at Lystra are mentioned.

The site of Derbe is unknown, though some suppose it to be the mound of Kerti Huyuk, about fifty miles southeast of Konya.

SCRIPTURAL ASSOCIATIONS

Acts 14:6, 20 Paul and Barnabas fled to Derbe to avoid threats to their lives; they taught many.

Acts 16:1 Paul visited Derbe on his second journey.

Acts 20:4 Gaius was from Derbe.

CILICIAN GATES

On his second and third journeys Paul walked north from Antioch and then west through his homeland of Cilicia, likely stopping each trip at Tarsus, and then up into the interior through the Taurus Mountains by way of the famous Cilician Gates. Just as Alexander the Great had marched with his thirty-five thousand troops through the Cilician Gates, so Paul hiked up through this strategic pass going forth to conquer in the name of Jesus Christ. After passing through the Cilician Gates, Paul then journeyed through Galatia (from *Galatai,* the Greek name for the Gauls, who had invaded Asia Minor in 278 B.C.). Paul traveled on through Phrygia and the Roman province of Asia and beyond.

TROAS

The harbor at Troas was Paul's link between the Roman province of Asia and Macedonia. It is now called "Alexander's Troy" (Alexandria Troas, or *Truva,* which is the Turkish word for Troy). It is situated ten miles south of the western end of the Dardanelles and ten miles south of the site of ancient Troy. Constantine the Great (about A.D. 324) thought to establish his capital at Alexandria Troas but decided in favor of the site of Byzantium, which came to be known as Constantinople. From Troas, Paul and company sailed to Samothracia, a small island (sixty-eight square miles) about fourteen miles farther on toward the Greek coast (see Acts 16:11). They went on to the port of Philippi, then called Neapolis (Macedonia) and now called Kavalla (Greece).

PHILIPPI

BRIEF HISTORY

The history of the site before the fourth century before Christ is obscure. Philippi was founded by King Philip II of Macedon in 357 B.C. His main interest was in the nearby gold mines of Mount Pangaeus. He annexed the entire region in 356 B.C. Philippi remained insignificant until after the Roman conquest of Macedonia in 168–167 B.C. It became the first of four districts of Macedonia and served as an important Roman colony. Latin was the official language, and Philippi was a stopping point on the Via Egnatia. In 42 B.C. Mark Antony and Octavian defeated the forces of Brutus and Cassius (Julius Caesar's assassins) in two separate battles on the plain west of Philippi. Mark Antony settled many of his veterans in Philippi and refounded it as a Roman colony. After the battle of Actium in 31 B.C. more veterans were settled in Philippi. It was formally named *Colonia Iulia Augusta Philippensis*, in honor of Julius Caesar. It was at Philippi that Christianity first entered what we call Europe.

GEOGRAPHICAL SETTING

Philippi is situated in northern Greece or Macedonia. The city-site is dominated by a high acropolis and is surrounded by mountains on three sides. It is twelve miles inland from the modern port city of Kavalla (ancient Neapolis). Twenty-two miles to the west of the city is the Nestos River and twenty-five miles to the southwest is the river Strymon (ancient Gangites). To the south and also to the west of the city are sizeable marshlands.

ARCHAEOLOGICAL REMAINS

Scholars date the remains of an archway at the west gate of the city to the time of Paul. The agora, or central marketplace, was uncovered in 1914. It was bounded by porticoes, temple facades, and public buildings. A large public lavatory has been

359

unearthed; it was equipped with stone seats and urinals—and even running water. The acropolis was situated on a nearby mountain spur more than one thousand feet above sea level. On the east slope of the spur stands the remains of a theater that once held up to five thousand people. On the north end of the agora, four steps leading up to the *bema*, or seat of judgment, have been discovered. This is possibly the place where the missionaries were sentenced. On the east side, what appear to be a library and reading rooms have been uncovered. Some Christian architectural remains in Philippi are an early fourth-century basilica outside the Neapolis Gate near a small stream (possibly where Paul first met with Lydia and friends; see Acts 16:13–14), and a crypt with seventh-century paintings depicting the imprisonment of Paul and Silas (possibly the jail where the missionaries were kept overnight). The Roman writer Vitruvius noted that prisons were usually located next to the forum (Harrison, *Major Cities of the Biblical World*, 207).

SCRIPTURAL ASSOCIATIONS:

Acts 16:16–34 Paul and Silas were beaten and imprisoned and then miraculously delivered by an earthquake; the jailor was baptized.

Acts 20:2–6 Paul was at Philippi on his third missionary journey.

1 Thessalonians 2:2 Paul was shamefully treated at Philippi.

Philippians Letter sent to the Saints at Philippi.

THESSALONICA

Paul and Silas passed through the cities of Amphipolis and Apollonia en route to Thessalonica (see Acts 17:1).

BRIEF HISTORY

Founded in 316 B.C. by Cassander, the city was named in

honor of Thessalonica, half sister of Alexander the Great, daughter of Philip II, and wife of Cassander. The new city included Therme and twenty-five other villages. When Macedonia became a Roman province in 146 B.C., Thessalonica was made the capital and the center of Roman administration. The city supported victorious Antony and Octavian before the battle of Philippi in 42 B.C. That battle began a new, prosperous time for Thessalonica. Various statesmen and generals took refuge in Thessalonica, including Cicero during his exile in 58 B.C. and General Pompey in 49 B.C. Its prosperity is exemplified by extensive coinage. Its status as a free city enabled it to enjoy such other privileges as tax concessions. Its location on the Via Egnatia provided significant commerce. In Paul's day Thessalonica had a thriving Jewish community in this commercial crossroads. In modern times, until World War II, many Spanish-speaking Jews lived in the city (modern Saloniki); they were descendants of Spanish Jews expelled from Spain in 1492 by Ferdinand and Isabella.

GEOGRAPHICAL SETTING

Thessalonica is situated in Macedonia at the head of the Thermaic Gulf (modern Thessaloniki features the largest gulf on the Balkan Peninsula), about eighty-five miles southwest of Philippi. It was accessible from all parts of Macedonia. Thessalonica spread out like a theater on the slopes surrounding the bay. It boasted secure, sturdy walls, an impregnable acropolis, and all the edifices and institutions of a thriving Hellenistic city—agora, hippodrome, gymnasium, and temples.

Thessalonica lay along the Via Egnatia, which originally extended five hundred miles from the Adriatic Sea to Thessalonica and later to Byzantium. "Traversing the tumbled mountain system of Inner Albania and Upper Macedonia, with considerable stretches at a level exceeding 6,000 feet, it was a remarkable feat of engineering. It was indispensable as a link on the shortest route from Italy to Macedonia, and eventually it became the main road to Rome's Asiatic provinces" (Cary, *Geographic Background,* 304).

ARCHAEOLOGICAL REMAINS

In 1962 the Roman forum, or marketplace, was uncovered. Some stretches of walls built during Byzantine times on earlier foundations still stand. One of two victory arches—part of a tetrapylon (four connected arches over the Via Egnatian) built in honor of Emperor Galerius about A.D. 305—is still standing; the other was destroyed in 1876.

SCRIPTURAL ASSOCIATIONS

Acts 17:1–9 Paul taught in the synagogue on his second missionary journey.

Acts 19:29; 27:2 Aristarchus (Paul's companion on his third journey through Asia Minor) was from Thessalonica (see also Philippians 4:16; 2 Timothy 4:10).

Thessalonians Letter sent to the Saints at Thessalonica.

Paul next preached successfully in Berea, though Thessalonian Jews pursued him there and caused trouble (see Acts 17:10–13; 20:1–5). Berea is modern Veroia, fifty miles southwest of Thessalonica.

ATHENS

BRIEF HISTORY

Athens was one of the first Greek city-states, and kings ruled it until 682 B.C. The city, it appears, was named after the Greek goddess Athena. In 508 B.C. Athens adopted a constitution that made it a democracy. Athens eventually became the head of the Delian League, which quickly developed into the Athenian Empire. Athens led the empire against Sparta and its allies in the Peloponnesian Wars but lost, never regaining political dominance. The city was destroyed in 480–479 B.C. during the Persian War, though still assisting with its maritime power in the defeat of the Persians. The city was immediately rebuilt under Pericles (462–429 B.C.) and flourished in a golden age. Pericles erected, among other important structures, the famous Parthenon on the Acropolis. With Alexander later carrying Greek culture throughout the eastern Mediterranean world all the way to southcentral Asia, Athens became a center of Hellenistic culture for more than three centuries. The once-renowned city was neglected in the Middle Ages and was ruled by various empires until 1834, when, after the Greek war of independence, it became the capital of the modern nation of Greece.

GEOGRAPHICAL SETTING

More than two hundred miles south of Thessalonica and five miles from the Aegean Sea, Athens was situated in the driest region of ancient Greece on a plain at the southern end of the Attican Peninsula. Mountains up to 4,600 feet rise on the west, north, and east. A large, flat-topped hill in the southwest, the center of ancient Athens, is called the Acropolis, from *Acro* ("high or upper") and *polis* ("city"), upon which were built many of the most famous temples and public buildings.

ARCHAEOLOGICAL REMAINS

Around 530 B.C. the Athenians built a temple to Athena, which was destroyed in 480 B.C. by the Persians. In 447 B.C. the Acropolis saw new building projects, including the Parthenon (Temple of Athena; the Greek word *parthenos* means "virgin"), the Propylaea (entrance to the Acropolis), the small temple of Athena Nike, and the Erechtheum. Nearby are the theater of Dionysus, the Odeon theater, the Agora (the marketplace and colonnade), the Temple of Olympian Zeus, and the Hephaesteum. Areopagus (*Ares,* the Greek god of war, was known to the Romans as Mars; *pagus,* "hill"; therefore, Mars' Hill) was 377 feet in elevation and the

Acropolis, 512 feet. Paul made his famous speech in full view of one of the most blatant settings of pagan idolatry the world has ever known.

SCRIPTURAL ASSOCIATIONS

Acts 17:15–34 Paul visited Athens: idolatry, Epicureans, Stoics, "Unknown God," the agora, Areopagus.

CORINTH

BRIEF HISTORY

The city of Corinth was founded by the Dorian Greeks in the tenth century before Christ. By 750 B.C. Corinth had become the wealthiest city in ancient Greece because its position on the Isthmus that connects the Peloponnesus with mainland Greece made it an ideal center for land and sea trade. In ancient times, ships were wheeled across the four-mile-wide land bridge on a five-foot-wide, rock-cut track that saved the ships from having to make the longer and more perilous journey around the southern coast of Greece. By the sixth century before Christ, the Corinthians had begun to fortify the mountain they called the Acrocorinthus, which became, until Roman times, a nearly impregnable fortress. With a secure defensive position and an ideal location for controlling trade from both the Adriatic and the Aegean Seas, Corinth maintained economic supremacy in ancient Greece for nearly thirteen hundred years, with the exception of two periods between 454 and 404 B.C. and 146 and 144 B.C. In 734 B.C. the Corinthians established colonies on the Ionian island west of Greece called Corcyra (now Corfu) and also at Syracuse on Sicily. In 581 B.C. the Corinthians instituted the Isthmian Games. By 400 B.C. long walls were built to connect the fortified city of Corinth with Lechaion on the coast, and the city probably approached a population of one hundred thousand people. In 147 B.C. Rome demanded the dissolution of the Achaian League. Corinth resisted, and the city was sacked and completely destroyed by 146 B.C. The Romans slaughtered the men and sold the women and children into slavery. For nearly one hundred years only squatters occupied the ruins. In 44 B.C. Julius Caesar renamed the city *Colonia Laus Iulia Corinthiensis* ("the praiseworthy Julian colony of Corinth") and began rebuilding it, populating it with Latin freed slaves and the poor of Rome. In 27 B.C. Corinth was named the capital of the province of Achaia by Augustus Caesar, and it became the administrative seat of the Roman proconsul. Despite earthquakes and conquests by the Goths and others in the third and fourth centuries after Christ, it remained an important center of commerce throughout the Middle Ages, though the city was largely confined to its citadel on the Acropolis.

GEOGRAPHICAL SETTING OF CORINTH

Corinth is situated at the southwest extremity of the narrow isthmus that connects the southern part of the Greek peninsula to the mainland, and it commands the land traffic between the two. It was the center of a city-complex that included Lechaeum on the Gulf of Corinth, one and a quarter miles to the north, and Cenchreae on the Saronic Gulf, six and a quarter miles to the east. The Greek geographer Strabo wrote, "It is situated on the Isthmus and is master of two harbors, of which the one [Cenchreae] leads straight to Asia, and the other [Lechaeum] to Italy, and it makes easy the exchange of merchandise from both countries that are so distant from each other" (Strabo, *Geography*, 8.6.20).

ARCHAEOLOGICAL REMAINS

Among the most prominent ruins is a Doric temple situated on a low hill overlooking most of the rest of the city. North of the temple lies a market complex that dates from the first half of the first century after Christ. Nearby is the theater of Corinth. In Paul's day, during a two-mile walk from the

Gulf of Corinth up to the forum, one would pass by shops, shrines, and baths that open onto the Via Lechaeum. The Lechaeum Road terminated at the Propylaea, through which one entered the forum proper. Inside the forum and to the left was the fountain of Peirine, a principal water source for the city. Another prominent feature of the ancient city was the *bema,* the speaker's rostrum, or judgment seat, from which formal announcements could be made by magistrates or judicial action taken. Some believe Paul was presented before Gallio at the *bema* (see Acts 18:12–17). For further information on the archaeology of Corinth, including photographs, see Furnish, "Corinth in Paul's Time."

SCRIPTURAL ASSOCIATIONS

Acts 18:1–18 Paul's second journey: he spent one and a half years at Corinth; taught in the synagogue every Sabbath; many were converted; was taken before Gallio.

Acts 18:24–28; 19:1 Apollos was influential in Achaia, the Roman province encompassing southern Greece (see also 1 Corinthians 1:12).

Corinthians Two letters sent to the Saints at Corinth.

1 Corinthians 1:14–16 Paul baptized some converts in Corinth.

1 Corinthians 4:17; 2 Corinthians 7:13–15 Timothy and Titus were sent to Corinth.

2 Corinthians 1:1 This letter was addressed to "all the saints which are in all Achaia."

At Corinth Paul apparently began his letter-writing activity, which is one of the greatest contributions of his earthly ministry.

Acts 18:18 Paul sailed to Ephesus from the Corinthian harbor at Cenchrea and made a vow there (see also Romans 16:1).

EPHESUS

BRIEF HISTORY

The eminent city of Ephesus was first colonized by the Ionian Greeks at the beginning of the first millennium before Christ; however, an ancient shrine, dedicated to the Anatolian mother goddess, already existed there. The Greeks identified the deity with their Artemis and the Romans later with their Diana, but the fertility goddess retained many of her attributes. In 560 B.C. Croesus of Lydia built the Artemision and moved the city from the north slopes of Mount Pion to the plain south of the Artemision. The Persian king Cyrus defeated Croesus in 547 B.C., and Ephesus remained under Persian rule until Alexander defeated the Persians in 334 B.C. During the Persian rule, the Artemision burned and a new temple was constructed; it endured through Hellenistic times and has come to be known as one of the seven wonders of the ancient world. In 287 B.C. Lysimachus moved the city to higher ground, between Mount Pion and Mount Koressos, because of possible floods. From 281 B.C. the Seleucids controlled Ephesus until it passed into the hands of the Romans. They, in turn, entrusted the rule of the city to the kings of Pergamum. Rome asserted direct control of Ephesus after the death of Attalos III in 133 B.C. With the exception of an unsuccessful revolt in 88 B.C., Ephesus was peacefully governed by the Romans and later by the Byzantines for the rest of its history. The city enjoyed prosperity during the first two centuries after Christ as a harbor city and the fourth largest city in the Roman Empire. At its peak it boasted a population of half a million, but as its harbor silted up during the Byzantine period, the city lost much of its prosperity and began its irreversible decline. The Turkish town of Selcuk is located near the site.

We know from monuments, inscriptions, coins, and literary sources that a host of deities was venerated at Ephesus, including Zeus, Apollo, Athena, Aphrodite, Dionysus, Hercules, Poseidon, Pluto, Asclepius, Cybele, and others from Egyptian cults. The parade of important people who lived in or passed through Ephesus is also impressive: Alexander the Great, Mark Antony, Cleopatra, Augustus Caesar, Domitian, Trajan, Hadrian, Paul, Luke, John, Mary, Silas, Timothy, Erastus, Titus, and the early Church Fathers. Most of Paul's missionary work was in the Aegean area; he spent three years in Ephesus—more time than he spent anywhere else in his thirty-five years of missionary service. John also apparently spent many years in Ephesus. It is possible that most of the New Testament was written or compiled in Ephesus, which may even have become the headquarters of the Church of Jesus Christ after the fall of Jerusalem in A.D. 70.

GEOGRAPHICAL SETTING

Ephesus lay between Smyrna and Miletus along the coast of the Aegean Sea. It was situated forty-five miles south of Smyrna (Izmir) and three miles from the sea on the banks of the river Cayster. The leading city of the Roman province of Asia, it was an important commercial center. Its harbor on the sea route of the international highway connected Rome with eastern lands. Ephesus lay at the center of the eastern Roman Empire. Today we might misunderstand its importance as the chief harbor of Roman Asia, because the Aegean waters are now more than three miles away. "The chronology of the city's decline is not entirely clear. In the first century Ephesus was at the height of its greatness, but the trends must already have been apparent, for Strabo speaks of an unsuccessful attempt to halt the progressive silting of the harbour as early as the time of Attalus Philadelphus [159–138 B.C.] (14.1.24). Yet extensive building schemes continued . . . when we must suppose that the problem of the city's future had become obvious and acute" (Hemer, *Letters to the Seven Churches,* 53). As the empire declined, harbor dredging was discontinued, and by the sixth century the inexorable process of silting had left the sea totally inaccessible through marshland.

ARCHAEOLOGICAL REMAINS

Ephesus is today the most impressive archaeological site in Turkey, with many structures, sculptures, mosaics, and frescoes. The city was artistically arranged with paved streets and large public buildings. The Great Theater on the west slope of Mount Pion had a capacity of approximately twenty-four thousand people; it took sixty years to build. It was originally constructed in the Hellenistic period but was extensively reworked in the imperial Roman era. From the theater that faces west, the site of the former harbor can be seen about a third of a mile away. A straight road, the marble-paved Arcadian Way—1,735 feet long and thirty-six feet wide—ran from the theater to the harbor. This street was lined with lecture halls, libraries, and minor temples. The marketplace was located at the junction of this street and Marble Street, which ran north to south. Ephesus was one of only three cities in the empire with street lighting (Antioch of Syria and Rome were the other two); one hundred street lamps on the two sides illuminated the way for evening strollers in the proud city.

Just north of the Harbor Baths, near the Church of the Virgin Mary, is the extensive area of ruins where the Third Ecumenical Council confirmed in A.D. 431 that Mary was the mother of Jesus, the Son of God. The Council noted that Mary lived and died near Ephesus; they labeled Nestor, the Patriarch of Constantinople, a heretic for his denial of the virgin birth.

The Temple of Diana is located not in the center of town but just north of the city. The temple was so large it could be seen from the sea. In the mid sixth century before Christ it became the first major building to be constructed completely of marble. Then, in the mid fourth century before Christ, after suffering extensive damage at the hand of an arsonist, the temple was restored exactly the same but larger, with exquisitely embellished columns and sculptures. The largest structure ever built in the Hellenic world, it was four times the size of the Parthenon in Athens. It took about 220 years to build and was thought to be the most spectacular of all the seven wonders of the ancient world. In the temple functioned a multitude of priestesses, who carried on the perversion of cultic prostitution. The widespread fame and adoration of Artemis/Diana, who was none other than the old Anatolian mother- and fertility-goddess Cybele, provides a dramatic backdrop for the success of Paul's missionary efforts in the region. The worship of Christ eventually supplanted the cults of Artemis and Caesar.

SCRIPTURAL ASSOCIATIONS

Acts 18:19–21 Paul was at Ephesus on his second missionary journey.

Acts 18:24–28 Apollos was converted completely at Ephesus.

Acts 19 Paul's third journey: he taught and organized the work throughout Asia; miracles were performed; books were burned; mob at theater; Demetrius.

Acts 20:17–38 (especially v. 31) The Ephesians met Paul at Miletus; touching farewell; warning of apostasy and "grievous wolves"; Paul spent three years at Ephesus; farewell.

Ephesians Powerful letter sent to the Saints at Ephesus.

1 Timothy 1:3–4 Timothy worked at Ephesus to curb apostasy.

2 Timothy 1:16–18 Onesiphorus' kindness to Paul at Ephesus is recorded.

Revelation 1:11; 2:1–7 Ephesus was one of John's seven cities, or churches: emphasis on the need to love Christ.

MILETUS

BRIEF HISTORY

Founded by the Ionians in the eleventh century before Christ, Miletus is the southernmost Greek city in Asia Minor. The Persians took control of the port city, but Alexander the Great freed it in 334 B.C. The city flourished during the Hellenistic and Roman periods (324 B.C.–A.D. 325), attaining a population of 100,000. Famous Miletians were the philosophers Anaximander and Thales, the latter also being the founder of Greek geometry and astronomy and author of the famous saying "know thyself." Miletus boasted the largest market in the ancient Greek world, and the city's most renowned temple, twelve miles south at Didyma, was the third largest structure ever built in the Hellenic world. Notwithstanding its former greatness (it is claimed by some to have been the greatest city in the Greek world), Miletus lost its importance in the fourth century after Christ when its port silted up. The great theater (dating to the second century after Christ) stills stands in the fairly isolated countryside and is probably the finest example of a Graeco-Roman theater in Turkey. On the fifth row from the stage on the south side of the theater is an inscription on the benches which reads "place of the Jews also called the God-fearers."

GEOGRAPHICAL SETTING

Miletus was once situated at the mouth of the Maeander River on the west coast of Asia Minor approximately thirty-five miles south of Ephesus. Over the centuries, the Maeander River inexorably silted up the whole of the basin, leaving the ancient city more than five miles inland.

SCRIPTURAL ASSOCIATIONS

Acts 20:15–38 Paul's touching farewell and warning to the Ephesians at Miletus.

2 Timothy 4:20 Trophimus was left sick at Miletus.

HIERAPOLIS

BRIEF HISTORY

Hierapolis (Greek, *hiero polis*, "holy city") possibly originated as a village center of a temple estate dedicated to the Phrygian mother goddess. Hierapolis grew and received formal city status from the King of Pergamum in the early second century before Christ. Attalus II ceded the city to Rome in 133 B.C., and it was made part of the province of Asia. It became a popular resort and a prosperous city based on textile and cloth dyeing industries. At the time of Augustus the name appears on coins as Hierapolis "Templeville." The city was virtually destroyed by the earthquake of A.D. 17. Paul referred to Hierapolis in his epistle to the Saints in Colossae (see Colossians 4:13).

GEOGRAPHICAL SETTING

The city of Hierapolis is located more than one hundred miles east of Ephesus, twelve miles northwest of Colossae, and six miles northeast of Laodicea on the north side of the Lycus Valley close to the hot springs now called *Pamukkale* (Turkish, "cotton castle"). Over the centuries the cascading hot mineral waters have built up the plateau on which the city rests with travertines, stepped terraces of brilliant white calcium deposits that look like a massive petrified cascade. One explorer wrote: "When the writer's party in 1939 proposed to pitch a tent for the night, an unexpected difficulty arose; it was almost impossible to drive the pegs into the ground. In fact the level plateau on which the city stands is not earth at all, nor even rock, but a solid calcareous mass deposited in the course of ages by the lime-charged springs and streams of the region. The process still continues, and in the last two thousand years has buried the lower parts of many ancient buildings to a depth of several feet in solid stone" (Bean, *Turkey beyond the Maeander*, 199).

ARCHAEOLOGICAL REMAINS

Extensive ruins abound at Hierapolis/Pamukkale. Besides the hot baths, the foundations of several churches are visible, particularly the Martyrium of Philip, the apostle traditionally connected with the early Church at Hierapolis. There is a long avenue of tombs, a necropolis in which no fewer than twelve hundred tombs have been counted. More than three hundred of its epitaphs have been read and published. Underneath the temple of Apollo, near the necropolis, explorers discovered what is called the Plutonium, an opening in the earth from which a deadly gas still rises. The city also had a large theater.

SMYRNA

BRIEF HISTORY

Smyrna, now known as Izmir, Turkey, is said to be the birthplace of Homer. Ancient Smyrna was destroyed by an earthquake in 627 B.C. Lysimachus, one of the successors of Alexander the Great, rebuilt the city in about 290 B.C.; as a result, Smyrna is one of the few planned cities of the ancient world. Around 195 B.C. a temple to the goddess of Rome was built, and Smyrna was one of the first cities to embrace the imperial cult, or emperor worship. Polycarp, a member of the Church and the bishop of Smyrna, is said to have been ordained by the apostle John near the end of the first century after Christ and to have learned much from the eyewitnesses of Jesus' ministry; he was martyred by Smyrnaean Jews. In A.D. 178 the city was leveled by the most severe earthquake in its history. Much later the Jewish false messiah, Shabbetai Zevi, was born in Smyrna (1626), and after erratic wanderings throughout the Near East, he proclaimed himself the long-awaited Messiah. When arrested and imprisoned he converted to Islam, as did many of his followers.

GEOGRAPHICAL SETTING

Smyrna is situated on the Aegean coast of Asia Minor, forty miles north of Ephesus, at the southeast edge of the Gulf of Smyrna, which reaches thirty miles inland. Because of its location it was an important trade center, and it is still one of the important ports of Turkey. The acropolis of Smyrna rises 525 feet above the port on Mount Pagus. The population of present-day Izmir is more than two million.

ARCHAEOLOGICAL REMAINS

Because the city has been continuously inhabited, few remains from antiquity are visible today. The Hellenistic acropolis was on Mount Pagus, from which the present-day Kadifekale (Velvet Castle) with its medieval fortress overlooks the city and gulf. The main archaeological site surviving from Graeco-Roman times is the agora situated midway between Mount Pagus and the port.

There is a traditional etymological link between the toponym Smyrna and *myrrh* (Greek, *smurna*). Myrrh was a gift of the wise men at the Nativity (see Matthew 2:11), and Nicodemus brought a great amount of it for the burial of Jesus (John 19:39). Myrrh was connected to the burial and preservation of the body—a prerequisite to resurrection. This use may also relate to the encouragement to Smyrnaean Saints: as the Savior died and is alive again, so they will suffer and die but be brought back to life again. For "ten days" (Revelation 2:10), apparently signifying a short duration, they would have tribulation and then they would receive a crown. Jesus' crown of thorns came before his crown of glory. So with the Saints of Smyrna: "after much tribulation come the blessings" (D&C 58:4). The Greek word for "crown," *stephanos,* is usually translated as "a garland of victory, honor, or worship." It is frequently used in reference to an athletic prize for victory and may transfer to the Christian concept of overcoming the world, the ultimate victory. There is evidence of a crown being a familiar inscriptional and numismatic, or monetary, motif referring to the city of Smyrna. The phrase "the crown of Smyrna" may have originated, according to the first-century Greek philosopher Appolonius of Tyana, from the appearance of the city—public structures rising from the rounded crest of Mount Pagus.

SCRIPTURAL ASSOCIATIONS

Revelation 2:8–11 Smyrna was one of John's seven cities, or churches; faithful endurance was praised. The central idea is triumph over tribulation and death.

PERGAMUM

BRIEF HISTORY

Pergamum became famous in the Hellenistic period. In the third century before Christ, during the Attalid dynasty, Pergamum became an independent kingdom because of its great manufacture of textiles and parchments. King Eumenes II (197–159 B.C.) founded a library with more than two hundred thousand volumes, second only to that of Alexandria. Readers could sit on stone seats in library gardens to study. Out of jealousy the Egyptians refused to send more papyrus, so the Pergamenes invented *parchment* (from *pergamena*), using animal skin for writing—sheeps' hides from Phrygia being used for the manufacture of the parchment. (Later, in 41 B.C. Antony carried off the library and transferred it to Alexandria as a wedding gift to Cleopatra.) The Attalids at first allied with Rome and then came under Roman control in 133 B.C. Under Augustus the kingdom was reconstituted as a senatorial province with a governor who ruled as proconsul. Although at the time John wrote the Revelation Pergamum was not the residence of the governor, court was still held in the city, and it served as the political capital of Asia. At the height of its power, in the second century after Christ, a large, new section of the city was developed at the foot of the hill (under present-day Bergama, Turkey), and the population increased to around two hundred thousand.

GEOGRAPHICAL SETTING

The city is situated in the Caicus Valley eighteen miles from the Aegean Sea and fifty miles north of Smyrna. The upper city is situated on a hill at an altitude of 1,300 feet above the plain. The biggest problem facing the city was its lack of water. Water had to be transported from mountains thirty miles to the north via an aqueduct, running through a triple-pipe system of 240,000 sections.

ARCHAEOLOGICAL REMAINS

Pergamum is one of the most completely excavated sites in all of Asia. The theater is one of the most spectacular and definitely the steepest in antiquity. The altar of Zeus is the largest (120 feet long, 112 feet wide, and 20 feet high) and the most impressive altar in the Greek world. The Asclepion ("health resort" or "hospital") was one of the famous healing centers in the Mediterranean world. Galen (A.D. 129–199) of Pergamum became the greatest physician and medical authority in the ancient world.

SCRIPTURAL ASSOCIATIONS

Revelation 2:12–17 Pergamum, or Pergamos, was one of the seven cities, or churches; false teachers are called to repentance.

THYATIRA

BRIEF HISTORY

Thyatira, the city known today as Akhisar, Turkey, was founded in 300 B.C. by Seleucus I Nicator and served to temporarily detain invaders, allowing the Seleucids time to concentrate military strength at other locations. Its setting at a crossroads made it a popular city for traders. Thyatira's history in the first century after Christ is obscure, almost totally unknown to us, except that it was renowned for its trade guilds (modern bazaars are also somewhat laid out in separate guilds).

GEOGRAPHICAL SETTING

Thyatira was about fifty-five miles northeast of Smyrna and about thirty miles north of Sardis. It was on the road between Pergamum and Sardis in Lydia on the Lycus River. Thyatira was the smallest of the seven cities of John's Revelation.

ARCHAEOLOGICAL REMAINS

Almost no ruins remain.

SCRIPTURAL ASSOCIATIONS

Acts 16:14 Lydia, "a seller of purple," was from Thyatira.

Revelation 2:18–29 Thyatira is one of John's seven cities, or churches; immoral practices are condemned.

SARDIS

BRIEF HISTORY

This city was the capital of the kings of Lydia in Asia Minor and was known for its beauty and wealth. Sardis was the residence of Gyges' descendant Croesus (560–546 B.C.), the last and richest of the Lydian kings. Herodotus wrote that he gave away more than ten tons of gold and financed the construction of the famous Temple of Artemis/Diana at Ephesus. It later served as a temporary residence of Cyrus when he conquered Sardis in 546 B.C. Alexander captured the city from the Persians, and it was again spoiled by Antiochus, in 214 B.C. Along with Philadelphia it experienced a catastrophic earthquake in A.D. 17, which Pliny described as the greatest disaster in human memory. Tacitus wrote that Sardis was hardest hit. Excavation shows extensive rebuilding after that calamity. At the time of John's writing, Sardis was considered a city of the past.

GEOGRAPHICAL SETTING

Located near Salihli, Turkey, seventy miles northeast of Ephesus and thirty miles south of Thyatira, at the crossroads of five major land routes, Sardis was an important inland trade center. It was spread out along the west slopes of the Pactolus River on the plain of the Hermus, which is bordered on the south by the ridge of Mount Tmolus. In front of the mountains are small hills. One of these hills is an elevated plateau that rises 1,500 feet above the plain; it is the original site of Sardis. The only approach to Sardis was on the south side; on all other sides the rock walls were smooth, almost perpendicular, and thought to be insurmountable. Even the southern approach is difficult to climb.

ARCHAEOLOGICAL REMAINS

More than eighty Jewish inscriptions have been found. Jews apparently had citizenship in this Greek city, which was an uncommon phenomenon. The unique acceptance of the Jewish community in pagan society at Sardis is evidenced by the largest and most opulent Jewish synagogue ever discovered anywhere (dating from the third century after Christ). It was built as part of a Greek gymnasium complex (which dates from the second century after Christ). Revelation 3:4 refers to a few who "have not defiled their garments," or accommodated the pagan milieu.

"The visible ruins of Sardis are extensive but fragmentary. The two gigantic unfluted columns yet standing of the Hellenistic temple of Artemis are the principal landmark of the Pactolus valley. But the heart of the Roman city occupied a terrace north of the Acropolis, and here may be seen the complex which includes the gymnasium and the recently excavated synagogue" (Hemer, *Letters to the Seven Churches of Asia,* 130).

The last several yards of the Persian Royal Road—the fifteen-hundred-mile paved road from Susa to Sardis—are still visible.

SCRIPTURAL ASSOCIATIONS

Revelation 3:1–6 Sardis is one of John's seven cities, or churches; Saints are called to a more spiritual life.

PHILADELPHIA

BRIEF HISTORY

The city anciently called Philadelphia ("brotherly love") is now the Turkish city of Alashehir, "the reddish city," from the red-brown hills around it. It was founded by King Attalus Philadelphus II (159–138 B.C.), who adopted the name *Philadelphus* because of his love for his brother. The city was founded to guard the important road on which it lay, and it was given the express purpose of disseminating Hellenism in Lydia and Phrygia. Philadelphia was destroyed, along with ten other western Asian cities, in the earthquake of A.D. 17; it was plagued by subsequent aftershocks for twenty years. For much of the first century after Christ the citizens of Philadelphia lived in fear of another great disaster, a "day of trial." There is almost no evidence of the ancient city of John's day. In modern times this is still an extremely active seismic region.

GEOGRAPHICAL SETTING

The city is located a hundred miles east of Smyrna, in Lydia in western Asia Minor. It attained cultural and military importance because of its position as the door to Phrygia—it has been called "the Gateway to the East."

SCRIPTURAL ASSOCIATIONS

Revelation 3:7–13 Philadelphia in one of John's seven cities, or churches: loyalty is praised; the Lord's second coming; New Jerusalem.

LAODICEA

BRIEF HISTORY

Near the modern Turkish village of Eskihisar was ancient Laodiceia-ad-Lycum, a prosperous commercial city in the region of Phrygia in Asia Minor. Laodicea was probably established by Antiochus II (261–246 B.C.) of the Seleucid dynasty; it was named after his wife, Laodice, and was built on the site of an older place first called Diospolis and then called Rhoas (according to Pliny). Nothing is known of those two cities. Laodicea was intended as a Seleucid stronghold. The original population may have been Syrian, but it probably included a group of Jewish citizens. Laodicea became the crossroads where the route from Ephesus to the east and the route from Pergamum and Sardis to the south met. Special attention was paid to Laodicea to maintain these highways. During Roman times, Laodicea appears to have been a judicial and administrative center. Cicero was in Laodicea in A.D. 50–51.

GEOGRAPHICAL SETTING

The Lycus Valley was home to three New Testament cities: Colossae, Hierapolis, and Laodicea. This last of John's seven cities was approximately one hundred miles east of Ephesus, nearly forty-five miles southeast of Philadelphia, and twelve miles southeast of the confluence of the Lycus (Curuksu) and Maeander (Buyuk Menderes) Rivers, near modern Denizli, Turkey. The Maeander River gave rise to the word *meandering*, for which the river is well-known.

ARCHAEOLOGICAL REMAINS

Still visible on the site are parts of a large building, probably a gymnasium, constructed during the reign of Hadrian, emperor of Rome from A.D. 117 to 138. There are also remains of a large Greek theater and a smaller one as well as an odeon, which was a small roofed theater used chiefly for competitions in music and poetry. The stadium amphitheater that was completed in A.D. 79 has an arena nine hundred feet long with seating around the circumference. Other interesting structures from antiquity are a water tower and aqueduct.

SCRIPTURAL ASSOCIATIONS

Colossians 1:7; 4:12, 13, 16 Epaphras worked among the Saints here; there was an epistle (now lost) to Laodicea.

Revelation 3:14–22 Laodicea is one of the seven cities or churches, condemned for lack of commitment: "neither hot nor cold."

MINOR CITIES AND OTHER SITES

On his third missionary journey, Paul stopped at several mainland and island sites.

Assos (modern Behramkoy) was a seaport of Mysia twenty miles south of Troas. Aristotle began his first school at Assos and taught for three years. In 344 B.C., he moved to the island of Lesbos, pioneering research in biology, botany, and zoology and laying the foundations of these life sciences; then he began tutoring Philip's son, Alexander. Paul stopped at Assos on his third missionary journey and last visit to Asia (see Acts 20:13–14).

Mitylene was the chief city of the island of Lesbos, the name of which continues into modern culture because of the reputed sensuality of the Lesbian people. A homosexual group associated with a woman named Sappho on the island about 600 B.C. Paul stopped at Lesbos on his third missionary journey (see Acts 20:14).

Chios is modern Khios, an island twelve miles west of Izmir, ancient Smyrna (see Acts 20:15).

Samos, an island in the Aegean Sea off the west coast of modern Turkey, was the home of Aesop and Pythagoras (see Acts 20:15).

Trogyllium is a promontory jutting out from the mainland opposite Samos (see Acts 20:15).

En route to Jerusalem, Paul passed by the island of *Cos* (or Coos), the birthplace of Hippocrates, the father of medicine.

Rhodes is a Greek island still called by the same name today. A gigantic statue, or colossus, that once stood at its harbor was considered one of the wonders of the ancient world.

Patara was the seaport of ancient Lycia (see Acts 21:1).

Myra, another Lycian port forty miles east of Patara, was the place where years later Paul transferred to an Alexandrian ship to continue his journey to Rome (see Acts 27:5). In the fourth century after Christ, the bishop of Myra became famous for giving generous gifts to needy people. He was Saint Nicholas, a name modified in some languages to *Sancta Nicholas,* to *Sinterklaas* in Dutch, and further changed in English to *Santa Claus.*

LIGHT, FIRE, AND CLOUDS WITH CELESTIAL BEINGS

OLD TESTAMENT

Exodus	3:2–4	Angel appeared in flame of fire; bush burned with fire, not consumed
	13:21–22	Pillar of cloud by day, pillar of fire by night
	14:19–20, 24	Pillar of fire and cloud
	19:9, 16–18, 21	"I come unto thee in a thick cloud"; "the Lord descended upon it in fire"—if the people broke through, they perished
	24:15–18	Cloud covered the mount—"glory of the Lord was like devouring fire"
	33:9–11	"Cloudy pillar" at door of the tabernacle
	40:34, 38	Cloud by day, fire by night
Leviticus	10:1–2	Aaron's sons devoured by "fire from the Lord"
Numbers	9:15–16	Cloud by day, "appearance of fire" by night
	14:14	Pillar of cloud by day, pillar of fire by night
Deuteronomy	5:4–5, 24–26	Lord talked out of midst of the fire—"this great fire will consume us"
1 Kings	8:10–11	Cloud filled the house of the Lord—"priests could not stand to minister because of the cloud" (the glory of the Lord)
2 Chronicles	5:13–14	
2 Kings	1:10–15	Elijah called down fire from heaven to consume soldiers
	2:10–12	Elijah taken up in a "chariot of fire" by "horses of fire"
	6:17	Elisha caused Syrians to be blinded by "horses and chariots of fire"
Psalm	68:17	"The chariots of God are . . . thousands of angels"
	104:4	"Who maketh his angels spirits; his ministers a flaming fire"
	78:14; 105:39	Cloud by day, light of fire by night

Isaiah 4:5	Cloud and smoke by day, shining of flaming fire by night
Daniel 7:13	"Son of man came with the clouds of heaven"

NEW TESTAMENT

Luke 9:28–36	Transfiguration: "countenance was altered," "raiment was white and glistering [Greek, 'as lightning']." Moses and Elias "who appeared in glory," "there came a cloud, and overshadowed them: and they feared as they entered into the cloud"; voice of the Father out of the cloud
Acts 1:9	Jesus "was taken up; and a cloud received him out of their sight"

BOOK OF MORMON

Ether 2:4–5, 14	"The Lord came down and talked with the brother of Jared; and he was in a cloud, and the brother of Jared saw him not"; the Lord went before this people in a cloud and gave them directions (he did the same with the Israelites).
1 Nephi 1:6	Lehi prayed, and "there came a pillar of fire and dwelt upon a rock before him"
1 Nephi 22:16–17	The righteous "shall be saved, even if it so be as by fire"
Mosiah 27:11	"Angel of the Lord appeared . . . and he descended as it were in a cloud"
Helaman 5:23–48	Nephi and Lehi "encircled about with a pillar of fire, and . . . it burned them not" (cloud of darkness over-shadowed the others); faces of Nephi and Lehi "did shine exceedingly, even as the faces of angels"; every-one encircled by flaming fire, no harm done; Holy Ghost came down "and they were filled as if with fire"; "they saw the heavens open; and angels came down"
3 Nephi 17:24	"They saw the heavens open, and they saw angels descending out of heaven as it were in the midst of fire"
18:38–39	"There came a cloud and overshadowed the multitude" as Jesus ascended

PEARL OF GREAT PRICE

Moses 1:11–14	"His glory was upon me; and I beheld his face, for I was transfigured before him. . . . I could not look upon God, except his glory should come upon me, and I were transfigured before him"
Abraham 2:7	"I cause the wind and the fire to be my chariot"
JS–H 1:16–17	"I saw a pillar of light exactly over my head, above the brightness of the sun, which descended gradually until it fell upon me. . . . When the light rested upon me I saw two Personages, whose brightness and glory defy all description, standing above me in the air"
JS–H 1:30–32, 43	"I discovered a light appearing in my room, which continued to increase until the room was lighter than at noonday . . . personage . . . standing in the air . . . whiteness beyond anything earthly . . . exceedingly white and brilliant . . . glorious beyond description, and his countenance truly like lightning. The room was exceedingly light, but not so very bright as immediately around his person." "I saw the light in the room begin to gather immediately around the person . . . and it continued to do so until the room was again left dark, except just around him; when instantly I saw, as it were, a conduit open right up into heaven, and he ascended till he entirely disappeared"
JS–H 1:68	"A messenger from heaven descended in a cloud of light"

DOCTRINE AND COVENANTS

5:19	"Inhabitants of the earth . . . destroyed by the brightness of my coming"
29:12	"The day of my coming in a pillar of fire"
34:7	"I shall come in a cloud with power and great glory"
45:45	"The saints that have slept shall come forth to meet me in the cloud"
76:102	"Caught up unto the church of the Firstborn, and received into the cloud"
78:21	"Ye are the church of the Firstborn, and he will take you up in a cloud"
84:5	"An house shall be built unto the Lord, and a cloud

shall rest upon it, which cloud shall be even the glory of the Lord"

88:97   "Caught up to meet him in the midst of the pillar of heaven"

109:75 "We shall be caught up in the cloud to meet thee"

On receiving light in our bodies, see Doctrine and Covenants 50:24; 88:12–13, 40–44, 50, 67–68.

On the "fire" that will destroy the world at the Second Coming, see Doctrine and Covenants 5:19, "destroyed by the brightness of my coming"; Doctrine and Covenants 133:41, "the presence of the Lord shall be as . . . fire that burneth"; Doctrine and Covenants 64:24, "the burning—this is speaking after the manner of the Lord"; see also Isaiah 66:15–16; Doctrine and Covenants 101:23–25; 29:12–13; 43:32; 130:7; 45:57; Joseph Smith–History 1:37.

English	Hebrew
light	*or*
fire	*esh*
pillar, column	*amud*
cloud	*anan;* Greek, *nephele* (the *Shekhinah* or Dwelling Cloud)

JEWS IN THE MEDITERRANEAN WORLD

The early Christians received a commission to be witnesses of Jesus not only in Jerusalem, Judaea, and Samaria, but also "unto the uttermost part of the earth." (Acts 1:8.) What would the "uttermost part of the earth" have meant to those Jewish Christians?

That phrase does appear in another context in the Gospels. Referring to the Queen of Sheba, Matthew and Luke indicate that "she came from the uttermost parts of the earth to hear the wisdom of Solomon." (Matt. 12:42; Luke 11:31.) The land of Sheba, or Seba—the land of the Sabaeans—was the southwestern part of today's Arabian Peninsula, specifically the modern land of Yemen. Was that the "uttermost part of the earth" to the Jews?

The Hellenistic-Roman world was as open and trafficable as the world had ever been. Land and sea routes crisscrossed each other in myriad directions; economic enterprises spanned the Empire. Great centers of learning dotted the Mediterranean lands. The Jews had made a particular mark on nations and societies everywhere. Diaspora communities still had great ties to the homeland, and Jerusalem wielded unique influence throughout the Empire. Strabo, a Greek historian and geographer writing in the first century after Christ, indicated that Jews had made their way "into every city, and it is not easy to find any place in the habitable world which has not received this nation and in which it has not made its power felt." [Josephus, *Antiquities,* tr. Ralph Marcus, in Loeb Classical Library (Cambridge: Harvard University Press, 1971), XIV:115.]

Philo, an Alexandrian philosopher and contemporary with Jesus, in issuing a veiled threat to Caligula (who wanted to set up his own statue in Jerusalem), wrote that the holy city of Jerusalem was "the mother city not of one country Judaea but of most of the others in virtue of the colonies sent out at diverse times to the neighbouring lands Egypt, Phoenicia, the part of Syria called Hollow [Coele-Syria; that is, the Lebanese Beq'a] . . . and lying far apart, Pamphylia,

Cilicia, most of Asia [Minor] up to Bithynia and the corners of Pontus, similarly also into Europe, Thessaly, Boeotia, Macedonia, Aetolia, Attica, Argos, Corinth and most of the best parts of Peloponnese. And not only are the mainlands full of Jewish colonies but also the most highly esteemed of the islands Euboea, Cyprus, Crete. I say nothing of the countries beyond the Euphrates. . . . So that if my own home city is granted a share of your goodwill the benefit extends not to one city but to myriads of the others situated in every region of the inhabited world." [*The Embassy to Gaius*, tr. F. H. Colson, in *Philo*, vol. X, in Loeb Classical Library, 281–83.]

Jews throughout the Empire looked to Jerusalem for calendar and legalistic questions. They sent money to Jerusalem from all parts of the Empire for the upkeep of the Temple and the Holy City.

Judaeans living in the time of Jesus likely had a wider compass of geographical knowledge than people in any previous era. In his own native land, the typical Judaean could have heard four different languages being used. He himself would have known Aramaic and Hebrew, and he might have had daily contact with those speaking Greek and Latin. So that all could read it, the superscription on Jesus' cross was "written in Hebrew, and Greek, and Latin." (John 19:20.)

THE DAY OF PENTECOST

At least yearly, Judaeans would expect to see fellow Jews and other curious tourists and travelers from all parts of the Roman world. Jerusalem was an international city. One of the most comprehensive lists of place names in the Bible recites the origin of those attending the Shavuot Festival, the day of Pentecost, shortly after Jesus' departure into heaven. Luke accurately reported that there were present: "Jews, devout men, out of every nation under heaven . . . Parthians, and Medes, and Elamites, and the dwellers in Mesopotamia, and in Judaea, and Cappadocia, in Pontus, and Asia, Phrygia, and Pamphylia, in Egypt, and in the parts of Libya about Cyrene, and strangers of Rome, Jews and proselytes, Cretes and Arabians." (Acts 2:5, 9–11.)

Following is a list of those geographical regions with modern equivalents:

ANCIENT NAME	MODERN EQUIVALENT
EAST	
Parthia	eastern Iran
Media	western Iran
Elam	southwest Iran
Mesopotamia	Iraq
NORTH	
Pontus	northern Turkey
Cappadocia	central Turkey
Asia	western Turkey
Phrygia	west-central Turkey
Pamphylia	southern Turkey
SOUTH	
Egypt	Egypt; northeast Africa
Libya	coastal Africa west of Egypt
Cyrene	a chief city of Libya or Cyrenaica
Arabia	great desert lands south and east of Judaea
WEST	
Crete	same as today; large island south of Greece
Rome	same as in Italy today

Judaeans, then, would have had some acquaintance with Jews and non-Jews from a rather wide compass, from beyond Mesopotamia to Rome and from the borders of Europe to north Africa.

NATIONS SURROUNDING THE HOLY LAND

EGYPT

The religious history of Israel is inextricably tied to the land of Egypt. The great patriarchs and prophets Abraham, Jacob, Joseph,

Moses, and Jeremiah all spent part of their lives in the land of pyramids, tombs, and temples. Egypt played a significant role as a place of refuge—either economic or political refuge. Abraham and Jacob had both gone down into Egypt to escape famine (because of the ever-flowing Nile, the land of Egypt knew famine less often than other lands). Jeroboam and Joseph, with Mary and Jesus, fled there to escape political dangers.

In the early Roman period, hundreds of thousands of Jews lived in Egypt, particularly in Alexandria. Some made annual pilgrimages to Jerusalem for the great festivals, like Pentecost. (Acts 2:10.) Jews from Alexandria debated with Stephen, one of the officials of the Christian Church in Jerusalem. (See Acts 6:9.) Interestingly, most references to Egypt in the New Testament come from the speech on the religious history of the Hebrew people that Stephen gave to his antagonists—ten occurrences in Acts 7.

CYRENAICA

The reference in Acts concerning the day of Pentecost is the only one mentioning the widespread nations until the accounts of Paul's journeys, with the exception of Cyrene. The New Testament contains a surprising number of allusions to Cyrenian Jews and Christians: "As they led him away, they laid hold upon one Simon, a Cyrenian, coming out of the country, and on him they laid the cross, that he might bear it after Jesus." (Luke 23:26.)

Cyrene was a Mediterranean port on the northern coast of Africa and the chief city of the Roman province Cyrenaica (or western Libya). Though in Africa, Cyrene had been settled as a Greek city, and by Jesus' day it had a large colony of Jews.

Many Cyrenians took an active stance either for or against the young Christian message. "Then there arose certain of the synagogue, which is called the synagogue of the Libertines, and Cyrenians, and Alexandrians, and of them of Cilicia and of Asia, disputing with Stephen." (Acts 6:9.) "Some of them were men of Cyprus and Cyrene, which, when they were come to Antioch, spake unto the Grecians, preaching the Lord Jesus." (Acts 11:20.) "Now there were in the church that was at Antioch certain prophets and teachers; as Barnabas, and Simeon that was called Niger, and Lucius of Cyrene." (Acts 13:1.)

MESOPOTAMIA

In addition to the single reference about residents of Mesopotamia being present at Pentecost, Stephen's historical review also alluded to Abraham's Mesopotamian homeland: "Men, brethren, and fathers, hearken; The God of glory appeared unto our father Abraham, when he was in Mesopotamia, before he dwelt in Charran [Haran in Genesis]." (Acts 7:2.) "Then came he out of the land of the Chaldaeans, and dwelt in Charran: and from thence, when his father was dead, he removed him into this land, wherein ye now dwell." (Acts 7:4.)

The only other New Testament reference to a place in Mesopotamia is Jesus' mention of the preaching of Jonah to the people of Nineveh, thus confirming the historicity of the prophet and the incident: "The men of Nineveh shall rise in judgment with this generation, and shall condemn it: because they repented at the preaching of Jonas; and, behold, a greater than Jonas is here." (Matt. 12:41.)

SYRIA-PHOENICIA

One of the benefactors of Jesus' healing power was a Greek woman, specifically a gentile woman, "a Syrophenician by nation." (Mark 7:26.) In Jesus' day, Phoenicia, the coastal region with the old cities Sidon, Sarepta, and Tyre, was part of the Roman province of Syria: "[Paul and company] sailed into Syria, and landed at Tyre." (Acts 21:3.)

Sites in Phoenicia also figured in the spread of the early Christian Church: "Now they which were scattered abroad upon the persecution that arose about Stephen travelled as far as Phenice, . . . preaching the word to none but unto the Jews only." (Acts 11:19.) "Being brought on their way by the church, they passed through Phenice and Samaria, declaring the conversion of the Gentiles." (Acts 15:3.) We have already seen how multitudes of people journeyed from the area around Tyre and Sidon to hear Jesus teach, and how Jesus himself visited the Tyrians and Sidonians in their cities.

Paul's missionary journeys later included stops at Tyre and Sidon: "[We] landed at Tyre: for there the ship was to unlade her burden. . . . And when we had finished our course from Tyre, we came to Ptolemais." (Acts 21:3, 7.) On Paul's voyage to Rome,

Luke recorded the itinerary in some detail: "The next day we touched at Sidon. And Julius courteously entreated Paul, and gave him liberty to go unto his friends to refresh himself." (Acts 27:3.)

The first reference to Syria (Old Testament Aram) in the life of Jesus is the mention by Luke of one Cyrenius, who was the Roman governor of the province of Syria at the birth of Jesus. Though there is some uncertainty about the dating of the census, or enrollment, that Luke mentioned, yet the service of Roman consul P. Sulpicius Quirinius as governor (legate) of Syria during the initial years of the first millennium A.D. is confirmed also by the Jewish historian Josephus.

Just as the old prophets of Israel had used their curative priesthood powers on foreigners—"Many lepers were in Israel in the time of Eliseus [Elisha] the prophet; and none of them was cleansed, saving Naaman the Syrian" (Luke 4:27)—so in Jesus' early ministry, "his fame went throughout all Syria: and they brought unto him all sick people that were taken with divers diseases and torments, and those which were possessed with devils, and those which were lunatick, and those that had the palsy; and he healed them" (Matt. 4:24).

Luke wrote that the ministries of John and Jesus began when Pilate was governor of Judaea, Herod Antipas the tetrarch of Galilee, his brother Philip the tetrarch of Ituraea and Trachonitis, and "Lysanias the tetrarch of Abilene." (Luke 3:1.) Abilene was a region, named after its capital city Abila (not to be confused with Abila, a city of the Decapolis further south), which was situated about twenty miles northwest of Damascus. The governor of Abilene, Lysanias, is mentioned not only by Luke but on an inscription at Abila dating from the reign of Tiberius.

The historic city of Damascus is mentioned seven times with a fair amount of detail (including the name of one of its streets, "Straight," in Acts 9:11). All the references to Damascus are in Acts 9, in connection with the conversion of Saul to Christianity. The city had a large number of Jews, and Saul felt the need to go there and root out the Jewish Christians: "Saul, yet breathing out threatenings and slaughter against the disciples of the Lord, went unto the high priest, and desired of him letters to Damascus to the synagogues, that if he found any of this way, whether they were men or women, he might bring them bound unto Jerusalem." (Vv. 1–2.) Instead, after his conversion, Saul ended up testifying of Jesus in those very synagogues. He so angered the Jews that they plotted to kill him, and Saul escaped by being let down in a basket over the walls at night.

The greatest city in Syria in the days of Jesus was its capital in the northwest corner of the province called Antioch (modern Antakya in Turkey). After Rome and Alexandria, Antioch was the third largest city in the Roman Empire and one of its greatest cultural and commercial centers. Jews from this city three hundred miles north of Jerusalem were quite active in the religious life of the Holy City. One of the seven Greeks chosen as leaders in the early Christian Church was a Jewish convert who had become Christian, "Nicolas a proselyte of Antioch." (Acts 6:5.)

Early persecution had caused some Christians to flee the Holy Land to other parts of the Empire. "They which were scattered abroad upon the persecution that arose about Stephen travelled as far as . . . Antioch, preaching the word to none but unto the Jews only." (Acts 11:19–20.) Antioch became pivotal in the growth of the Church. "They sent forth Barnabas, that he should go as far as Antioch. . . . When he had found [Paul], he brought him unto Antioch. And it came to pass, that a whole year they assembled themselves with the church, and taught much people. And the disciples were called Christians first in Antioch. And in these days came prophets from Jerusalem unto Antioch." (Acts 11:22, 26–27.)

ASIA

The catalog of countries represented on the day of Pentecost includes Cappadocia, Pontus, and Asia. (See Acts 2:9.) The province referred to as "Asia" meant the westernmost region of modern Turkey, extending west to the Aegaean Sea. There were Jews of Asia disputing with Stephen in Jerusalem (Acts 6:9), as well as "Jews which were of Asia" stirring up the people against Paul in the Temple (Acts 21:27; 24:18).

Another specific region mentioned frequently in Acts was Cilicia, the home province of Paul: "I am a man which am a Jew of Tarsus, a city in Cilicia, a citizen of no mean city." (Acts 21:39; see also 22:3; 23:34.) Paul labored among his own native Cilicians: "He went through Syria and Cilicia, confirming the churches." (Acts 15:41.)

CYPRUS

One of the early leaders of the Christian Church in Jerusalem was a diaspora Jew named Joseph, who was from Cyprus: "Joses, who by the apostles was surnamed Barnabas, (which is, being interpreted, The son of consolation,) a Levite, and of the country of Cyprus." (Acts 4:36.) Some of the Jewish Christians who fled the persecutions surrounding Stephen's martyrdom also traveled to Cyprus (see Acts 11:19), and some Christian Cypriots traveled to Antioch to preach about Jesus (Acts 11:20).

Another reference to the island is given in the story of Paul's last trip to Jerusalem: "Now when we had discovered Cyprus, we left it on the left hand [that is, to the north], and sailed into Syria, and landed at Tyre." (Acts 21:3.)

Having identified the neighboring countries of the Holy Land referred to in the Gospels and Acts, we can see that Judaeans living at the time of Jesus had a geographical perspective of the world that was broad indeed. They had contact with Jews and non-Jews from the states contiguous with Israel—that is, Syria (including Phoenicia and Transjordan), Arabia, and Egypt—from Mesopotamia and beyond, from Asia Minor and Greece, from Rome, from the islands of the Mediterranean, and from north Africa. The commission to take the gospel to the "uttermost parts of the earth" was an expansive challenge issued out of the humble hill country of Judaea.

From D. Kelly Ogden, *Where Jesus Walked: The Land and Culture of New Testament Times* (Salt Lake City: Deseret Book, 1991), 43–50.

A P P E N D I X   3

THE NUMBER SEVEN IN REVELATION

	THE SEVEN CHURCHES	THE SEVEN SEALS	THE SEVEN TRUMPETS
1	Opening vision (1:1–20) Ephesus (2:1–7)	White Horse conquest (6:1–2)	First Angel hail, fire, blood (8:7)
2	Smyrna (2:8–11)	Red Horse war (6:3–4)	Second Angel great burning mountain (8:8–9)
3	Pergamos (2:12–17)	Black Horse famine (6:5–6)	Third Angel great burning star (8:10–11)
4	Thyatira (2:18–29)	Pale Horse death, hell, war, famine (6:7–8)	Fourth Angel sun, moon, stars darkened (8:12–13)
5	Sardis (3:1–6)	Souls of martyred Saints (6:9–11)	Fifth Angel bottomless pit opened (9:1–12)
6	Philadelphia (3:7–13)	Great calamities (6:12–17)	Sixth Angel massive army (9:13–21)
7	Laodicea (3:14–22)	Interlude—sealing of God's servants (7:1–17)	Interlude—little book, two witnesses (10:1–11:14)
Summary	Opening vision of God and Christ (4:1–5:14)	Angels pour fire and desolation (8:1–6)	Seventh Angel destruction of the wicked (11:15–19)

THE SEVEN PERSONS	THE SEVEN VIALS	THE SEVEN JUDGMENTS ON THE HARLOT	THE SEVEN GREAT EVENTS
Woman with crown (12:1–2, 14–17)	Instruction to seven angels (15:1–8) First vial Grievous sore (16:1–2)	Kings make war with Lamb; are conquered (17:14–15)	Christ comes as King of Kings (19:11–16)
Great red dragon (12:3–4, 13)	Second vial Sea of blood (16:3)	Kings turn against the harlot (17:16–18)	Final victory over beast (19:17–21)
The man child (12:4–6)	Third vial Rivers and fountains of blood (16:4–7)	The fall of Babylon (18:1–7)	Satan bound for 1,000 years (20:1–3)
Michael (12:7–12)	Fourth vial Scorching fire (16:8–9)	Plagues sent on Babylon (18:8–17)	Resurrection of faithful Saints, Millennium (20:4–6)
Beast from the sea (13:1–10)	Fifth vial Darkness and pain (16:10–11)	Burning of Babylon (18:18–20)	Satan's final loosening, battle of Gog and Magog (20:7–10)
Beast from the earth (13:11–18)	Sixth vial Unclean spirits, Armageddon (16:12–16)	Great millstone cast into sea (18:21)	Final judgment of earth (20:11–15)
Lamb on Mt. Zion (14:1–6)	Seventh vial Great earthquake (16:17–21)	Silence and desolation (18:22–24)	New heaven and earth (21:1–22:5)
Interlude— Angel, voices, visions (14:6–20)	Interlude— The great harvest and beast (17:1–13)	Interlude— Song of triumph over fall of Babylon (19:1–10)	Closing instructions and testimony (22:6–21)

THE SEVEN CHURCHES OF REVELATION

The following chart shows at a glance the consistent internal structure and carefully crafted organization of the first part of the book of Revelation. Chapters 1 through 3 contain the messages to the seven churches of Asia Minor that John was commanded to deliver. Though each was individualized, common themes run through all seven. Each message was constructed around the same organizing principles: John's commission to write to each church, a condemnation and admonition for each church, and so forth. Each description of the speaker (or the one who commissioned the letters) presents an attribute of the Lord Jesus Christ found in other portions of the Revelation as well as in other scripture, especially in scripture of the Restoration.

The phraseology of the "call to hear," issued to each of the seven branches of the Church, is the same for all seven churches and precedes seven separate blessings or rewards that are the same as those promised to modern Saints in latter-day Temples. The Temple-centered language is striking. It helps us realize that the seven letters (chapters 1–3), as well as the Revelation itself (chapters 4–22), were addressed to members of the kingdom in two different dispensations who understood the nature of Temple covenants. It is therefore not unreasonable to suppose that the messages and ideas of the book of Revelation will be better understood by those in our own day who attend the Temple.

STRUCTURE	TO EPHESUS (2:1–7)	TO SMYRNA (2:8–11)	TO PERGAMOS (2:12–17)
Commission or Charge	Unto the angel of the church of Ephesus write;	Unto the angel of the church in Smyrna write;	To the angel of the church in Pergamos write;
Description of the Speaker (Christ)	These things saith he that holdeth the seven stars in his right hand, who walketh in the midst of the seven golden candlesticks;	These things saith the first and the last, which was dead, and is alive;	These things saith he which hath the sharp sword with two edges;
Description of each city's activity	I know thy works, and thy labour, and thy patience, . . . and for my name's sake hast laboured, and hast not fainted.	I know thy works, and tribulation, and poverty, (but thou art rich)	I know thy works, and where thou dwellest, even where Satan's seat is: and thou holdest fast my name, and hast not denied my faith. . . .
Condemnation	Nevertheless I have some-what against thee, because thou hast left thy first love.	and I know the blas-phemy of them which say they are Jews, and are not, but are the synagogue of Satan. Fear none of those things which thou shalt suffer . . . :	But I have a few things against thee, because thou hast there them that hold the doctrine of Balaam. . . . So hast thou also them that hold the doc-trine of the Nicolaitans, which thing I hate.
Admonition	Remember therefore from whence thou art fallen, and repent, and do the first works. . . .	be thou faithful unto death, and I will give thee a crown of life.	Repent; or else I will come unto thee quickly, and will fight against them with the sword of my mouth.
Call to Hear	He that hath an ear, let him hear what the Spirit saith unto the churches;	He that hath an ear, let him hear what the Spirit saith unto the churches;	He that hath an ear, let him hear what the Spirit saith unto the churches;
Promise and Blessing	To him that overcometh will I give to eat of the tree of life, which is in the midst of the paradise of God.	He that overcometh shall not be hurt of the second death.	To him that overcometh will I give to eat of the hidden manna, and will give him a white stone, and in the stone a new name written, which no man knoweth saving he that receiveth it.

TO THYATIRA (2:18–29)	TO SARDIS (3:1–6)	TO PHILADELPHIA (3:7–13)	TO LAODICEA (3:14–22)
Unto the angel of the church in Thyatira write;	Unto the angel of the church in Sardis write;	To the angel of the church in Philadelphia write;	Unto the angel of the church of the Laodiceans write;
These things saith the Son of God, who hath his eyes like unto a flame of fire, and his feet are like fine brass;	These things saith he that hath the seven Spirits of God, and the seven stars;	These things saith he that is holy, he that is true, he that hath the key of David, he that openeth, and no man shutteth . . . ;	These things saith the Amen, the faithful and true witness, the beginning of the creation of God;
I know thy works, and charity, and service, and faith, and thy patience, and thy works; and the last to be more than the first.	I know thy works, that thou hast a name that thou livest, and art dead.	I know thy works: behold, I have set before thee an open door, and no man can shut it: for thou hast a little strength, and hast kept my word, and hast not denied my name.	I know thy works, that thou art neither cold nor hot: I would thou wert cold or hot. So then because thou art lukewarm, and neither cold nor hot, I will spue thee out of my mouth.
Notwithstanding I have a few things against thee, because thou sufferest that woman Jezebel . . . to teach and to seduce my servants to commit fornication. . . . I will cast her . . . and them that commit adultery with her into great tribulation, except they repent. . . .	Be watchful, and strengthen the things which remain, that are ready to die: for I have not found thy works perfect before God.	Behold, I will make them of the synagogue of Satan, which say they are Jews, and are not, but do lie; behold, I will make them to come and worship before thy feet, and to know that I have loved thee. . . .	Because thou sayest, I am rich . . . , and have need of nothing; and knowest not that thou art wretched, and miserable, and poor, and blind, and naked: I counsel thee to buy of me gold tried in the fire, that thou mayest be rich; and white raiment, that thou mayest be clothed. . . .
But unto you I say, . . . as many as have not this doctrine, . . . I will put upon you none other burden. But that which ye have already hold fast till I come.	Remember therefore how thou hast received and heard, and hold fast, and repent. If therefore thou shalt not watch, I will come on thee as a thief, and thou shalt not know what hour I will come. . . .	Behold, I come quickly; hold that fast which thou hast, that no man take thy crown.	As many as I love, I rebuke and chasten: be zealous therefore, and repent. Behold, I stand at the door, and knock: if any man hear my voice, and open the door, I will come in to him. . . .
He that hath an ear, let him hear what the Spirit saith unto the churches.	He that hath an ear, let him hear what the Spirit saith unto the churches.	He that hath an ear, let him hear what the Spirit saith unto the churches.	He that hath an ear, let him hear what the Spirit saith unto the churches.
And he that overcometh, and keepeth my works unto the end, to him will I give power over the nations: And he shall rule them with a rod of iron. . . . And I will give him the morning star.	He that overcometh, the same shall be clothed in white raiment; and I will not blot out his name out of the book of life, but I will confess his name before my Father.	Him that overcometh will I make a pillar in the temple of my God . . . : and I will write upon him the name of my God, and the name of the city of my God, which is new Jerusalem . . . : and I will write upon him my new name.	To him that overcometh will I grant to sit with me in my throne, even as I also overcame, and am set down with my Father in his throne.

COMMENTARY ON ARMAGEDDON

"Who are these witnesses, and when will they prophesy? 'They are two prophets that are to be raised up to the Jewish nation in the last days, at the time of the restoration, and to prophesy to the Jews after they are gathered and have built the city of Jerusalem in the land of their fathers.' (D&C 77:15.) Their ministry will take place after the latter-day temple has been built in Old Jerusalem, after some of the Jews who dwell there have been converted, and just before Armageddon and the return of the Lord Jesus. How long will they minister in Jerusalem and in the Holy Land? For three and a half years, the precise time spent by the Lord in his ministry to the ancient Jews. The Jews, as an assembled people, will hear again the testimony of legal administrators bearing record that salvation is in Christ and in his gospel. Who will these witnesses be? We do not know, except that they will be followers of Joseph Smith; they will hold the holy Melchizedek Priesthood; they will be members of The Church of Jesus Christ of Latter-day Saints. It is reasonable to suppose, knowing how the Lord has always dealt with his people in all ages, that they will be two members of the Council of the Twelve or of the First Presidency of the Church" (McConkie, *Millennial Messiah*, 390).

"One host opposes the other. One host is for God and his cause; the other fights against him. Both hosts are comprised of wicked and worldly men, but one is defending freedom, and the other would destroy liberty and enslave men. One defends free institutions, freedom in government, freedom to worship the god of one's choice according to one's own conscience, and the other, Lucifer-like, seeks to overthrow liberty and freedom in all its forms. And the Lord himself is interceding to bring to pass his own purposes" (McConkie, *Millennial Messiah*, 457).

"Armageddon is a holy war. In it men will blaspheme God. They will be in rebellion against Jehovah. The armies that face each other will have opposing philosophies of life. It will be religious instincts that cause them to assemble to the battle. And the plagues poured out upon them will not cause them to repent.

"Such—sadly—is the destiny that lies ahead.

"And such—providentially—is not right at hand. It is some years away. It shall come to pass by and by" (McConkie, *Millennial Messiah*, 398).

"The valley of Megiddo (once Megiddon), meaning place of troops, is part of the plain of Esdraelon (or plain of Jezreel), which is some twenty miles long and fourteen miles wide. . . . Armageddon is the hill of the valley of Megiddo west of Jordan on the plain of Jezreel. And Armageddon is the place where the final war will be fought, meaning, as we suppose, that it will be the focal point of a worldwide conflict, and also that as a place of ancient warfare, it will be a symbol of the conflict that will be raging in many nations and on many battlefronts.

"Having these things in mind, let us turn to the prophetic word relative to Jerusalem and the final great battle during which our Lord will return. 'Behold, I will make Jerusalem a cup of trembling unto all the people round about,' saith the Lord, 'when they shall be in the siege both against Judah and against Jerusalem.' Armageddon is in process; all nations are at war; some are attacking Jerusalem and others are defending the once holy city. She is the political prize. Three world religions claim her—Christianity, Islam, and Judaism. Emotion and fanaticism run high; it is a holy war" (McConkie, *Millennial Messiah*, 464).

"'And it shall come to pass, that in all the land, saith the Lord, two parts therein shall be cut off and die; but the third shall be left therein.' This is Israel of whom he speaks. These are the armies who are defending Jerusalem and whose cause, in the eternal sense, is just. Two-thirds of them shall die.

"'And I will bring the third part through the fire, and will refine them as silver is refined, and will try them as gold is tried: they shall call on my name, and I will hear them: I will say, It is my people: and they shall say, The Lord is my God.' (Zech. 13:8–9.) We repeat: It is a religious war. The forces of antichrist are seeking to destroy freedom and liberty and right; they seek to deny men the right to worship the Lord; they are the enemies of God. The one-third who remain in the land of Israel are the Lord's people. They believe in Christ and accept Joseph Smith as his prophet and revealer for the last days" (McConkie, *Millennial Messiah*, 465–66).

"'And again shall the abomination of desolation, spoken of by Daniel the prophet, be fulfilled.' That which once happened to Jerusalem and its inhabitants shall happen again. . . .

". . . 'And when ye shall see Jerusalem compassed with armies, then know that the desolation thereof is nigh.' So shall it be again. . . . Is this the way the saints shall be saved in the last days when two-thirds of the inhabitants shall be cut off and die and only one-third be left? If more than a million were put to the sword in A.D. 70, how great shall be the slaughter when atomic bombs are used?" (McConkie, *Millennial Messiah*, 473).

"The kings of the earth and of the whole world will gather to fight the battle of that great day of God Almighty. Their command center will be at Armageddon, overlooking the valley of Megiddo. All nations will be gathered against Jerusalem. Two hundred thousand thousand warriors and more—two hundred million men of arms and more—shall come forth to conquer or die on the plains of Esdraelon and in all the nations of the earth. At the height of this war, the Lord Jesus will put his foot on the Mount of Olives and save his ancient covenant people. . . .

"Now it is our purpose to show that this war will be a religious war, a war in which the servants of Satan assail the servants of the Lord and those allied with them" (McConkie, *Millennial Messiah*, 476).

"We do not speculate as to what nations are involved in these wars. It is well known that the United States and Great Britain and the Anglo-Saxon peoples have traditionally been linked together in causes designed to promote freedom and guarantee the rights of man. It is also well known that there are other nations, ruled by a godless communistic power, that have traditionally fought to enslave rather than to free men. It is fruitless to try and name nations and set forth the alliances that are to be" (McConkie, *Millennial Messiah*, 477).

"Armageddon will be a holy war. There will be political overtones, of course. Wars are fought by nations, which are political entities. But the underlying causes and the moving power in the hearts of men will be their views on religious issues. . . .

". . . These events shall go forward over a long period of time; there will be ample opportunity for all nations to choose the course they will pursue" (McConkie, *Millennial Messiah*, 478).

"Daniel describes the anti-gospel, anti-Christ, anti-God nature of the king and his armies from the north. 'He shall exalt himself, and magnify himself above every god,' the scripture saith, 'and shall speak marvellous things against the God of gods, and shall prosper till the indignation be accomplished: for that that is determined shall be done.' Already the communistic nations exhibit this spirit. As the polarization between good and evil continues apace in the last days, we may expect to see even more resistance manifest by them toward God and his laws. . . . By then billions of earth's inhabitants (even more so then than now) will be in open rebellion against the gospel and every principle of truth and virtue found therein" (McConkie, *Millennial Messiah*, 478–79).

"Armageddon will be a war of aggression instituted by Gog and Magog. Theirs will be an evil cause. Those nations that defend Israel and Jerusalem will be doing what the Lord wants done. To them it will be a righteous war" (McConkie, *Millennial Messiah*, 482).

TEN DOCTRINES OF SALVATION

1. *Justification*

Justification is being put back into a right relationship with God, to be declared righteous: "Accounted or adjudged righteous." We are justified by faith, which includes works (see McConkie, *Doctrinal New Testament Commentary,* 2:229–40; McConkie, *Mormon Doctrine,* 408; Sperry, *Paul's Life and Letters,* 164, 171–78).

2. *Sanctification*

Sanctification is the process of becoming clean, pure, spotless, renewed by rebirth of the Spirit. We are sanctified by blood (see Moses 6:60), the blood of Christ (see McConkie, *Doctrinal New Testament Commentary,* 3:49–50, 185–89; McConkie, *Mormon Doctrine,* 675).

3. *Reconciliation*

Through the intercession or mediation of Christ, through his expiation or propitiation on our behalf, we enjoy reconciliation with God once again. We are ransomed from a state of sin. Though spiritually fallen, we are restored to harmony and unity with God. Reconciliation is made possible through the Atonement (see McConkie, *Doctrinal New Testament Commentary,* 2:421–23; 3:77–78; McConkie, *Mormon Doctrine,* 620).

4. *Election (covenant people)*

Election to a chosen lineage is based on premortal worthiness, obedience, conformity, and preparation before this life (see McConkie, *Doctrinal New Testament Commentary,* 2:271–78, 283–85, 291, 494, 513; 3:322–55).

Calling and election: membership in the Church.

Calling and election made sure: the same as being justified and sealed by the Holy Spirit of Promise. It immediately precedes receipt of the Second Comforter. We are sealed to eternal life, which is the promise of exaltation in the celestial kingdom, or guaranteed Godhood. Anyone who commits the unpardonable sin is disqualified from the sealing promises.

5. *Foreordination*

Premortal spirits were called or assigned, not by compulsion, to special missions in this world, all according to the foreknowledge of God regarding their valor, worthiness, talent, and capacity. All Melchizedek Priesthood holders, as well as Abraham, Moses, Cyrus, John the Baptist, Mary, Jesus, Columbus, the American Founding Fathers, Joseph Smith, and others were foreordained to their missions (see McConkie, *Doctrinal New Testament Commentary,* 2:267–69; 3:64; McConkie, *Mormon Doctrine,* 290–92, 588–89).

Predestination is a spurious, sectarian substitute for foreordination. Predestination teaches, falsely, that individuals through no acts of their own are inevitably and invariably scheduled for salvation or damnation, thus dismissing the eternal concept of agency.

6. *Adoption*

In connection with joint-heirship, the term *adoption* is used in two senses:

1. When Gentiles believe and repent, they are adopted into the house of Israel (see Jacob 5).

2. By righteous living we may be adopted into the family of God, becoming joint-heirs with his Son (see McConkie, *Doctrinal New Testament Commentary,* 2:275, 285–89, 474–75, 490–91; McConkie, *Mormon Doctrine,* 23).

7. *Joint-heirship with Christ*

Christ is the natural heir of God the Father. It is his right to inherit and possess all his Father has. By righteousness we may be adopted into the family of God and become joint-heirs with Christ in all things (see McConkie, *Doctrinal New Testament Commentary,* 2:261–62, 474–75; Smith, *Doctrines of Salvation,* 2:24, 35–40; McConkie, *Mormon Doctrine,* 394–95).

8. *Intercession, or Mediation*

Jesus Christ is the Intercessor and Mediator (sometimes the Spirit fills this role also). He intercedes, mediates, prays, petitions, and entreats the Father for us. Those who reject Christ's mediation, the Atonement, must pay the penalty for their own sins (according to the law of justice) and sometimes even being destroyed in the flesh and delivered over to the buffetings of Satan till the day of redemption (see D&C 45:3–5; McConkie, *Doctrinal New Testament Commentary,* 2:265–66, 269–71; 3:77–78, 344; McConkie, *Mormon Doctrine,* 387–88, 472).

9. *Sealing by the Holy Spirit of Promise*

When the Holy Spirit seals our calling and election, it is *made sure.* Righteous acts are justified, approved, or ratified by the Holy Ghost to be binding on earth and in heaven. The action of having our calling and election being made sure, or being sealed up to eternal life, is accompanied by the sealing of the Holy Spirit of Promise (see McConkie, *Doctrinal New Testament Commentary,* 2:493–95, 513; 3:333–37; Smith, *Doctrines of Salvation,* 1:45, 55; 2:94–95, 98–99; McConkie, *Mormon Doctrine,* 361–62).

10. *The Second Comforter*

The Second Comforter follows sealing by the Holy Spirit of Promise or having our calling and election made sure—all three are parts of the same process. The personage of Jesus Christ himself may then attend us and teach us face to face, appearing from time to time to manifest the Father; visions of the heavens are opened; mysteries of the Kingdom are learned perfectly (see McConkie, *Doctrinal New Testament Commentary,* 1:734–41; 3:337–42; Smith, *Doctrines of Salvation,* 1:55; McConkie, *Mormon Doctrine,* 687).

SOURCES

The Anchor Bible Dictionary. 6 vols. Edited by David Noel Freedman. New York: Doubleday, 1992.

Anderson, Richard Lloyd. "Guide to Acts and the Apostles' Letters." Unpublished syllabus. Provo, 1990.

———. *Understanding Paul.* Salt Lake City: Deseret Book, 1983.

Aratus. *Phaenomena.* Translated by G. R. Mair. Loeb Classical Library. Cambridge, Mass.: Harvard University Press, 1921.

Backman, Milton Vaughn, Jr. *The Heavens Resound: A History of Latter-day Saints in Ohio, 1830–1838.* Salt Lake City: Deseret Book, 1983.

Bean, George. *Turkey beyond the Maeander.* New York: W. W. Norton, 1980.

Beitzel, Barry J. *The Moody Atlas of Bible Lands.* Chicago: Moody Press, 1985.

The Book of Mormon. Salt Lake City: The Church of Jesus Christ of Latter-day Saints, 1981.

Brown, Raymond E., Joseph A. Fitzmyer, and Roland E. Murphy. *The Jerome Biblical Commentary.* 2 vols. in 1. Englewood Cliffs, N. J.: Prentice-Hall, 1968.

Bruce, F. F. *New Testament History.* Garden City, N. Y.: Doubleday, 1980.

———. *The New Testament Documents—How Reliable Are They?* Grand Rapids, Mich.: Eerdmans, 1985.

Bullinger, E. W. *Figures of Speech Used in the Bible.* Grand Rapids, Mich.: Baker Book House, 1968.

Burton, Theodore M. *Ensign,* November 1974, 54–56.

Calvin, John. *Institutes of the Christian Religion.* Translated by Henry Beverage. 2 vols. Grand Rapids, Mich.: Eerdmans, 1957.

Cannon, George Q. *Gospel Truth: Discourses and Writings of President George Q. Cannon.* 2d ed. 2 vols. Salt Lake City: Deseret Book, 1974.

Cary, M. *The Geographic Background of Greek and Roman History.* Oxford: Clarendon Press, 1949.

Charles, R. H. *The Apocrypha and Pseudepigrapha of the Old Testament.* Vol. 2. Oxford: Clarendon Press, 1976.

Cobern, Camden M. *The New Archaeological Discoveries and Their Bearing upon the New Testament and upon the Life and Times of the Primitive Church.* New York; London: Funk and Wagnalls, 1917.

Cowley, Matthias F. *Wilford Woodruff: History of His Life and Labors.* 1909. Reprint, Salt Lake City: Bookcraft, 1964.

Cross, F. L., and E. A. Livingstone, eds. *The Oxford Dictionary of the Christian Church.* 2d ed. Oxford: Oxford University Press, 1984.

Doctrine and Covenants. Salt Lake City: The Church of Jesus Christ of Latter-day Saints, 1981.

Draper, Richard D. *Opening the Seven Seals: The Visions of John the Revelator.* Salt Lake City: Deseret Book, 1991.

Encyclopedia of Mormonism. Edited by Daniel H. Ludlow. 5 vols. New York: Macmillan, 1992.

Eusebius. *Ecclesiastical History.* Translated by Kirsopp Lake. 2 vols. Loeb Classical Library. Cambridge: Harvard University Press, 1992.

———. *The History of the Church from Christ to Constantine.* Translated by G. A. Williamson. London: Penguin Books, 1989.

Evans, Richard L. *Improvement Era* 67, no. 4 (April 1964): 306.

Franklin, Benjamin. *The Autobiography of Benjamin Franklin.* New Haven, Conn.: Yale University Press, 1964.

Furnish, Victor Paul. "Corinth in Paul's Time." *Biblical Archaeology Review* 15, no. 3 (May/June 1988): 14–27.

Galbraith, David B., D. Kelly Ogden, and Andrew C. Skinner. *Jerusalem, the Eternal City.* Salt Lake City: Deseret Book, 1996.

Ginzberg, Louis. *The Legends of the Jews.* Philadelphia: Jewish Publication Society of America, 1906–38.

Graham, Billy. *Christianity Today* 25, no. 13 (17 July 1981): 18–24.

"Great Events." *Times and Seasons* 3, no. 6 (15 January 1842): 662.

Harrison, R. K., ed. *Major Cities of the Biblical World.* Nashville: Thomas Nelson, 1985.

Hemer, Collin J. *The Letters to the Seven Churches of Asia in Their Local Settings.* Sheffield: JSOT, 1986.

Hinckley, Gordon B. *Ensign,* June 1971, 71–72.

Holy Bible. Authorized King James Version.

Holy Bible. The New American Bible.

Holy Bible. New International Version.

Howe, Julia Ward. "Battle Hymn of the Republic." In *Hymns of The Church of Jesus Christ of Latter-day Saints,* no. 60. Salt Lake City: The Church of Jesus Christ of Latter-day Saints, 1980.

Hunter, Howard W. *Church News.* 11 June 1994, 3, 14.

Jagersma, H. *A History of Israel from Alexander the Great to Bar Kochba.* London: SCM Press Ltd., 1985.

Joseph Smith's "New Translation" of the Bible [JST]. Independence, Mo.: Herald, 1970.

Josephus. *Complete Works.* Translated by William Whiston. Grand Rapids, Mich.: Kregel Publications, 1973.

———. *Jewish Antiquities.* Translated by H. St. J. Thackeray, et al. 10 vols. Loeb Classical Library. Cambridge: Harvard University Press, 1930–65.

———. *Jewish War.* Translated by H. St. J. Thackeray. 2 vols. Loeb Classical Library. Cambridge: Harvard University Press, 1927–28.

Journal of Discourses. 26 vols. Liverpool: Latter-day Saints' Book Depot, 1854–86.

Kimball, Spencer W. *Faith Precedes the Miracle.* Salt Lake City: Deseret Book, 1972.

———. *The Miracle of Forgiveness.* Salt Lake City: Bookcraft, 1969.

———. Conference Report, October 1943, 15–19.

———. Conference Report, October 1953, 51–56.

———. Conference Report, April 1969, 27–31.

———. *Ensign,* November 1977, 76–79.

———. "Marriage Is Honorable." In *Speeches of the Year: BYU Devotional Addresses, 1973.* Provo: Brigham Young University Press, 1973.

———. *Peter, My Brother.* Brigham Young University Speeches of the Year. Provo, 13 July 1971.

Lectures on Faith. Independence, Mo.: Price Publishing, 1988.

Lee, Harold B. *Stand Ye in Holy Places: Selected Sermons and Writings of President Harold B. Lee.* Salt Lake City: Deseret Book, 1974.

———. Conference Report, October 1967, 98–108.

———. Conference Report, October 1973, 3–10.

———. "Put on the Whole Armor of God." Era of Youth section, *Improvement Era,* October 1962, n.p.

Leith, John H., ed. *Creeds of the Churches.* Richmond, Va.: John Knox Press, 1973.

Lewis, C. S. *Mere Christianity.* New York: Macmillan, 1960.

Lyon, T. Edgar. "Greco-Roman Influences on the Holy Land." *Ensign,* September 1974, 20–21.

MacArthur, John F. *Faith Works: The Gospel According to the Apostles.* Dallas: Word Publishing, 1993.

Madsen, Truman. "The Temple and the Restoration." In *The Temple in Antiquity: Ancient Records and Modern Perspectives,* edited by Truman G. Madsen. Provo: Brigham Young University Religious Studies Center, 1984.

Matthews, Robert J. *"A Plainer Translation": Joseph Smith's Translation of the Bible, A History and Commentary.* Provo: Brigham Young University Press, 1985.

Maxwell, Neal A. "Taking Up the Cross." In *Speeches of the Year, 1976.* Provo: Brigham Young University Press, 1976, 249–63.

McConkie, Bruce R. *Doctrinal New Testament Commentary.* 3 vols. Salt Lake City: Bookcraft, 1966–73.

———. *The Millennial Messiah.* Salt Lake City: Deseret Book, 1982.

———. *Mormon Doctrine.* 2d ed. Salt Lake City: Bookcraft, 1966.

———. *The Promised Messiah: The First Coming of Christ.* Salt Lake City: Deseret Book, 1978.

———. "The Bible, a Sealed Book." Supplement to *A Symposium on the New Testament, 1984.* Salt Lake City: The Church of Jesus Christ of Latter-day Saints, 1984, 1–7.

———. "The New Revelation on Priesthood." In *Priesthood.* Salt Lake City: Deseret Book, 1981, 126–37.

———. Conference Report, April 1979, 130–33.

———. *Ensign,* September 1975, 85–89.

McGuire, Meade. "Father, Where Shall I Work Today?" Quoted in Thomas S. Monson, *Ensign,* May 1986, 39.

Meinardus, Otto F. A. *St. Paul in Greece.* Athens: Lycabettus Press, 1973.

Metzger, Bruce M. *The New Testament: Its Background, Growth, and Content.* Nashville: Abingdon Press, 1965.

Monson, Thomas S. *Ensign,* November 1975, 20–22.

Neusner, Jacob. *The Glory of God Is Intelligence.* Provo: Brigham Young University Religious Studies Center, 1978.

Ogden, D. Kelly. *Illustrated Guide to the Model City and to New Testament Jerusalem.* 2d ed. Jerusalem: The Jerusalem Center for Near Eastern Studies, 1990.

———. *Where Jesus Walked: The Land and Culture of New Testament Times.* Salt Lake City: Deseret Book, 1991.

Packer, Boyd K. *The Holy Temple.* Salt Lake City: Bookcraft, 1980.

———. *Ensign,* November 1980, 20–22.

The Pearl of Great Price. Salt Lake City: The Church of Jesus Christ of Latter-day Saints. 1981.

The Personal Writings of Joseph Smith. Compiled and edited by Dean C. Jessee. Salt Lake City: Deseret Book, 1984.

Philostratus. *Life of Apollonius of Tyana.* Translated by J. S. Phillmore. Oxford: Clarendon Press, 1912.

Pliny the Elder. *Natural History.* 10 vols. Translated by H. Rackham. Cambridge: Harvard University Press, 1938–63.

Pratt, Orson. "Past and Future Existence." *Millennial Star* 28 (17 November 1866): 721–23.

Ramsay, W. M. *The Cities of St. Paul: Their Influence on His Life and Thought—The Cities of Asia Minor.* London: Hodder and Stoughton, 1907.

———. *The Historical Geography of Asia Minor.* New York: Cooper Square, 1972.

Richardson, Alan, ed. *A Dictionary of Christian Theology.* Philadelphia: Westminster Press, 1969.

Roberts, Alexander, and James Donaldson, eds. *The Ante-Nicene Fathers: Translations of the Writings Down to* A.D. *325.* 9 vols. 1885. Reprint, Grand Rapids, Mich.: Eerdmans, 1993.

Roberts, B. H. Conference Report, October 1912, 30–35.

Romney, Marion G. Conference Report, October 1954, 65–70.

———. Conference Report, October 1965, 20–23.

Ryken, Leland. *How to Read the Bible as Literature.* Grand Rapids, Mich.: Academie Books/Zondervan, 1984.

Sill, Sterling W. "Dedication." *Church News,* 22 April 1967, 13.

Smith, Hyrum M., and Janne M. Sjodahl. *Doctrine and Covenants Commentary.* Salt Lake City: Deseret Book, 1950.

Smith, Joseph. *History of The Church of Jesus Christ of Latter-day Saints.* Edited by B. H. Roberts. 2d ed. rev. 7 vols. Salt Lake City: Deseret Book, 1980.

———. *Joseph Smith's Commentary on the Bible.* Compiled and edited by Kent P. Jackson. Salt Lake City: Deseret Book, 1994.

———. *Teachings of the Prophet Joseph Smith.* Selected by Joseph Fielding Smith. Salt Lake City: Deseret Book, 1976.

Smith, Joseph F. *Gospel Doctrine.* Compiled by John A. Widtsoe. Salt Lake City: Deseret Book, 1919.

Smith, Joseph Fielding. *Answers to Gospel Questions.* 5 vols. Salt Lake City: Deseret Book, 1957–66.

———. *Doctrines of Salvation.* 3 vols. Compiled by Bruce R. McConkie. Salt Lake City: Bookcraft, 1954–56.

———. Conference Report, April 1967, 119–23.

Snow, LeRoi. *Improvement Era* 22, no. 8 (June 1919): 653–62.

Sperry, Sidney B. *Paul's Life and Letters.* Salt Lake City: Bookcraft, 1955.

Steinberg, Milton. *Basic Judaism.* New York: Harcourt, Brace, 1947.

Stern, David H. *Jewish New Testament.* Jerusalem: Jewish New Testament Publications, 1989.

Strabo. *Geography.* Translated by Horace Leonard Jones. 8 vols. Loeb Classical Library. Cambridge: Harvard University Press, 1950.

Talmage, James E. *Jesus the Christ.* Salt Lake City: Deseret Book, 1962.

Talmon, Shemaryahu. *The "Dead Sea Scrolls" or "The Commentary of the Renewed Covenant."* Tucson: University of Arizona, 1993.

Turner, Rodney. "Grace, Mysteries, and Exaltation." In *Acts to Revelation,* edited by Robert L. Millet. Vol. 6 of Studies in Scripture Series. Salt Lake City: Deseret Book, 1987.

Walker, Williston. *A History of the Christian Church.* 3d ed. New York: Charles Scribner's Sons, 1970.

Woodruff, Wilford. *The Discourses of Wilford Woodruff.* Compiled by G. Homer Durham. Salt Lake City: Bookcraft, 1946.

———. *Wilford Woodruff: History of His Life and Labors.* Prepared by Matthias F. Cowley. Salt Lake City: Deseret News, 1909.

Young, Brigham. *Discourses of Brigham Young.* Compiled by John A. Widtsoe. Salt Lake City: Deseret Book, 1978.

INDEX

Aaronic Priesthood, 47–48, 249, 252. *See also* Priesthood

Abel, 259

Abraham: covenant to, 23–24, 40, 165–66; as viewed by Jews, 174; receives priesthood, 254–56; acts on faith, 259–60; is justified, 268; time of, symbolized by black horse, 326–27

Accountability, 171–72, 174, 206–7, 287

Aceldama, 32–33

Achaia, 83

Achaicus, 130

Acts, The, meaning of, 27–29

Adam, 275, 175–76, 325–26. *See also* Michael

Adam-ondi-Ahman, 329

Adoption, into house of Israel, 182–83

Afflictions: necessary for salvation, 151–53, 328–29; helps perfect us, 175, 262, 277–78, 288–92; be grateful for, 283–84. *See also* Persecution

Agabus, 97

Agrippa. *See* Herod

Albinus, 21

Alexander the Great, 7–8

Ananias: of Jerusalem, 42–43; of Damascus, 53

Ananus, 264–65

Andrew, 38

Angels: appearance of, in latter days, 35; worshipped by Colossians, 192–93, 195; Christ superior to, 246–47; nature of, 263; who did not keep first estate, 274–75; as messengers, 314; seven, pour out judgments, 330, 336; of restoration, 335–36; destroying, 336

Anger, 268–69

Annas, 40

Anointings, with oil, 271–74

Anthropomorphism, 193

Anti-Christs, 300, 339–40

Anti-Marcionite Prologue, 28

Antioch (Antakya, Turkey), 60–61; 352–54

Antioch of Pisidia, 67, 355

Antiochus III (the Great), 8–9

Antiochus IV, 10

Antipas, 317

Antipater, 16–17

Antonia Fortress, 20, 99

Apocalypse, 305, 323–349

Apollos, 90–91, 129

Apostasy, the Great, 96, 118–22, 129, 294, 333

Apostates, in early Church, 96, 119–21; 222–23, 274, 276

Apostles: necessity of, 2, 203; challenges of, 22–25; empowerment of, 30–31; qualifications for, 33; receive gift of Holy Ghost, 34; heal sick, 37–38; proclaim gospel, 41–42; delegate authority, 44–45; hold keys of kingdom, 121; have disagreements, 161–62; in early and latter days, 170

Apphia, 198

Aquila, 88, 90, 237

Archelaus, 18, 62

Archippus, 198
Areopagus, 85
Aristarchus, 109, 199, 237
Aristobulus, 62
Aristotle, 381
Armageddon, 330, 337
Armor of God, 208–11
Articles of Faith, 192
Assos, 381
Assumption of Moses, The, 275
Athens, 83–87, 362–64
Atonement: proof of, 30;
    reconciliation is part of,
    153–54, 247–48; necessary for
    salvation, 164, 324–25;
    understanding, 175–76; as
    taught by Paul, 232–33;
    rejection of, by sons of
    perdition, 250; Mosaic
    ordinances prefigured, 256–59,
    279; olive oil symbolic for,
    271–74; show gratitude for,
    283; elements of, 296; red
    symbolic for, 341–42
Attalia (Antalya, Turkey), 71,
    354–55
Augustus, 18, 20, 317
Authority, line of, 217

Babylon, 284, 336, 339–40
Baptism(s): of three thousand, 37;
    by immersion, 49; of Saints in
    Ephesus again, 91–92; for the
    dead, 145–46, 282–83;
    symbolism of, 176; as saving
    ordinance, 282
Barnabas, Joses: identity of, 42,
    284; as Paul's missionary
    companion, 65–66, 237; leaves
    with John Mark, 76; disagrees
    with Paul, 161–62, 236
Barsabas, Judas, 76
Beasts, meanings of, 324, 335–36
Beatitudes of the epistles, 183–86
Beautiful Gate, 102
Berea, 83
Bernice, 62, 108
Bethesda pools, 103

Bishops, 205, 215–16
Blacks, receiving priesthood, 58–59
Boaz, 104
Body, views of, 297–99
Book of Mormon, 1
Book, sealed, 324
Brimstone, 343
Burial place, 46

Caesar. See Augustus, Claudius,
    Nero
Caesar, Julius, 3–4, 16–17
Caesarea, 55, 107–8
Caesarea Philippi (Panias), 8
Cain, 259
Calling and election made sure:
    meaning of, 196, 202, 206,
    221–22; Paul's, 223–24;
    conditions for, 284–85; mark
    of, 328
Calvin, John, 179
Cassander, 360–61
Catachresis, 314
Charity, 141–43, 283, 295–96
Chester Beatty Biblical Papyri, 4–5,
    244
Chios, 381
Chloe, 130
Christian Church(es), early:
    functioning of, 2; survives fall of
    Jerusalem, 15; fate of, under
    Roman rule, 22–23; embraces
    Hellenistic culture, 23; parallels
    Church of Jeus Christ of Latter-
    day Saints, 26–27; meeting
    places of, 31–32, 38; members
    of, live form of law of
    consecration, 37; debates over
    circumcision, 74–75; epistles to,
    89–90; Jewish members of,
    follow Mosaic law, 97–99; in
    Thessalonica, 112–14, 117–18;
    in Corinth, 128–30; referred to
    as temple, 132, 140; practices
    baptisms for the dead, 146; in
    Rome, 169–70; in Philippi,
    187–88; in Colossae, 192–93;
    in Ephesus, 200; unites Gentiles

and Jews, 203–4; name of,
205–6; understood crucifixion,
261–62; confused by
Gnosticism, 297–300; John
pleads with, 310–11; John
writes to seven, 314–22; woman
as symbol of, 333
Christians, definition of, 60–61
Church of Jesus Christ of Latter-
day Saints, 26–27, 29, 205–6
Church of the devil, 338–39
Cilician Gates, 358
Circumcision, 74–77, 158–59, 203
City of God, 344–46
Claudius, 20, 22, 61, 88–89
Clayton, William, 196
Clement, 120–21, 191–92, 244,
301
Cleopatra, 62
Clothing, symbolism of, 47
Codex Sinaiticus, 4
Codex Vaticanus, 4
Colossae, 192–93, 320–22
Condescension of God, 189
Consecration, law of, 37, 42–43
Conversation, meaning of, 279,
281
Corinth, 87, 128, 364–66
Cornelius, 55–56
Cornerstone, 40–41, 203, 280
Cos, 382
Courts of the Temple, 98–99,
102–3
Cowdery, Oliver, 170, 240–41
Creation, 258
Crete, 220
Crispus, 89, 130
Criticism, 287
Crucifixion, 36, 261–62

Damascus, 51–52, 63
Daniel, 13, 307
David, King, 31, 36–37
Day of Atonement, 110, 257–58
Deacons, 44
Dead Sea Scrolls, 15–16, 206, 246
Deceivers, 300
Deeds, 171, 174–75

Degrees of glory, 147–48
Delegation, 44
Demas, 199, 237, 224
Derbe, 357–58
Destruction, 342
Dionysius, 87
Diotrephes, 301
Discipleship, 267–68
Dispensation of the fulness of
times, 201–2
Docetism, 295–96, 298
Doctrine and Covenants, 240–42,
307
Dogs, symbolism of, 191
Dome of the Rock, 103–4
Domitian, 310
Dragon, 333, 335
Drusilla, 62, 107
Dyes, 78–79

Earth, 336–38
Earthquakes: during other
dispensations, 80–81, 287,
319–20, 322; of apocalypse,
326, 330, 332–33, 337
Elders, twenty-four, 323–24
Election, law of, 179–80
Elias, 328
Emperors of Rome, 22–23
Enoch, 254, 259–60, 275–76,
325–27, 344
Epaphras, 193, 237
Epaphroditus, 190–91, 237–38
Ephesus, *91–96, 200–201;* 238,
314, 367–70
Epicureans, 85
Epistles, 89–90, 212–13
Erastus, 185–86, 237
Essenes, 15–18
Eternal life, sealed unto, 284–85,
296–97. *See also* Calling and
election made sure
Ethiopian officer, 49
Eusebius, 28, 244–45, 301
Evangelists, 205, 223
Eve, 215
Exaltation, 279
Ezekiel, 307

Faith: combines with works, 175, 202; gaining of, 182; definition of, 258–61; to ask God, 266; being justified through, 270; for healings, 272–74; demonstrated through trials, 278, 288–92

Fall, the, 232

Famine, 61

Fasting, 35–36

Feast of the Unleavened Bread, 63

Feet, shaking dust off, 69

Felix, Antonius, 21, 107, 235

Festus, Porcius, 21, 108, 235

Fire, 34, 343

First Jewish Revolt, 19, 22

Flattery, 206

Foreordination, 52–54, 178–79, 181, 200–201

Forgiveness, 198, 270

Fortunatus, 130

Fruit of the Spirit, 167

Gaius, 130, 237, 300–301

Galatians, 158

Galilee, 16–19

Gallic Wars, 3–4

Gallio, Lucius Junius, 88–89

Gamaliel, 43, 94

Genealogy, endless, 214

Gentiles: gospel to go among, 56–60, 67–68; adopted into house of Israel, 182–83; united with Jews in Church, 203; can be fellow heirs with Christ, 233

Gerousia, 8

Gioras, Simon bar, 19

Gnosticism: Simon associated with, 48; teachings of, 195–96, 213, 216, 297–300; John preaches against, 293–94

Goat, sacrificial, 258

Godhead, 194–95, 230, 246, 296

Gods, plurality of, 137

Gog and Magog, 343

Gospel of Jesus Christ: principles of, 37; to go among the Gentiles, 56–60; taught in Athens, 86–87; taught to

Corinthians, 130–32; based on higher principles, 151; preached by Paul, 239–40; taught by word of God, 280. *See also* Christian Church(es), early

Governments, early Judean, 7–13

Governors, 20–21

Grace, 173–76, 202

Grass, symbolism of, 279–30

Grecians, 45

Greek language, 23

Gymnasium in Jerusalem, 10

Handkerchiefs of healing, 93–94

Hanukkah, 12

Hasidim, 9–11

Hasmonean dynasty, 12–14, 16

Healing of sick: by apostles, 37–38, 41, 43; by Paul, 92; by Joseph Smith, 92–93; by faith, 270; through anointings, 272–74

Hell, 343

Hellenistic culture, 8–9, 16, 23

Hermas, 282

Herod (the Great), 17–18, 62. *See also* Temple of Herod

Herod Agrippa I, 21–22, 24, 61–64

Herod Agrippa II, 22, 62, 108, 235

Herod Antipas, 18, 62

Herodias, 62

Herodotus, 4

Herod Philip, 18, 62

Herod's Basilica, 101

Hezekiah, 18

Hierapolis, 192, 320–22, 372–73

Holy Ghost: departs from Israel, 7; apostles endowed with, 30; apostles receive gift of, 34–35, 41; received by Samaritans, 48; converts Cornelius, 56; warns Paul and Silas, 77; given to baptized Saints in Ephesus, 91–92; is Holy Spirit of Promise, 140, 202; Paul close to, 237

Holy of Holies, 104, 257. *See also* Temple of Herod
Horses of the apocalypse, 325–26
Huntington, Prescindia, 35
Hypocrisy, 269, 287
Hyrcanus, John, 16

Iconium (Konya, Turkey), 69, 356
Idolatry: in Lystra, 70; in Athens, 85–87; in Ephesus, 93–94; in eating sacrificial meat, 137, 139, 318
Idumea, 16
Independence, Missouri, 335
Irenaeus, 28, 301, 310
Isaac, 253, 255, 260
Israel: as a light to the Gentiles, 68; distinct in premortal life, 180; adoption into house of, 182–83; apostasy of ancient, 248; James writes to lost tribes of, 266; known as peculiar people, 280; tribes of, saved, 328; has covenant with Lord, 340–41
Isthmian games, 138

Jachin, 104
Jackson County, Missouri, 344
Jambres, 222
James the Less, 264–65
James: brother of John, 24, 61–63, 264–65; brother of Jesus, 32, 63, 75, 97, 144, 264–65
Jannes, 222
Jason, 83
Jeremiah, 41
Jerusalem, 15, 20, 97–99, 332; celestial, 344–46. *See also* New Jerusalem, Temple of Herod
Jesus Christ: earliest records of, 2; teachings of, 16, 32; during reign of Herod Antipas, 19–20; gospel of, 26–27, 37; life of, chronicled by Luke, 28–29; prophecies concerning, 39–40, 46; Second Coming of, 113, 340–42; salvation through, 117, 131–32, 138, 158–65, 173–74,

296; brings justification, 176; nature of, 192–94, 231, 314; testified of by Paul, 229–30; law of, superior to Mosaic, 246–49, 256–59; scourging and crucifixion of, 261–62, 281; olive oil symbolic for, 271–74; premortal knowledge of, 279; Gnostic beliefs in, 295–98; designations of, 312, 324–25; will reign over earth, 344. *See also* Atonement; Christian Church, early; Gospel of Jesus Christ; Second Coming; Resurrection
Jewish Christians, 75–76, 97–99, 129, 158–62, 245
Jews: destruction of, 11–12; resist Christianity, 23–25; messianic expectations of, 30–31, 40; crucify Christ, 37; try to stop apostles, 43–44; laws of, 49–50; expelled from Rome, 87–88; God's love for, 180; united with Gentiles through church, 203
Jezebel, 318
John Mark: identity of, 32, 63, 237, 284; goes on missions, 66, 76, 236; reconciles with Paul, 199, 224
John: the Baptist, 33; the Beloved: is arrested, 40; witnesses Apostasy, 120; writes to Saints, 293–94, 300–301; story of, 301–4; as Revelator, 305–6; bears testimony of Christ, 310–12; given special mission, 331–32
Jonathan, 12
Joppa, 55
Joseph Caiaphas, 40
Joseph Smith Translation of Bible, 122–27
Joseph: father of Jesus, 32; who was sold into Egypt, 283
Joshua, 46
Judaea, 16–17

Judah, tribe of, 7
Judaism, 9–11, 15, 50–51
Judas: son of Hezekiah, 18; the
    Galilean, 19; Iscariot, 31–33
Jude, brother of Jesus, 274
Judgments, 171, 330, 336–37,
    343–44
Justification, 159, 163–64,
    172–74, 232, 268
Justus, Jesus, 130, 237

Kirtland Temple, 35
Koine, 23

Lamb, Christ as, 324–25
Land ownership, 19
Language, of Romans and Greeks,
    23
Laodicea, 192, 320–22, 380–81
Last Supper, the, 31–32, 140
Law of gospel, 171–72, 174
Lesbos, 381
Levitical Priesthood, 252. *See also*
    Aaronic Priesthood
Light-dark metaphor, 206
Linus, 225
Livy, 4
Locusts, 330–31
Lots, casting, 33
Love, 141–43, 183–84, 238–39,
    295–96, 345–46
Luke: as author of the Acts, 27–29;
    joins Paul and Silas, 77, 237; in
    Ephesus, 94–96; in Rome,
    109–11, 224; writes of James,
    264–65
Luther, Martin, 159
Lycus Valley, 320–22
Lydia, 78–79, 187, 191
Lysias, Claudius, 99, 105
Lystra, *70,* 357–58

Maccabees, 10–11
Maccabeus (the Hammerer), 12
Macedonia, 77
Malthace, 62
Mariamne(s), 62
Mark Anthony, 17, 350–51, 359

Marketplace, 80
Marriage: Paul's teachings on,
    134–37, 139, 206–8, 216–18;
    in the Temple, 209–10; Peter's
    counseling on, 281; symbolic of
    covenant making, 340–41
Martyrs, 45–46, 61–62, 179
Mary: mother of Jesus, 32; mother
    of John Mark, 32, 63
Materialism, 339–40
Mattathias, 11–12
Matthias, 33
Melchizedek Priesthood, 45,
    251–53
Melchizedek, 250–54
Menander, 299
Messiah, 30–31, 40. *See also* Jesus
    Christ
Metalepsis, 167
Metonymy, 314
Michael, 246, 275, 343. *See also*
    Adam
Miletus, *95*–96, 371
Millennium, 39, 326–27, 329–30,
    342–43
Mishnah, 49–50
Missionary work, 136–37
Mitylene, 381
Modi'in, 11–12
Monson, Thomas S., 77
Morality, sexual, 133–36
Moriah, Mount, 253
Mosaic law: of Sabbath travel, 31;
    of stoning, 47; of stages of a
    man's life, 49–50; Paul attempts
    to keep, pure, 52; of
    circumcision, 74–75; not to be
    followed by converts, 75–76;
    still followed by Jewish
    Christians, 97–99, 158–62,
    165–66; as a lesser law, 151; is
    dead, 176–77; Christ is greater
    than, 246–48; as preparatory
    law, 256–59
Moses, 39–40, 46, 275–76
Muratorian Canon, 28
Myra, 382

Myrrh, 274
Mythology, Greek, 87, 93–94, 145

Nazarite vow, 90, 102
Neapolis (Kavalla, Greece), *78*
Nehemiah, 7
Nero, 22, 224, 277
New Jerusalem, 320, 339–40, 344
New Testament, authenticity of,
    1–5
Nicaea, Council of, 194
Nicanor, Gate of, 103
Nicholas, Saint, 382
Nicolaitans, 314–15
Nicopolis, 221
Nike, 315
Noah, 326–27
Numbers, in Revelation, 307–9,
    334–35

Obedience, 202–3, 206–7
Octavian, 17
Oil, consecrated olive, 271–74
Old Testament, 245–46
Olive tree, 182–83
Onesimus, 192, 197–99
Onesiphorus, 222, 238
Oral Torah (oral tradition), 13, 24,
    50–51

Pagan worship, 316–17
Palace, in Jerusalem, 20
Panias (Caesarea Philippi), 8
Parchment, 375
Passover, 63
Pastors, 205
Patara, 382
Patience, 270
Patmos, isle of, 310
Patriarchs, 205
Paul: persecutes Christians, 47,
    49–50; conversion of, 52–55;
    preaches gospel, 65; on first
    missionary journey, 66–71;
    preparation and focus of,
    71–73, 160; travels of, 73–74;
    on second missionary journey,
    76–90; imprisoned with Silas,
    80–82; in Thessalonica, 82–83;
    in Athens, 83–87; in Corinth,
    87–90; in Ephesus, 91–96; in
    Jerusalem, 97–99; addresses
    Sanhedrin, 104–6; on trial in
    Caesarea, 107–9; travels to
    Rome, 109–11; writes to
    Thessalonians, 112–13;
    discusses the Second Coming,
    116–18; writes to Corinthians,
    128–30, 148–49; discusses
    marriage and sexual relations,
    131–37; discusses spiritual gifts
    and charity, 140–43; teaches
    about resurrection, 144–48;
    preaches endurance, faith and
    repentance, 152–57; writes to
    Galatians, 159–60; teaches
    justification through Christ,
    161–63, 172–76; writes to
    Romans, 169–71; trials of,
    177–78; writes to Philippians,
    187–88; writes to Colossians,
    192–93; writes to Ephesians,
    200; writes to Timothy,
    212–13, 221, 240; writes to
    Titus, 219–220; is martyred,
    223–24, 277; tribute to,
    226–29; as witness to Christ,
    229–33; tribute to missionary
    work of, 233–40; as author of
    Hebrews, 244–45
Paulus, Sergius, 66
Peace, 282
Pentateuch, 13
Pentecost, 33–34
Perdition, sons of, 250
Perea, 16
Perfection, of Christ, 250, 261,
    290
Perga, *72,* 354–55
Pergamum, 316–1*7, 318,* 375–76
Persecution, 113–15, 117–18,
    282–84, 288–92
Persian empire, 7
Peter (Simon): sought and jailed,
    22, 24, 40; leader of early

church, 27, 32, 38–39; rebukes
Simon Magus, 48; tours mission
of Church, 55; to teach to the
Gentiles, 56–60; exempts
Gentiles from law of Moses, 75;
disagrees with Paul, 161–62,
236; is martyred, 224, 277;
testifies of Christ, 286
Pharisees, 9, 12–14, 17–18
Phasael, 17
Phebe, 185
Philadelphia (Alashehir, Turkey),
319–20, 379
Philemon, 192, 197–99
Philip, 45, 47–49, 97
Philippi, 78–80, 187–88, 359–60
Pilate, Pontius, 21
Pisidia, 67–68
Politarchs, 83
Polycarp, 373
Pompey, 16–17
Prayers, 63, 238–39, 270, 295,
325
Predestinate, 178–79, 200–201
Premortal life, 86, 180–81,
221–22, 274–75
Pricks, kicking against, 52
Priesthood: used in righteousness,
206–7; organization of, 213,
215–16, 220; duties of,
249–50; anointings through,
272–74; given to Adam, 275.
See also Aaronic Priesthood,
Levitical Priesthood,
Melchizedek Priesthood
Priscilla, 88, 90, 237
Procurator, 20
Prophets: false, 66; foundation of
Church, 203–5; two slain, 332
Provinces, 20
Ptolemies, 8

Qumran, 15–16

Rabbis, 14–15, 24, 50–51
Rahab, 261, 268
Records, opened, 343
Red, symbolism of, 341–42

Reformation, Protestant, 159
Repentance, 153–54, 179–80
Restoration, 39, 122, 122–27,
201–2, 327–28
Resurrection: of Christ, 29; signs
of, 30; of others at time of
Christ's, 36–37; Paul taught,
107, 116, 144–48, 193–94,
231–33; state of bodies after,
191; of two witnesses, 332; at
times during Millennium,
342–43
Revelation, 197, 312–13, 346
Revelation, book of, 126, 347–49
Rhodes, 382
Roman empire, 16–18, 20–23,
87–88
Rome, 169–70, 224, 284

Sabbath, 31, 95, 195
Sacrament, 140
Sacrifices: in Temple, 103–4; of
animals, 256–59; foreshadowed
Christ's sacrifice, 279; of
faithful, 288–92, 328–29. See
also Idolatry, Persecution
Saddok, 19
Sadducees, 9, 13–14, 145
Saints, 205–6. See also Christian
Church(es), early
Salem, 253. See also Jerusalem
Salt, symbolism of, 197
Salvation: through Christ only,
173–74, 176, 232–33, 296;
plan of, 178–79, 233; is
conditional, 180; is not easy,
191; as a goal, 210–11, 278; for
the dead, 282–83; trials
necessary for, 288–92, 328–29
Samaria, 16
Samos, 381
Sanctification, 115, 163–64
Sanctuary, Holy, 104. See also
Temple of Herod
Sanhedrin, 8, 46, 103, 107
Sapphira, 42–43
Sardis, 318–19, 320, 377–79
Satan: as leader of rebellious, 120,

295; guarding against, 208–11; followers of, 274–75; introduced Gnostic movement, 299; throne of, 316–17; in the last days, 333–35; to be bound, 342; final battle with, 343

Saul, 47, 227. *See also* Paul

Scarlet, significance of, 338–39

Scribes, 14

Scriptures, 32, 223, 346

Seals, 324–26

Second Coming: taught by Paul, 112–13, 116–19, 233; shall be in fire, 262–63; taught by Jude, 276; taught by Peter, 287–88; events prior to, 329–31; at time of, 340–42

Secundus, 237

Seleucids, 8

Sepphorus, 18

Sergius Paulus, 354

Sermon on the Mount, 268–70

Seven, symbolism of, 313–14

Sexuality: of Hellenism, 9–10, 129; of Romans, 171; of Gnostics, 298

Sicarii, 21

Signs or tokens, 30

Silas (Silvanus), 76, 112–13, 237, 284

Simon Magus, 48, 299

Simon Peter. *See* Peter

Simon, son of Mattathias, 12, 16

Sin, 167, 175–76, 206

Slavery, 197–99, 208

Smith, Joseph: quotes Paul, 1, 242–43; has First Vision, 53, 241; describes Paul, 66; relates to Paul, 70–71; translates the Bible, 122–27; identifies Paul as author of Hebrews, 245; show gratitude for trials of, 283; verifies scripture, 312

Smyrna (Izmir, Turkey), 315–*16*, 373–75

Snow, Lorenzo, poem of, 189

Sodom and Gomorrah, 275, 286–87

Solomon's Pools, 103

Solomon's Porch, 31–32, 38, 101

Solomon's Stables, 100

Solomon's Temple, 100, 104

Sopater, 237

Sorcery, 48, 79–80

Sosthenes, 89, 130, 237

Spirit of Christ, 171–72

Spirit prison, 282

Spirits, 93, 297–300

Spiritual gifts, 140–41, 143

Spiritual rebirth, 297

Stephanus, 130

Stephen, 45–46

Stoics, 85

Stones, symbolism of, 180. *See also* Cornerstone

Stoning, 47

Submission, 206–7

Suffering, 54. *See also* Afflictions

Susa Gate, 101

Symbolism, 306–9

Tabitha (Dorcas), 55

Tanakh, 151

Tarsus, 63, 72, 350–52

Teaching of the Twelve Apostles, The, 120

Telestial world, 344

Temple Mount, 100, 103, *105*, 253–54

Temple of Herod: destroyed, 3, 15; desecration of, 11; restored, 12; Paul's visit to, 97–99, 245; description of, 100–4, *106*; sacrifices made at, 256–59

Temple worship, 310–11, 315

Temptations, 267, 278

Testimony, 182, 271

Theophilus, 30

Thessalonica (Saloniki, Macedonia), 82–83, 89, 112–13, 360–62

Thorns, 250–51

Thucydides, 4

Thyatira (Akhisar, Turkey), 317, 376–77
Time, reckoning of, 35–36
Timothy: Paul befriends, 76–77; is circumcised, 236; goes to Thessalonica, 112–13, 237–38; letters to, 212–13, 221, 228–29, 240; at death of Paul, 224; in Hebrews, 245
Titus, 76, 150, 212–13, 219–20, 224
Tolerance, 137
Tongues, gift of, 35, 143–44
Torah, 13
Transfiguration, Mount of, 286
Transgressions, 174
Transjordan, 17
Tree of life, 315
Tribulation. See Affliction
Troas, 77–78, 358
Trogyllium, 382
Trophimus, 237
Trumpet, meaning of, 143
Tychicus, 237

Unity of Church, 203–5
Urim and Thummin, 317, 337

Vanity, 214–15, 219
Varus, 18
Veil, symbolism of, 251

Vials, golden, 336–37
Vows, 90

Warfare, 330–31, 337
Water, lukewarm, symbolism of, 320–22
Weaknesses, 177
Wealth, 219, 266–67, 269
Welfare system, early, 217, 267–68
Whitmer, David, 170, 240–41
Whore. See Church of the devil
Widows, 217
Witnesses, two slain, 332
Woes, 330, 332
Women, 144, 214–15, 218. See also Marriage
Woodruff, Wilford, 81–82, 93
Work, 119
Works of the flesh, 167. See also Sin
Works, good, 171, 174–75, 202

Yoke, 154
Yom Kippur, 110, 248, 257–58

Zadokim, 9–11, 13–14
Zealot movement, 19–20, 44
Zechariah, 307
Zelotes, Simon, 19
Zevi, Shabbetai, 373
Zion, 335, 344